Global Land Grabs

Since the 2008 world food crisis a surge of land grabbing swept Africa, Asia and Latin America and even some regions of Europe and North America. Investors have uprooted rural communities for massive agricultural, biofuels, mining, industrial and urbanisation projects. 'Water grabbing' and 'green grabbing' have further exacerbated social tensions.

Early analyses of land grabbing focused on foreign actors, the biofuels boom and Africa, and pointed to catastrophic consequences for the rural poor. Subsequently scholars carried out local case studies in diverse world regions. The contributors to this volume advance the discussion to a new stage, critically scrutinizing alarmist claims of the first wave of research, probing the historical antecedents of today's land grabbing, examining large-scale land acquisitions in light of international human rights and investment law, and considering anew longstanding questions in agrarian political economy about forms of dispossession and accumulation and grassroots resistance.

Readers of this collection will learn about the impacts of land and water grabbing; the relevance of key theorists, including Marx, Polanyi and Harvey; the realities of China's involvement in Africa; how contemporary land grabbing differs from earlier plantation agriculture; and how social movements—and rural people in general—are responding to this new threat.

This book was originally published as a special issue of *Third World Quarterly*.

Marc Edelman is Professor of anthropology at Hunter College and the Graduate Center, City University of New York.

Carlos Oya is Senior Lecturer in Political Economy of Development at SOAS, University of London.

Saturnino M Borras Jr is an Associate Professor at the International Institute of Social Studies (ISS), The Hague, The Netherlands.

Thirdworlds
Edited by Shahid Qadir, *University of London*

THIRDWORLDS will focus on the political economy, development and cultures of those parts of the world that have experienced the most political, social, and economic upheaval, and which have faced the greatest challenges of the postcolonial world under globalisation: poverty, displacement and diaspora, environmental degradation, human and civil rights abuses, war, hunger, and disease. **THIRDWORLDS** serves as a signifier of oppositional emerging economies and cultures ranging from Africa, Asia, Latin America, Middle East, and even those 'Souths' within a larger perceived North, such as the U.S. South and Mediterranean Europe. The study of these otherwise disparate and discontinuous areas, known collectively as the Global South, demonstrates that as globalisation pervades the planet, the south, as a synonym for subalterity, also transcends geographical and ideological frontiers.

Global Land Grabs

History, Theory and Method

Edited by
**Marc Edelman, Carlos Oya and
Saturnino M Borras Jr**

Routledge
Taylor & Francis Group

LONDON AND NEW YORK

First published 2015
by Routledge

2 Park Square, Milton Park, Abingdon, Oxon OX14 4RN
711 Third Avenue, New York, NY 10017, USA

Routledge is an imprint of the Taylor & Francis Group, an informa business

First issued in paperback 2016

British Library Cataloguing in Publication Data
A catalogue record for this book is available from the British Library

ISBN 978-1-138-83053-0 (hbk)
ISBN 978-1-138-69130-8 (pbk)

Typeset in Times New Roman
by RefineCatch Limited, Bungay, Suffolk

Publisher's Note
The publisher accepts responsibility for any inconsistencies that may have
arisen during the conversion of this book from journal articles to book chapters,
namely the possible inclusion of journal terminology.

Disclaimer
Every effort has been made to contact copyright holders for their permission to
reprint material in this book. The publishers would be grateful to hear from any
copyright holder who is not here acknowledged and will undertake to rectify
any errors or omissions in future editions of this book.

Contents

Citation Information

The chapters in this book were originally published in *Third World Quarterly*, volume 34, issue 9 (November 2013). When citing this material, please use the original page numbering for each article, as follows:

Chapter 1
Global Land Grabs: historical processes, theoretical and methodological implications and current trajectories
Marc Edelman, Carlos Oya and Saturnino M Borras Jr
Third World Quarterly, volume 34, issue 9 (November 2013) pp. 1517–1531

Chapter 2
The Land Rush and Classic Agrarian Questions of Capital and Labour: a systematic scoping review of the socioeconomic impact of land grabs in Africa
Carlos Oya
Third World Quarterly, volume 34, issue 9 (November 2013) pp. 1532–1557

Chapter 3
Land Grabbing, Large- and *Small-scale Farming: what can evidence and policy from 20th century Africa contribute to the debate?*
Elena Baglioni and Peter Gibbon
Third World Quarterly, volume 34, issue 9 (November 2013) pp. 1558–1581

Chapter 4
Primitive Accumulation, Accumulation by Dispossession and the Global Land Grab
Derek Hall
Third World Quarterly, volume 34, issue 9 (November 2013) pp. 1582–1604

Chapter 5
The New Enclosures? Polanyi, international investment law and the global land rush
Lorenzo Cotula
Third World Quarterly, volume 34, issue 9 (November 2013) pp. 1605–1629

Chapter 6
Human Rights Responses to Land Grabbing: a right to food perspective
Christophe Golay and Irene Biglino
Third World Quarterly, volume 34, issue 9 (November 2013) pp. 1630–1650

Chapter 7
The Global Politics of Water Grabbing
Jennifer Franco, Lyla Mehta and Gert Jan Veldwisch
Third World Quarterly, volume 34, issue 9 (November 2013) pp. 1651–1675

Chapter 8
Green Dreams: Myth and Reality in China's Agricultural Investment in Africa
Deborah Bräutigam and Haisen Zhang
Third World Quarterly, volume 34, issue 9 (November 2013) pp. 1676–1696

Chapter 9
Cycles of Land Grabbing in Central America: an argument for history and a case study in the Bajo Aguán, Honduras
Marc Edelman & Andrés León
Third World Quarterly, volume 34, issue 9 (November 2013) pp. 1697–1722

Chapter 10
Global Land Grabbing and Political Reactions 'From Below'
Saturnino M Borras Jr and Jennifer C Franco
Third World Quarterly, volume 34, issue 9 (November 2013) pp. 1723–1747

Please direct any queries you may have about the citations to
clsuk.permissions@cengage.com

Global Land Grabs: historical processes, theoretical and methodological implications and current trajectories

MARC EDELMAN[a], CARLOS OYA[b] & SATURNINO M BORRAS JR[c1]

[a]Department of Anthropology, Hunter College, City University of New York, New York, USA;
[b]Department of Development Studies, SOAS, University of London, London, UK;
[c]International Institute of Social Studies, The Hague, The Netherlands.

ABSTRACT   Scholars, practitioners and activists generally agree that investor interest in land has climbed sharply, although they differ about what to call this phenomenon and how to analyse it. This introduction discusses several contested definitional, conceptual, methodological and political issues in the land grab debate. The initial 'making sense' period drew sweeping conclusions from large databases, rapid-appraisal fieldwork and local case studies. Today research examines financialisation of land, 'water grabbing', 'green grabbing' and grabbing for industrial and urbanisation projects, and a substantial literature challenges key assumptions of the early discussion (the emphasis on foreign actors in Africa and on food and biofuels production, the claim that local populations are inevitably displaced or negatively affected). The authors in this collection, representing a diversity of approaches and backgrounds, argue the need to move beyond the basic questions of the 'making sense' period of the debate and share a common commitment to connecting analyses of contemporary land grabbing to its historical antecedents and legal contexts and to longstanding agrarian political economy questions concerning forms of dispossession and accumulation, the role of labour and the impediments to the development of capitalism in agriculture. They call for more rigorous grounding of claims about impacts, for scrutiny of failed projects and for (re)examination of the longue durée, social differentiation, the agency of contending social classes and forms of grassroots resistance as key elements shaping agrarian outcomes.

Land grabbing? Large-scale land acquisitions? Enclosures? Global land rush? Scholars, policy practitioners and activists rarely agree on how to describe the current interest in land, although they generally concur that since 2007 investor interest has skyrocketed. While the underlying minimalist consensus about a worldwide upsurge in land deals is notable, the disagreements go beyond terminology, are far from academic and need to be aired. The present collection of new research and analysis sits uneasily at the intersection of this unity and discord. Current policy analysis and scholarly research are marked by explicit and implicit differences over the causes, character, mechanisms, meanings, trajectories and implications of contemporary land deals.

Among the contested aspects of 'land grabbing' are:

(1) What to include in the definition and what to exclude. This question, discussed extensively by Derek Hall in this collection, is not trivial, because it has important implications for where we turn our analytical gaze. [2]

(2) How do we count land deals and how do we measure the extent of the phenomenon?[3]

(3) How do we understand processes of social change—including antecedents, 'drivers', legal frameworks, contentious politics and impacts of land grabbing? These issues have major implications for how we explain existing and emerging social structures. For example, some observers limit their examinations of land grabbing to land transactions dedicated to food production by foreign (state and/or corporate) entities,[4] while others broaden the definition to include 'green grabbing' or deals aimed at profiting from carbon sequestration, bio-prospecting in forests or the creation of various kinds of protected zones (national or private parks, watersheds, ecotourism projects).[5] Still others include projects that appropriate farmland for industry or urbanisation.[6]

(4) What is the range of actors involved? What relations, for example, link (or not) foreign and domestic capital, old and new investors, or state and non-state players?[7]

(5) How may we understand the varied political reactions to land deals by affected social groups?

Sensational media reports and NGO agit-prop fact-finding missions turned the global spotlight on land grabbing in the immediate aftermath of the 2007–08 worldwide food price spike. The initial perspective on land grabbing therefore was directly linked to surging commodity prices, particularly those of internationally traded staple foods, such as maize, wheat, rice and soy.[8] The 2007–08 crisis has remained a key analytical point of departure for most observers and the sole one for some. The central concern was and is that food-insecure countries are appropriating land overseas in order to secure their own food supply and that, in doing so, they are displacing poor people in host countries, who are generally food insecure themselves, from their lands.

Since 2008, however, scholars and activists have analysed the scope and context of global land grabbing in greater depth. Dimensions that have received increasing attention include 'green grabbing',[9] 'water grabbing',[10] biofuels and biomass,[11] the financialisation of agriculture,[12] and the seizing of land used by peasants, indigenous communities and pastoralists for industrial, mining and urbanisation projects.[13] A growing body of research now challenges (or at least nuances) several claims that figured prominently in the initial salvo of journalistic and NGO fact-finding research. Among these assumptions are the dominance of foreign grabbers, especially China and the Gulf states, the centrality of deals related to food production, and the near-exclusive focus on sub-Saharan Africa, as well as the notion that people are necessarily and always expelled and displaced from their lands. For example, new and more reliable data have started to come in showing that China's and the Gulf states' involvement might have been overstated. Deborah Bräutigam, whose article with Zhang Haisen forms part of this collection, has been the leading scholar to question the problematic, inflated claims about China in Africa. The involvement of North Atlantic governments and companies has been slowly but steadily incorporated into emerging literature, whether of the fact-finding type or the more academic variety.[14] Nor is land grabbing just about food and biofuels or solely a result of the 2007–08 commodity price spikes. Several contributions to this collection (particularly those by Baglioni & Gibbon, Edelman & León, Hall, and Oya) emphasise the need for longer temporal frames and more sophisticated and historically specific approaches to periodisation. Land grabbing, moreover, is occurring not just in Africa but also in other regions, such as post-Soviet Eurasia, Southeast Asia and Latin America,[15] and in some big powerful countries, notably China, Russia and India.[16] Land grabbing frequently involves both domestic and foreign actors— even if it is the latter that have received most media and other attention—and state and corporate entities. Finally, people are not necessarily and always expelled or displaced from their lands. Some are subsumed into contract farming schemes or other kinds of 'partnership' arrangements. Some sell their holdings with little or no coercion and even with relief and enthusiasm. The contributions here build on these critical and more nuanced approaches.

The media and NGOs, especially GRAIN, have played a critical role during the initial period—and up to now—in putting land grabbing under the global spotlight and onto the (official) agenda. NGOs, however, almost always view research as a function of their advocacy work and, as a consequence, focus selectively on particular issues and employ corresponding methodologies.[17] This inherently imposes limits on what they can contribute towards a fuller understanding of the causes, conditions, character, mechanisms, meanings, trajectories and implications of the new global land rush.

There is usually a time lag between media or NGO fact-finding and agit-prop reports and the catch-up effort of academics. We have seen this in the past with various topics in agrarian studies, including the GATT negotiations and genetically modified organisms (GMOs). In the case of land grabbing academics entered the conversation with relative speed. In mid-2011 the first large-scale academic conference on land grabbing was held at the Institute for Development Studies (IDS) in the UK, organised by the loose academic network working on land grabs, the Land Deal Politics Initiative (LDPI, www.iss.nl/ldpi). The second international conference organised by LDPI was held at Cornell University in late 2012. The entry of academic researchers into the land grab discussion has shifted the initial parameters established by NGOs and the media, since many academics are not comfortable with, and have started to question, sensational anecdotal media accounts and NGO reports. The *Journal of Peasant Studies*' 'Forum on Global

Land Grabbing', published in March 2011, in some ways signalled the significant and systematic entry of academics into land grab research. It was followed by the publication of two special issues on land grabs in the same journal in 2012.

The period between 2007 and 2012 is what we can call the 'making sense period': media, NGOs, policy experts and academics were grappling with basic questions: what is happening, where and when, who is involved, how much land is involved, and how many people are being expelled from their land? How do we define land grab? What do we count? How do we count? How do we interpret our sources? Perhaps unsurprisingly to this day there is no consensus on these fundamental epistemological and methodological questions. Fact-finding research missions were appropriate and useful for answering basic questions (eg what, where, when, who, how much, how many?) and indeed became quite popular. But 'quick and dirty' or rapid appraisal research also easily led to competing initiatives and perspectives, as different organisations sought to quantify ever more shocking 'killer facts'—particularly dramatic numbers of people displaced and hectares grabbed. Theoretically quantification is important; it ought to provide us with a sense of the extent of the phenomenon and its implications for broader questions about agrarian change. But whether it is methodologically possible or desirable is another matter—and one that is especially contentious in the current land grabbing debate.

Several flaws were evident in much of the initial 2007–12 research into land grabbing, including major disconnects between some conclusions on outcomes or impacts and available evidence, and between declared research purposes and adopted research methodologies. Nevertheless, this first wave of research also achieved impressive results, particularly in terms of the quantity of material produced and the number of different situations and issues reported in a relatively short time span. It called public attention to the urgency of understanding and addressing global land grabbing. It facilitated our initial critical understanding of the phenomenon and eventually allowed us to ask better and more rigorous questions and to explore more appropriate research methodologies. The latter part of this period has been marked by consensus around two fundamental points. First, agreement remains firm and widespread that a renewed land rush is indeed happening worldwide, albeit unevenly. Second, a growing number of researchers agrees that the initial set of basic questions has served its purpose and its era has ended. A newer set of questions began to emerge towards the end of the initial period of land grab research. The *Journal of Peasant Studies* 'Forum on Global Land Grabbing, Part 2: on methodologies', published in June 2013, attempted to both initiate and instigate this new era of research. In the current collection, Oya, as well as Bräutigam & Zhang, deal extensively with these newer issues in their articles.

The guest editors and contributors to this special issue of *Third World Quarterly* believe that land grab research—after some five years of the 'making sense period' and a growing accumulation of case studies—is now at a critical juncture. The next phase of work will require taking stock of where we are now in research on land grabs and identifying the key challenges. This issue differs from other recent journal special issues because it is a collection of synthetic papers—and not strictly country and thematic case studies—which examine broad trends and conceptual questions and seek to deepen and profoundly alter prevailing theoretical assumptions. It builds on previous special issues on land grabs in the *Journal of Peasant Studies* (March 2012 and May 2012), *Canadian Journal of Development Studies* (December 2012), *Development and Change* (March 2013) and *Globalizations* (March 2013). We have organised the remainder of this short introduction into four sections: common themes, diverging views, silences, and a concluding section that focuses on the research challenges.

Common themes

There are at least five broadly distinct but closely interlinked themes common to several papers in this collection that have not been fully and systematically addressed in previous publications on land grabbing. We will focus our brief discussion on these themes. They are: the long history of land grabbing, the theoretical implications of the contemporary land rush for agrarian political economy and for social theory more broadly, the plurality of legal institutions implicated or potentially implicated in today's land deals, the differentiated outcomes of grabs and the political reactions of those affected, and the methods most appropriate for carrying out rigorous, relevant research.

Long history

Perhaps the most important theme that cuts across all contributions to this collection—and that has so far received insufficient attention in the emerging literature on land grabbing—is the central importance of an historical analytical framework. Contributors to this collection share the view that most research (academic or otherwise) tends to neglect the importance of history, and over-emphasises the 'here and now'. The concern is not just that a longer temporal perspective is needed and that it may call into question some claims about the 'newness' of land grabbing. Rather, it is essential to restore a sense of the agency of contending social classes, as well as an appreciation of how historical contingencies may affect agrarian outcomes (as both Hall and Edelman & León argue). The spaces in which land grabbing occurs have almost always been created and shaped by earlier processes of political contention, longstanding patterns of land tenure and use, and pre-existing social formations.

Several of the papers concern outcomes. This too needs to be linked to the historicising theme. One big question, explicit in Oya, Hall, and Edelman & León, and implicit in several of the other contributions, is whether it is possible to ascribe certain outcomes to land grabbing when the processes that led there originated well before the recent wave of appropriation and indeed may have helped to facilitate it. Moreover, impacts can only really be assessed when the pre-land grab situation is thoroughly understood and documented.

To reassert the importance of historical, processual analysis and broader temporal frames is not to deny or minimise the reality of the 'renewed global land rush'. On the contrary, viewing today's land rush in greater historical perspective permits both a more profound analysis of its origins and dynamics and a greater appreciation of the specificity that may characterise contemporary land grabs in general and certain land grabs in particular.

Implications for agrarian political economy and social theory

All the papers here have underscored the importance of taking the dynamics of agrarian change and of global capital accumulation as key reference points. Such a broad agrarian political economy framework critically examines the dynamics of production and reproduction, and how power, property and labour are politically contested and transformed over time. This poses questions about the relations between different forms of agrarian capital (foreign and domestic, old and new wealth, land-rich/money poor, money-rich/land poor, and so on) and about the possibilities and impediments that exist in any given context to the development of capitalist social relations in agriculture (see Hall's and Oya's papers). While the question of landed property relations is central to our understanding of agrarian change, it is not the only important issue that requires careful scrutiny. A broader agrarian political economy perspective goes beyond a land property relations-centric analysis to include other closely linked agrarian issues.

The dynamics of labour regimes, for example, may be just as important as the land issue. Building on Tania Li's argument for 'centering labor in the land grab debate', we can take on the question of labour from two broad perspectives.[18] On the one hand, people are expelled from their land when and where the land is needed but the labour is not (in Li's formulation). This brings us back to classical debates around 'primitive accumulation' and its more recent incarnation in Harvey's 'accumulation by dispossession'.[19] While expulsion and displacement are issues that have received much attention to date in the emerging land grabs literature, the labour dimension remains under-explored.[20] In the current collection, Hall, Oya, and Baglioni & Gibbon analyse these questions thoroughly, pointing out the need for more careful and systematic research on labour and on forms of subsumption more generally.

On the other hand, there are situations where capital needs the land *and* the labour. The most obvious result is the turning of peasants into wage labourers, thereby contributing to rural labour market formation. Evidence is, however, still patchy about the extent and dynamics of wage employment creation as a result of land acquisitions. But investors may not need to directly employ wage labour since the labour of smallholder producers can be mobilised through contract farming. Smallholder participation in the emerging land-grab-related plantation or agribusiness enclaves (or subsumption, as opposed to displacement) has received surprisingly little attention in the debate, particularly given the existence of a substantial earlier body of research on contract farming.[21]

This neglect is indicative of a lingering dilemma connected to the problem of defining land grabs: are land deals 'land grabs' only when they expel or displace people from their land? Sometimes smallholders may be agents of or complicit with land grabbers, and they may even eagerly join the crop booms that are driving land grabbing in their vicinity. Several contributions to our collection address these questions critically, bringing greater complexity to both the substantive and definitional discussions (see especially the papers by Baglioni & Gibbon, Edelman & León, Oya, and Hall). Land grab studies highlight the usefulness of returning to some fundamental themes in agrarian political economy, including the large-scale-versus-small-scale farms debate (see Baglioni & Gibbon), contract growing schemes and questions of power relations, domination and subordination (see Edelman and León, and Oya), the nature of 'primitive accumulation' and 'accumulation by dispossession', and expulsion and displacement not through any extra-economic coercion, but through the 'dull compulsion of economic relations', or simply by 'dispossession by social differentiation', as Farshad Arraghi puts it (see Hall in this issue).

The use of a broad political economy lens also brings into view resources other than land, such as water and minerals. Land is key, no doubt, since control of land is essential in order to control and make use of other coveted resources, whether water, minerals or forests, which can supply not only timber and natural products but also tradable carbon sequestration credits. Many contributions in this issue touch on these concerns. But perhaps one of the most interesting angles linked to land grabbing is the question of water. Pioneering work on water grabbing has been carried out by Philip Woodhouse, Tony Allan and colleagues, and by Lyla Mehta and colleagues.[22] Here Franco, Mehta & Veldwisch offer further analysis of the water question, and in particular what it implies for the political economy of land and resource grabbing and what it requires in terms of future research. Among other things, they argue that 'For water grabbing, the fixation on size has a parallel in a too narrow focus on the volume of water involved, ignoring the fact that access to water concerns distribution in time and space'.

Finally, a broad agrarian political economy perspective views contemporary land grabbing as a valid and urgent agrarian issue—but not the only important such issue today. Borras & Franco's paper discusses three broadly distinct but interlinked perspectives around political reactions from below that connect back to key agrarian political economy processes emphasised by most of the other contributors, namely: 1) the struggle against expulsion, displacement and dispossession; 2) the struggle for incorporation and against exploitation; and 3) the struggle for land redistribution and recognition. What this implies, aside from the question of displacement versus subsumption discussed earlier, is that the issue of land concentration affects the great majority of rural people worldwide and often provokes mass mobilisation for land redistribution or recognition (of rights, especially but not only by indigenous peoples). The key is to first acknowledge that land grabbing and land concentration are *not* always the same thing, the respective struggles therefore not being equivalent, and, second, to study both in an interlinked manner and take into account how they shape each other. This point is emphasised by most authors here but especially in the papers by Edelman & León, Borras & Franco, and Oya.

Plurality of legal institutions

Several of the contributions focus on legal regimes, most notably those by Cotula and Golay & Biglino, but also those by Franco *et al* and Edelman & León. Legal regimes constitute both part of the context for enabling land deals and an object of political contestation. Law making, as Cotula suggests, has been used both to facilitate the creation of new commodities (eg in land, one of Polanyi's 'fictitious commodities') and to rein in market forces. Different national traditions of law reflect different histories and imply different conditions of possibility for land grabbing. Cotula points as well to the 'legal pluralism' on the ground that has multiple bodies of law—from global to local—interacting and overlapping.

At the international level scholars and activists are devoting increasing attention to possible global governance mechanisms for administering and slowing the land rush.[23] The papers by Cotula and by Golay & Biglino throw into stark relief an even more fundamental question: what kind of international law will be paramount? Agrarian movements and their allies have struggled to prioritise human rights law, broadly conceived and including economic, social and cultural rights. Agribusiness interests and sympathetic governments, on the other hand, emphasise the primacy of trade and investment law. As Cotula points out, the ways land in which is conceptualised and transacted are profoundly influenced by international investment law (and—we might add—by national property law and local practices). He also indicates, however, that, notwithstanding opposition between the principles of trade and investment law and human rights law, both share similar features inasmuch as they protect private actors against government interference and provide remedies for those actors to challenge government actions. Nonetheless, the tension between trade and investment versus human rights law at the international level is nothing less than a manifestation of the ongoing tension between market and society, reminiscent of the famous 'double movement' described by Polanyi nearly 70 years ago and adeptly applied to the land grab discussion by Cotula. Indeed, Cotula detects 'recent evolutions' in investment law that portend a shift back in the direction of favouring state regulation over investor protections.

International human rights law—particularly in the area of economic, social and cultural rights—tends to be incorporated selectively and unevenly into regional conventions and national laws (because of the peculiarities of national politics), while international trade and investment law is generally applied more thoroughly, in part because of the universalising pretensions of liberal economic doctrine but more importantly because of strong elite interests. The way these contradictions play out in any specific case of land grabbing cannot, however, be predicted from an analysis of 'drivers' or of legal frameworks. Golay & Biglino's paper addresses how the widely recognised right to food in international law has recently been employed to argue for land tenure security. They also detail how activists have worked within the United Nations Human Rights Council, various UN treaty bodies and regional human rights systems to articulate human rights-based responses to land grabbing in diverse Asian, African and Latin American countries. Finally, they call for mainstreaming human rights considerations in analyses of land transactions and remind us that states have legal obligations under international human rights law and cannot shed these commitments simply by pressuring investors to abide by voluntary commitments.

The consideration of legal frameworks in the papers in this collection is integrally connected to our broader commitment to bringing a more in-depth historical approach to the land grabbing discussion. Agrarian outcomes, after all, are always the result of historically determined balances of class and sectorial forces, which are in turn reflected in and shaped by legal frameworks and practices, including the institutionalised illegality that sometimes accompanies and facilitates land grabbing (as described, for example, in Edelman & León's analysis of Honduras).

Differentiated outcomes, differentiated political reactions

One of the most striking findings of recent critical research on land deals is that many projects—sometimes announced to great fanfare in the business press or in government ministers' press conferences—are blocked by public outcries, at home or abroad, or simply never implemented. Variation in the degrees of implementation, the groups affected and the reactions is substantial and calls for a research agenda that looks at these processes and their outcomes with fresh eyes and new questions. Outcomes may be differentiated and sometimes contradictory for many reasons: whether there has been displacement or not; the extent to which wage employment has been created and who has mostly benefited; whether investors actually invest substantial capital and commit to the long term or are merely there for speculative reasons; the extent to which states put conditions on the nature of projects or simply facilitate the entry of any kind of investor with an attractive project; whether the land being acquired is a site of long-standing land or labour struggles; and the extent to which new investors opt for 'incorporation' of smallholders for political reasons or considerations of risk. Much depends on the nature of the investor, the scale, the political-economic context and the time taken since the transaction was initiated. Several papers in this collection, notably Edelman & León, Baglioni & Gibbon, Oya, and Borras & Franco emphasise the importance of variation and the need to provide an empirically and historically grounded analysis of specific land grabbing stories, in order to make sense of the political, social and economic implications of differentiated outcomes with different time horizons.

Borras & Franco provide a thorough analysis illustrated with concrete examples of how differentiated and contradictory outcomes give rise to differentiated political reactions. Understanding mobilisation and contestation around land grabbing may be complicated by the possible convergence and contradictions between different types of struggles, against expulsion, against exploitation (or for better incorporation) and against land concentration and for recognition. The actors involved are themselves differentiated, even though they are often assumed to be part of homogeneous entities ('local communities') opposed to the outsider. As Borras & Franco put it: 'The configuration of actors and the intersections, character and trajectory of political contestations are far more diverse and complex than casual claims in the current media and popular literature on land deals would suggest'. This poses a major empirical challenge for researchers and activists, as there is a serious need for systematic research into the dynamics of inter- and intra-class tensions and synergies, to ascertain the issues that unite and divide and therefore make sense of the panoply of political reactions to different processes of land acquisition.

On research methodology

The methodological and conceptual concerns that several of the papers express are not merely calls for fine tuning land deal research in the post-'making sense' period, which we hope we are now entering. A focus on methodologies, as exemplified in Bräutigam and Zhang's paper on Chinese investment in Africa, permits not just a greater understanding of how the (frequently erroneous) conventional wisdom—and indeed 'fact'—has been constructed so far, but also significantly qualifies and even potentially upends key elements of the prevailing alarmist picture of an inexorable advance of massive foreign land grabbing.

Oya, similarly, points out 'that in much of the literature published so far the methods used seem limited with respect to the difficulty, breadth and depth of the questions asked'. There is, he declares, 'no shortcut to good quality evidence'. Despite pervasive claims in the literature about deleterious impacts of land grabs, Oya's scoping review of some 2000 published reports could not find a single study that had 'an evaluation of impact with a rigorous baseline and a before and after comparison'. Given the high political stakes, more and better research on new and more challenging questions can indeed be carried out, building on the knowledge accumulated so far as well as reflecting upon and avoiding the common biases and shortcomings of previous work.

As Hall points out in his paper, three sets of concepts have shaped research on land deals: a common-sense understanding of 'land grab', the more precise definitions in academic writings, and diverse interpretations of 'primitive accumulation' and 'accumulation by dispossession'. These frames both create possibilities and restrict researchers' gaze and imaginations. They very probably contributed, for example, to the focus on foreign capital as a 'driver' of land grabbing and to a concomitant tendency to ignore or downplay domestic actors. Moreover, as Hall emphasises:

> One of the great strengths of the primitive accumulation framework is its analysis of the centuries-long process by which capitalism has become truly global, but the framework can simultaneously encourage us to ignore the effects of that history of capitalist expansion on the places where land grabs are now taking place.

In a related admonition Bräutigam & Zhang warn that 'the nature of knowledge circulation is such that the first papers written on the initial analysis of (problematic) data often... have much greater impact than papers written later, with revised and better data'. This intellectual and political inertia—the product in part of a deliberately constructed conventionality—is one of the central challenges that land deal scholars now confront in seeking to advance beyond the 'making sense' phase of research. It will take some time until new ideas, questions and evidence shake up the epistemic communities that have emerged around debates on land grabbing.

Diverging views

The papers in this collection employ widely varying methods and occasionally manifest considerable disagreement. Oya, for example, sees the land grabbing field as dominated by neoclassical and neo-populist paradigms, while Hall believes that critical agrarian political economy is the dominant approach. These different interpretations are also driven by the kind of material reviewed and the questions addressed, so that, for example, the use of the concept of 'primitive accumulation' can be seen primarily centred in contributions within political economy, while a broader literature on land deals and their impact arises from a wider pool of researchers and activists, many of whom are deeply influenced either by neo-populist views or by neo-classical economics assumptions. As land grab research begins to move beyond the 'making sense' phase of the past several years, this heterogeneity of views and methods needs to be celebrated as a strength and as one element of what might be considered the way forward in land grabbing research. The heterogeneity of approaches to some extent grows out of different disciplinary and regional academic traditions, but it also reflects highly diverse objects of study—numerous varieties of land grabbing in distinct contexts—that require different approaches in their analysis.

Silences

Any consideration of the agenda for the next stage of land deal research must acknowledge that there are continuing gaps and silences in the literature that necessitate sustained attention and analysis (as Oya's paper maintains). Gender and generational dimensions of land grabbing need more in-depth study, not just in terms of possible differential impacts of displacement on women and men or on young or older populations, but also in relation to the politics of resistance. Edelman & León's paper, for example, documents how the complicity of some male cooperative leaders in agrarian counter-reform and associated land grabbing in Honduras fuelled the emergence of a new generation of militant women activists. This doubtless has parallels elsewhere, even in similarly patriarchal societies.

Questions of scale are also beginning to receive more critical scrutiny, but there is still a long way to go (see papers by Oya and by Edelman & León).[24] The massive land appropriations documented in some regions do not always have effects commensurate with their size, while small grabs sometimes give rise to widespread displacement and intense social conflicts. Much of the difference has to do with pre-existing land tenure and use, the types of projects implemented or planned on the appropriated plots, how these are acquired, and the levels of capital applied to them. The rush to create special economic zones (SEZS) in India after 2005, for example, generated bitter widespread conflict, but the total hectares devoted to the 600 or so SEZS in the entire country is quite small in comparison with some of the more spectacular land grabs in other world regions.

The question of alternatives to land grabbing, while implicit in much of the literature during what we have called the 'making sense' period of research, deserves more concrete analysis. This involves complex issues of governance, democracy and environmental sustainability, as well as a detailed knowledge of the grabbers and their backers and a genuine effort to hear the voices and acknowledge the views of the affected populations. Diverse forms of resistance to and incorporation into land grabbing (systematised in Borras & Franco's contribution) need to be studied from the ground up rather than assumed *a priori* from a distance.

Concluding remarks: challenges

The beginning of this introductory essay briefly traced the short but rich and lively story of the 'research rush on the global land rush' for the period 2007–12, which we term the 'making sense period'. During this time a large body of literature has emerged, with media, NGOs, policy experts and academics grappling with basic questions about the nature and dynamics of land grabbing: what is happening, where and when, who is involved, how much land is involved, and how many people are being expelled from their land? How do we define land grab? What do we count? How do we count? How do we interpret our sources? All these questions are important and, thanks to the drive and interest of researchers and activists alike, much knowledge has been accumulated in a short time and with limited resources. We have argued that the initial set of basic questions has served its purpose and its era has ended, now giving way to new questions and new approaches to addressing these questions. The papers in this collection reflect on this rising research agenda and on the challenges posed by the first wave of research and work on land grabbing.

As argued in this article, a number of key themes runs through this collection, giving a flavour of some of the key challenges ahead. The articles point to the need to take history seriously and to place the current 'land rush' in the *longue durée* of the development of capitalism, so that key continuities and shifts are clearly grasped with due attention to agency and contingency. This in itself requires a deepened engagement with long-standing discussions in agrarian political economy. These include debates on landed property relations, the dynamics of accumulation, the nature and dynamics of 'agrarian capital', the impediments to and drivers of capitalist development, the shifts in labour regimes, the complex interactions between different forms of capitalist and non-capitalist production, whether small, medium or large-scale, and the actual struggles against dispossession and around incorporation that have historically characterised the development of capitalism and which underpin the responses and reactions to the current land rush. The challenge is particularly daunting when one attempts to connect these long-standing themes and questions to new conditions and scenarios where the 'global' and the 'local' cannot be neatly separated—either in terms of the origins of the investors (see Edelman & León's article) or of the relevant legal regimes (see Cotula's and Baglioni & Gibbon's articles). Similarly, an emphasis on the centrality of land, capital and labour cannot ignore the current significance of water, climate and speculative capital (as Franco *et al* insist).

The 'making sense' period commenced with broad assertions about a global land grab that were not wrong, but which nonetheless implicitly contributed to a vision of uniform processes across time and space. The contributions to this collection, written with the benefit of a vast research bibliography published in the past five years, instead emphasise the necessity of acknowledging diversity across time and space and the limits of our ability to know some things with certainty. These cautions do not mean that the imperative to deepen and extend knowledge about land grabbing is any less urgent. Land grabbing (and associated other forms of grabbing) constitutes a recent intensification of an historic threat to rural livelihoods, to democratic governance and equity, and to long-term environmental sustainability. The challenge will be to understand it in all of its complexity and to build on those more complex understandings to propose viable and durable alternatives. This collection suggests that, in order to understand the complexity of the phenomenon and the contradictions it raises, researchers and activists must face challenging questions about what is to be known and how best to know it. In other words, the 'making sense' period has seen various attempts to provide some answers to a phenomenon that is not easy to grasp. This is now the time to consider new questions and new ways of formulating old questions.

Notes

1 The three authors share equal contributions to the article and to the editorship of the issue. The order of names was decided by random selection between different combinations (picked by a five-year old child) in order to avoid the conventional tyranny of the alphabetical order

2 See initial but basic discussion in S Borras, J Franco, S Gómez, C Kay & M Spoor, 'Land grabbing in Latin America and the Caribbean', *Journal of Peasant Studies*, 39(3-4), 2012, pp 845–872.

3 This is one of the most complicated and debated issues in global land grabbing today. The *Journal of Peasant Studies*' 'Forum on global land grabbing, Part 2' has been dedicated to jump-starting a more rigorous debate on this matter. See, specifically, I Scoones et al 'The politics of evidence: methodologies for understanding the global land rush', *Journal of Peasant Studies*, 40(3), 2013, pp 469–483; M Edelman, 'Messy hectares: questions about the epistemology of land area and ownership', *Journal of Peasant Studies*, 40(3), 2013, pp 485–501; and C Oya, 'Methodological reflections on land "grab" databases and the land "grab" literature "rush"', *Journal of Peasant Studies*, 40(3), 2013, pp 503–520.

4 See, for example, H Akram Lodhi, 'Contextualising land grabbing: contemporary land deals, the global subsistence crisis and the world food system', *Canadian Journal of Development Studies*, 33(2), 2012, pp 119–142.

5 J Fairhead, M Leach & I Scoones, 'Green grabbing: a new appropriation of nature?', *Journal of Peasant Studies*, 39(2), 2012, pp 237–261.

6 M Levien, 'Regimes of dispossession: from steel towns to Special Economic Zones', *Development and Change*, 44(2), 2013, pp 381–407.

7 All contributors to this collection take a broader perspective on the issue of drivers and actors, to include foreign and domestic, state and non-state. For an extensive discussion on foreign and domestic land grabbers, see M Murmis & MR Murmis, 'Land concentration and foreign land ownership in Argentina in the context of global land grabbing', *Canadian Journal of Development Studies*, 33(4), 2012, pp 490–508. For the role of the state in either directly grabbing land or facilitating corporate land grabbing, see W Wolford et al, 'Governing global land deals: the role of the state in the rush for land', *Development and Change*, 44(2), 2013, pp 189–210; and Levien, 'Regimes of dispossession'.

8 For an excellent critical examination of the 2007–08 food price spike, see the contributions to the Symposium in *Journal of Agrarian Change*, 10(1), 2010, pp 69–129.

9 Fairhead et al, 'Green grabbing'.

10 L Mehta, GJ Veldwisch & J Franco, Introduction to the special issue: water grabbing? Focus on the (re)appropriation of finite water resources', *Water Alternatives*, 5(2), 2012, pp 193–207.

11 S Borras, P McMichael & I Scoones, *Biofuels, Land and Agrarian Change*, London: Routledge, 2010.

12 J Ghosh, The unnatural coupling: food and global finance', *Journal of Agrarian Change*, 10(1), 2010, pp 72–86.
13 See Levien, 'Regimes of dispossession'.
14 See, for example, the critical discussion on the role of some European governments and companies in the case of Chikweti tree plantation in Niassa, Mozambique in Foodfirst Information and Action Network (FIAN), *The Human Rights Impacts of Tree Plantations in Niassa Province, Mozambique: A Report*, Heidelberg: FIAN, 2012. More academically, in the context of Europe, both as host of land grabbing and as land grabber, see J Franco & S Borras (eds), *Land Concentration, Land Grabbing and People's Struggles in Europe: A Report by the European Coordination Via Campesina (ECVC) and Hands-Off The Land (HOTL)*, Amsterdam: Transnational Institute (TNI), 2013.
15 For Eurasia, see O Visser & M Spoor, 'Land grabbing in post-Soviet Eurasia: the world's largest agricultural land reserves at stake', *Journal of Peasant Studies*, 38(2), 2011, pp 299–323; S Borras & J Franco, *Political Dynamics of Land-grabbing in Southeast Asia: Understanding Europe's Role*, Amsterdam: TNI, 2011; and S Borras, C Kay et al (eds), 'Land grabbing in Latin America', *Canadian Journal of Development Studies* (special issue), 33(4), 2012.
16 For Russia, see O Visser, N Mamonova & M Spoor, 'Oligarchs, megafarms and land reserves: understanding land grabbing in Russia', *Journal of Peasant Studies*, 39(3–4), 2012, pp 899–931. For India, see Levien, 'Regimes of dispossession'.
17 For a discussion on how they frame their datasets, for what purposes, and with what limitations, see W Anseeuw et al, 'Creating a public tool to assess and promote transparency in global land deals: the experience of the Land Matrix', *Journal of Peasant Studies*, 40(3), 2013, pp 521–530; and GRAIN, 'Collating and dispersing: GRAIN's strategies and methods', *Journal of Peasant Studies*, 40(3), pp 531–536.
18 TM Li, 'Centering labor in the land grab debate', *Journal of Peasant Studies*, 38(2), 2011, pp 281–298.
19 K Marx, *Capital*, Vol 1, New York: Modern Library, 1906; and D Harvey, *The New Imperialism*, Oxford: Oxford University Press, 2003.
20 See also relevant discussions in M Levien, 'Special Economic Zones and accumulation by dispossession in India', *Journal of Agrarian Change*, 11(4), 2011, pp 454–483; Levien, 'The land question: Special Economic Zones and the political economy of dispossession in India', *Journal of Peasant Studies*, 39(3–4), 2012, pp 933–969; and M Kenney-Lazar, 'Plantation rubber, land grabbing and social-property transformation in southern Laos', *Journal of Peasant Studies*, 39(3–4), 2012, pp 1017–1037.
21 See, for example, PD Little & M Watts (eds), *Living Under Contract: Contract Farming and Agrarian Transformation in Sub-Saharan Africa*, Madison, WI: University of Wisconsin Press, 1994; EF Fischer & P Benson, *Broccoli and Desire: Global Connections and Maya Struggles in Postwar Guatemala*, Stanford, CA: Stanford University Press, 2006; and C Oya, 'Contract farming in sub-Saharan Africa: a survey of approaches, debates and issues', *Journal of Agrarian Change*, 12(1), 2012, pp 1–33.
22 P Woodhouse, 'New investment, old challenges: land deals and the water constraint in African agriculture', *Journal of Peasant Studies*, 39(3-4), 2012, pp 777–794; L Mehta, GJ Veldwisch & J Franco, 'Introduction to the special issue: Water grabbing? Focus on the (re)appropriation of finite water resources', *Water Alternatives*, 5(2), 2012, pp 193–207; and T Allan et al (eds), *Handbook of Land and Water Grabs in Africa: Foreign Direct Investment and Food and Water Security*, London: Routledge, 2012.
23 SM Borras, JC Franco & C Wang, 'The challenge of global governance of land grabbing: changing international agricultural context and competing political views and strategies', *Globalizations*, 10, 2013, pp 161–179; and P Seufert, 'The FAO voluntary guidelines on the responsible governance of tenure of land, fisheries and forests', *Globalizations*, 10, 2013, pp 181–186.
24 See Scoones et al 'The politics of evidence'; Edelman, 'Messy hectares'; and Oya, 'Methodological reflections'.

Notes on Contributors

Marc Edelman is Professor of Anthropology at Hunter College and the Graduate Center, City University of New York. His books include *The Logic of the Latifundio* (1992), *Peasants Against Globalization* (1999), *Social Democracy in the Global Periphery* (coauthored, 2007), and *Transnational Agrarian Movements Confronting Globalization* (coedited, 2008).

Carlos Oya is Senior Lecturer, Department of Development Studies, SOAS, University of London. He has undertaken primary research mostly in sub-Saharan Africa, particularly Mozambique, Senegal, Mauritania, Uganda and Ethiopia, focusing on the political economy of agrarian change, capitalist accumulation, rural wage labour and poverty. He is also co-editor of the *Journal of Agrarian Change*.

Saturnino M Borras Jr is Associate Professor at the International Institute of Social Studies, The Hague, Adjunct Professor at China Agricultural University, Beijing, and Fellow at the Transnational Institute in Amsterdam and at Food First in California. He is co-editor of *Land Grabbing and Global Governance* (with M Margulis and N McKeon, 2013) and of *Governing Global Land Deals: The Role of the State in the Rush for Land* (with W Wolford, R Hall, I Scoones and B White, 2013), and co-coordinator of the Land Deal Politics Initiative (LDPI, www.iss.nl/ldpi).

The Land Rush and Classic Agrarian Questions of Capital and Labour: a systematic scoping review of the socioeconomic impact of land grabs in Africa

CARLOS OYA

Department of Development Studies, SOAS, University of London, London, UK

ABSTRACT   *This paper has two main objectives. First, to address the problematic of the socioeconomic impact of land deals in sub-Saharan Africa by looking at what we know from the available literature so far, namely what has been claimed and how much research has been done, as well as why we do not know very much despite the quantity of material published. This is done via a systematic scoping review, which aims to avoid some of the biases inherent in conventional literature reviews and to provide evidence for some basic features of the emerging research on land grabs in Africa, with specific reference to their contribution to the understanding of livelihood impacts. Second, the article links empirical questions about the impact and implications of land grabs with a discussion of alternative (neglected) research questions, notably the implications of the current land rush phenomenon for the classic agrarian questions of capital and labour, as understood in agrarian political economy. Thus the paper proposes a re-engagement with debates on the classic agrarian questions in a Marxist political economy tradition in order to move the land grab research agenda towards more conceptually and empirically challenging research questions.*

There has been a literature 'rush' concomitant with the widely reported 'land rush' that has swept extensions of territory worldwide and particularly in Africa. The volume of the literature on 'land grabs' is indeed remarkable, considering the fluid nature of the phenomenon and the short timespan involved.[1] Initially spurred by a number of NGO reports, the creation of the first global land grab database (GRAIN 2008) and rising media attention in the wake of the global food crisis 2007–08, the literature has been growing at considerable speed, involving academics, activists, NGOs, media, business publications, international organisations and international financial institutions. The systematic scoping review of the literature on (sub-Saharan) Africa presented in the following section provides quantitative evidence of this literature rush,[2] as well as its sequence in terms of the rise of peer-reviewed academic publications since 2009.

The accelerated growth in publications on the topic has obviously also come with a shifting focus on different issues and a broadening of the coverage, thematically, conceptually and geographically. Thus, from initial anecdotal and highly sensationalist accounts of large-scale land acquisition deals we have been gradually moving towards greater engagement of the academic community, starting from more 'activist' networks to more ambivalent institutional accounts. Because of the important role of large NGOs and transnational agrarian movements, intergovernmental organisations have also intervened, the World Bank being a prime mover with its widely cited publication in 2011.[3] Networks of academics and activists, particularly the Land Deal Politics Initiative (LDPI, www.iss.nl/ldpi), and journals like the *Journal of Peasant Studies* in particular, have also contributed through two major conferences,[4] and several special issues[5], reflecting an exponentially growing interest among academics in the subject. In some ways this is a welcome development, since the breadth and depth of the literature has been improving over time.[6] Cotula suggests in a paper in this special issue that 'more in-depth analyses have emerged that emphasise the historical roots of the global land rush'. While this is true in terms of the quantity and quality of land grab research gradually improving over time, and of debates and claims also becoming also more nuanced, what we learn from a systematic scoping review of the literature until mid-2013 is that there are still major thematic and analytical gaps and methodological problems with what is being published, particularly with regard to evidence on socioeconomic impacts, a central issue in debates on 'land grabs'. It is also clear that there has been a preference for certain types of themes and questions—partly logical because of the nature of the phenomenon and how recent it is—and less interest in long-standing debates in agrarian political economy, as argued below.

This paper has two main objectives. First, the question of the socioeconomic impact of land deals is addressed by looking at what we know from the available literature so far, namely what has been claimed and how much research has been done on the issue, as well as why we do not know very much, despite the quantity of material published. This task is undertaken via a systematic scoping review, which aims to avoid some of the biases inherent in conventional literature reviews and to provide evidence on some basic features of the emerging research on 'land grabs', with reference to their contribution to the understanding of livelihood impacts. Second, the article contributes through a discussion of alternative (neglected) research questions, notably the implications of the current land rush phenomenon for the classic agrarian questions of capital and labour, as understood in agrarian political economy.[7] In other words, the paper proposes a re-engagement with debates on the classic agrarian question in a Marxist political economy tradition in light of the recent experience of large-scale land deals.

The article therefore has two distinct parts, one dealing with the review of the literature's claims on impact and outcomes and the other devoted to discussion of the implications for classic agrarian questions. The article is thus organised as follows. The next section provides a brief discussion of trends in the literature on land grabs and some key methodological and epistemological implications of the rise of this research in agrarian studies. This is followed by a more substantive section, which presents the methods and results of a systematic scoping review of the literature published between 2005 and the end of March 2013, with a focus on land deals and their livelihood outcomes. The following section then tackles the relevance of the debates on the classic 'agrarian questions', engaging with the debate between Bernstein and Byres on the relevance or not of the 'agrarian question of capital', and asking whether the current land rush signals a return of this question or not. This is followed by some concluding remarks and a research agenda.

The literature rush on land grabs: some basic questions of methods and epistemology

As mentioned above, the growth of the literature on land grabs has been remarkable, and has evolved in terms of focus, themes, methods and claims, although some general features have persisted over time. The main points of continuity are the following. First, the practice of denunciation of large-scale land deals and the fascination with big numbers has driven much of the research conducted by NGOs, activist networks and *some* academics in agitprop-type publications. This continues today but is now less central, especially to the academic literature. Some of the interest in monitoring deals and engaging a wider audience was driven by the publication of several 'killer facts' facilitated by the creation of global databases of land deals that a wide audience could both use and contribute to in various forms of 'crowd-sourcing'. The 'killer facts' contributed to creating an image of massive scale and almost a turning point for agrarian societies in poor countries, especially in Africa, an image that has recently been substantially qualified and corrected.[8] From this a series of potentially damaging scenarios has been drawn by activists and the media.[9] Although the focus on scale and drivers has somewhat waned, in fact this initial drive in the 'land grab' literature, plus the big numbers and associated campaigns, have created the conditions for the kind of research and questions that have dominated the literature in the past four to five years. This publication period (roughly 2007–12) can also be seen as a phase in a longer-term narrative of research on the land rush, a phase in which the dominant questions have been about who, where, when and how much, questions that are largely descriptive but have the imperative aim of starting to make sense of a new and rapidly evolving phenomenon.

Second, in this phase much of the literature continues to pay great attention to the *process* of land deals, describing its main actors, what is in the contracts, and the governance issues raised in relation to the negotiation and approval of these deals. This is not surprising, considering that many researchers and activists are particularly interested in land rights and how these are defined and protected. Moreover, international organisations have also contributed to this debate by proposing actions in the form of voluntary guidelines, which essentially focus on the governance of these deals.[10] This means that the literature has indeed provided some useful evidence with rich descriptions of processes, scope and of the nature of deals, the contracts, promises, expectations, negotiations and actors involved.

Third, (though in decline because thanks to consensus and because this phase of 'salvo' research is being exhausted), besides trying to establish the magnitude of the phenomenon, most of the work on land grabs has paid particular attention to its causes and drivers, especially in relation to global processes affecting the political economy of food production and distribution, and the various 'narratives of crisis' beyond food, whether articulated to favour large-scale deals or to oppose them.[11] As the literature has evolved, there has been a move away from simplistic, single-driver analyses (whether biofuels, or the food crisis, for example) towards the characterisation of a multifaceted and multi-caused phenomenon where context specificity is very important.[12]

Many of the questions and themes briefly presented above were often geared towards establishing the range of negative consequences, whether in terms of the governance of these deals or in terms of potential impacts on 'local communities'. A lot of research and advocacy work was also driven by a deliberate aim to debunk the simplistic win-win scenarios sometimes depicted by those advocating the need for large-scale private agricultural investment in poor countries, including some of the recent accounts by intergovernmental organisations.[13] In the end, both pro- and anti-land acquisition deals sometimes converged in a superficial and over-simplified presentation of the potential benefits of these deals, without candidly addressing the complex and contradictory ways in which such benefits might actually materialise over time. In any case many of the early engagements with the question of 'impacts' or 'outcomes' emerged around potential or expected vs actual outcomes, but readers and the media may typically have interpreted them as real outcomes.

The questions and themes dominating the 'land grab' literature therefore tend to ignore a number of long-standing debates and questions in agrarian political economy, notably the prospects for and impediments to the development of capitalist agriculture in developing countries. One reason for this is that this initial wave of research mainly tried to engage with the emerging phenomenon by attempting to ascertain its scale and actors. Another is that many of the (more populist) participants in these debates simply oppose capitalist development on ideological grounds and set out to denounce the consequences of it if it comes through large-scale land deals from foreign investors. Another reason is that Marxist scholars, who are more interested in these debates, have largely ignored the literature on recent large-scale land deals.

Before moving to the next section, which more systematically explores the emerging literature in relation to questions of impact, it is worth emphasising two basic epistemological and methodological challenges. The first is matching research questions with appropriate methods. This is a general challenge in social science research, where problems of reductionism and ecological fallacy are sometimes hard to avoid.[14] In the case of research and publications on land grabs many of the questions asked are very broad and hard to pin down, even more so when information on deals is often opaque or simply biased by misreporting. Such questions (on the scale and dynamics of deals, their drivers and governance and their impact) require the deployment of methods, tools and resources that are seldom available to many researchers. In this sense, then, it is surprising that so much research has been published. The key point at this stage (see more below) is that for much of the literature published so far the methods used seem limited with respect to the difficulty, breadth and depth of questions asked. Questions such as 'who', 'when', 'where' and 'how much' may be tackled through a variety of largely descriptive methods, that is, they do not necessarily require a sophisticated quantitative framework, but the room for error is significant and effective triangulation and probing are crucial.

In this regard there is of course a variety of approaches, with some studies being far more heedful of the need for triangulation and empirical caveats in contrast with others, which easily jump to conclusions from limited research. Indeed, a fundamental problem in any exercise that reviews a mix of academic and NGO 'agitprop' research material is the heterogeneity in quality and methods. Much of the NGO–grey literature is unfortunately driven by small and badly designed studies which essentially add some circumstantial detail to pre-cooked conclusions. NGO 'agitprop' campaign surveys are certainly not the same as a serious piece of social science. Some academic publications, especially in the past two years, are very different in terms of the depth and methodological care involved.[15] Although there is space for different kinds of research on these issues, there is no shortcut for good quality evidence.[16]

The second, and associated, challenge is identifying the influence of ideology on research questions, themes and methods. This is particularly important in the context of polarised debates also shaped by the intensive participation of the mass media, which tend to over-simplify and distort facts and narratives. A basic problem with some of the literature on land grabs (especially NGO material and campaigns) is its tendency to present a caricature of capitalism, agrarian capital and the relations between corporate agribusiness and the developing world. Therefore, the simplification of discourses around the impact of land grabs (whether negative or positive) is not surprising, given that much of the initial push for the literature and reporting on large-scale acquisition was action-oriented and driven by condemnation of land deals.

This simplification tends to obscure some basic features of agrarian change and capitalist development which are at the heart of long-standing agrarian questions, as will be argued below. First, capitalist development is not a harmonious monotonic process of change, but tends to happen unevenly, in spurts and through varying cycles depending on local, national and global conditions. Capitalist development in agriculture sometimes manifests itself as a roller-coaster with episodic instances of 'rush', economic and extra-economic coercion, while sometimes it is a much more gradual process that slowly evolves behind the scenes. Second, history shows that many of the rushed changes associated with the penetration of capitalism tend to be conflictual, especially in relation to land use, primitive accumulation and labour exploitation. Capitalism and conflict go hand in hand.[17] While many contributions to the land grab literature are well aware of this basic feature of capitalism, conflict is often presented and analysed in Manichean terms. Third, by focusing on simple binaries (capital vs 'other' or 'peasant', corporate industrialised agriculture vs peasant smallholders, 'local, vs 'outsider', etc) the dominant wisdom eschews the analysis of contradictions and ambiguities both within capitalism and within those who oppose it.[18] Missing out on the nuances of capitalist expansion and its contradictions, as well as of resistance to, it runs the risk of leading debates to a simple world of 'baddies' (the 'grabbers'), usually synonymous with large transnational agribusiness or sovereign funds, and 'goodies' (or 'affected communities', displaced smallholders and so on).

At the heart of this problematic dichotomy are assumptions and claims about impacts and 'winners' and 'losers'. Impacts can take many forms but it is usually socioeconomic impact that is likely to have more relevance, even though justified attention is also paid to environmental impacts. The next section presents the results of a systematic scoping review on research and evidence on livelihood impacts from the research published between 2005 and March 2013, the period when the literature on land grabs emerged and grew very quickly.

Evaluating the socioeconomic impact of land deals in Africa: what do we know? And why don't we know much?

Impact evaluation has become central to much research in international development. Funding agencies, NGOs and academics are increasingly involved in various forms of impact evaluation. It is therefore not surprising that debates about methods on impact evaluation have also become more prominent and lively. In the jargon of evaluation studies a 'land deal' could be seen as an 'intervention', which may be driven by a variety of actors, such as states, companies and international organisations. Debate thus arises on the outcomes and impact of such intervention. As suggested in the previous section, methodological debates about land grabs and the land rush have recently been initiated around issues of quantification of deals and doing research on large-scale land acquisitions, rather than on the latter's impacts.[19] Impacts on the ground have not received the same attention from researchers, for reasons discussed below, but claims about outcomes and impacts abound in the available literature, especially in reports and studies published by NGOs and international organisations. Before proceeding to report on the systematic scoping literature review described below, two caveats are worth noting. First, this is not an exhaustive review of the whole literature on land grabs: it is limited to studies that make any claims on outcomes and impact (even if these are not the main research questions) and to studies that make any such claims in relation to sub-Saharan Africa.[20] Second, the literature reviewed is not just academic or that found in peer-reviewed publications, but also includes a rich range of 'grey literature', for instance reports from (national and international) NGOs as well as international organisations. It therefore comprises an epistemological and methodological mix of sources.

This section presents the preliminary results of a basic systematic scoping review of the literature on land acquisitions in sub-Saharan Africa published between 2005 and March 2013. Systematic literature review is an increasingly popular method in evaluation research and is here deployed to partly assess the emerging literature in relation to claims about impact and outcomes of existing land deals. This is still a work in progress, since the usual strict criteria used in systematic reviews have been somewhat relaxed to accommodate more studies and to learn more about the nature of the research done rather than on the reported outcomes, therefore opting for the technique of 'lumping' as opposed to 'splitting' reviews.[21] First, the methods of the systematic scoping review are described in some detail. Second, some basic results on the kind of research underpinning claims on impact are discussed, followed by a more general reflection about the interpretation of these claims and the inherent challenges in conducting impact evaluation on land deals.

Methods

This scoping review aims primarily to explore and synthesise key aspects of the emerging literature on 'land grabs' with a focus on its main claims about socioeconomic (livelihood) impacts and the methods used to support these claims. In a way, it is a mapping exercise of the state of the emerging and fast-growing literature on this subject though within a narrower scope, that is, studies that have something to say about the *impact* of land deals on livelihoods of the affected 'communities', published within a given timeframe (1 January 2005 to 31 March 2013) and with evidence from sub-Saharan Africa. As a *scoping* review, the aim is not to directly evaluate individual studies, or to compare specific statistical results to provide a synthesis, as in conventional systematic reviews. The scope is broader and allows for the inclusion of a wide range of studies from different disciplinary and epistemological traditions.[22] Scoping reviews also constitute preliminary examinations of a field of research (in this case, land grabs in Africa), in terms of the size, scope and nature of the research, as well as the nature and extent of the relevant research evidence and the methods used to obtain it.

This review is *systematic* in the sense of being undertaken according to a fixed plan or system or method, often presented in the form of a 'protocol'.[23] A review can also be systematic in terms of its methods being both explicit and replicable. Usually a systematic review is expected to involve the 'mapping' of research, specifically identifying and describing relevant sources, a systematic critical appraisal based on some explicit criteria, which leads to a selection of studies according to such criteria, and a synthesis of extracted data, which brings together findings into a coherent statement. In its conventional use in natural sciences and now increasingly in the field of development, a systematic review aims to assess what is known through a synthesis of available results and to make recommendations for policy and practice based on a statistical or qualitative aggregation of results from selected studies.

The review undertaken for this paper partly aimed to assess 'how what is known is known' with reference to a specific question but without the aspiration of synthesising results for policy recommendations, as the nature of the published research and the phenomenon analysed would not make this possible. This is a common challenge in systematic reviews of international development issues, as different types of research provide different types of evidence on outcomes, which is not always quantifiable. Other challenges are the heterogeneity of studies reviewed, making comparisons and selection difficult unless very clear criteria are used; the need to search beyond academic and bibliographic databases, since much research is published in institutional repositories and websites and therefore not always peer-reviewed; and the difficulty of obtaining information on methods used and the unavoidable reliance on researchers' own description thereof, because of the impossibility of interviewing each researcher to probe the nature of methods and their application.[24] All these challenges were encountered in the exercise undertaken for this review. The paucity of information on methods was particularly problematic, an issue that will be discussed in more detail below. Therefore this review can be seen as a scoping review following a systematic approach to the relevant literature.

Any review of this nature requires a clear and relevant research question. The key guiding research question that was addressed by the review was: what is the nature of the evidence on the socioeconomic impacts of recent and current land acquisition (in terms of both positive and negative livelihood outcomes)? Put differently, what do we know about the livelihood impacts of land grabs and how do we know it? The focus is specifically on the dialectic between the possible threats and displacement of existing livelihoods and the opportunities being created, thus 'new' livelihoods, as a result of land acquisitions. Cotula is right when he states that 'livelihood options are not created—they are transformed... the question is whether this transformation is for the better'.[25] The main aim of this review was therefore to assess how the literature tackled this question. This is a key empirical question that should underpin efforts at establishing impacts (rather than a singular impact). In particular, and consistent with the main focus of this paper, it is a question essentially centred on labour outcomes, where access to land is an important issue as long as it constitutes a central source of livelihoods. As Li strongly suggests, it is important to centre land grab debates on labour, particularly in terms of understanding whether the interest in farmland is accompanied and complemented by interest in labour or not, and not only on what happens to those displaced but also on what happens to those who are not displaced.[26]

A key motivation for this exercise was the abundance of claims about the livelihood impact of land grabs in much of the available literature and especially in NGO reports. Although there is a wide range of themes and issues that have been researched around the phenomenon of recent land acquisitions, many publications say something about the implications of these deals for livelihoods. What is not clear at first glance is whether the evidence to support these claims is solid and systematic or flimsy and patchy. This is particularly important in a debate that is polarised and where the interests of 'groups' and 'communities' are often referred to.

In order to produce a systematic review, even if for scoping purposes, there is a need for an explicit systematic review protocol where the concrete aims, the search methods, key terms, inclusion and exclusion criteria are explicitly shown, as detailed below. The review had two complementary aims. First, it tried to find studies that specifically provided some evidence on impact with a minimum of a before and after quantitative framework. This is because claims about impacts often referred to numbers of people displaced or given jobs but it was not clear on what basis these claims were being made. In the context of conventional systematic reviews in the natural sciences and increasingly in international development, there is a ranking of study designs for quality appraisal and, at the minimum, we have studies with some comparator (in the form of constructed control groups through data analysis matching) or a before and after framework. These methods are often considered *less* reliable than experimental methods such as Randomised Control Trials (RCTs).[27] In the case of land deals, and given the nature of the phenomenon, experimental designs are unlikely if not impossible. However, a before and after comparison with the use of a baseline in order to assess outcomes would be a reasonable expectation if the goal is to establish a relatively precise *quantitative* impact. While many studies make claims that implicitly refer to a before and after framework, it was not initially clear whether these claims were based on study designs with baselines and follow-up surveys. This was therefore used as a 'strict' criterion of final inclusion for the assessment of outcome results. In fact, we wanted to know whether we could find any study containing these characteristics.

The second aim, once all relevant studies were screened, was to ascertain the type of claim in relation to outcomes (whether negative, positive or both) and the nature of the research methods used. This was more important in terms of understanding the nature of emerging research on 'land grabs' and ascertaining what we really know about their impacts and why we know what we know.

As happens with most literature in development studies research, many studies are of a qualitative nature, and often based on limited interviews. A before and after comparison does not necessarily require a quantitative survey approach, although it would be hard to establish a clear 'net' impact with a qualitative approach only. The challenge is that land deals are likely to produce a variety of effects, some positive and some negative depending on the issue and depending on whose well-being or whose interests one pays attention to. Moreover, time matters, as negative outcomes may be more common in the initial stages, whereas positive outcomes, like employment creation and spill-over effects from new production and infrastructure may only materialise after some time. There may be winners and losers and establishing an overall impact is a challenging exercise that would require a careful in-depth investigation of the phenomenon.[28]

Findings

The protocol of the review included an initial phase of comprehensive literature 'mapping', including sources that met the following criteria: 1) studies that reported on land grabs in sub-Saharan Africa; 2) studies that reported on impacts or aspects of impacts, even if this was not necessarily the main focus of the research; 3) studies focusing on impacts relevant to people's livelihoods, eg employment and displacement; thus studies on environmental impact were not selected; d) studies published between 1 January 2005 and 31 March 2013; 5) peer-reviewed literature identified through bibliographical database searches, and non-peer-reviewed reports and studies that were well cited and well known in the relevant literature. The search strategy therefore included the following sources:

- multidisciplinary bibliographic databases of peer-reviewed literature, eg Web of Science, EBSCOhost, JSTOR, EconLit, IBSS, Taylor & Francis, ScienceDirect etc;

- Entries from Google Scholar with a minimum of 10 citations in the first 10 pages of entries;
- databases, repositories or websites of organisations such as Oxfam, the Oakland Institute, the IIED, International Land Coalition, ActionAid, World Bank and GRAIN, among others;
- through 'snowballing', ie consulting key informants for any key missing studies, as well as using the citations in the previously searched items to expand the list of entries.

This systematic scoping review, unlike more conventional such reviews, which only search bibliographic databases, did not limit the search to peer-reviewed publications, because much cited material and influential reports have been produced and published by international organisations and NGOs and not by academics.[29] Key search terms were carefully selected to make sure the net was cast wide enough, so that all relevant material was included, but also to avoid unnecessary irrelevant material. The combination of various search terms narrowed down the scope of the search to favour literature with some claims or information on impact, so the review did not search for publications on 'land deals' or 'land grabs' but for those with 'impact' and related search terms in their keywords and abstracts. Despite somewhat narrowing down the scope of the search, the initial result yielded over 2000 entries, excluding duplicates (see Figure 1).

Once the screening for eligibility had been performed, a substantial number of publications was excluded, mainly for reasons of different topic, or no evidence on Africa, or because information or claims on impacts were lacking. The main screening yielded 176 publications, which were then screened again with abstracts and full-text for two purposes: first, to undertake a basic methodology review to characterise the nature of the publication and the evidence base; and, second, to establish how many studies would meet the strict inclusion criterion of impact assessment with baseline and before and after comparison. Given the nature of the literature, the challenges involved in studying this phenomenon (see above) and the short timeframe for impact assessments, at best a very small number of publications would be expected to meet the strict inclusion criterion. In the end, the finding is nonetheless striking. *The review could not find a single study meeting this criterion, ie one presenting an evaluation of impact with a rigorous baseline and a before and after comparison.* Of course, this is partly a result of the nature of the criteria, which necessarily excluded all studies that were only based on rapid qualitative assessments of perceptions about impact or on short-term qualitative research. It is, however, a significant finding, since much has been said and published about the impacts of land grabs, especially in NGO reports, but there is no rigorous *quantitative* evidence to support these claims.

After the screening for first-stage eligibility, and also after confirming that there were no studies meeting the 'strict' quantitative methodology criterion, a methodology review was undertaken, which initially included 176 publications that were browsed based on their focus and claims on socioeconomic impacts in Africa, regardless of the sources and methodology used. Only 170 were finally

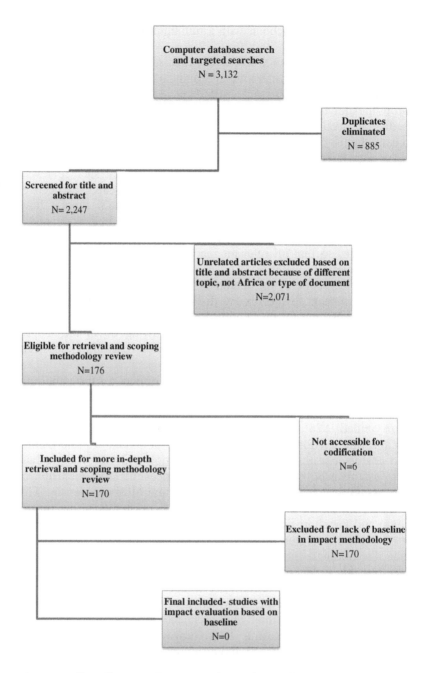

FIGURE 1. PRISMA flow diagram of a systematic scoping review of literature.

found to be fully accessible and these are the object of the basic descriptive analysis shown below. This 'methodology review' was particularly challenging because of the unfortunate practice of many publications in this field of not

TABLE 1. Basic results of systematic scoping review

Categories	Attributes	% within each category	Count
Type of document	Book, whole	2%	3
	Journal article	52%	89
	Report (NGO, institutional, website, etc)	46%	78
Research type (sources)	Primary research (at least *some*)	37%	62
	Secondary sources only	63%	107
Rapid appraisal or not	Rapid appraisal ('quick and dirty research')	50%	31
	Other primary research (qualitative, quantitative)	50%	31
Total		100%	170

Note: The percentages for 'rapid appraisal or not' categories are in relation to the 62 publications that were based on some primary research as shown above.

explaining or only partially describing their research methods. Sometimes these had to be inferred from a reading of the report/article or through additional searches. The paucity of information on research methods, especially when primary data collection is undertaken, is not unusual in the field of international development but it makes the appraisal of methods and results very difficult and raises some questions about transparency and consistency.[30] The categorisations presented here are therefore unavoidably broad, since it was generally hard to discern concrete study designs.

The findings about the type of research and methods that made the 'cut' for this scoping review are also striking, though not entirely surprising for someone familiar with the debates and literature on land grabs. First, the total number of publications is very significant, given how recent the phenomenon is, how hard it is to do primary research and the political sensitivities involved. A total of 89 peer-reviewed journal articles met the eligibility criteria, among many more published on land grabs but beyond the specific boundaries of the initial search. This is remarkable given the time that it usually takes for articles to go through peer-review processes and between first submission and final publication. It also reflects a rapidly growing interest in the topic as more and more academics of different generations have engaged in current debates on land acquisitions. This growth and the speed of publication turnover may also indicate political urgency, as well as indirect pressure from global media interests and its indirect effects on research agendas.

Second, the review showed that much of the published material meeting the eligibility criteria was actually not based on *primary* research, namely data directly collected from the 'field'. Only about 37% (or 62) of the relevant publications contained some primary evidence directly collected by the authors. The depth and breadth of this primary evidence obviously varied a lot (hence our term 'at least *some* primary research'). This means that almost two-thirds of the publications were essentially based on secondary sources and the citation of empirical material from other sources included in this review. This is also noteworthy, since lack of primary evidence is a major constraint on knowledge and a relative abundance of secondary research reflects a mismatch between the evidence accumulated and the amount of published literature. On the other hand, it is also not entirely surprising, since much of the literature of the first phase of research on the 'land rush' did not primarily focus on impact and where claims were made on impact these were often based on a few selected field studies undertaken by other researchers.

Third, much of the primary evidence was collected through rapid appraisal or so-called 'quick and dirty research'. This practice would include a few days or weeks of mostly semi-structured or open interviewing with selected informants, generally among a range of different stakeholders but sometimes with a particular focus on representatives of groups negatively affected by land acquisition processes, particularly displaced people. Out of the 62 studies that contained some primary data collection half were based on rapid appraisals conducted over short fieldwork periods and with a limited number of interviews with selected informants, as far as methods were described. This partly reflected the quick fact-finding nature of many of these studies, which often deliberately focused on issues of displacement and not on medium or long-term socioeconomic impact. Although this kind of research has some value in itself, providing in particular information on early outcomes or on perceptions of potential effects, and thus may be adequate for a range of research questions and interests, it is certainly worrying that, given how much published material has made claims about the impact of land acquisitions, the depth of the evidence accumulated is still so limited.

Fourth, an analysis of trends in time of publication also suggests a literature rush that almost mirrors the quantification of the land rush in available databases like the Land Matrix and GRAIN (see Figure 2). Between 2011 and 2012 more than 100 publications were recorded out of the 176 included since 2005. It is interesting that both journal articles and non-peer-reviewed reports peaked in 2011–12, with around 75% of all items published since 2011. However, there is a slight lag in journal articles, which tend to be concentrated more in 2012, when one-third of all such publications came out, whereas other non-academic publications peaked in 2011. In sum, there is a clear consistency between the land rush and a related literature rush on the phenomenon in terms of quantities of material. This is not surprising. The relatively short lag between the ongoing phenomenon of land acquisitions and the publication of academic peer-reviewed

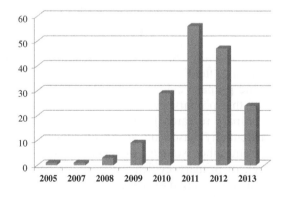

FIGURE 2. Frequency of items by year of publication.

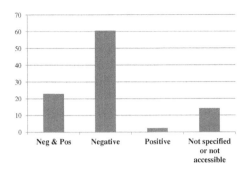

F<small>IGURE</small> 3. Reported impact, dominant conclusion (% of publications).

material is somewhat more surprising, because of the usually long time between submission and publication in most peer-reviewed academic journals.

Fifth, some journals and organisations have played a leading role in terms of the promotion of material on land grabs. On the academic front the *Journal of Peasant Studies* (JPS) stands out, with 36 articles out of the total count of 89, almost 30% of all journal articles and nearly 15% of all reviewed publications. In fact, a few journals account for a very large proportion of all articles published. The JPS, *Globalisations* and *Review of African Political Economy* contain over 50% of all journal articles recorded in the scoping review. This shows that there are some 'prime-movers' with substantial mobilisation capacity to attract researchers working on land acquisition, and also reflects the use of special issues to organise this mobilisation of academic research.

Sixth, a large majority of the works reviewed reported negative outcomes as their dominant conclusion (60%), while fewer than 3% reported mainly positive outcomes (see Figure 3). This can be viewed in three ways. First, that these were the results of various case studies reported by different publications without any particular bias. Second, that there may be a selection and reporting bias, especially considering that virtually all NGO reports focus on negative outcomes— unsurprising given that most of these were produced as part of an advocacy agenda against 'land grabs' and attempted to focus on issues of displacement and land rights, or on whether 'communities' were consulted or not, rather than on overall impact *per se*. The third view is that the bias is not deliberate but arises from the nature of the phenomenon of land grabs, whereby negative outcomes (for instance displacement) tend to appear earlier in the lifetime of the investment project, while benefits arrive in the medium term (see further discussion below).

Discussion

The paucity of evidence on impact and the dominance of 'rapid appraisal' methods in addition to use of secondary sources, while alarming, also reflects a number of features of the land grab phenomenon and the challenge of data collection on it. It is a relatively recent phenomenon on processes that often last a long time. Therefore, different conclusions and impressions can be reached depending on the time when interviewing is done. In the early stages the sorts of questions that dominate may not refer to long-term effects, but rather to short-term outcomes such as displacement or to issues like lack of consultations with potentially affected groups. Land grabbing is also a controversial issue on which access to reliable information is complicated. Some potential respondents are hard to find or to persuade to be interviewed, especially managers and workers in investing companies, who fear the use of information in the media. The reliance on case study material is also not surprising given the difficulty in accessing systematic evidence on land acquisitions processes, and the lack of statistical systems to provide a systematic account of land deals, their *ex-ante* assessments and their processes. Researchers, constrained by their own limited resources, are thus inclined to conduct case study research and rapid appraisals. This is also partly because the advocacy drive of much of this research has led to a rush to investigate as many case studies as possible and as quickly as possible but with limited resources, which have been spread thinly among multiple groups of researchers and activists.

In light of the problems with empirical evidence on impact, Cotula is perhaps too quick to conclude that 'as a broad generalisation, local livelihoods tend to be disrupted in ways that are not offset by the new agricultural venture'.[31] Discussions in several studies rely on patchy (sometimes anecdotal) evidence used to provide broad comparative narratives of large-scale deals versus small-scale farming, which are then cited by some studies based on secondary sources. A contrast is often made between a romanticised notion of 'local livelihoods' and a reality of failed deals, with new livelihoods highly vulnerable to international market vagaries, or partial implementation without devolution of land. Any impact assessment would require a candid analysis of the existing situation, namely a balanced unpacking of the nature and vulnerability of 'local livelihoods' before deals start to be implemented. This normally requires a baseline, if researchers aim to provide numbers and 'net' overall outcomes. The review presented here shows that no study has been able to provide such an in-depth analysis of the *ex-ante* situation compared with emerging data on differentiated effects on different groups of people. There is more reporting of cases of failed deals, some with innocuous results when enclosures have not taken effect, and some leading to a worst-case scenario of displacement, followed by abandonment of the project and land but without devolution of the land.[32] However, in the absence of 'harder' evidence, the polarisation of views between the public relations optimism of some of the new investors with regard to their expectations of benefits for 'local communities', on the one hand, and the celebration of and support for existing 'local livelihoods', in the form of small-scale 'subsistence' farming and other uses of land and forests by the 'local populations', on the other hand, is likely to continue. The main conclusion of this review is that neither the investing companies trying to sell their projects nor their critics trying to debunk these promises provide rigorous evidence based on solid research methods of impact assessment, whether quantitative or qualitative or both.

The most important point made by Cotula and others is the idea that impacts are unavoidably differentiated, namely there are 'winners and losers' and, often, when and how groups of people gain or lose out depends much on the type of deal and project, the investors, the speed of the process and other macro- and micro-structural conditions.[33] It is a highly contextual issue. Differentiated impacts also have implications for the sorts of reactions from below that are found in a variety of contexts. Borras and Franco (in this collection) provide compelling evidence that these reactions from below are differentiated and at times contradictory. It is precisely in terms of providing more nuanced and in-depth research into how particular groups benefit and why, and how some others are negatively affected, that a serious research gap seems to exist. The gap is not merely related to the type of field research conducted and the methods deployed. It derives directly from the kinds of questions asked and debates addressed, and which ones remain neglected, which will be discussed below.

As the land rush literature moves into a new phase of more academically and analytically oriented research, new research questions around 'why', 'how' and 'with what consequences' are likely (or ought) to take over the research agenda on large-scale acquisition. New contributors from a variety of epistemological and theoretical traditions may add new angles to the debates. It is in this spirit that a revival of classic agrarian questions in the agrarian political economy tradition is suggested here. This revival is necessary to give more depth to our knowledge of impact and long-term implications of the land rush and to frame this phenomenon historically and conceptually. This is perhaps also an opportunity for Marxist scholars immersed in this tradition to engage more actively with current debates on the implications and impact of so-called land grabs for both the prospects for agrarian transformations and processes of rural class formation.

The land rush in relation to agrarian questions of capital and labour: the return of agrarian capital?

This section takes up the challenge of moving on from the knowledge gap on the impact and outcomes of the land rush towards framing the analysis of land deals and the current rush and their outcomes within a broad agrarian political economy framework, where research questions focus on the processes of agrarian transition and how the questions of capital and labour (see below) are solved or not. It provides some pointers to what kind of questions and evidence are relevant in understanding the impact of land deals, and their implications for contemporary questions of capital, that is, the development of agrarian capitalism and its obstacles, and of labour, namely the crisis in the social reproduction of labour because people leave (or are economically forced to leave) agriculture without their labour being absorbed elsewhere in the economy.[34]

In classic agrarian political economy the 'agrarian question of capital' has been central. Byres describes it in its broadest terms as 'the continuing existence in the countryside of a poor country of substantive obstacles to an unleashing of the forces capable of generating economic development, both inside and outside agriculture'.[35] Central to the agrarian question of capital is the 'production problematic', in Bernstein's terms,[36] which essentially refers to the drivers of and impediments to the development of capitalist agriculture in agrarian transitions to capitalism. This problematic involves the gradual generalisation of wage labour as a way of survival and the gradual separation of workers from their means of production, especially land, a key outcome of which is usually called 'primitive accumulation' and is also related to the 'agrarian question of labour' mentioned above. Indeed, the 'production problematic' in the agrarian question lies at the centre of current debates on land grabs, but is rarely tackled directly. Much of the literature in fact makes reference to the implications of land grabs in terms of *transforming* livelihoods towards wage employment, namely 'proletarianising the peasantry' or simply as displacement to leave space for corporate agri-capital (usually foreign but also national) to exploit the land.

It is interesting that there are no contributions to the vast recent literature on land grabs attempting to engage with long-standing debates about the agrarian question of capital and whether the current land rush marks a turning point in the resolution (or not) of this question. In fact, extreme interpretations of the land rush as capital's renewed commitment to dispossess the peasantry would contradict the basic proposition defended by Bernstein that the agrarian question of capital is now redundant.[37] Bernstein's basic point is that agrarian questions evolve as capitalism evolves. Thus agrarian transitions in contemporary developing countries are affected by earlier transitions to capitalism elsewhere, as well as by subsequent changes in the dynamics of capitalism globally. Global forces may therefore shape and constrain the speed and nature of agrarian transitions in countries where agrarian capital has not emerged as a major force. Contemporary globalisation and transformations in global agribusiness mean capital (global and national) is no longer interested in agriculture and therefore in direct exploitation of land for production purposes, and thus agrarian capitalist transformations in developing countries are no longer necessary for the spread of capitalist commodity relations worldwide. Other sectors (especially finance) provide the key *loci* of contemporary accumulation. The corollary of this situation is that 'agrarian transition is no longer a necessary precondition of the development of capitalism' and 'Bernstein thus prioritises the rural politics problematic over the rural production and accumulation problematics'.[38]

Bernstein's position is, however, debatable, especially if one takes it to an extreme interpretation, which would deny the possibility of the development of capitalist agriculture in developing countries. In fact, Bernstein's argument that agrarian transition, in the 'classic' sense, is no longer a necessary precondition for the development of capitalism does not necessarily mean that capitalist transformation of agriculture is not happening or not going to happen. The key term is 'necessary'. Empirical evidence on processes of economic development and structural change in many developing countries suggests that there may be cases where capitalist development takes place without a concomitant radical transformation of agriculture along capitalist lines. However, there is also empirical evidence suggesting that these transformations are taking place, even in poor countries in Africa where the agricultural sector is typically portrayed as a reservoir of small-scale non-capitalist farmers, and even in a context of limited structural change or industrialisation. If in discussing the development of agrarian capital we do not limit ourselves to the emergence of large-scale corporate agriculture but we consider the wide range of small-, middle- and large-scale indigenous and foreign investors and capitalist farmers, then the realities of and scope for capitalist transformations are more significant than implied in Bernstein's arguments.[39]

Byres, on the other hand, remains sceptical about the validity of Bernstein's arguments for the impact of globalisation on the relevance of the 'classic' agrarian question. He notes, in particular, that 'Bernstein places great stress on the possible access of contemporary developing economies to "external sources of external accumulation"';[40] and that Bernstein argues that 'imperialism/globalisation [will] industrialise backward agrarian formations, and without reference to agriculture'.[41] Byres further notes that 'Bernstein's point runs the danger of reductionism…and world system determinism', and adds that 'one unfortunate danger of Bernstein's argument, indeed, is that it leads to the ignoring of "national capitals" which, under the thrall of "global capital", have no autonomous role'.[42] This is an important point that is especially relevant to current debates on land grabs in Africa. For one significant finding in some of the emerging literature concerns the role and dynamics of 'national capitals' in recent processes of land acquisition for agricultural purposes. While Byres focuses on the industrialisation experiences of India and China and the role of agrarian transitions there to question the death of the 'agrarian question of capital', the argument here is that both agrarian questions of capital and labour, whether conflated in one question or addressed separately, are central to the land grab debate but have actually received little direct empirical attention, as the systematic review presented in the section above suggests. However, if the phenomenon of land grabs is of such spectacular scale as is often portrayed, it should perhaps mark a renewal of the 'agrarian question of capital'. Are current agrarian transformations in parts of Africa being spurred by the 'external forces of accumulation' at a speed not seen thus far? Are 'national forces' also behind this renewal of the 'agrarian question of capital'?

These are now relevant analytical and empirical questions that require more long-term research and a renewal of interest in the processes of the development of capitalism in agriculture in the contemporary world. One can of course speculate about the reasons why these questions have not been tackled with substantive evidence in the land grab literature. In light of the results of our systematic scoping review, one of the most plausible reasons is that it is hard to gather high-quality evidence on these questions without greater time, more resources and more interest in the classic agrarian questions and how relevant they are for a more nuanced interpretation of land grabs. Part of the problem is also the fact that literature on agrarian capital in Africa has been sorely lacking in the past three decades and is only emerging in isolated instances now.[43] It is a scholarly tradition that has attracted little interest in a field influenced by neoclassical economics, neo-populist perspectives and livelihood approaches. These are also questions that have not been tackled by authors who work within a broadly Marxist political economy tradition, because their focus has been on globalisation, the politics of resistance and 'accumulation by dispossession' at a very general level, and on the features and dynamics of international food regimes.[44] At the moment there are many more questions than answers and, while the fast-growing literature on 'land grabs' has provided some evidence to suggest that the agrarian questions of capital and labour are highly relevant, the contributions in this regard have so far been limited.

A key question is whether the scale is quantitatively and qualitatively significant. Unfortunately, even the global numbers on large-scale land acquisitions suffer from serious problems of reliability.[45] If the magnitude of the phenomenon is much less significant than implied by the literature rush on the land rush, and if the phenomenon of land acquisitions turns out to be an ephemeral episode in the history of investors' interest in land in developing countries, in Africa in particular, then we may be left with the same unanswered questions and continuing discussion like the Bernstein–Byres debate on the relevance of the classic agrarian questions until new evidence is produced. This would require a more effective and independent monitoring system of land deals, with better verification processes that explicitly aim to distinguish between failed or fake deals and real deals.

A related question is whether this still 'limited' return of global capital to agriculture is driven by the prospects of agriculture-based accumulation or by speculation on land (and all its ramifications). If speculation is a significant driver, and we do not know enough about it to address this question, then this phenomenon is likely to be ephemeral and to have little effect on the dynamics of capitalist transformation in African agrarian societies. Although a failed deal is not necessarily speculative, there are consequences for the evaluation of its impacts and their relevance for the classic agrarian questions. Indeed, Cotula's strongest argument about the relative failure of large-scale land deals is the high incidence of failed projects.[46] If the gap between plans and reality is large or, in other words, if the land rush does not finally materialise in terms of real and sustained farm ventures, then, of course, the whole debate about impact becomes reduced to the negative impact of a speculative rush for land on material realities of land access and livelihood. The stories of failures would also then corroborate some of Bernstein's more pessimistic conclusions. It remains, however, an empirical question for which there is some evidence, but certainly not enough. We still don't know the proportion of reported deals that have had some kind of impact on the ground, in the form of displacement, enclosure or conflict, but have turned out to be speculative. On the one hand, neglecting this question implies a serious bias in the assessment of large-scale land deals. On the other hand, over-emphasising this possibility without sufficient evidence may also obscure our understanding of land deals and their impact on social differentiation and agrarian class formation.

In any case, showing cases of failure among large-scale land deals driven by foreign capital does not necessarily disprove the existence of an ongoing but slow agrarian transformation towards capitalist forms of production. Arguably this transformation has been taking place slowly and unevenly but it is taking place regardless of the current land rush. So, even if the land 'rush' is only episodic, it will have opened researchers' eyes to current processes of rural accumulation and differentiation and thus may have made existing 'agrarian capital' and ongoing transformations more visible. For the land rush does not happen in a historical and political-economic vacuum. The example of Ethiopia is noteworthy in this regard, since this is one of the more frequently investigated countries within the literature on land grabs in Africa. The emerging literature on land deals has increasingly emphasised the centrality of national agrarian capital (whether large, medium or small-scale) in the processes of land acquisition, despite media interest in high-profile cases of 'land grab' by large multinational agribusiness like Karuthuri.[47] In reality, little is known about the emergence of an increasingly powerful class of agrarian capitalists with interests in different regions and commodities, and a variety of linkages with the state and foreign capital. Some sectors and regions have received more attention as a result of the emerging 'land grab' literature, but many other important instances of the rise of domestic agrarian capital in sectors like coffee, flowers and cotton, where domestic capital accumulation pre-dates the land rush are worth researching in much more depth. An important research question, therefore, is the extent to which these emerging capitalists will play a leading role in spurring agrarian transformations, land acquisition and employment creation in rural Ethiopia, and ultimately with what social, economic and political effects.[48]

A further critical question is what kind of agrarian capital, whether domestic or foreign? Unsystematic evidence on foreign investors suggests that some new entrants have little track record in agribusiness in Africa, are under-capitalised in relation to the land requested and are excessively reliant on lending.[49] In reality, this may also characterise many of the thousands of national investors willing to expand agricultural activities, who start with little capital and lots of energy and face much uncertainty.[50] The history of indigenous agrarian capitalism in Africa is plagued with such under-capitalised capitalists, so it is not necessarily a new trend. Nor is it a sufficient reason to dismiss their viability in the long term.[51] The origins of emerging agrarian capitalists, whether from the ranks of smallholder farmers or of established rural elites and landowners, are also important, as different trajectories of transition and accumulation, from 'above' or 'below', may be evolving in different directions during the current 'land rush'.[52]

Evidence to shed light on the questions raised above requires the sort of meticulous and long-term mixed-method research that has not been particularly abundant in the recent land grab literature. Indeed researchers working on contemporary agrarian and development studies would learn much from the careful work of (economic) historians on the rise of agrarian capitalism and methodological problems with the definition of categories and evidence.[53] In current debates on land grabs the use of categories such as 'large farms', 'mega farms', 'small-scale farmers', 'family farms', 'peasant producers', 'local livelihoods' are elusive at best, inconsistent and misleading at worst. There is little effort either to engage with debates on definitions or to assess whether the evidence we have (official statistics or survey data) is good enough to help us with these methodological debates. The reality in sub-Saharan Africa is that occupational and labour market data for rural areas are very poor.[54] Data on agrarian capital and emerging capitalist farmers, for different scales and sizes, are also hard to come by. Without reliable data for these aspects of social structures and their trends over time it is hard to say much about the dynamics of agrarian capitalism and the main tendencies and counter-tendencies. The use of farm-size is not the best option for ascertaining trends in the rise or decline of agrarian capital, since this takes many forms and farm size does not directly correspond to a particular form of production. It is hard to find reliable and disaggregated statistics on the proportion of labour-employing farms (employing hired labour regardless of size), which is a crucial indicator of the development of capitalist relations of production in agriculture across geographical and historical contexts. This is a missed opportunity, since the widespread interest in the impact of land deals could have triggered a drive to collect this kind of evidence on capital and labour in rural Africa.

For example, much of the debate on land grabs has centred on what some call 'mega farms', which are then opposed analytically and empirically to 'small farms'. However, the reality of farm size in Africa is far more complex and what is 'large' and 'small' depends much on the specific context, crop and dominant social structures. In historical accounts of agrarian capitalist development in pre-industrial Europe such methodological issues also loom large.[55] So, while a 20 ha tea farm in Uganda is presented as a 'tea smallholder', because there are tea plantations of more than 1000 ha, in fact a 20 ha tea farm is essentially a capitalist farm reliant on wage labour. A 2 ha capital- and labour-intensive (but not land-intensive) flower farm in Ethiopia, implying perhaps over US$900 000 of start-up investment is certainly a capitalist farm, given how much work is done by hired labourers and the business scale of the farm. Many groundnut farmers cultivating over 10–20 ha of land in Senegal are in fact middle- to large-scale producers who use some family labour but also employ a lot of casual and seasonal hired labour. In many respects this is another type of non-mechanised capitalist farm, though very different from the examples above.[56] A given farm size may correspond to a very wide range of farms in terms of turnover, level of capitalisation, farmer's net income and dominant labour relations. A particular size range (for example 0–5 ha or 10–20 ha) may in indeed be consistent with a range of labour relations, as employment of hired labour per hectare can vary a lot with the degree of farm intensification, crop choice and available technology. However, this does not imply that 'capitalist farms', as defined in terms of labour relations, should be a homogeneous group in terms of all those criteria. There may be different types of 'capitalist farms' according to crop, use of land, agro-ecological context and level and type of capitalisation, but they will all be characterised by a tendency to rely more on wage labour. The foreign-owned 'mega-farms' often discussed in the land grab literature may in fact be a very small proportion of what we can call 'agrarian capital' in rural Africa, but media and activist priorities have created blinkers that impair a broader look at the realities of agrarian capitalism, emerging or old.

In sum, a key question is whether the recent 'land rush' is having any kind of impact on this variety of 'agrarian capitals' whose long trajectories in rural Africa should not be ignored. Is the kind of slowly emerging capitalist farming accelerating as part of the current 'land rush' or not? Does this mean more and better employment opportunities for the poorest of the poor who cannot hope to survive by micro-holding farming or not? Here, the empirical counterfactual is crucial and the need for rigorous comparisons more pressing. Without the post-2007 land rush, would this agrarian capitalism have continued to expand at the same rhythm, would it have accelerated or declined? How are rural labour relations affected? These are key empirical questions needed for a more solid and up-to-date empirical engagement with the Bernstein–Byres debate, and in light of the emerging land grab debate. However, these are also empirical questions that so far, unfortunately, studies on land grabs in Africa have failed to tackle and for which they have not yet provided relevant and reliable evidence.

Conclusions

This article has attempted to address two objectives. First, it has provided some systematic evidence of the state of knowledge about the socioeconomic impact of land deals from the emerging literature on the land rush in Africa, showing that the evidence gap is still very large. This is partly because the first wave of 'salvo' research has focused on other types of research questions, essentially trying to grasp the scale, drivers and actors of this emerging phenomenon. So far, studies of land grabs in Africa have provided very limited and often biased evidence on impacts. The article has then proposed a series of alternative questions and arguments around the extent to which current land acquisition processes mark a return of the agrarian question of capital, thereby contradicting Bernstein's argument about the death of the 'classic' agrarian question. First, if the scale and significance are warranted by the sheer size of the literature devoted to this phenomenon we would definitely be witnessing a 'return' of the agrarian question of capital. Second, if the impressions from the media and emerging literature were true, it would also mark a substantive role for the external forces of accumulation to speed up processes of agrarian transition in low-income developing countries. Third, if the usual claims on impact are supported by evidence, it would seem that the return of capital to agriculture and the renewal of the agrarian question of capital would not bring a resolution of the agrarian question of labour, since displacement is seen as more significant than the creation of any new livelihood opportunities, notably in the form of wage employment.

The systematic review of part of the literature (with a focus on claims about impacts) and a re-engagement with the Bernstein–Byres debate take this article in a different direction. The following points have been made or can be raised from the previous discussion. First, as stated above, a systematic scoping review of the literature on land grabs shows an alarming scarcity of primary research and excessive reliance on rapid appraisal-type work, which can only tackle a limited number of questions in a somewhat selective fashion. Second, much has been learned about processes, actors, possible drivers and the governance of land deals but, in reality, very little has been learned about their actual, as opposed to their potential or perceived, socioeconomic impacts, both in terms of livelihoods of the 'poor' and in terms of prospects for rural accumulation. Third, there is insufficient evidence to demonstrate that the scale of land acquisitions is such as to mark a dramatic structural shift in the relation between (agrarian) capital and labour in Africa. Although figures on land acquisition are being constantly revised downwards, there is no doubt that in some cases there is a renewed interest on the part of global capital in agricultural production and the direct use of land in Africa. This is not totally new or unprecedented, as the paper by

Baglioni and Gibbon in this collection shows. Nonetheless, a toning down of the impressionistic portrayal of global capitalists investing in land in Africa could *potentially* provide support for Bernstein's point that global capital is still bypassing agrarian transformations in today's poorest countries, if not enough attention is given to other processes of rural class formation taking place before the recent rush. Fourth, the focus on land grabs has shed some light on what is going on under the radar, namely a steady and in some cases rather accelerated process of capitalist accumulation at a smaller scale than usually catches the media's attention, whereby 'national capitals' are assuming an important role alongside and sometimes in joint ventures with global capital. This is even more significant for 'agrarian questions of capital' than the rising interest of global capital in farmland. For it shows that processes of class formation in the country-side are under way, often blurring the boundaries between the rural and the urban, since many of these 'national capitals' straddle the rural–urban divide.

In this sense the article disputes the overly pessimistic interpretations of Bernstein's argument on the agrarian questions of capital and labour, and suggests that current agrarian change in many parts of Africa is more dynamic and contradictory than often assumed in the literature on land grabs. These are largely empirical questions, though informed by the long tradition of a rich con-ceptual debate on the major forces driving or impeding agrarian transitions in African social formations. The article therefore calls for more attention to the twin agrarian questions of capital and labour through more in-depth and rigorous research on socio-economic impact, from survival at one end of the social spectrum to accumulation at the other end. Given the neglected importance of 'national capitals' in these processes and to their interaction with classes of labour in rural Africa, the article also proposes that more attention be paid to the 'internalist problematics' of the agrarian question, to use Bernstein's terms.

There are obvious implications of the discussion and arguments in this article for a future research agenda on the land rush. The rise of the land grab literature and its various debates provides research opportunities that have so far remained unexplored or sorely neglected. The first of these is a more seri-ous and solid approach to impact evaluation with a focus on livelihoods and, more specifically, on labour, as a way of engaging with the difficult 'agrarian question of labour' that has become so important in today's poor countries. This requires in-depth research and the deployment of evaluation methods that can provide hard evidence on trends and baseline situations. Second is a direct engagement with the 'old' agrarian questions and, in particular, with the agrarian question of capital. This requires, again, solid in-depth quantitative and qualitative research on the various forms of agrarian capital prevailing in different rural African contexts and how they are evolving in light of the causes and consequences of the recent land rush. Indeed, if more empirical attention is devoted to understanding the tendencies in African agrarian capital-ism as a result of the debates on the land rush, this is a welcome outcome. It is also an opportunity to revive old debates in agrarian political economy that seem to have waned in the recent past because of the growing dominance of neo-classical neo-populism in agrarian debates, and because many Marxist scholars have considered these questions obsolete.

Notes

The author is particularly grateful for the excellent research assistance provided by Thomas Muddimer for the systematic scoping review of the literature. An earlier version of this material was presented at the Centre of African Studies, University of Copenhagen, and received valuable feedback from an engaging audience, particularly from Christian Lund and Amanda Hammar. The article has also benefited from very useful comments and suggestions by Borras Saturnino Jr, Marc Edelman, Terence J Byres and an anonymous reviewer. I am, however, solely responsible for the analysis, and any errors, in the final paper.

1 For the sake of simplicity 'land rush' and 'land grabs' will be used interchangeably to characterise the key topic of discussion, even if their respective meanings are quite different. Indeed, the use of these two terms also reflects the variety of approaches to the phenomenon of recent large-scale land acquisitions in developing countries. For a discussion of these definitions, see SM Borras Jr, C Kay, S Gómez, & J Wilkinson, 'Land grabbing and global capitalist accumulation: key features in Latin America', *Canadian Journal of Development Studies*, 33(4), 2012, pp 402–416.

2 C Oya, 'Methodological reflections on "land grab" databases and the "land grab" literature "rush"', *Journal of Peasant Studies*, 40(3), 2013, pp 503–520.

3 K Deininger, D Byerlee, J Lindsay, A Norton, H Selod & M Stickler, *Rising Global Interest in Farmland: Can it Yield Sustainable and Equitable Benefits?*, Washington, DC: World Bank, 2011.

4 The 'Global Land Grabbing Conference I' at the Institute of Development Studies (IDS), September 2011, and the 'Global Land Grabbing Conference II' at Cornell University, October 2012.

5 Note, particularly, special issues in the *Journal of Peasant Studies*, 40(3), 39(3–4), 39(2), 38(2), 37(4); *Development and Change*, 44(2); *Globalisations*, 10(1); and the *Canadian Journal of Development Studies*, 33(4). Within these issues see, in particular, introductory essays by B White, S Borras Jr, R Hall, I Scoones & W Wolford, 'The new enclosures: critical perspectives on corporate land deals', *Journal of Peasant Studies*, 39(3-4), 2012, pp 619–647, on the political economy of land grabbing; W Wolford, S Borras Jr, R Hall, I Scoones & B White, 'Governing global land deals: the role of the state in the rush for land', *Development and Change*, 44(2), 2013, pp 189–210, on the role of the state in land grabbing; J Fairhead, M Leach & I Scoones, 'Green grabbing: a new appropriation of nature?', *Journal of Peasant Studies*, 39(2), 2012, pp 237–261, on 'green grabbing', ME Margulis, N McKeon & S Borras Jr, 'Land grabbing and global governance: critical perspectives', *Globalisations*, 10 (1), 2013, pp 1-23, on global governance and land grabbing; and Borras *et al*, 'Land grabbing and global capitalist accumulation', on land grabbing in Latin America.

6 However, thus far progress has not been so impressive on methodological grounds. See Oya, 'Methodological reflections on "land grab" databases and the "land grab" literature "rush"'; and M Edelman, 'Messy hectares: questions about the epistemology of land grabbing data', *Journal of Peasant Studies*, 40(3), 2013, pp 485–501, a point to which I will return in the next section.

7 For some explanations of the classic 'agrarian questions', see TJ Byres, 'The agrarian question and the peasantry', in B Fine & A Saad-Filho (eds), *The Elgar Companion to Marxist Economics*, Cheltenham: Edward Elgar, 2012, pp 10–15; H Bernstein, 'Agrarian questions from transition to globalisation', in H Akram-Lodhi & C Kay (eds), *Peasants and Globalisation*, London: Routledge, 2009, pp 239–261; Bernstein, *Class Dynamics of Agrarian Change*, Halifax: Fernwood Publishing, 2010; and H Akram-Lodhi & C Kay, 'Surveying the agrarian question (Part 2): current debates and beyond', *Journal of Peasant Studies*, 37(2), 2010, pp 255–284.

8 See L Cotula, *The Great African Land Grab? Agricultural Investments and the Global Food System*, London: Zed Books, 2013, pp 35–81; and the debate in the *Journal of Peasant Studies'* 'Forum on Global Land Grabbing Part 2', 2013. See also media reports on land deal data revisions at http://www.bbc.co.uk/news/science-environment-22839149.

9 See, for example, Oxfam GB, *Land and Power: The Growing Scandal Surrounding the New Wave of Investments in Land*, Briefing Paper 151, Oxford: Oxfam, 2011, at http://policy-practice.oxfam.org.uk/publications/download?Id=428754&dl=http://oxfamilibrary.openrepository.com/oxfam/bitstream/10546/142858/32/bp151-land-power-rights-acquisitions-220911-en.pdf ; and 'The surge in land deals: when others are grabbing their land', *The Economist*, 5 May 2011, at http://www.economist.com/node/18648855.

10 The special issue of *Globalisations* is particularly focused on the governance of land deals, with an analysis and proposals that go beyond what has essentially emerged from interventions by international organisations like the Food and Agriculture Organization (FAO) and the World Bank. See Margulis *et al*, 'Land grabbing and global governance'.

11 See, for example, S Borras Jr, JC Franco & C Wang, 'The challenge of global governance of land grabbing: changing international agricultural context and competing political views and strategies', *Globalisations*, 10 (1), 2013, pp 161–179; and P McMichael, 'The land grab and corporate food regime restructuring', *Journal of Peasant Studies*, 39(3–4), 2012, pp 681–701.

12 In particular, see Borras *et al*, 'Land grabbing and global capitalist accumulation'; and Wolford *et al*, 'Governing global land deals'.

13 For example, some win-win scenarios are presented in FAO, *Trends and Impacts of Foreign Investment in Developing Country Agriculture: Evidence from Case Studies*, Rome: FAO, 2013. They can also be seen in some of the descriptions of investment projects to be found in company websites, for example http://www.agrisoltanzania.com; and http://www.youtube.com/watch?v=cBtJmGXTGnU.

14 RL Miller & JD Brewer, *The A–Z of Social Research*, London: Sage, 2003.

15 For examples of this, see Cotula, *The Great African Land Grab?*; and T Lavers, '"Land grab" as development strategy? The political economy of agricultural investment in Ethiopia', *Journal of Peasant Studies*, 39(1), 2012, pp 105–132; and, particularly, work focused on non-African contexts, such as M Levien, 'The land question: special economic zones and the political economy of dispossession in India', *Journal of Peasant Studies*, 39(3–4), 2012, pp 933–969; and TM Li, 'Centering labor in the land grab debate', *Journal of Peasant Studies*, 38(2), 2011, pp 281–298. See also some of the more recent special issues in the *Canadian Journal of Development Studies*, 33(4), on Latin America; *Development and Change*, 44(2), on the role of the state; and *Globalisations*, 10(1), on the governance of land deals.

16 See Scoones et al 'The politics of evidence: methodologies for understanding the global land rush', *Journal of Peasant Studies*, 40(3), 2013, pp 469–483; Oya 'Methodological reflections on "land grab" databases and the "land grab" literature "rush"'; and Edelman, 'Messy hectares' for an extensive discussion of this challenge. These articles pay particular attention to the problems of addressing the question of 'how much' and 'where', particularly in the case of international land deal databases. In the emerging academic literature published in this period there are of course several examples of solid research that deal with the 'who', 'where' and 'how much' questions, such as SM Borras Jr & JC Franco, 'Global land grabbing and trajectories of agrarian change: a preliminary analysis', *Journal of Agrarian Change*, 12(1), 2012, pp 34–59; Levien, 'The land question'; and Cotula, *The Great African Land Grab?*

17 C Cramer, *Civil War is Not a Stupid Thing: Accounting for Violence in Developing Countries*, London: Hurst & Company, 2006.

18 See Oya, 'Methodological reflections on "land grab" databases and the "land grab" literature "rush"'; and Borras & Franco, this issue. Consider, for example, peasants who use 'modern' technology in traditional cultivation systems, investors who are domestic but widely reported as foreign (like Sheikh Al-Amoudi in Ethiopia), or alliances between domestic and foreign capital. Thanks to Marc Edelman for raising this important point.

19 See the *Journal of Peasant Studies'* 'Forum on Global Land Grabbing Part 2', 2013.

20 It is important to point out that, while the first wave of 'salvo' research did not focus on research questions on impact but rather on questions of process, magnitude of deals and their main actors, claims have been made about impacts, often conflating actual and potential effects, a point that will be discussed later in the paper.

21 See H Waddington, H White, B Snilstveit, J Garcia Hombrados, P Davies, A Bhavsar *et al*, 'How to do a good systematic review of effects in international development: a tool kit', *Journal of Development Effectiveness*, 4(3), 2012, pp 359–387.

22 V Terstappen, L Hanson & D McLaughlin, 'Gender, health, labor, and inequities: a review of the fair and alternative trade literature', *Agriculture and Human Values*, 30(1), 2013, p 2. For an extended discussion of the challenges for systematic reviews in international development research, see also R Mallett, J Hagen-Zanker, R Slater & Maren Duvendack, 'The benefits and challenges of using systematic reviews in international development research', *Journal of Development Effectiveness*, 4(3), 2012, pp 445–455.

23 D Gogh, S Oliver & J Thomas, *An Introduction to Systematic Reviews*, London: Sage, 2012, p 5; and Waddington *et al*, 'How to do a good systematic review'.

24 Mallet *et al*, 'The benefits and challenges of using systematic reviews in international development studies', pp 448–450.

25 Cotula, *The Great African Land Grab?*, p 145.

26 Li, 'Centering labor in the land grab debate'.

27 See Waddington *et al*, 'How to do a good systematic review', p 366.

28 For an extended discussion of potential positive and negative outcomes, see Cotula, *The Great African Land Grab?*, pp 125–172.

29 Mallett *et al*, 'The benefits and challenges of using systematic reviews in international development research', also strongly recommend this practice for systematic reviews in development studies.

30 See *ibid*; and Terstappen *et al*, 'Gender, health, labor and inequities', p 6.

31 Cotula, *The Great African Land Grab?*, p 145.

32 *Ibid*, pp 142–144.

33 *Ibid*, pp 135–138. For non-African contexts, see also Li 'Centering labor in the land grab debate'; and JF McCarthy, 'Processes of inclusion and adverse incorporation: oil palm and agrarian change in Sumatra, Indonesia', *Journal of Peasant Studies*, 37(4), 2010, pp 821–850.

34 On the agrarian question of labour, see H Bernstein, '"Changing before our very eyes": agrarian questions and the politics of land in capitalism today', *Journal of Agrarian Change*, 4(1–2), 2004, pp 190–225. This question has been partly addressed by some contributions to land rush research, particularly by studies on

Asia, such as Li, 'Centering labor in the land grab debate'; and McCarthy, 'Processes of inclusion and adverse incorporation'.

35 Byres, 'The agrarian question and the peasantry', p 13.

36 Bernstein, 'Agrarian questions from transition to globalisation', p 241.

37 See Akram-Lodhi & Kay, 'Surveying the agrarian question (Part 2)' for a clear explanation of Bernstein's idea of the 'decoupled question', which essentially means that the emergence of agrarian capital is no longer relevant to global capital accumulation. See also Bernstein, 'Agrarian questions from transition to globalisation', for the author's own explanation.

38 Akram Lodhi & Kay, 'Surveying the agrarian question (Part 2)', pp 264, 267.

39 For examples of such instances and documented evidence, see C Oya 'Stories of rural accumulation in Africa: trajectories and transitions among rural capitalists in Senegal', *Journal of Agrarian Change*, 7(4), 2007, pp 453–493.

40 TJ Byres, 'Structural change, the agrarian question and the possible impact of globalisation', in J Ghosh & JH Chandrasekhar (eds), *Work and Well-being in the Age of Finance*, 2003, p 207.

41 *Ibid*, p 207.

42 *Ibid*, p 209.

43 See Oya, 'Stories of rural accumulation in Africa', for a discussion of this neglect.

44 See, for example, McMichael, 'The land grab and corporate food regime restructuring'.

45 *Journal of Peasant Studies*' 'Forum on Global Land Grabbing Part 2', 2013.

46 Cotula, *The Great African Land Grab?*, p 142.

47 See, for example, T Lavers, 'Patterns of agrarian transformation in Ethiopia: state-mediated commercialisation and the "land grab"', *Journal of Peasant Studies*, 39(3–4), 2012, pp 795–822; and R Lefort, 'Free market economy, "developmental state" and party–state hegemony in Ethiopia: the case of the "model farmers"', *Journal of Modern African Studies*, 50(4), 2012, pp 681–706. The recent revisions of the Land Matrix data on land deals also confirm the substantial role of national investors.

48 See also Cotula, *The Great African Land Grab?*, pp 53–54, for more examples of domestic capital playing a major role in large-scale land acquisitions.

49 *Ibid*, p 144.

50 See Oya, 'Stories of rural accumulation in Africa', for examples in Senegal and in the wider literature on agrarian capital in Africa.

51 See also Baglioni & Gibbon, this issue, on the relative 'constancy' of large-scale and plantation farming in Africa, with a growing role of national capital since independence in most countries.

52 See the classic work by TJ Byres, *Capitalism from Above and Capitalism from Below: An Essay in Comparative Political Economy*, New York: St Martin's Press, 1996; and discussion of such trajectories in Oya 'Stories of rural accumulation in Africa'.

53 See, for example, L Shaw-Taylor, 'The rise of agrarian capitalism and the decline of family farming in England', *Economic History Review*, 65(1), 2012, pp 26–60; and the classic contribution by R Brenner, 'Agrarian class structure and economic development in pre-industrial Europe', in TH Aston & CHE Philpin (eds), *The Brenner Debate: Agrarian Class Structure and Economic Development in Pre-industrial Europe*, Cambridge: Cambridge University Press, 1985, pp 10–63. See also Byres, *Capitalism from Above and Capitalism from Below*; and, more recently, J Banaji, *Theory and History: Essays on Modes of Production and Exploitation*, Leiden: Brill, 2010.

54 See C Oya, 'Rural wage employment in Africa: methodological issues and emerging evidence', *Review of African Political Economy*, 40(136), 2013, pp 251–273, for an extended discussion.

55 See Shaw-Taylor, 'The rise of agrarian capitalism and the decline of family farming'.

56 All these examples are taken from the author's own fieldwork experiences in Senegal, Uganda and Ethiopia and are used for illustrative purposes.

Notes on Contributor

Carlos Oya is Senior Lecturer in the Political Economy of Development, soas, University of London. He has undertaken primary research mostly in sub-Saharan Africa, particularly Mozambique, Senegal, Mauritania, Uganda and Ethiopia, focusing on the political economy of agrarian change, capitalist accumulation, rural wage labour and poverty. He is also co-editor of the *Journal of Agrarian Change*.

Land Grabbing, Large- *and* Small-scale Farming: what can evidence and policy from 20th century Africa contribute to the debate?

ELENA BAGLIONI[a] & PETER GIBBON[b]

[a]*School of Business and Management, Queen Mary, University of London, London UK;*
[b]*Danish Institute for International Studies, Copenhagen, Denmark*

ABSTRACT   *This article examines the contemporary phenomenon of 'land grabbing' in relation to the history of plantation and large- and small-scale farming (PF, LSF and SSF) in sub-Saharan Africa. It looks at the extent of PF and LSF over the 20th century, as well as the policy narratives that have justified, supported or circumscribed their development. Many characteristics of the current land rush and its interpretation reveal elements of continuity with some of the general trends marking the history of PF and LSF up to recent years. In particular, the heterogeneity of PF and LSF, subsuming quite different relations to SSF, and the pivotal role played by the combination of private capital (whether foreign, domestic or combined) with the state represent organisational continuities. Meanwhile continuities in supporting narratives centre on the prevalence of generic prescriptions for either LSF/PF or SSF. Refuting these generic prescriptions is a precondition for more nuanced analysis and policy proposals.*

Recent years have seen a strong, generally highly critical, political and academic focus on land deals and transactions in Africa. Supposedly idle, land-abundant Southern countries, especially in sub-Saharan Africa (SSA), have been the objects of a global land rush involving domestic and foreign actors. The literature on land grabbing is inundated with accounts of more or less transparent purchases, confirmed and unconfirmed deals, arm twisting, allocations and dispossessions, as well as instances of redistribution and employment creation. Rather than a global land grab, the picture that emerges is one of a scramble and reshuffling, of significant but unstable restructuring of land access and control, or what resembles an ongoing and unfinished process of capital restructuring. While unravelling this complex landscape is a great challenge, comprehension of these phenomena is becoming progressively more complex and articulate.

Much scholarly analysis has so far linked this land rush to a more general crisis of neoliberal capitalism, unleashing capital's appetite for new sources of accumulation.[1] According to this interpretation, land grabs are driven by global capital accumulation dynamics and strategies in response to a convergence of multiple crises concerning finance, environment, energy and food.[2] The diversity and intricate intertwining of these crises attest to the complexity of the forms, mechanisms and scale of land transactions observed, debated and often challenged. Notwithstanding this heterogeneity and the importance of 'green grabbing' and speculation,[3] a significant proportion of these deals is aimed at the establishment of agricultural production.[4] Although most of this production is driven by the corporate agro-export industry, channelled in complex global supply chains,[5] the production of food, biofuels and other resources for consumption and exchange on the domestic markets as commoditisation advances has been another important driver.[6] Multiple actors seek land: foreign governments, sovereign wealth funds, state-owned enterprises from new (BRICS and other powerful middle-income countries) and old players (OECD countries), private actors such as agribusiness and agrifood companies, corporate players interested in developing biofuels, as well as private institutional investors such as banks and a plethora of mutual, pension, hedge and private equity funds.[7] Again, Africa appears as the ultimate investment frontier, a new paradise where an unlimited supply of land and labour can yield profits in times of crisis.

This new land rush phase represents the culmination of a period where the interest in land has constantly grown, generating widespread conflicts and struggles all over the continent.[8] However, while large-scale farming investments are nothing new, the recent debate emphasises how the speed and rate at which land changed hands between around 2004 and 2009 is unprecedented in the history of postcolonial Africa. This poses new challenges at many different levels. One of the most important is that of 'development'. Supporters of this new wave of land deals depict attractive scenarios characterised by rapid agricultural modernisation, mechanised farming, employment creation, and positive spill-overs across the economy. Critics are fiercely hostile and highlight widespread land alienation, evictions and destruction of livelihoods. It is still early days for understanding what paths and types of development, if any, might result from the current phase. It is equally difficult to forecast whether, as a result, capitalism in Africa will enter a new and more ideal-typical phase and if so with what implications, gains and costs. This new phase of accelerated agrarian change, and the enormous question marks arising from it, may be better illuminated by exploring the extent and significance of earlier instances of land concentration, their countermovements, as well as the economic thinking and political claims supporting or opposing them. This entails analysing different farming 'models' historically linked to distinctive agrarian policies and narratives and how they rise and wane in popularity.

To achieve a deeper understanding of the current land rush and highlight possible elements of change and continuity, this article considers some historical experiences of large-scale and plantation farming (LSF and PF) in SSA. LSF is understood as a type of land ownership and use involving generally local citizens producing temperate and/or semi-tropical crops, partly or mainly for the domestic market, with predominantly hired labour. PF is considered here as a type of land ownership and use involving generally foreign investors producing tropical crops, mainly or wholly for export, with hired labour. These definitions are indicative rather than exhaustive. Inevitably—and perhaps increasingly—some enterprises fall between them. Deliberately no mention is made of cut-off points in terms of size of holding or number of hired labourers. This makes it possible to consider the inherent diversity of PF and LSF throughout the continent, while avoiding the trap of equating investment scale merely with land size,[9] a tendency which 'tends to miss or de-emphasise in its analysis the underlying broader logic and operations of capital'.[10] By maintaining a focus on crop production, the article underestimates the full historical extent of large-scale land concentration and seizure for farming and exploitation of natural resources, as it does not consider livestock production (which in many African countries account(s)ed for most of the area under large-scale farming), nor timber, mining, nor other exploitation of natural resources, which are again in high demand from 'grabbers'. On the other hand, by concentrating on the historical lineages of contemporary PF and LSF, the analysis inevitably reveals how both need to be considered alongside what is most often categorised as their 'opposite', that is small-scale farming (SSF). The latter also covers an immense variety of situations, land use and ownership, farming practices carried out by local and migrant farmers, as well as food and cash cropping. SSF is considered here as a type of farming entailing limited capital investment and very limited employment of *permanent* wage workers, but which is nevertheless integrated with the commoditisation of land, other inputs and markets.

Before providing a historical overview of farming models in Africa and of their politics, the article focuses on some of the main features of contemporary land grabbing, and how its analysis has developed over time. The recent rush for land in SSA and other developing countries is approached by looking at the main actors involved and issues emerging from the unfolding, buoyant debate. This is followed by an examination of the political economy of PF and LSF during the 20th century, extrapolating some tentative general trends. It is suggested that, during the 20th century, PF and LSF were a constant in African agriculture. Their development was uneven and shifting but their overall share of the cultivated area remained roughly the same. The heterogeneity of PF/LSF is emphasised, as is the decisive participation of the state both in its making and its circumscription. While the current land grabbing phase shows that the state still has a constant hand in large-scale farming, its main role has shifted back to that of broker. Moreover, the resilience of LSF subsumes the vitality of domestic capital, often overlooked in the literature. Meanwhile, the basic rationales fostering and containing the expansion of PF and LSF were historically provided by specific techno-economic policy narratives that continue to dominate much of the current discussion. A key continuity theme is the generic character of the prescriptions they provide for one type of farming system rather than another.

Land grabbing and its analysis

The idea of 'pristine' African land awaiting exploitation has been exceedingly resilient over the years. The World Bank has followed others in rekindling Joseph Chamberlain's image of the continent as a sleeping giant awaking from a long-lasting lethargy, which has prevented the exploitation of immense resources and rapid development.[11] It also suggests that the current land rush offers a precious opportunity to unbridle unexploited potential and resources: 'the steep rise in prices of food and agricultural commodities that occurred in 2008 has led to a realisation that new opportunities may be opening for countries that are endowed with the land, labour, and other resources needed to respond to the growing demand for food and biofuels feedstock'.[12] According to another World Bank study, SSA is particularly suited to make the most of such opportunity as 'none of the Sub-Saharan African countries of most interest to investors is now achieving more than 30 percent of the potential yield on currently cultivated areas. So, increasing productivity on existing farmland would have a much bigger impact than simply expanding the land area at current yields.'[13]

A strong sense of *déjà-vu* is awakened by these accounts, as once again crises at the core of capitalism are depicted as offering new and attractive possibilities for the peripheries, or even requiring that these be seized. Food, environmental and financial crises have troubled Western capitalist development in the past,[14] and although the early development of capitalism in Western Europe had a global dimension from the outset, many capitalism crises were temporarily 'solved' by further geographical expansion. Thus, as the current debate on land grabbing emphasises, the current land rush features the familiar lever of foreign capital resorting to 'idle' land and resources in Africa and other developing countries to overcome shrinking opportunities for accumulation.

Yet, while the extent of land deals and alienation in Africa remains substantial, it seems that many of the claims made in this regard have been exaggerated.[15] Initially there was commonly confusion between areas of land applied for by investors and those for which concessions were actually granted—not to mention those that were actually cultivated. Further confusion occurred between development aid projects and private investment.[16] As Hanlon observes,[17] investors may encourage such confusion, since the 'area game' can stimulate interest in financing land deals. This relates to another limitation to land grabbing: many of the investors involved, like many of Africa's colonial settlers in the past, suffer from undercapitalisation, as is illustrated by their under-utilisation of the areas allocated them. Hanlon suggests that, while the combination of the food crises and fuel prices with the financial crisis made land speculation more attractive, it also made it more difficult to finance.[18] Hence the inherent uncertainty and ambiguity of data on land grabs often masks the extent of intended and unsuccessful deals.[19]

Despite the tendency to depict current land acquisitions as a threat, it is worth noting the diversity of the current and prospective uses of the land acquired. Not all land deals fall under the category of intended food and biofuel production for distant markets. Indeed, as Borras and Franco show, some deals imply a move in the opposite direction, that is, from food production for export or from 'marginal' or forest land to food and biofuel production for local consumption and domestic exchange.[20] Furthermore, although several accounts describe African land as being sold into entirely foreign hands, the picture is strikingly more complex thanks to the presence of multiple and diverse land tenure and organisational arrangements (purchase, leases of different durations, contract farming with or without nucleus estates, etc).[21]

Furthermore, it is important to emphasise how, as the demand for land has increased, so has the supply. Land-seeking capital has often encountered a willingness on the part of African states (or at least elites) to cede large portions of land. In much of SSA the convergence of different global crises, combined with a long-term impasse in rural development unresolved by structural adjustment, has led to a revival of arguments concerning the superiority of large-scale investment by African politicians and planners. Thus, a crisis of neoliberal capitalism has encountered one of neoliberal development. This revival draws on a combination of earlier narratives supporting LSF/PF and the exemplary status of new islands of vibrant and intense growth linked to the development of non-traditional cash-crops stimulated by Northern markets. Faced with a lagging capitalist transition,[22] often fostering conflicting projects and policies such as agricultural modernisation and the preservation of family farming,[23] the role of African states in the restructuring of land access and control appears more contradictory than ever.[24]

As for domestic or 'African' capital, this has never been dormant, as illustrated by the resilience of LSF over the 20th century (see below). The contribution of domestic investors to land concentration processes has never been limited to small- and medium-scale farming and commercial capital,[25] nor to settler economies, especially since the 1960s. Today probably the most clamorous examples of domestic capital involvement emanate from the most advanced areas of capitalist development within the continent. Here indigenous capital may be more acutely affected by and responsive to the contradictory logics inherent in agrarian restructuring. As Hall shows for South Africa, the combined pressures of agricultural deregulation, advancing class struggle in the form of labour rights and minimum wage legislation, as well as timid instances of land redistribution and de-concentration, have stimulated a relocation of South African capital to other African countries, including the Congo, Mozambique, Malawi, Botswana and Kenya.[26] Elsewhere involvement of indigenous capital has a lower profile but remains relentless and cumulatively significant.[27] For example, in Benin, Burkina Faso and Niger, 95% of all (as opposed to the very largest) recent land transactions involve local civil servants, politicians, traders and business people.[28] In Senegal domestic 'accumulators' remain dominant players in the groundnut sector,[29] as well as in export horticulture, and have increasingly accumulated land with both the manifest and hidden help of state officials.[30] In other circumstances local players have sought to leverage their access to state support by seeking alliances with foreign capital. Combined investment of local and foreign capital on this basis has also been observed in Ethiopia, Liberia, Mozambique, Nigeria and Sudan.[31] In yet other instances, rather than becoming allies, foreign and domestic investors have competed over land access. While further exposing the complexity of state structures, which are far from a uniform and coherent expression of voices and interests, the existence of competing investors might indicate the intersection and clashing of different accumulation logics.

Thus, while several authors encompass land grabs under more or less different, enlarged or revised understandings of 'accumulation by dispossession' processes,[32] it is still unclear whether the surge in land deals consistently falls under this 'common' roof. Correspondingly, the extent to which different 'classes of capital' operate according to the same logic is also limited.[33] The deep extent of (both labour *and* capital) socioeconomic differentiation in African rural and urban areas, the different accumulation circuits, via commercial and/or productive capital, the different processes of acquisition involved, the varying magnitude of capital invested, the different organisational forms it takes and the diverse sectors targeted, all ultimately contribute to the *heterogeneity* of land grabbing and the 'new' LSF/PF.

Equally ambiguous is the current, unfolding 'question of labour'.[34] Much of the debate on land grabs has oscillated between the two poles of poverty reduction and poverty creation.[35] Overall, critics generally agree that labour conditions and rights cannot just be left to the goodwill of investors and codes of conducts emanating from corporate capital.[36] They highlight the need for strong action on the part of the state. As elsewhere, however, African independent states have historically hindered the emergence of labour movements. Meanwhile, among both states and critics, while in the 1950s and 1960s the labour question was shoehorned into the broader development question,[37] attempts to squeeze labour movements into the rather different 'peasant question' that spans the whole 20th century have reappeared today. Thus old and new variants of populism are typically exclusivist and problematically bundle together the broad categories of labourers, the poor and smallholders in various notions of peasants and 'people of the land'.

Overall, the combined development of both LSF and SSF in Africa contributed to the unfolding of farming models and narratives—and the representations of farming populations structuring them (eg a rural population as a mass of homogeneous peasants, or as an army of wage labourers)[38]—as powerful ideological tools advancing different and contradictory interests and concerns, whether from different state officials, donors and agencies, or small- and large-scale investors. Contemporary land grabbing, as it unrolls unevenly and problematically, continues this tradition. The current prevalence of policy narratives favouring SSF (contrary to the claims of Peters)[39] manifests the ambiguity towards land grabbing of at least some sections of national political elites and foreign donors. Therefore, instances postulating the superiority of one farming model over the other may overlook the politics behind them. Ultimately small- and large-scale farming should both be read historically as manifestations of capitalist development, often politically and economically complementary, rather than alternative to one another.

A short history of PF and LSF in 20th century Africa

This section briefly outlines the history of PF/LSF in Africa during the 20th century. It underlines the long-established and resilient nature of farming of these kinds, as well as their heterogeneity over time and place. It further underlines how PF/LSF in Africa is far from universally an externally imposed phenomenon. Non-white African private individuals and independent African governments have been among the leading sponsors since 1960.

Efforts to quantitatively trace the development over time of PF and LSF crop production in SSA are hampered by the inconsistent definitions of LSF,[40] of cultivated area and of employment in published sources.[41] In terms of coverage, data or estimates based on secondary sources are available for PF and LSF crop areas for only about a quarter of the countries in SSA, whatever period is considered in the 20th century. Estimates for employment are available for still fewer. Those countries for which figures are available are generally those where privately owned PF or LSF has been important, but there are countries (particularly in West Africa) known to have (had) PF, but where information is scarce or non-existent.[42] Even for those countries where figures are available, often these cover only one or two crops. A further problem is validity. Some of the figures in Table 1 below, particularly the aggregates for Africa provided for each period, fall into the category of 'guesstimate' rather than estimate.[43]

With these caveats, Table 1 and this section endeavour to trace some general trends, based on observations drawn from three periods: around the outbreak of World War I, during the early 1960s (the time of independence for most of the continent), and from the 1990s or after. Unfortunately, because its heyday occurred between the second and third of these sets of observations, the rise and fall of state-owned PF and LSF is not generally reflected in the data (see below).

An initial observation from Table 1, notwithstanding the issue of coverage, is the consistently uneven distribution of PF and LSF over the continent. PF and LSF are absent from large parts of it, notably the Sahel and land-locked Africa south of the Sahel—with the exception of Congo, the inland settler economies of southern Africa (Southern Rhodesia/Zimbabwe, Northern Rhodesia/Zambia and Nyasaland/Malawi) and Ethiopia. PF predominantly occurs in countries with seaboards, especially West African ones, and within these in regions with easy access to ports. Conversely, where present, LSF—and to a lesser extent PF—often dominates both the agricultural land area and national employment (Southern Rhodesia/Zimbabwe, South Africa, Liberia and São Tomé and perhaps increasingly Sudan and Malawi).

Second, while data on employment is too sparse for meaningful comparisons over time, the share of SSA cultivated under PF/LSF apparently remained broadly constant at 5% to 7.5% for almost a century up to the commodity boom beginning in 2004. Although the period before World War I is commonly considered the golden age of PF in Africa, and the inter-war period saw a turn in colonial economic policy in favour of SSF, between 1920 and 1960 the area under PF/LSF crop production increased in line with the cultivated area generally. This was mostly the result of an expansion of LSF in Kenya, Southern Rhodesia and South Africa. After 1960 the substantial contraction in the LSF crop area in Kenya, Zimbabwe and South Africa was more than compensated for by its growth in Sudan and, to a lesser extent, Ethiopia and Malawi.

Third, although this is not visible from Table 1, there has been a narrowing of the range of crops produced. The period 1900–14 saw substantial production

TABLE 1. Combined LSF and PF crop area and employment in Africa (000 ha and 000 workers), c 1914–c 2000

Country	1900–20 Area (employment)	Year (source)	1960s Area (employment)	Year (source)	Latest available Area (employment)	Year (source)
Angola	11 (11, slaves)	1903-11[1]	n/k		n/k	
Belgian Congo/DRC	350 α (n/k)	1920[2]	58 + 350 α (41.6)	1959[3]	n/k	
Cameroon	75 (n/k)	1913[4]	40 (25 permanent)	1960s[5]	40 (18 permanent) β	1990[6]
Côte d'Ivoire	75 (n/k)	1913[7]	n/k		75 (n/k)	2002[8]
Ethiopia	0		5 (n/k)	1970[9]	616 (15 permanent) γ	2010;[10] 2007[11]
Fernando Po/Equatorial Guinea	11 (n/k)	1909[12]	n/k		n/k	
French Congo/Congo Brazzaville	n/k		200 (n/k)	'1960s'[13]	200 (n/k)	2010[14]
Gold Coast/Ghana	10 (n/k)	1920[15]	165 (n/k)	1965-70[16]	n/k	
Guinea	50 (n/k)	1913[17]	n/k		n/k	
Kenya	n/k (71)	1923[18]	615 (252)	1960[19]	535 (>95) δ	area 1980;[20] empl c 2000 δ
Liberia	0		87 (n/k)	1960[21]	110 (53)	1990[22]
Nigeria	n/k		14 (6) ε	1959[23]	n/k	
Northern Rhodesia/Zambia	n/k		n/k		n/k (7 permanent) η	2004;[24] 2009[25]
Nyasaland/Malawi	n/k		26 (n/k)	1962[26]	360 (157)	area 1997;[27] empl 1981[28]
Portuguese East Africa/Mozambique	n/k (36) ζ	1908[29]	25 (n/k) ζ	1965[30]	n/k	
Rwanda	n/k		n/k		3 (n/k) θ	2010[31]
São Tomé & Príncipe	n/k (40, incl slaves)	1908[32]	n/k		n/k	

(Continued)

TABLE 1. (Continued)

Country	1900–20		1960s		Latest available	
	Area (employment)	Year (source)	Area (employment)	Year (source)	Area (employment)	Year (source)
Southern Rhodesia/Zimbabwe	75 (58)	1914 (area[33]), 1921 (labour[34])	450 (216)	1965[35]	100 (n/k)	2009[36]
South Africa	2665 (341 males)	1918 (area), 1925 (labour)[37]	6500 (756 'regular')	1960[38]	4682 š (378 'full time')	area 2007;[39] empl 2007[40]
Sudan	0		504 (86 'half yearly')	area 1960,[41] empl 1960[42]	5880 (n/k)	2005[43]
Tanganyika/Tanzania	n/k (140 registered)	1912[44]	260 (75) τ	1956–57[45]	63 (n/k)τ	1986[46]
Uganda	14 (n/k)	1920[47]	n/k		0.2 (6) υ	2005[48]
Zanzibar/Tanzania	25 (n/k)	1916[49]	24 (n/k)	1940s[50]	clove plantations broken up and redistributed	
Estimated total area	<5000		8000–12 000		10 000–15 000	

Notes: 'N workers' denotes all workers except where stated.

[1] W Clarence-Smith, *Slaves, Peasants and Capitalists in Southern Angola, 1840–1926*, Cambridge: Cambridge University Press, 1979.

[2] D Fieldhouse, *Unilever Overseas: The Anatomy of a Multinational, 1895–1965*, London: Croom Helm, 1978.

[3] *Ibid.*

[4] Estimate based on F Cooper, *Decolonisation and African Society: The Labour Question in French and British Africa*, Cambridge: Cambridge University Press, 1996.

[5] P Koning, 'Plantation labour and economic crisis in Cameroon', *Development and Change*, 26, 1995, pp 525–549.

[6] *Ibid*; and E Graham with I Floering, *The Modern Plantation in the Third World*, London: Croom Helm, 1984.

[7] Estimate based on Cooper, *Decolonisation and African Society.*

[8] United States Department of Agriculture (USDA), 'Favourable palm oil production for Cote d'Ivoire', Foreign Agricultural Service, Production Estimates and Crop Asessment Division, 2002, at http://www.fas.usda.gov/pecad2/highlights/2002/09/cote_divoire/index.htm, accessed 13 September 2010.

[9] J Cohen, 'Effects of green revolution strategies on tenants and small-scale landowners in the Chilalo Region of Ethiopia', *Journal of Developing Areas*, 9, 1975, pp 335–358.

[10] Government of Ethiopia, 'Large and medium scale commercial farms sample survey: results at county and regional levels', Central Statistical Agency, *Statistical Bulletin*, 505, Addis Ababa, 2011.

[11] A Melese & A Helmsing, 'Endogenization or enclave formation? The development of the Ethiopian cut flower industry', *Journal of Modern African Studies*, 48(1), 2010, pp 35–66.

[12] I Sundiata, 'Equatorial Guinea: the struggle for a cocoa economy, 1880–1930', in W Clarence-Smith (ed), *Cocoa Pioneer Fronts since 1800: The Role of Smallholders, Planters and Merchants*, Basingstoke: Macmillan, 1996, pp 105–118.

[13] R Hall, 'The next Great Trek? South African commercial farmers move north', *Journal of Peasant Studies*, 39(3-4), 2011, pp 823–843.

[14] *Ibid.*

[15] A Pim, *Colonial Agricultural Production: The Contribution made by Native Peasants and by Foreign Enterprise*, London: Oxford University Press, 1946.

[16] A Asamoa, *Socio-economic Development Strategies of Independent African Countries: The Ghana Experience*, Accra: Ghana University Press, 1997; and A Shepherd, 'Agrarian change in northern Ghana: public investment, capitalist farming and famine', in J Heyer et al (eds), *Rural Development in Tropical Africa*, London: Macmillan, 1981, pp 168–192.

[17] Estimate based on Cooper, *Decolonisation and African Society*.

[18] P Mosley, *The Settler Economies: Studies in the Economic History of Kenya and Southern Rhodesia, 1900–63*, Cambridge: Cambridge University Press, 1983.

[19] L Brown, *Agricultural Change in Kenya, 1945–60: Studies in Tropical Development*, Food Research Institute, Stanford University, 1968.

[20] Government of Kenya, *Agricultural Census of Large Farms, 1979 and 1980*, Central Bureau of Statistics, Ministry of Economic Planning and Development, Nairobi, 1982.

[21] S Voll, *A Plough in Fields Arable: Western Agribusiness in Third World Agriculture*, Hanover, NH: University Press of New England, 1980.

[22] *Africa South of the Sahara, Liberia*, London: Europa Publications, 2004, pp 611–617.

[23] Fieldhouse, *Unilever Overseas*.

[24] S Barrientos, A Kritzinger, M Opondo & S Smith, 'Gender, work and vulnerability in African horticulture', *IDS Bulletin*, 36(2), 2005, pp 74–79.

[25] B Richardson, 'Big sugar in southern Africa: rural development and the perverted potential of sugar/ethanol exports', *Journal of Peasant Studies*, 34(4), 2010, pp 917–938.

[26] T Mkandawire, *Agriculture, Employment and Poverty in Malawi*, ILO/SAMAT Policy Paper 9, Harare, 1999.

[27] *Ibid.*

[28] F Pryor & C Chipeta, 'Economic development through estate agriculture: the case of Malawi', *Canadian Journal of African Studies*, 24(1), 1990, pp 50–74.

[29] L Vail & L White, *Capitalism and Colonialism in Mozambique: A Study of Quelimane District*, London: Heinemann, 1980.

[30] *Ibid.*

[31] C Huggins, *A Historical Perspective on the 'Global Land Rush': Commercial Pressures on Land Initiative*, Rome: International Land Coalition, 2011, p 35.

[32] Clarence-Smith, *Slaves, Peasants and Capitalists in Southern Angola*.

[33] R Palmer, *Land and Racial Domination in Rhodesia*, London: Heinemann, 1977.

[34] I Phimister, *An Economic and Social History of Zimbabwe, 1890–1948*, London: Longman, 1988.

[35] H Dunlop, *The Development of European Agriculture in Rhodesia, 1945–65*, Department of Economics Occasional Paper No 5, Salisbsury: University of Rhodesia, 1971.

[36] Estimate based on I Scoones, N Marongwe, B Mavedzenge, J Mahenehene, F Murimbarimba & M Sukume, *Zimbabwe's Land Reform: Myths & Realities*, Oxford: James Currey, 2010.

[37] Estimates based on M Morris, 'The development of capitalism in South African agriculture: class struggle in the countryside', *Economy and Society*, 5(3), 1976, pp 292–343.

[38] Estimate based on F Wilson, 'Farming, 1866–1966', in M Wilson & L Thompson (eds), *The Oxford History of South Africa, Vol II, 1870–1966*, Oxford: Clarendon Press, 1971, pp 104–171.

[39] Statistics South Africa, *Census of Commercial Agriculture, 2007: Financial and Production Statistics*, Pretoria, 2010.

[40] *Ibid.*

[41] J O'Brien, 'Agricultural labour and development in Sudan', PhD dissertation, University of Connecticut, 1980.

[42] Estimate based on M Simpson, 'Large-scale mechanized rainfed farming development in the Sudan', in Centre of African Studies (CAS) (ed), *Post-Independence Sudan*, CAS Seminar Proceedings, University of Edinburgh, 1981, pp 197–212.

[43] R Mustafa, 'Risk management in the rainfed sector of Sudan: case study, Gedaref area, eastern Sudan', Dr Agr dissertation, Institute of Agriculture and Food Systems Management, Justus-Liebig University, Giessen, 2006.

[44] J Iliffe, *A Modern History of Tanganyika*, Cambridge: Cambridge University Press, 1979.

[45] C Guillebaud, *An Economic Survey of the Sisal Industry of Tanganyika*, Welwyn: Tanganyika Sisal Growers' Association and James Nisbet & Co, 1958.

[46] A Hartemink, *Soil Fertility Decline under Sisal Cultivation in Tanzania*, Technical Paper No 28, International Soil Reference and Information Centre, Wageningen, 1995.

[47] R van Zwanenberg & A King, *An Economic History of Kenya and Uganda, 1800–1970*, Atlantic Highlands: Humanities Press, 1975.

[48] World Bank, 'Uganda, standards and trade: experiences, capacities and priorities, paper prepared for Uganda Diagnostic Trade Integration Study, World Bank, January 2006.

[49] F Cooper, *From Slaves to Squatters: Plantation Labour and Agriculture in Zanzibar and Coastal Kenya, 1895–1925*, New Haven, CT: Yale University Press, 1980.

[50] *Ibid.*

[51] B Dinham & C Hines, *Agribusiness in Africa*, London: Earth Resources, 1983.

[52] The source for pineapple is S Jaffee, *How Private Enterprise Organised Agricultural Markets in Kenya*, Policy Research Paper 823, Washington, DC: World Bank, 1992. The source for cut flowers and fresh vegetables is J Humphrey, N McCulloch & M Ota, 'The impact of European market changes on employment in the Kenyan horticulture sector', *Journal of International Development*, 16, 2004, pp 63–80.

Key: n/k = not known; α refers to Unilever (HCB) plantations only; '350' denotes area of additional concession for collection of natural fruit; β excludes plantations owned by United Brands referred to in Dinham and Hines;[51] γ employment data refers to cut flowers only; δ cut flowers, fresh vegetables and pineapple only for employment;[52] ε excludes Dunlop rubber plantation; ζ refers to Sena Sugar Co only; η refers to cut flowers and fresh vegetables in 2004 plus sugar in 2009; θ refers to sugar only; š this figure is based on aggregating the total LSF area under all crops in South Africa. It may therefore overstate the crop area as more than one crop may be grown on the same area during a calendar year, depending on season; τ refers to sisal only; υ refers to cut flowers only.

of cocoa, coffee, spices, copra, cotton and tobacco on plantations. With the partial exception of tobacco, SSF came to dominate production of all these crops by around 1960. More recently a similar process has occurred with maize, sugar and tea, although sugar and tea also remain plantation crops. The fall, since 1980, in the LSF cultivated area in South Africa is largely accounted for by the decline in maize production following deregulation.[44] A notable development since 1980 has been the expansion of the LSF/PF area in Africa under higher-value crops such as fresh vegetables, cut flowers, citrus and grapes. In some cases this has replaced SSF production of the same crops. These crops occupy a relatively tiny share of the overall LSF/PF area but account for a very high share of LSF/PF investment, revenue and employment.[45]

Fourth, although this is again not visible from Table 1, there has been substantial growth since 1960 in the share of LSF/PFS owned by Africans of non-white descent. The bulk of this category of operations was established *ex-initio* from this time, notably the large-scale sorghum farms of Sudan and the tobacco and tea estates in Malawi. Simultaneously Africans of non-white descent acquired ownership of the majority of LSFS in Kenya, formerly owned by white settlers. More recently a new wave of non-white African investment has occurred in Kenya through leasing of sections of existing LSFS for production of higher-value crops.[46] These developments are distinct from a further wave of non-white African investments associated with privatisation of state-owned LSF/PFS (see below).

Turning to state-owned PF and LSF in Africa, its history follows two main strands.[47] One is nationalisation of property owned by white settlers or enterprises based in the colonial power by post-independence governments. In most cases this represented a pragmatic and sometimes temporary response to spontaneous evacuations. Where white settlers were not a factor, expropriation of European-owned corporate landed property after independence was the exception. The largest single purposive nationalisation of this kind in terms of scale was that affecting almost all Tanzanian sisal plantations (around 0.25 million ha) in 1967.

A second strand dates from the same period, but concerns the establishment from scratch of large-scale state farms producing food crops, mainly or exclusively for the domestic market. The main focuses here were on rice,[48] wheat, maize and, especially, sugar.[49] Typically there were heavy supporting investments in irrigation and milling plants, financed by donors ranging across the political spectrum from PR China to Japan and Canada. In a handful of West African countries new state farming for export crops was also initiated.[50] Systematic data on state-owned PF and PF crop production is unavailable, but it appears that it reached its African zenith in Ethiopia under the Derg, exceptionally in this case with relatively little foreign support.[51]

African state-owned PF and LSF ceased expansion around 1980 and began declining soon after. This often reflected problems in servicing heavy recurrent expenditure demands in an emerging context of adjustment and withdrawal of subsidies. Related to this and to a general lack of ideological investment in state-owned agriculture (see below), the sale of public plantations and LSFS were typically the first steps in the privatisation programmes in many African countries in the early 1990s. But these offers only provoked a strong response from private investors as of 2004, meaning that state-owned agriculture limped on in the absence of proper finance for a considerable period.

Since 2004 privatisation of state-owned PF and LSF has contributed substantially to the 'land grabbing' phenomenon; indeed, it has probably been the main channel for those new investments that have actually been implemented.[52] In terms of crops this has been particularly evident in sugar, where, for example, the South African-owned Illovo and Tongaat-Hulett companies have since the 1990s purchased or leased state-owned estates in Tanzania, Malawi, Mozambique, Mauritius, Swaziland and Zambia.[53]

Policy narratives on PF/LSF in Africa

This section explores the argument that, in addition to recognising African PF/LSF's historical resilience, heterogeneity and partially internal origins, the 'land grabbing' discussion would do well to acknowledge the policy dependence of both PF/LSF's and SSF's presence. Prototypes for the main forms of LSF and SSF were imagined by policy makers in Africa and disseminated through interventions on land distribution, tenurial relations, public revenue allocation and market regulation, though of course not normally simultaneously. The latter is already widely recognised in the case of LSF/PF but much less so for SSF.

A number of recurrent policy narratives, some extending back to the 19th century, underwrote the unfolding of LSF/PF and SSF during the 20th century.[54] In support of LSF/PF was a narrative assuming economies of scale and technical superiority. In support of SSF was the 'Indian civil service doctrine', which combined a critique of these assumptions with considerations of political stability. Pro-SSF narratives later elaborated the Indian civil service doctrine by adding the claims that LSF in Africa was inextricably dependent on racially allocated rents and that SSF had intrinsically higher productivity. The most recent stage in the development of these policy narratives has involved advocates of LSF/PF accepting that large numbers of LSFs were indeed historically dependent on racially allocated rents, and advocates of SSF admitting the existence of important exceptions to the rule of higher productivity. All these narratives refer to work by economists, not just administrators.

Regardless of the validity of the arguments deployed, it should be noted that recent developments represent a significant departure from earlier periods, when discussion was dominated by generic support for either LSF or SSF as such. On the one hand, these modifications make it less likely that the worst fears of those alarmed by 'land grabbing' will be realised. On the other, again regardless of the validity of the arguments deployed, they serve as a model for taking seriously the heterogeneity of both LSF and SSF.

Pro-LSF narratives

Claims for LSF's superiority on grounds of technology and economies of scale date from contributions by Arthur Young (1741–1820) and JR McCulloch (1789–1864). Both saw the English model, combining hereditary landed property with LSF by tenants holding long leases for large units, as both natural and the most productive possible. Granting leases for larger rather than smaller units meant proprietors could reap the scale benefits of draft animals, machinery and scientific agronomy, as well as organise workers using a scientific division of labour. Moreover, together with long terms, it provided those possessing them with incentives to 'improve'. In contrast, SSF by (pre-revolutionary) French share-croppers and Irish and Scottish 'cottiers', peasants holding half a hectare or less on annual leases, provided neither economies of scale nor incentives for improvement (see Dewey for a summary[55]).

The core argument of the Young–McCulloch position was repeated by the standard textbook on tropical agronomy of the first half of the 20th century,[56] and in the late 1930s and early 1940s in international discussions on optimal pro-duction organisation for palm oil. In Germany and The Netherlands, where this perspective enjoyed its greatest support, it was for example deployed by ADA de Kat Angelino in 1931 as the cornerstone of his definitive statement of a Dutch colonial development model, commissioned by the Ministry of the Colonies.[57]

In Britain pro-LSF narratives had lost their dominance over colonial policy before the end of the 19th century, although they did experience a revival during the palm oil discussion when, together with claims about the success of the 'Dutch model' in Southeast Asia, they were embraced both by the British Association,[58] and by large corporate users of vegetable oils. The debate is referred to in Lord William Hailey's 1938 *African Survey*, sponsored by the Colonial Office,[59] and in more detail in Sir Alan Pim's definitive restatement in 1946 of British colonial agricultural policy, sponsored by Chatham House.[60] While Hailey's book can be interpreted as a riposte to LSF narratives, Pim's indi-cated acceptance of their claims to technical superiority. However, rather than leading to a blanket endorsement of LSF/PF this was employed to promote the idea of 'marrying' LSF and SSF in systems combining 'nucleus estates' and small-scale outgrowers, organised in ways that could facilitate their 'scientific assistance'.[61] This was to prove perhaps the most enduring agricultural policy proposal of the 20th century and it will be returned to below.

With its claims for technical superiority apparently accepted, and with the gradual toning down of its 19th century claims for the unique investment incentives attached to large-scale property, advocates of LSF/PF continued to search for new arguments to support the economies-of-scale thesis. One that was increasingly deployed was that such economies might be extrinsic in nature as well as intrinsic, that is, they might be 'transmitted' upstream, as in the case of those crops tradable only after processing.[62] As will be seen, a version of this argument was to become accepted in the course of the 'land grab' debate by SSF's main international institutional advocate, the World Bank.[63]

A footnote to pro-LSF narratives is their persistent links to Malthusian doctrines of population. Young and McCulloch referred to a race between agricultural productivity and population growth, in a context where Irish peasants were held to combine 'low propensity to improve' with high propensity to pro-create. Likewise, recent restatements of the narrative cite an urgent need for 'something to be done' in relation to food security and employment, against the background of abnormal population growth.[64]

Pro-SSF narratives to 1960

Twentieth century British colonial policy regarding land and agricultural production was dominated by the Indian Civil Service (ICS) doctrine. It derived from policies instituted in British India in the second half of the 19th century and shaped personally by Richard Jones, WT Thornton and John Stuart Mill, who were all either officials in the East India Company or its successor (the ICS) or were employed to train its leadership. Leading British administrators in Africa were drawn from the ICS's ranks, ensuring the transmission of the doctrine. Its central feature was a presumption in favour of peasant proprietorship, on the basis of a series of economic arguments against Young and McCulloch and a political critique of Cornwallis's land reform in Bengal.

According to Jones and Thornton, Young and McCulloch were mistaken in believing that scale contributed to propensity to 'improve'. This was instead attributable to a combination of security of tenure and functioning land and labour markets. Where both were absent, as in Ireland, landlords could make more money from using peasant competition for SSF land to continuously raise (or 'rack') rents, than from encouraging 'improvement'. At the same time there was no incentive for SSFs to invest, since they could not be sure of renewing their tenancies, nor expect a Ricardian rent,[65] nor use profit to buy land from a landlord. Where SSFs were not hampered by rack rents, they were able to exhibit higher levels of unit investment than LSFs.[66]

Mill completed this critique by arguing that LSF enjoyed no natural economies of scale. There were few agricultural machines whose use was economical only for LSFs, and these could also be used economically by SSFs through cooperative ownership. Moreover, a peasant household of average size could achieve a level of internal specialisation corresponding to the optimal division of agricultural labour.[67] Importantly, he added, in the absence of market regulation, landlordism led to an inefficient pattern of resource allocation and to political instability. The latter case was illustrated in relation to both Ireland and Cornwallis's failed 'Permanent Settlement' of 1800 in Bengal, which created a new class of landlords living off the rents of insecure cultivators.[68]

An important moment in the ICS doctrine's dissemination in British Africa was the West Africa Land Commission of 1914–18, appointed to decide what tenurial system Britain should endorse in the region. Although the detailed recommendations of the Commission were never implemented, its rejection of freehold concessions for PF was accepted, while its justification for doing so was to become implanted in the 'official mind'. This repeated Mill's link between the economic inefficiency of large-scale property and extended his argument concerning political destabilisation. Not only land alienation, but also hired labour and labour migration were presented as threatening the indirect rule system.[69]

Developments in the West African cocoa sector were also in favour of the ICS doctrine. SSF production overtook PF production of cocoa in the Gold Coast between 1900 and 1908. This, and related price considerations,[70] encouraged the British Cotton Growing Association and Cadbury Bros to switch from operating their own plantations to sourcing crops overwhelmingly from SSFs.[71] Daviron notes the dissemination of the Gold Coast peasant cocoa story in international scientific journals from 1909, and partly attributes the fading allure of PF also in French colonial circles at this time as a reflection of it.[72] Lever Bros (forerunner of Unilever) maintained support for PF but were denied plantation land in British West Africa, and therefore invested in the Belgian Congo, where policy remained PF-friendly until 1945.[73]

As noted earlier, concerns about the unassisted competitiveness of SSF for palm oil led in the late 1940s to Pim's proposals to support its integration with LSF through a mechanism that would provide both technical and organisational support to small-scale farms. While Pim's model of nucleus estates and outgrower schemes was to become widely disseminated, for example in the sugar and tea sectors, British and French colonial authorities also explored a series of instruments aimed at SSF technical and organisational 'modernisation' that could be applied independently of a link to LSF. Over the next two decades in Kenya and Sudan the main vehicle for these instruments was to be resettlement schemes, incorporating subdivision of settler land and/or consolidation of peasant holdings,[74] and use of farm plans, model budgets, target incomes and public marketing systems.[75] As former British officials disseminated the now revised doctrine in international organisations, Integrated Rural Development (IRD) planning proliferated along these lines.[76] The World Bank alone sponsored more than 70 IRD projects and programmes in independent black Africa between the late 1960s and the 1980s.

Pro-SSF narratives post-1960

Pursuit of the project to 'modernise' SSF (lending it features considered to be hitherto confined to LSF/PF) without a direct link to LSF/PF was underwritten by the emergence or wider dissemination of two additional pro-SSF narratives during the 1960s. The first of these updated the critique of African LSF/PF by underlining its links with white settler power, the other updated the Gold Coast peasant cocoa story by proposing a generically superior productivity for SSFS.

Although partially rehearsed by Hancock,[77] Wilson's 1971 contribution was the first systematic statement of the argument that LSF in settler Africa was primarily a political rather than an economic phenomenon, aimed at promoting white domination of rural areas.[78] This proceeded first through forcible expropriation of African land, then by stabilising white agricultural incomes, and finally by supporting these incomes at levels equivalent to (white) urban ones. The first two stages of this process involved undermining the conditions of black SSF; all three entailed subsidising white LSF, initially through cheapening access to land, then through discriminatory labour, output and credit market interventions.[79] The unsustainability of LSF in the absence of discriminatory interventions was demonstrated with reference to its high attrition rates before these interventions.[80]

Claims for the superior economic efficiency of SSF revived in the early 1960s following publication of the first Indian Farm Management Surveys and the Inter-American Committee for Agricultural Development reports on seven Latin American countries.[81] Both pointed to a generally higher SSF output per unit. This was explained at the time by reference to SSF's ability to command (family) labour at sub-market prices, thanks to labour market segmentation, in turn allowing cultivation of more land per unit.[82]

Two studies published between 1979 and 1985 provided more comprehensive LSF–SSF empirical comparisons.[83] Both claimed to provide clear evidence across Asia, Latin America and Africa and, in the case of Berry and Cline, time periods for what the authors called the 'Inverse Relation' (IR) between farm size and agricultural productivity in developing countries. Sen and Mabro's arguments were reinforced by one concerning capital market imperfections.[84] From Feder's 1985 paper onwards a third argument was added, which thereafter came to displace that of dual labour markets.[85] This is that the higher productivity of SSF resulted from a superior capacity to supervise labour, allowing farms to select optimal factor combinations (more labour, capital only in the form of labour-based improvements, and less purchased or hired inputs).[86] The majority of subsequent contributions on developing countries have supported the IR proposition;[87] on the other hand, as Sender and Johnston point out, there is less support for it from African studies.[88]

More recent contributions to the discussion assert a need to recognise limitations to the validity of both these new narratives. In the case of the 'racial rents' narrative, following suggestions by Dunlop and Mosley,[89] Vink and Kirsten argue that there was always a segment of LSF in settler Africa that was efficient and profitable, regardless of policy interventions (at least after land alienation). Furthermore, these interventions were aimed not at white LSF in general but specifically at its least efficient components.[90]

In the case of the IR narrative the point has been made that, even if the narrative's many methodological criticisms are overlooked,[91] there are a series of empirical circumstances where it is difficult to credibly maintain that SSF will have higher productivity than LSF. These include farming for crops that require industrial post-harvest treatment or processing immediately after harvesting, where economies of scale in processing may be transmitted to production;[92] participation in global supply chains where buyers demand sophisticated standards entailing high fixed costs such as traceability, or sophisticated logistical systems where high fixed costs and economies of scale apply; and utilisation of advanced technologies such as remote sensing, which can substitute or even improve the imputed 'local knowledge' advantages of SSFS.[93]

The policy conclusions of the first set of these more recent contributions favour LSF but only in a 'structurally adjusted' form. Full liberalisation of land and output markets would allow separation of the efficient from the inefficient, rent-dependent component of LSF, thereby realising the sector's underlying economic advantages. This narrative gained ground among agricultural economists in South Africa from the early 1980s and formed the discursive basis for the reforms of the South African agricultural sector in the late 1980s and mid-1990s. The result was that subsidies and opportunities for rent were indeed severely reduced, resulting in a shakeout of large numbers of producers.[94]

The policy conclusions of the second are that proposals to introduce LSF/PF in regions where these were not previously present should be assessed both in terms of their financial viability independent of the deployment of public resources, and with reference to which crop(s) will be grown, which value chains they will be integrated into and which technologies they will employ. Both point broadly towards a selective rehabilitation of LSF.

Conclusion

What is the legacy of the practice of PF and LSF and the policy narratives that supported them in 20th century SSA? Both supporters and critics of land deals borrow significantly from past ideas to support their views. In general, the supporters invoke the technological superiority of large-scale operations as well as the spectre of Malthusian scenarios, reinforced by reference to the food crisis. However, the assumption that much land in SSA is indeed 'idle' land, which if exploited could potentially solve several global problems, has been exposed with some authority.[95]

It is widely known that, compared to Asia and Latin America, LSF has historically been less important in SSA. On the other hand, outside of Zanzibar in the 1960s, Ethiopia in 1975 and Zimbabwe in 2002–03, so too have far-reaching land reforms. This has supported both the curious resilience of LSF/PF, despite efforts to contain its development, and various efforts to 'modernise' SSF. The result has been an uneven combination of LSF and SSF that continues today. While press and some NGO reports provide an overwhelming image of growth in highly mechanised large-scale exploitations based on low absorption of wage labour, the evolving debate on land grabbing increasingly acknowledges a much more complex picture, including instances of redistribution and productive investment alongside others of acquisition without productive investment, investor withdrawal or even expulsion, and contract farming with or without nucleus estates.

As in the past, much of today's debate still revolves around a comparison between LSF and SSF, their economic efficiency and political consequences. Since the 1960s the claim of an inverse relation between scale and productivity has dominated economic views and policy debates over developing country farming. This trend continues in the current land grabbing debate. The World Bank still acclaims the benefits of family labour as compared to wage labour, which implies lower worker incentives and hence higher supervision costs, although critics have also pointed out that family labour is rarely found in undiluted forms, especially for export crops.[96] On the other hand, the conviction that SSF would benefit from organisational and technical modernisation also survives, giving rise as in earlier periods to proposals to facilitate this via links to LSF/PF. Middle-ground solutions of this kind reflect a historical impetus to contain rather than dismantle PF and LSF in SSA. In this sense, whereas in the colonial period support for SSF was partially motivated by fears associated with the formation of masses of wage labourers, currently support for contract farming can be read as a new substitute and surrogate for more radical opposition to LSF/PF. By linking SSF (under non-specified conditions) to supposedly dynamic and affluent markets, by forging new and lucrative commodity chains and by widening access to more advanced technologies, contract farming can provide PF and LSF with a human face and recast a SSF model of development without resorting to politically difficult land distribution.

While doubt surrounds the underlying premise that scheme participation will bring about technological spill-overs and welfare benefits, it must be acknowledged that support for such solutions represents an advance over positions of blanket support for either LSF/PF or SSF. This attitude hinders a reflection on the heterogeneity of both forms of agriculture. Indeed, only by unbiased reflection can the different forms of LSF/PF and SSF be fully examined, providing a sounder basis for understanding the long-term consequences for economic development, employment and labour conditions.

Notes

1   P McMichael, 'The land grab and corporate food regime restructuring', *Journal of Peasant Studies*, 39(3–4), 2012, pp 681–701.
2   SM Borras & JC Franco, 'Global land grabbing and trajectories of agrarian change: a preliminary analysis', *Journal of Agrarian Change*, 12(2), 2012, pp 34–59.
3   J Fairhead, M Leach & I Scoones, 'Green grabbing: a new appropriation of nature?', *Journal of Peasant Studies*, 39(2), 2012, pp 237–261; O De Schutter, 'Forum on global land grabbing: how not to think land grabbing—three critiques of large-scale investments in farmland', *Journal of Peasant Studies*, 38(2), 2011, pp 249–279; and M Levien, 'The land question: special economic zones and the political economy of dispossession in India', *Journal of Peasant Studies*, 39(3–4), 2012, pp 933–969.
4   B White, SM Borras, R Hall, I Scoones & W Wolford, 'The new enclosures: critical perspectives on corporate land deals', *Journal of Peasant Studies*, 39(3–4), 2012, pp 619–647.
5   K Amanor, 'Global resource grabs, agribusiness concentration, and the smallholder: two West African case studies', *Journal of Peasant Studies*, 39(3–4), 2012, pp 731–750.
6   Borras & Franco, 'Global land grabbing and trajectories of agrarian change', pp 34–59.
7   D Shepard, 'Situating private equity capital in the land grabbing debate', *Journal of Peasant Studies*, 39(3–4), 2012, pp 703–729.
8   P Peters, 'Inequality and social conflict over land in Africa', *Journal of Agrarian Change*, 4(3), 2004, pp 269–314.
9   P Woodhouse, 'New investment, old challenges: land deals and the water constraint in African agriculture', *Journal of Peasant Studies*, 39(3–4), 2012, pp 777–794.
10 SM Borras, JC Franco, S Gomez, C Kay & M Spoor, 'Land grabbing in Latin America and the Caribbean', *Journal of Peasant Studies*, 39(3–4), 2012, pp 845–872.
11 World Bank, *Awakening Africa's Sleeping Giant: Prospects for Commercial Agriculture in the Guinea Savannah Zone and Beyond*, Washington, DC: World Bank, 2009.
12 *Ibid*, p 2.
13 World Bank, *Rising Global Interest in Farmland: Can it Yield Sustainable Benefits?*, Washington, DC: World Bank, 2010, p xiv.
14 H Friedmann & P McMichael, 'Agriculture and the state system: the rise and decline of national agricultures, 1870 to the present', *Sociologica Ruralis*, 29(2), 1989, pp 93–117; JW Moore, '"Amsterdam is standing on Norway" Part I: the alchemy of capital, empire, and nature in the diaspora of silver, 1545–1648', *Journal of Agrarian Change*, 10(1), 2010, pp 33–68; Moore, '"Amsterdam is standing on Norway" Part II: the global North Atlantic in the ecological revolution of the long seventeenth century', *Journal of Agrarian Change*, 10(2), pp 188–227; and G Arrighi, *The Long Twentieth Century: Money, Power and the Origins of our Times*, New York: Verso, 1994.
15 See the latest revision of data by Land Matrix, at http://www.landmatrix.org. A special issue of the *Journal of Peasant Studies*, 40(3), 2013, questions some of the methodologies of data collection that have hitherto fuelled the debate on land grabbing. See also L Cotula, *The Great African Land Grab? Agricultural Investment and the Global Food System*, London: Zed Books, 2013, and Oya (this issue).
16 S Ekman, 'Myth and reality: Chinese investment in the Mozambican agricultural sector', paper presented at the SIANI Expert Group meeting on Chinese global land investment, Stockholm Environment Institute, January 2012, at www.slideshow.net/SIANIAgri/sigrid-ekmand-Chinamoz.
17 J Hanlon, *Understanding Land Investment Deals in Africa: Mozambique, A Country Study*, San Francisco, CA: Oakland Institute, 2011.
18 This has applied especially to non-sugar biofuel projects, for which profitability was dependent upon oil prices at $120 or above (not to mention over-optimistic estimates of yields from feedstock, particularly Jatropha).

19 As of May 2013, according to the Land Matrix, 'intended' and 'failed' land deals represent, respectively, 17% and 7% of recorded global land deals. See http://www.landmatrix.org.

20 Borras & Franco, 'Global land grabbing and trajectories of agrarian change', pp 34–59.

21 It has been argued that the notion of 'control grabbing' captures the wider spectrum of resources at stake, including 'green grabs' and 'water grabs'. Borras *et al*, 'Land grabbing in Latin America and the Caribbean'. A focus on control rather than ownership also enables recognition that African states remain *de jure* landowners and consideration of land deals not entailing dispossession or expulsion of local occupiers.

22 H Bernstein, 'Agrarian questions of capital and labour: some theory about land reform (and a periodization)', in L Ntsebeza & R Hall (eds), *The Land Question in South Africa: The Challenge of Transformation and Redistribution*, Cape Town: HSRC Press, 2006.

23 White *et al*, 'The new enclosures', pp 619–647; and C Oya, 'Contract farming in sub-Saharan Africa: a survey of approaches, debates and issues', *Journal of Agrarian Change*, 12(1), 2012, pp 1–38.

24 W Wolford, SM Borras, R Hall, I Scoones & B White, 'Governing global land deals: the role of the state in the rush for land', *Development and Change*, 44(2), 2013, pp 189–210; and L Alden Wily, '"The law is to blame": the vulnerable status of common property rights in sub-Saharan Africa', *Development and Change*, 42(3), 2011, pp 733–757. Unlike in the 1960s there are today only a few examples of African states dispossessing occupiers to initiate publicly owned LSF/PF. The special issue of *Development and Change*, 44(2), 2013, explores the complexities of states' role in land grabbing.

25 P Hill, *Studies in Rural Capitalism in West Africa*, London: Cambridge University Press, 1970; and N Swainson, *The Development of Corporate Capitalism in Kenya, 1918–1977*, Berkeley, CA: University of California Press, 1980; J Iliffe, *The Emergence of African Capitalism*, London: Macmillan, 1983; P Kennedy, *African Capitalism: The Struggle for Ascendancy*, Cambridge: Cambridge University Press, 1988; BJ Berman & C Leys, *African Capitalists in African Development*, London: Lynne Rienner, 1994, and S Ellis & YA Fauré (eds), *Entreprises et entrepreneurs africains*, Paris: Karthala, 1995.

26 R Hall, 'The next Great Trek? South African commercial farmers move north', *Journal of Peasant Studies*, 39(3–4), 2011, pp 823–843.

27 W Anseeuw, L Alden Wily, L Cotula & M Taylor, *Land Rights and the Rush for Land: Findings of the Global Commercial Pressures on Land Research Project*, Rome: International land Coalition, 2012.

28 T Hilhorst, J Nelen & N Traoré, 'Agrarian change below the radar screen: rising farmland acquisitions by domestic investors in West Africa—results from a survey in Benin, Burkina Faso and Niger', LDPI Paper, 2011.

29 C Oya, 'Stories of rural accumulation in Africa: trajectories and transitions among rural capitalists in Senegal', *Journal of Agrarian Change*, 7(4), 207, pp 453–493.

30 E Baglioni, 'Straddling contract and estate farming: accumulation strategies of Senegalese horticultural exporters', *Journal of Agrarian Change* (forthcoming).

31 World Bank, *Rising Global Interest in Farmland*.

32 D Harvey, *The New Imperialism*, Oxford: Oxford University Press, 2003.

33 H Bernstein, *Class Dynamics of Agrarian Change*, Black Point/Sterling, VA: Fernwood/Kumarian Press, 2010.

34 T Li, 'Centering labor in the land grab debate', *Journal of Peasant Studies*, 38(2), 2011, pp 281–298.

35 While some emphasise the poverty reduction potential of large-scale investment in Southern 'unexploited' land, others expose its labour-displacing outcomes, whether involving the formation of a reserve army of labour or simply its elimination of a surplus population ultimately irrelevant to 'capital needs'. See, respectively, World Bank, *Rising Global Interest in Farmland*; F Araghi, 'The invisible hand and the visible foot: peasants, dispossession and globalisation', in AH Akram-Lodhi & C Kay, *Peasants and Globalization: Political Economy, Rural Transformation and the Agrarian Question*, London, Routledge, 2009; and T Li, 'To make live or let die? Rural dispossession and the protection of surplus populations', *Antipode*, 41(1), 2009, pp 66–93. Others more cautiously emphasise the current lack of hard evidence on this question. See C Oya, 'Methodological reflections on land "grab" databases and the land "grab" literature "rush"', *Journal of Peasant Studies*, 40(3), 2013, pp 503–520.

36 J Franco & S Borras, 'From threat to opportunity? Problems with the idea of a "Code of Conduct" for land-grabbing', *Yale Human Rights and Development Law Journal*, 13(2), 2010, pp 507–523.

37 F Cooper, *Decolonisation and African Society: The Labour Question in French and British Africa*, Cambridge: Cambridge University Press, 1996.

38 P Peters, 'Land appropriation, surplus people and a battle over visions of agrarian futures in Africa', *Journal of Peasant Studies*, 40(3), 2013, pp 537–562. Challenges to these persistent views can be found in TJ Byres, 'Neo-classical neo-populism 25 years on: déjà vu and déjà passé—towards a critique', *Journal of Agrarian Change*, 4(1), 2004, pp 17–44; and Bernstein, *Class Dynamics of Agrarian Change*.

39 While narratives favouring LSF are equally generic and sketchy, historically these have not enjoyed comparable influence.

40 In Malawi, for example, some holdings as small as 10 ha are officially classified as 'estates'. By the same token this problem applies also to SSF.

41 The authors have used figures for 'permanent' labour where these are available (usually the period since 1990 only). Where they are not, they have used those for 'regular' labour. Where these are also not available, they have used those for male labour. And (only) where these also are unavailable, have they used those for registered labourers.

42 Examples are Gabon, Sierra Leone, and Gambia and Senegal. See, respectively, D Fieldhouse, *Unilever Overseas: The Anatomy of a Multinational, 1895–1965*, London: Croom Helm, 1978; A Pim, *Colonial Agricultural Production: The Contribution made by Native Peasants and by Foreign Enterprise*, London: Oxford University Press, 1946; and B Dinham & C Hines, *Agribusiness in Africa*, London: Earth Resources, 1983.

43 So too do those on area for South Africa in 1900–20 and the 1960s.

44 A classic PF crop that has seen a downward trend has been sisal, although this relates primarily to demand and prices rather than to a shift to SSF production.

45 For greater detail, see P Gibbon, *Experiences of Plantation and Large-scale Agriculture in Twentieth Century Africa*, Working Paper 20, Copenhagen: Danish Institute for International Studies, 2011.

46 S Jaffee, How Private Enterprise Organised Agricultural Markets in Kenya', Policy Research Paper, 823, Washington, DC: World Bank, 1992.

47 Other, minor strands include confiscation of enemy (German and Italian) property in several countries following World War II.

48 In Senegal, Mali, Cameroon, Madagascar and Congo-Brazzaville. See P Hugon, 'Multi-channel food supply systems to francophone African cities: FAO Inter-regional Programme on Food Supply and Distribution to Cities', mimeo, Rome, nd. Rice was also the focus in Ghana and Tanzania.

49 Tanzania, Malawi, Zambia, Benin, Togo, Madagascar, Sierra Leone, Liberia, Mali and Ethiopia among others.

50 In Ghana, for example, publicly owned palm oil, coconut, kola nut, rubber and cotton plantations were established on around 15 000 ha. A Asamoa, *Socio-economic Development Strategies of Independent African Countries: The Ghana Experience*, Accra: Ghana University Press, 1997.

51 By 1980 there were 240 000 ha of state farms under grains. H Abera, 'Adoption of improved tef and wheat production technologies in crop–livestock mixed systems in northern and western Shewa zones, Ethiopia', PhD dissertation, Faculty of Natural and Agricultural Sciences, University of Pretoria, 2008. There were 38 000 under cotton. M Demeke, T Negash, S Damte, A Bersufehad & T Aklilu, *Decent Work Deficits in the Ethiopian Cotton Sector*, Geneva: ILO, 2004. A similar area was under sugar and smaller ones under oil seeds and pulses.

52 L Cotula, 'The international political economy of global land rush: a critical appraisal of trends, scale, geography and drivers', *Journal of Peasant Studies*, 39(3–4), 2012, pp 649–680.

53 Hall, 'The next Great Trek?'.

54 The condensed account offered here overlaps with the important contribution of M Cowen & R Shenton, *Doctrines of Development*, London: Routledge, 1996, especially in highlighting the influence of Mill and of the Indian experience. However, it also departs from this by downplaying the role of the doctrine of 'trusteeship' and relatedly of Fabian socialist thinking.

55 C Dewey, 'The rehabilitation of peasant proprietorship in nineteenth century economic thought', *History of Political Economy*, 6(1), 1974, pp 17–47.

56 JC Willis, *Agriculture in the Tropics: An Elementary Treatise*, Cambridge: Cambridge University Press, 1909, pp 179–90, 200–216. JC Willis was Director of the Royal Botanical Garden at Kew, the institutional reference for agricultural extension services in British Africa until World War II. His book was reprinted twice. It should be noted that, while endoring LSF/PF's overall superiority, he did not entirely reject SSF for the cultivation of some export crops.

57 ADA de Kat Angelino, *Colonial Policy*, The Hague: Martinus Nijhoff, 1931.

58 The premier association of British scientists, founded in opposition to the more conservative Royal Society.

59 W Hailey, *An African Survey: A Study of Problems Arising in Africa South of the Sahara*, Oxford: Oxford University Press, 1938.

60 Pim, *Colonial Agricultural Production*.

61 *Ibid*, pp 141–142.

62 For example sisal, palm oil, sugar, rubber and tea. See M Tiffen & M Mortimore, *Theory and Practice in Plantation Agriculture: An Economic Review*, London: Overseas Development Institute, 1990, p 27.

63 World Bank, *Rising Global Interest in Farmland*.

64 P Collier, *The Bottom Billion: Why the Poorest Countries are Failing and What can be Done about it*, Oxford: Oxford University Press, 2008.

65 Ricardo's theory states that rent for agricultural land is mainly determined by the natural fertility of the soil. Ricardo himself accepted that Ireland was an exception to his theory, which he explained as a result of normal tenurial relations being confounded by the 'racial' behaviour of landlords. R Collison Black, 'Economic policy in Ireland and India in the time of JS Mill', *Economic History Review*, 21(2), 1968, pp 321–336.

66 Thornton cited several European examples and also introduced the idea that 'labour-based', in addition to capital-based, improvements be counted as investments. He further postulated a link between recognition of peasant property rights, spontaneous land consolidation, improved productivity and stabilisation of population growth. For a summary, see C Dewey, 'The rehabilitation of peasant proprietorship in nineteenth century economic thought'.

67 *Ibid.*

68 Collison Black, 'Economic policy in Ireland and India in the time of JS Mill'.

69 A Hopkins, *An Economic History of West Africa*, London: Longman, 1973; and A Phillips, *The Enigma of Colonialism: British Policy in West Africa*, Oxford: James Currey, 1989, pp 72–76, 97–100. Hired migrant labour was held to lead to a series of 'problems of population' including 'promiscuity and prostitution, instability of native marriage, venereal disease and probable decline in native population'. See E Ardener, S Ardener & W Warmington, *Plantation and Village in the Cameroons*, Oxford: Oxford University Press, 1960, p 219. Daviron mentions similar concerns in France. B Daviron, 'Mobilising labour in African agriculture: the role of the International Colonial Institute in the elaboration of a standard of colonial administration, 1895–1930', *Journal of Global History*, 5, 2010, pp 479–501.

70 In *The Enigma of Colonialism,* Phillips quotes George Cadbury observing after a visit that 'self-employed Africans were willing to work longer and for lower returns than day labourers'. Cadbury Bros's reservations about PF were reinforced by popular boycotts of chocolate and cocoa from plantations on São Tomé, following exposure of labour conditions there in 1908. Clarence-Smith, *Slaves, Peasants and Capitalists in Southern Angola.*

71 Phillips, *The Enigma of Colonialism*, p 70.

72 Daviron, 'Mobilising labour in African agriculture'. PF/LSF's low priority in French Africa was reaffirmed in 1944 at the Free French Brazzaville conference, held to determine postwar colonial policy. PF/LSF 'received virtually no support…The colons [settlers] were reviled for their inefficiency and greed and for putting officials in the position of slave traders'. Cooper, *Decolonisation and African Society.*

73 Fieldhouse, *Unilever Overseas*; Phillips, *The Enigma of Colonialism*, pp 72–76, 97–100; and Clarence-Smith, *Slaves, Peasants and Capitalists in Southern Angola.*

74 Based in turn on individual surveying and titling.

75 A Gaitskell, *Gezira: A Story of the Development in the Sudan*, London: Faber & Faber, 1959, ch 25; W Rendell, *A History of the Commonwealth Development Corporation*, London: Heinemann, 1976, pp 275–278; and T Phillips, 'Nucleus plantations and processing factories: their place in the development of organized smallholder production', *Tropical Science*, 1965, pp 99–108.

76 J Hodge, 'British colonial expertise, post-colonial careering and the early history of international development', *Journal of Modern European History*, 8(1), 2010, pp 24–46.

77 W Hancock, *Survey of British Commonwealth Affairs, Vol II, Problems of Economic Policy, 1918–39, Part 2*, Oxford: Oxford University Press, 1941.

78 F Wilson, 'Farming, 1866–1966', in M Wilson & L Thompson (eds), *The Oxford History of South Africa, Vol II, 1870–1966*, Oxford: Clarendon Press, 1971, pp 104–171.

79 On land alienation, see R van Zwanenberg & A King, *An Economic History of Kenya and Uganda* for Kenya; Phimister, *An Economic and Social History of Zimbabwe* for Southern Rhodesia; and E Francis & G Williams, 'The land question', *Canadian Journal of African Studies*, 27(3), 1993, pp 380–403 for South Africa. On labour market interventions, see M Cowen, 'Before and after Mau Mau in Kenya', *Journal of Peasant Studies*, 16(2), 1989, pp 260–275 for Kenya; R Loewenson, *Modern Plantation Agriculture: Corporate Wealth and Labour Squalor*, London: Zed Books, 1992 for Southern Rhodesia; and M Morris, 'The development of capitalism in South African agriculture: class struggle in the countryside', *Economy and Society*, 5(3), 1976, pp 292–343 for South Africa. On output market interventions, see P Mosley, *The Settler Economies: Studies in the Economic History of Kenya and Southern Rhodesia, 1900–63*, Cambridge: Cambridge University Press, 1983 for Kenya and Southern Rhodesia; and Wilson, 'Farming, 1866–1966' for South Africa. On credit market interventions see references to output markets.

80 Phimister, *An Economic and Social History of Zimbabwe*, pp 127–129; R Hodder-Williams, *White Farmers in Rhodesia, 1890–1965: A History of the Marandellas District*, London: Macmillan, 1983, pp 129, 127; and R Palmer, 'White farmers in Malawi: before and after the depression', *African Affairs*, 84 (335), 1985, pp 211–245.

81 M Lipton, *Land Reform in Developing Countries: Property Rights and Property Wrongs*, London: Routledge, 2009.

82 AK Sen, 'Peasants and dualism with or without surplus labour', *Journal of Political Economy*, 74, 1996, pp 425–450; and R Mabro, 'Employment and wages in dual agriculture', *Oxford Economic Papers*, 23, 1971, pp 401–417.

83 R Berry & W Cline, *Agrarian Structure and Productivity in Developing Countries*, Baltimore, MD: ILO and Johns Hopkins University Press, 1979; and G Cornia, 'Farm size, land yields and the agricultural production function: an analysis for fifteen developing countries', *World Development*, 13(4), 1985, pp 513–534.

84 Since LSFS enjoyed cheaper access to capital they over-substituted capital for labour, thus reducing their productivity further.

85 G Feder, 'The relation between farm size and farm productivity', *Journal of Development Economics*, 18, 1985, pp 297–313.

86 Lipton, *Land Reform in Developing Countries*, deploys additional arguments to the effect that SSFS have superior capacity to select productive labourers and that they have lower costs of disposing of over-output (since this will be shared between family members).

87 For examples, see R Netting, *Smallholders, Householders: Farm Families and the Ecology of Intensive, Sustainable Agriculture*, Stanford, CA: Stanford University Press, 1993; F Ellis, *Peasant Economies: Farm Households and Agrarian Development*, Cambridge: Cambridge University Press, 1993; K Deininger & G Feder, *Land Institutions and Land Markets*, Policy Research Paper 16, Washington, DC: World Bank, 1998; and K Griffen, A Khan & A Ickowitz, 'Poverty and the distribution of land', *Journal of Agrarian Change*, 2(3), 2002, pp 279–330.

88 See J Sender & D Johnston, 'Searching for a weapon of mass production in rural Africa: unconvincing arguments for land reform', *Journal of Agrarian Change*, 4(1–2), 2004, pp 142–165. The main references are D Hunt, *The Impending Crisis in Kenya*, Farnham: Gower, 1984; and I Livingston, *Rural Development, Employment and Incomes in Kenya*, Farnham: Gower, 1986, using Kenyan data from the late 1960s and early 1970s; S Pearson, J Stryker & C Humphreys, *Rice in West Africa*, Stanford, CA: Stanford University Press, 1981, using Nigerian data from the 1970s; C Barrett, *On Price Risk and the Inverse Farm Size–Productivity Relationship*, Department of Agricultural Economics Staff Paper No 369, University of Wisconsin-Madison, 1993, on Madagascar; D Sahn & J Arulpragsam, 'Land tenure, dualism and poverty in Malawi', in J van der Gaag & M Lipton (eds), *Including the Poor*, Washington, DC: World Bank, 1993, pp 306–334, on Malawi; A Adesina & K Djato, 'Farm size, relative efficiency and agrarian policy in Côte d'Ivoire: a profit function analysis of rice firms', *Agricultural Economics*, 14, 1996, pp 93–102, on Côte d'Ivoire; A Dorward, 'Farm size and productivity in Malawian smallholder agriculture', *Journal of Development Studies*, 35(5), 1999, pp 141–161, on Malawi; and J Pender, E Nkonya, P Jagger, D Sserunkuuma & H Ssali, 'Strategies to increase agricultural productivity and reduce land degradation: evidence from Uganda', *Agricultural Economics*, 31(2–3), 2004, pp 181–195, on Uganda. Of these, only Hunt, Livingston and Pender *et al* provide clear support for the IR, while Dorward supports its rejection.

89 H Dunlop, *The Development of European Agriculture in Rhodesia, 1945–65*, Department of Economics Occasional Paper No 5, Salisbsury: University of Rhodesia, 1971; and Mosley, *The Settler Economies*, pp 176–78. Mosley showed a high level of internal differentiation in LSF yields in the settler economies, with a majority of high volume, high yield producers and a majority of low volume, low yield ones.

90 The mechanisms included allocating loans in sizes too low to interest larger LSFS, distributing sales quotas whose size related inversely to output, and calculating production costs for subsidy purposes from surveys biased toward smaller LSFS. See N Vink & J Kirsten, *Deregulation of Agricultural Marketing in South Africa: Lessons Learned*, Monograph 25, Sandton: Free Market Foundation, 2000; Mosley, *The Settler Economies*, pp 179–181; and Dunlop, *The Development of European Agriculture in Rhodesia*, p 34.

91 These include lack of control for crop mix or—more importantly—for differences in agro-ecological conditions and failure to consider methods by which LSFS might reduce supervision costs. See, respectively, G Dyer, 'Redistributive land reform—no April rose: the poverty of Berry and Cline and GKI on the Inverse Relation', *Journal of Agrarian Change*, 4(1–2), 2004, pp 45–72; and Sender & Johnston, 'Searching for a weapon of mass production in rural Africa'. A further criticism is the artificiality of the exclusive identification of SSF labour with family labour.

92 This argument is attributed to Binswanger and Rosenzweig. H Binswanger & M Rosenzweig, 'Behavioral and material determinants of production relations in agriculture', *Journal of Development Studies*, 22(3), 1985, pp 503–539.

93 World Bank, *Rising Global Interest in Farmland*.

94 See M de Klerk, 'The financial crisis in South African agriculture and post-apartheid agricultural transformation', *Canadian Journal of African Studies*, 27(3), 1993, pp 361–380; H Bernstein, 'The political economy of the maize filière', *Journal of Peasant Studies*, 22 (2–3), 1996, pp 120–145; J Van Zyl, N Vink, J Kirsten & D Poonyth, 'South African agriculture in transition: the 1990s', *Journal of International Development*, 13(6), 2001, pp 725–739; and Vink & Kirsten, *Deregulation of Agricultural Marketing in South Africa*.

95 De Schutter, 'Forum on global land grabbing'; and White *et al*, *The New Enclosures*.

96 World Bank, *Rising Global Interest in Farmland*.

Notes on Contributors

Elena Baglioni is lecturer in Global Supply Chains at the School of Business and Management, Queen Mary, University of London. She is also an early career fellow at the Future Agriculture Consortium, where she research land grabbing issues in relation to sub-Saharan Africa.

Peter Gibbon is Senior Researcher, Danish Institute for international Studies, Copenhagen. His current research interests include labour in large-scale agriculture in developing countries and the relation between finance, financialisation and commodity trade.

Primitive Accumulation, Accumulation by Dispossession and the Global Land Grab

DEREK HALL

Department of Political Science and Balsillie School of International Affairs, Wilfrid Laurier University, Waterloo, ON, Canada

ABSTRACT   *Critical scholars have made extensive use of the concepts of primitive accumulation and accumulation by dispossession to analyse the global land grab. These concepts have been crucial to efforts to understand the land grab in terms of the creation, expansion and reproduction of capitalist social relations, of accumulation by extra-economic means, and of dispossessory responses to capitalist crises. This paper provides an overview of these approaches. It also argues that there are substantial challenges involved in the use of primitive accumulation and accumulation by dispossession, including tensions and ambiguities over what the concepts mean, the assumptions embedded within them and problems of fit with other conceptualisations of the land grab. The paper also highlights resources for engaging with these challenges in the land grab literature.*

A central feature of the academic literature on the 'global land grab' is the explanation of the post-2006 surge in large-scale land acquisitions for (especially) crop production and resource extraction in terms of the dynamics and contemporary transformations of capitalism. Two key concepts scholars have used to understand these processes are Marx's 'primitive accumulation' and David Harvey's updating and reconstruction of it as 'accumulation by dispossession'.[1] For some authors, indeed, the land grab can be understood substantially in terms of one or both of these concepts. Sam Moyo, Paris Yeros and Praveen Jha write that the 'new scramble' for Africa's land and resources 'consists in the geopolitical escalation of an ongoing process of primitive accumulation'.[2] Wendy Wolford and her co-authors argue that contemporary land deals are 'productively analysed through the lens of' accumulation by dispossession, while Jun Borras and Jennifer Franco state that the 'massive enclosures' of private and public lands that constitute the land grab 'manifest "accumulation by dispossession" [...] driven by the imperatives of capitalist development and expansion in the context of converging food, energy, financial and environmental crises'.[3] Lyla Mehta *et al* observe that 'most critical analysts working on land grabbing today draw on political economy and Marxist traditions, in particular David Harvey's notion of "accumulation by dispossession"'.[4]

The relevance of primitive accumulation and accumulation by dispossession (ABD) to the analysis of the land grab will be clear to anyone familiar with these concepts. The processes by which land and other resources are enclosed, and their previous users dispossessed, for the purposes of capital accumulation are central to both. Land grab researchers have noted the resemblances between many current land acquisitions and the enclosures of land and dispossession of peasants in England that Marx placed at the heart of his analysis of primitive accumulation and, thus, at the very origin of capitalism.[5] They have linked today's 'new enclosures' to the land seizures crucial to centuries of imperialism and capitalist expansion.[6] The role of the state in capital accumulation and dispossession, too, is at the core of both the theorisation of primitive accumulation and ABD and of land grab research. That research has also built on the innovations of a vibrant recent literature on primitive accumulation and ABD in critical political economy and geography to analyse 'water grabs' and 'green grabs' as part of the land grab.[7]

Primitive accumulation and ABD have been used to develop fruitful and theoretically informed accounts of the global land grab. Their use is also, however, fraught with challenges. There are substantial tensions and ambiguities over their meanings in the foundational texts by Marx and Harvey, and they are employed to mean quite different (and sometimes unclear) things, and in pursuit of diverse intellectual projects, by different authors.[8] Understandings of primitive accumulation and ABD also contain potentially problematic assumptions about land grabbing (including what it is, whether it is a unified phenomenon, who carries it out, and how), and conceptualise it in ways that sit awkwardly with prominent definitions and empirical findings in the land grab literature. Borras and Franco have critiqued a 'dominant discourse' about 'the current wave of land grabs' that can encourage mischaracterisations of contemporary agrarian change in part because of its assumptions about land grab-related dispossession.[9] Analyses that use primitive accumulation and ABD face similar problems.

I do not seek in this paper to develop a new account of the global land grab in terms of primitive accumulation and ABD. Rather, I provide an overview of the three main uses of these terms in land grab research, identify key challenges associated with each of them, and highlight theoretical and empirical resources in the land grab literature for grappling with these challenges. The first project, the use of (usually) ABD to analyse dispossessory responses to capitalist crises, raises questions about the balance between global and domestic forces in driving land grabbing and about the agency of (global) capital, states and smallholders. The second, which analyses extra-economic means of capital accumulation, has a difficult relationship with scholarly definitions of the land grab, and invites queries about the boundaries between the economic and the extra-economic. The challenges of the third project, the study of the creation, expansion and reproduction of capitalist social relations, include the assumptions embedded in primitive accumulation and ABD as concepts and the difficulties of distinguishing capitalism's 'inside' from its 'outside'. I conclude the paper with a discussion of the implications of these findings for future land grab research.

The literature consulted here consists primarily of papers published in special journal issues on land grabbing, together with other important contributions that explicitly analyse it. While I naturally focus on works that refer to primitive accumulation and ABD, I do not limit the analysis to them. One reason for this relates to how these concepts fit into broader literatures. Debates over primitive accumulation and ABD do not take place in isolation, but intersect with those over related concepts like enclosure, commodification, the double movement, neoliberalism, privatisation and capitalism in general.[10] (There has also been a proliferation of terms similar to accumulation by dispossession, including 'accumulation by displacement' and 'dispossession by displacement',[11] 'accumulation by encroachment',[12] 'accumulation by denial',[13] 'primitive accumulation by dispossession',[14] and 'dispossession by accumulation'.[15]) Some land grab research, similarly, discusses core issues of concern to this paper in ways that resonate with work on primitive accumulation and ABD without using those terms, and it would be a mistake to ignore it.[16] I also draw on the broader land grab literature for concepts and empirics.

Some words of warning: even though problematising 'land grabbing' is a central goal of this paper, for ease of exposition I sometimes take 'the land grab' for granted as a phenomenon. The interconnected nature of different conceptions of primitive accumulation and ABD means that some of the arguments I make under the heading of one of the three main senses of the term apply to other senses as well. Space limitations mean that I can only sketch the contours of debates over primitive accumulation and ABD outside the land grab literature;[17] I also assume some background on the land grab itself. Most importantly, scholars who use primitive accumulation and ABD to study land grabbing generally employ these terms in diverse ways, and alongside other concepts, in developing multifaceted analyses of land grabbing. I have had to isolate specific statements about primitive accumulation and ABD to highlight the different meanings of the concepts, and hope that in doing so I have not taken them too far out of context.

Finally, a central project in this paper is the comparison of conceptions of primitive accumulation and ABD with explicit definitions of 'land grabbing' in the scholarly literature. I introduce the definitions I draw on here by exploring their (dis)agreements on eight points.[18] First, while early research focused on foreign land acquisitions,[19] none of the definitions considered here does this, and some explicitly include domestic and foreign investments. Second, the definitions almost all require that land acquisitions be large in order to count, with some setting a lower bound in hectares and others using qualitative terms like 'large-scale'. Borras *et al* argue that acquisitions need not be large as long as the capital involved is.[20] Third, some definitions insist that acquisitions be for specific purposes like crop production and/or resource extraction; there is disagreement over whether, in particular, acquisitions for urban development and industry count.[21] Fourth, none of them puts geographical restrictions on where land grabs can take place. Fifth, some define 'current' or 'contemporary' land grabbing, while others make no reference to time. Sixth, only some definitions mention the actors involved (these include capital, states, state-owned enterprises and non-profit entities). Seventh, none of them specifies that land must be acquired in any particular way for the acquisition to be a 'grab'. Eighth, some state that the key process is the grabbing of *control* over land, a broader concept than the acquisition of formal rights to (use) it. A final point to bear in mind is that, while such definitions usefully seek to delimit the land grabbing phenomenon, the papers published in the land grab special issues discuss as 'land grabs' a broader range of cases than any of them would suggest.

Four uses of primitive accumulation and accumulation by dispossession

There is substantial variation in understandings of primitive accumulation and ABD in the land grab literature in terms both of how they are conceptualised individually and of their relationship to one another. ABD, for instance, is used by Mine Islar to refer to the ways 'common resources are enclosed and transformed into exclusive places', by James Fairhead, Melissa Leach and Ian Scoones (quoting Karen Bakker) to involve 'the enclosure of public assets by private interests for profit, resulting in greater social inequity', and by Haroon Akram-Lodhi to denote market-driven processes of dispossession.[22] Similarly, some authors take primitive accumulation and ABD to mean essentially the same thing, while others differentiate sharply between them.[23] These divergences are grounded in the four approaches to primitive accumulation and ABD in the literature on these terms (largely, with the exception of *Capital*, published since 2000) referenced in land grab research.[24] I describe all four here, but focus on three for the remainder of the paper.

The first project asks how capitalist social relations are created (Marx's central question in the section of *Capital* on primitive accumulation), how they spread, and how they are reproduced in the face of resistance and obstacles. It is often framed as asking how people and resources previously 'outside' capitalist social relations are brought and kept within them. Many accounts refer to these processes as primitive accumulation, although ABD is also used in this way.[25] Asking these questions implies some sense of what capitalist social relations are, an issue on which there is substantial variation and ambiguity.[26] What might be called the 'classical' approach analyses the formation of two main classes: property-less proletarians who must sell their labour to survive, and capitalists who control the means of production (including land). Such accounts focus especially (though with varying degrees of emphasis) on the enclosure of common land, and the concomitant separation from the means of production of the people who previously held it; on the creation of private property rights to the land; and on the (eventual) proletarianisation of the dispossessed. Recent research extends the key enclosures involved well beyond land. It also largely argues that primitive accumulation is not a finished historical stage, but rather is ongoing both in that new people and resources are still being incorporated into capitalist social relations, and in that those social relations need to be reproduced.

The second main use of primitive accumulation and ABD has been to understand capitalist responses to crisis. One of Harvey's core projects in *The New Imperialism* was the analysis of neoliberalism as a response to the over-accumulation crisis that began in the 1970s. He developed the concept of ABD to unite the ways in which assets are 'released' at minimal cost through 'predation, fraud and violence' so that 'overaccumulated capital can seize hold of

[them] and immediately turn them to profitable use'.[27] Harvey highlighted the financial and credit systems, backed by state power, as mechanisms of ABD; emphasised the diverse objects to which ABD is applied under neoliberalism; and conceptualised dispossession in terms not only of the enclosure of the commons but also of the privatisation of public (state-owned) property. He argued, finally, that crises do not simply occur, but are created and manipulated by dominant states in order to facilitate ABD, which thus denotes both a process and a strategy.[28]

Primitive accumulation and ABD have also been understood, in a third approach, in terms of extra-economic means of capital accumulation, especially political and legal power and violent force.[29] Such extra-economic means, which allow resources to be forcefully expropriated and redistributed to capital, are usually directly employed by state actors, although other organisations (including gangs and capitalist firms themselves) may also mobilise them. Here again some authors argue that there will never come a time when all accumulation takes place through expanded reproduction within 'the economy', but rather that political and/or violent expropriations will always play a role in capital accumulation. I discuss Michael Levien's important reconstruction (in a land grab special issue paper) of ABD as accumulation by extra-economic means below, but note here his point that the process may involve not only the expropriation of commons or even public property but 'the dispossession of more "traditional" capitalist forms by more "advanced" ones'.[30] Such an approach thus does not require a distinction between capitalism's 'inside' and 'outside'.

While these three understandings can be distinguished for analytical purposes, they are not always so easily separable in practice. This is in part because empirical processes can be instances of two or three of them. There are also differences of opinion on their interrelationships, with some authors, for instance, arguing that transitions to capitalism can take place in the absence of extra-economic coercion, while for others it is precisely the use of such means that makes the process 'primitive'.[31] A third reason is that some authors do not clearly differentiate between these understandings. Harvey's use of ABD in *The New Imperialism* engages with all three of them, a fact that helps to explain the many different interpretations of his concept. I expand on some of these issues in my further discussion of the approaches below.

Fourth and finally, 'primitive accumulation' and 'ABD' can be used without engaging with broad theoretical questions. Brief and *en passant* uses do not necessarily mean that the author has no clear and specific understanding in mind, only that the reader is not told what it is. They can, however, imply that primitive accumulation and ABD are more or less synonymous with enclosure and dispossession in general. Miles Kenney-Lazar has highlighted this tendency in uses of ABD that focus on 'the unjust acquisition of assets without analyzing the resulting transformations of social-property relations'.[32] While I do not devote extensive attention to in-passing references to primitive accumulation and ABD in the land grab literature,[33] I do discuss similarly un-theorised use of the term 'land grab'.

Land grabbing and responses to crisis

Much research frames land grabbing as a response to crisis, and many scholars use ABD to theorise the process. While crisis arguments sometimes reference the accumulation crisis that began in the 1970s, they more often emphasise the 'multiple crises' that intersected around 2006–08. Philip McMichael argues in an important and detailed statement that 'this rush to acquire land—however varied (in origin, destination and impact) and inconclusive—is symptomatic of a crisis of accumulation in the neoliberal globalization project'.[34] Borras *et al.* state that:

> what is distinct in the current land grabs is that these occur primarily because, and within the dynamics, of capital accumulation strategies largely *in response to* the convergence of multiple crises: food, energy/fuel, climate change, financial crisis [...] as well as the emerging needs for resources by newer hubs of global capital, especially BRICS and some powerful middle income countries (MICS).[35]

The same authors find that the 'need to embed land grabs within our analysis of contemporary global capitalist development (Harvey 2003), in the specific context of the convergence of multiple crises' is a 'common thread' in the literature.[36] These crises are widely seen to drive land grabbing through, for instance, the impetus given to agricultural land acquisitions by spikes in food prices and export bans, and the way that the post-2007 financial crisis encouraged capital fleeing Western financial markets to invest in commodities, agriculture and land. Fairhead *et al*, meanwhile, organise their theorisation of 'green grabs' substantially around Harvey's ABD, highlighting privatisation, financialisation, 'the management and manipulation of crises' and state redistributions; White *et al* analyse the overall land grab in similar terms.[37] Catherine Corson and Kenneth MacDonald examine international conservation policy with reference to Harvey's 'argument that market liberalization will produce chronic crises of over-accumulation, which require the continual release of new assets that over-accumulated capital can seize and convert to profit'.[38] As some of the above quotations show, the crises highlighted by the land grab literature are not exclusively ones of capital accumulation.

How do such frameworks relate to other approaches to the land grab? Initial answers can be gleaned by comparing the ABD/multiple crises thesis to the definitions of land grabbing surveyed above. Key elements of some or all of the definitions fit well, including the focus on the contemporary period as distinctive and the insistence that deals (or the capital involved) be large in scale. The absence of a distinction between land acquisitions by foreign and domestic actors may at first glance seem to sit awkwardly with accounts of the land grab rooted in global crises. This lack of concern for nationality, however, reflects the argument that domestic capital is as affected by, and as likely to respond to, 'multiple crises' as is transnational. Critical political economists have opposed the nationalist assumption that foreign land acquisition is uniquely problematic, an assumption which has characterised much of the public outcry over land grabbing.[39] (It is worth noting, however, that given this argument, foreign acquisitions are probably over-represented in empirical land grab research.)

The ABD/multiple crises approach to land grabbing can also be compared to the lack of attention in the surveyed definitions to *how* grabs occur. Conceptualising land grabs in terms of accumulation by dispossession obviously implies that dispossession must occur when land is grabbed, and seeing grabs as responses to massive and multiple crises encourages assumptions that the dispossessions, too, will be massive. I defer discussion of the first point to the next section, but take up the second here. The extent of the land grab is usually measured in terms of the amount of land acquired (an approach that Edelman calls 'the fetishization of the hectare').[40] Little is known, however, about how many *people* are being dispossessed by large-scale land acquisitions.[41] Further, while it is difficult to imagine that there has not been a rise since 2006 in dispossession resulting specifically from large-scale land acquisitions for agriculture with foreign involvement, it is much harder to know whether there has been (as is often argued) a surge of land-related dispossession in general. Two estimates of such dispossession in previous eras may serve as partial baselines here: one states that 60 million people were displaced by development projects in India between 1947 and 2004, the other that 50 to 66 million Chinese had land expropriated by local governments between 1990 and 2002.[42] My point is not that land grab-driven dispossession is not massive, but that understanding the land grab as crisis-driven ABD assumes that it *must* be.

Crises, causes and actors

A third issue requires more extended discussion. There has been much debate over whether the land grab is ultimately, in Madeleine Fairbairn's words, 'a top-down phenomenon driven by global markets and foreign states'.[43] The ABD/multiple crises thesis suggests, obviously, that we see the land grab as deriving from global forces. There are at least three possible formulations of this position, each of which sees crises as causes, while taking a different position on the actors at work (a point that is also a source of variation between the land grab definitions). The first does not specify who is responding to 'multiple crises'; the second focuses on (global) capital and investing states as the key actors; the third agrees with the second, but puts more emphasis on the land grab as a relatively unified *strategy* of global capital. Formulations consistent with the latter approach to land grabbing, as 'an effort to create a change in the character of accumulation',[44] include Utsa Patnaik's description of it as involving 'a concerted attempt by global capital to acquire control' over peasant lands and Corson and MacDonald's argument that 'international conservation policy is orchestrating spatial fixes for over-accumulated capital'.[45]

Many scholars have critiqued the argument that land grabbing is fundamentally a response to crises and a project (unified or otherwise) of global capital and investing states. Philip Woodhouse writes in the African context that 'at least in terms of understanding the impacts of the "land grab" on rural poverty, viewing land deals primarily in terms of a conjuncture of crises in financial markets, energy and food supply, or governance of global trade, misses an important part of the story'. Rebecca Smalley and Esteve Corbera argue that situating 'the land rush within the political economy of global agro-food networks and capital's search for frontiers of accumulation' understates 'the contribution of local actors in making or resisting land deals and the complicit role of domestic states and developers'. Thomas Sikor, too, makes the case that 'narrow readings of commodification, market expansion or accumulation by dispossession may not fully explain the occurrence of land grabs in some circumstances, and their absence in others'.[46] These statements resonate with Nancy Peluso and Christian Lund's position that there is 'no one grand land grab, but a series of changing contexts, emergent processes and forces, and contestations'.[47]

As the quotation from McMichael at the beginning of this section shows, however, statements of the 'multiple crises' thesis can accommodate substantial variation in the dynamics of actual land grabs. While there is now a rich and important body of work showing how actors and structures in recipient states influence land acquisitions (thus demonstrating that capital and investing states do not always get their way), the use in such analyses of terms like 'shape', 'filter', 'channel', 'modify' and 'mediate' to describe this influence is, I would argue, compatible with the argument that land acquisitions originate from, and are driven by, global forces. Tom Lavers, for instance, writes that 'in Ethiopia, commercial pressures resulting from international drivers are filtered through the state as it attempts to promote its own developmental objectives and manage the competing interests of dominant groups in society'.[48] Fairbairn puts the logic clearly: 'though the increase in foreign demand for land is the ultimate cause of the "land rush" across the African continent and the world, a closer look at the case of Mozambique reveals the importance of domestic institutions and actors in shaping the land acquisition process.'[49] Such an approach seems still to fit within Borras *et al*'s claim that 'while land grabbing occurs in Latin America and the Caribbean within the same logic and processes of global capitalist development that underpinned land grabs elsewhere, it has taken different forms and character—and trajectories—in this region'.[50]

Other arguments, however, challenge the multiple crises thesis more directly. One strand focuses on land acquisitions that seem, in terms of their timing, their goals and the actors involved, to have little to do with global crises, or indeed with 'global' forces at all. Levien criticises approaches to land grabs in India that see them as a 'strategy of global capital'. He argues that they derive rather from the characteristics of the Indian political economy and the needs of domestic capital at different times, an analysis he develops through the concept of 'regimes of dispossession'.[51] Shelley Feldman and Charles Geisler similarly focus overwhelmingly on domestic political-economic dynamics in analysing land expropriation and displacement in Bangladesh, and warn that 'a focus solely on high-profile, off-shore "land grabbing" runs the risk of consigning internally generated land deals and everyday displacement practices of vast numbers of people to semi-oblivion'.[52]

A second riposte sees actors in investment-receiving countries not just as shaping and/or resisting exogenously generated land demand, but as stimulating that demand themselves. States have long encouraged land investment in pursuit of goals as diverse as agricultural development, political stability, military security, territorial control, conservation or simple predation and rent seeking.[53] They provide substantial incentives to corporate actors (domestic and, increasingly, foreign) in pursuit of these goals. The land grab literature also emphasises that large-scale land deals (particularly in sub-Saharan Africa) often take place on land claimed by the state, and finds that, when such deals involve expropriation, it is usually the state that carries it out.[54] States may acquire this land for their own reasons, and expropriations may take place in advance of any interest demonstrated by capital.[55]

These two broad arguments show that demand for land is generated not just by exogenous forces but by state priorities and opportunities for corruption. John McCarthy and his co-authors, for instance, trace the importance of state subsidies in generating 'virtual land grabbing' in Indonesia (see below).[56] Kevin Woods explores the promotion of land concessions in Burma's borderlands with China by the Burmese military state 'as an act of creating effective national state and military authority, sovereignty and territory', and argues that the military state 'uses businessmen as one of their contemporary strategies of territorial control in ceasefire zones'.[57] The most striking example I know, however, is Oane Visser, Natalia Mamanova and Max Spoor's discussion of the Russian state's use, in promoting agricultural investments, of both carrots and sticks. They note an implicit state promise 'not to investigate the dubious practices of the oligarchs in return for their investment in the countryside'. Observers have framed this as a threat: one stated that 'either you pay tax arrears or you start producing food', while a German investor stated of one project that 'the land was almost forced on us'.[58]

Smallholders as land grabbers?

The first possible formulation of the 'multiple crises' thesis described above does not specify which actors are responding to those crises. The actions of (global) capital, investing and 'target' states, and local elites have all received extensive study. Those of smallholders, however, have not. While some studies show smallholders consenting to land deals or joining contract farming schemes,[59] the possibility that smallholders might migrate (locally or over longer distances) to clear new land or claim land currently used by others to grow newly lucrative export crops is almost never considered. This is a striking omission, given that migrations of (would-be) smallholders have for centuries been one of the key processes behind global agricultural expansion.

The lack of attention to smallholders as potential land grabbers has theoretical and empirical aspects. On the theoretical side the identification of capital and states as the forces behind dispossession and enclosure in theories of primitive accumulation and ABD, combined with the agreement among land grab definitions that acquisitions (or the capital involved) must be large in scale, make 'smallholder land grabs' an oxymoron. Even the careful analytical framework for the study of land use change developed by Borras and Franco, which encompasses both smallholder commodity production and smallholder-driven agricultural expansion, does not explicitly consider the possibility that smallholders might acquire new land to grow export crops.[60] Empirical land grab research, on the other hand, frequently refers to past histories of migration in study areas (see below), but rarely considers the possibility of post-2006 smallholder land acquisitions.

There are, of course, strong reasons to suspect that smallholder migration plays a limited role in contemporary agricultural expansion. Smallholder and peasant agriculture has been in crisis for decades across the South.[61] Intensifying corporate demands for food quality and certification make it harder for smallholders to sell export crops. States have reduced their support for migration to agricultural frontiers and intensified conservationist efforts to place land off limits to smallholders. Recognising that smallholder-driven agricultural expansion and land grabbing have been critical in the past does not mean arguing that they are important today.

Developments in Southeast Asia during the 1990s and 2000s, however, show that smallholders can still drive rapid growth of export-oriented food, fibre and fuel crop production. Regional production of coffee, cocoa, rice and rubber is substantially or overwhelmingly in smallholder hands.[62] Even crops more characterised by large-scale production, like oil palm and fast-growing trees, have seen substantial smallholder involvement, and would see more if policy was not usually biased towards plantations.[63] Smallholder cocoa, coffee and rubber expansion in particular has involved people making new and contested claims to private control of land. Acquisitions have taken place in situations in which large numbers of people are migrating to new areas to take part in 'crop booms', but also through *in situ* 'intimate exclusions', which see formerly communal land converted into private holdings by relatively long-term residents of the area in question.[64]

The ABD framework, with its focus on capital, states and their strategies, contributes to the lack of research on whether smallholders are responding to 'multiple crises' by grabbing land. More attention could also be paid to smaller-scale land acquisitions by actors other than smallholders, another question on which we lack much sense of what is happening. It is worth noting Lorenzo Cotula's reference to a study on Benin, Burkina Faso and Niger, which found that 'the aggregate land area acquired by many small deals can be larger than that involved in fewer, larger deals', and Laurence Becker's argument that, while large-scale deals make headlines, 'more common, but less-publicized, small-scale land acquisitions are transforming long-standing human–land relations' in peri-urban West Africa.[65] More broadly, the ABD/multiple crises thesis provides powerful insights into the land grab, but its assumptions tend to direct attention away from both domestic states and smallholders. I have argued elsewhere that analyses that take 'crop booms', rather than land grabs, as their starting point will likely catch a broader (or at least different) range of processes; the same could be said about studies organised around frontiers.[66]

Land grabbing and accumulation by extra-economic means

The previous section raised questions about what 'land grabs' should be taken to be. I tackle this issue more directly here by turning to the distinction between 'economic' and 'extra-economic' forms of accumulation. Research in critical agrarian studies often identifies two basic means by which people (especially poor farmers and peasants) lose their land. In the first, people who cannot keep their heads above water as farmers take on more and more debt and, eventually, have to sell their land to survive. Such 'economic' or 'market' sales are 'voluntary' in the sense that people are not coerced or legally obliged to sell to any particular party or at any particular price. 'Extra-economic' land acquisitions, on the other hand, involve the use of legal or political power and/or (the threat of) force. The people losing land may receive compensation, but there is no market transaction between a willing buyer and a willing seller. Akram-Lodhi uses essentially this distinction in analysing the land grab, and views 'market-led' processes that see 'the expropriation of producers from their assets through the normal, everyday workings of imperfect markets' as 'similar to' Harvey's ABD, while labelling as primitive accumulation 'the expropriation of producers through extra-economic means'.[67]

Land grabs might be assumed to involve accumulation by extra-economic means. Taken at face value, 'land grab' straightforwardly (and dramatically) conveys the idea of land being seized by force. This sense of the term can be used in a great many contexts, including non-capitalist ones: Peter Heather uses it to describe land seizures in first-millennium Europe.[68] In the land grab literature, too, the term is often used in this common-sensical way. Shapan Adnan identifies numerous non-capitalist motivations for land grabs, including 'political and particularistic conflicts based on race, ethnicity, caste or religion', on the desire for pre-capitalist ground rent, and on considerations of 'traditional social status and political power among the peasantry'. Adnan points out that the term must be narrowed through the condition that grabbed land be 'deployed in capitalist production' for grabs to count as (to use his preferred term) primitive accumulation.[69] Such a move might still be expected, however, to retain the idea of forceful seizure. Levien conceptualises land grabs in very much this way, writing that 'it only makes sense to talk about a "grab" when land is expropriated using means other than voluntary market purchase', and that the term provides 'little more than a self-evident descriptive label' for the phenomenon in which 'capital in general requires—or more precisely attempts and achieves—forceful expropriation at any given place and time to sustain accumulation'.[70]

No other definition of land grabbing surveyed in this paper, however, specifies that land acquisitions must happen in some particular *way* to count as 'grabs'. Some use broad terms like 'acquisition' or 'taking control' to describe the process, while some explicitly include sales and leases as possible mechanisms. As a result, sales or leases of large parcels of land by, say, a rancher or large landlord to a foreign corporation[71]—transactions which are not only 'economic' but which take place between capitalists—are defined as 'grabs'. While an Oxfam briefing note gives a list of characteristics that would make a 'land acquisition' a 'land grab', this distinction is not made in the scholarly definitions cited here (although it is made in the broader literature).[72] These definitions thus cannot be read as stipulating that land grabbing takes place through extra-economic means. Similarly, while land grabs have been described as the 'new enclosures', these definitions mean that enclosure and dispossession are not necessary elements of land grabs (even if they are commonly are). This point is in fact made explicit by understandings of land grabbing as the grabbing of *control* over land (and the resources associated with it), a process that, as Borras *et al* write, does not 'always require expulsion of peasants from their lands; [it does] not always result in dispossession'.[73]

As the quotations above suggest, Levien takes a different approach, and does so in a series of papers that constitute not just a contribution to land grab research but a major theoretical intervention in broader debates over primitive accumulation and ABD.[74] Levien critiques several aspects of Harvey's formulation of ABD, the most important of which here is the latter's explicit claim that the role in ABD of (especially) the financial and real estate markets means that it is primarily an economic rather than an extra-economic process. Levien argues that it is on this point in particular that ABD loses its conceptual specificity and 'definitively falls apart'. He does not want to abandon ABD, however, but to reconstruct it. He does this by detaching the term from the debate over transitions to capitalism and defining it instead as 'the use of extra-economic coercion to expropriate means of production, subsistence or common social wealth for capital accumulation'. This reconstruction leads to Levien's central question of why, in a given situation, 'capital would need to dispossess land rather than purchase it through the ordinary operation of real estate markets'.[75]

Levien thus makes a rigorously argued case for an outlier position in the land grab literature: that land acquisitions are only grabs (and ABD) when they take place through extra-economic coercion. His approach holds out the promise of a more clearly framed analysis of the relationship between ABD and the land grab, and it is one that will work well in many cases. I would also suggest, however, that there may be circumstances in which a dichotomous conception of economic and extra-economic means of accumulation in land acquisition will be difficult to maintain.[76] I give two examples. First, markets (and especially land markets in the South) are rarely 'ordinary' spaces of straightforwardly 'economic' relations. Philip Hirsch, Tania Murray Li and I have argued that, in peri-urban Southeast Asia, land sales are usually shaped by the powers of legitimation, regulation and force.[77] Li has written elsewhere about regulation's role:

> Ruling regimes can intervene by calibrating tariffs, prices, taxes, rents, wages, and interest to adjust the rate at which farmers hold on to, or lose, their land. Put another way, the conditions governing the so-called 'free market' are always set. When they are set to work against small-scale farmers, currently the case in much of the global South, the result is pervasive land loss and 'depeasantization'.[78]

Force also complicates the boundaries of 'economic' transactions because of the often implicit nature of its threat. Land grab research tends to refer to force in terms of its actual application or direct threat in pursuit of expropriation. Sales can be motivated, however, by a diffuse sense that land seizure could occur. People in Southeast Asian 'crop boom' areas can be prompted to sell their land by the likelihood that someone else will seize it if they don't.[79] The economic/extra-economic distinction is also tricky with respect to contract farming schemes, which supposedly see landholders freely contracting with corporations or the state but may involve offers that are hard to refuse.[80] Things are further complicated by questions of representation in situations in which customary leaders negotiate land access with corporations or the state; a 'voluntary' market transaction for leaders may essentially be imposed upon other members of the group.[81] Land transactions that appear to capital to be 'ordinary', 'economic' purchases, leases or contracts may thus, from the point of view of the land holders, be shot through with political, legal and coercive power.

Even when transactions seem clearly 'voluntary' and market-driven, meanwhile, fraud and unkept promises can complicate the picture. Fraud is a core mechanism of ABD for Harvey,[82] and unkept promises are a constant refrain in the land grab literature (and in that on land relations in the South more generally). In land deals between corporations and smallholders, agreed-upon payments for land and crops may not be made, undertakings to set aside land for smallholders may not be abided by (or the land provided may be of poor quality),[83] and promised schools, roads and jobs may never materialise. Unkept promises frequently extend to the failure of the corporate project to go ahead at all. Uneven access to judicial power and, often, vague or unwritten contracts mean that it is usually difficult for affected people to hold companies (and the state) to account. Surprisingly little conceptual work has been done on such processes in the land grab literature; the most systematic effort I know is Smalley and Corbera's analysis of how people weigh up how much trust to put in company promises.[84] In general, then, the economic/extra-economic distinction may be better seen as a continuum than as a dichotomy.

Land grabbing and the expansion of capitalism

I turn, finally, to the analysis of the land grab's relationship to the creation, expansion and reproduction of capitalist social relations, and especially to the use of primitive accumulation and/or ABD for this purpose. This has been a prominent project in the literature. Wolford et al approach land grabs partly in terms of ABD understood as an updated and expanded primitive accumulation, and involving processes 'whereby direct producers were separated from the means of production, common property rights were privatized and non-capitalist modes of production were either harnessed or destroyed'.[85] Mehta et al conceptualise water grabbing along similar lines, calling it 'a particular form of accumulation by dispossession under neo-liberalisation leading to the commodification and privatisation of resources, the eviction of certain groups and the conversion of various forms of property rights into exclusive private property rights'.[86] Saskia Sassen describes foreign demand for land as 'part of the systematic deepening of the current phase of capitalism' and 'an expansion of the operational space for advanced capitalism through the expulsion of people from a range of institutional settings in both the Global South and North'.[87] Finally, Borras and Franco locate their 'analysis of land-use changes in the latest wave of capitalist penetration of the countryside', and they and Haroon Akram-Lodhi in particular have contributed sophisticated frameworks for understanding this process to the land grab literature.[88]

In this section I focus on land (with some reference to other resources) and labour (people) by taking up two questions about the relationship between land grabbing and the creation of 'the conditions under which capitalist production takes place'.[89] The first asks what the literature finds is being brought 'inside' capitalism, what is not, and how this happens. The second discusses the assumptions analyses of bringing things 'into' capitalism make about their previous status 'outside' it. Before turning to these issues, however, I briefly discuss an argument notable in the land grab literature mainly for its absence. It is often claimed in the post-2000 debate over primitive accumulation, ABD and related concepts that capitalism (or capital) has an inherent drive to commodify and colonise more and more of the lifeworld.[90] Such arguments suggest a causal account of the land grab as an expression, ultimately, of the remorseless expansion of capital. This position, however, is not common. Liz Alden Wily argues that the 'overarching explanation' for the vulnerability of people in sub-Saharan Africa to the loss of their land 'clearly lies in the ever-expanding and now globalised capitalist transformation'. Kojo Amanor makes a somewhat different case in opposing 'multiple crises' narratives, writing that 'the dynamic towards land grabbing arises internally from the logic of agribusiness accumulation rather than from exogenous developments'.[91] Most explanations, however, focus either on capitalist dynamics in the specific context of multiple crises, or on local and national dynamics that call unified explanations into question.

Land and labour

The global land grab is making available for purchase, lease or use (control) much land previously out of capital's reach. While this process resonates with classic accounts of primitive accumulation, the land grab literature also shows differences from earlier analyses. One is that, while earlier accounts study how land becomes private property owned by capitalists, many contemporary large-scale land acquisitions in the South take place on state-claimed land.[92] Investors access such land through leases or concessions (albeit often very long-term ones) rather than purchase, which in some countries is not legally possible. Much of this land is, of course, used and claimed by people whose rights are recognised partially or not at all by the state, and they may need to be dispossessed for the acquisition to proceed. Alice Kelly explores an even greater divergence from classic analyses by showing that turning land into *public* property can create and expand capitalist social relations, as the enclosures and dispossessions involved in establishing conservation areas separate people from their means of production and make park resources available for capitalist investment through tourism and other activities.[93]

Financialisation, which (as noted above) is for Harvey a key mechanism of ABD, is also relevant to the study of land grabbing and capitalism's expansion. There is still relatively little empirical work on the opening up of farmland for capitalist investment not simply through purchases, leases and concessions allowing its use, but through its conversion into an object of financial investment and speculation. Fairbairn gives an account of such moves since the 2007–08 financial crisis, including securitisation and the emergence of private equity funds dealing in farmland.[94] Research on 'green grabs' has also taken up 'the deepening financialisation of nature' through the creation of new commodities like carbon and wildlife. Leach *et al* use ABD to theorise carbon trading schemes involving biochar that bring 'into the sphere of financial exchange phenomena that once lay outside it'.[95] John

McCarthy *et al* take up related issues by studying 'virtual land grabbing', in which 'actors engage in land acquisitions without the intention to use the land for the purpose mentioned in the plan or development license'. The goals of such acquisitions include accessing subsidies and using land permits for speculative purposes or as collateral; in West Kalimantan (Indonesia), for instance, there is a secondary market for unused oil palm plantation licences. One implication of this analysis is that 'virtual grabs' can allow new land to serve as the basis for profits and accumulation even without much actual enclosure and dispossession.[96]

The incorporation (or otherwise) of new labour into capitalism, meanwhile, can be discussed first in terms of the extent to which capitalist labour relations are being established in land grab areas. While it seems reasonable to assume that they are, there is still little research on contemporary (post-2006) grabs that engages in empirical detail with this question. Levien takes on this issue with respect to acquisitions for industrial, residential and commercial purposes at his field site in Rajasthan.[97] It is also prominent in two papers on large-scale agricultural expansions in Laos: Ian Baird's examination of rubber concessions in Bachieng District, and Kenney-Lazar's research on a 10 000-hectare timber and rubber concession granted to a Vietnamese company in 2008.[98] Both papers deal theoretically and empirically with the extent to which capitalist social relations are expanding in the targeted areas. Tania Murray Li's study of labour in Indonesian oil palm plantations also takes up related issues.[99]

A second issue arising from 'classic' primitive accumulation work has received more attention: the extent to which land grabs aim to create 'free', proletarianised labourers. Critical political economy sees such workers as vital to capitalist firms both because of their direct role as labour and because the unemployed form a labour reserve that suppresses wages. Farshad Araghi makes the case that dispossession is central to contemporary capitalist accumulation in part because it helps constitute such a reserve.[100] Land grab research, however, generally sees people dispossessed by land acquisitions as a 'surplus population' with limited prospects of finding work, and finds few indications of a 'strategy' to generate a labour reserve. People are being separated from their means of production simply because they are in possession of land and other resources to which capital wants access. Li writes that 'their land is needed but their labour is not', while Kenney-Lazar calls dispossession 'merely a tactic for getting people out of the way'.[101] Baird does argue that 'turning people into labour' has motivated recent Lao government policy towards land and agriculture in the uplands, but also finds that companies investing in Laos have shown little interest in hiring local labour.[102]

Assumptions

What assumptions can be embedded in analyses of primitive accumulation (or ABD) in terms of the expansion of capitalism? First, such approaches can encourage the assumption that people dispossessed by land grabs were previously and straightforwardly 'outside' capitalism. A strong version of this tendency takes it for granted that they were self-sufficient peasants producing for subsistence and/or holding their land in common. Such assumptions can be built into definitions of primitive accumulation. Chris Sneddon's paraphrase of David Moore's definition, for instance, includes as an element of primitive accumulation 'the separation of producers engaged in pre-capitalist, or subsistence, production from the means of production and their subsequent proletarianization'.[103] Weaker versions involve assuming that the people being dispossessed live in communities that are internally homogeneous, and/or that they have been 'in place' since time immemorial. Examples of these tendencies can be found in the land grab literature. As noted above, Islar takes ABD to be a process in which 'common resources are enclosed and transformed into exclusive places'.[104] Sosa and Zwarteveen define land and water grabbing in terms of 'the enclosure of commons by multinational companies and government agencies, dispossessing peasants and indigenous people and altering the environment'.[105] Araghi's definition of 'accumulation by displacement' refers to the 'dispossession of formerly self-reproducing peasantries'.[106]

The danger here, put starkly, is that drawing on Marx's analysis of primitive accumulation may make us assume that people being dispossessed today live under the same conditions as did the medieval English peasantry. The danger is a somewhat ironic one. One of the great strengths of the primitive accumulation framework is its analysis of the centuries-long process by which capitalism has become truly global, but the framework can simultaneously encourage us to ignore the effects of that history of capitalist expansion on the places where land grabs are now taking place. Assuming that land grabs go on in areas 'outside' capitalism can also lead to mischaracterisations of the politics of and resistance to land grabbing.

The land grab literature also, however, contains substantial challenges to and explicit critiques of such assumptions. Woodhouse argues that 'foreign investment projects cannot be assumed to take place within rural areas made up of smallholders dependent on household labour and non-commodified access to land via customary tenure', and emphasises the role of labour markets and mobility in the rural African economy.[107] Adnan finds that before the onset of primitive accumulation, poor peasants in the *chars* of Bangladesh accessed land substantially through quite brutal clientelistic relationships with what were essentially gangs.[108] Borras and Franco provide a nuanced account of the internal differentiation that generally characterises agrarian political economies, although they have less to say about migration and mobility.[109] More generally, many case studies trace the relationships between migrations and land-holding, and show how these histories shape land deals.[110]

I am not arguing that (relatively) self-sufficient peasantries and common lands no longer exist, or that they are not threatened by land grabs. My point, rather, is that analyses of transitions to capitalism need to show that they exist rather than assuming that they do. Baird's paper on primitive accumulation in Laos provides a model. Baird states that many people affected by the land deals he studied had, 'until quite recently, been heavily reliant on mixed subsistence and semi-subsistence agriculture' involving both family farming and use of common resources, and that their relationship with the labour market had remained limited. He makes this argument, however, with reference to the literature on agrarian Southeast Asia, which claims such circumstances are now unusual, and provides evidence to back it up.[111]

Similar assumptions can be made, too, about the land and other resources being 'grabbed'. I argued above that land purchased or leased from one capitalist concern by another cannot be seen as 'extra-economic' accumulation. The argument also holds here: such transactions do not extend capitalism's scope or bring anything into it from the 'outside'. A variant of this argument can be made with respect to some instances of financialisation. While financialisation may generate new investment opportunities for capital by creating new commodities and new markets, it is often applied to things that are already held by capitalists as private property. Some of Fairbairn's examples of farmland financialisation seem to fit this argument. Financialisation may thus 'expand' capitalism without bringing new resources into it from 'outside'.

A further issue involves not the enclosure of commons but the seizure or privatisation of public assets. The land grab literature follows Harvey in highlighting such moves, with White *et al* discussing Harvey's ABD in general terms as a process in which 'public assets are enclosed [...] in an important extension of the classic process of primitive accumulation described by Marx'.[112] There are various concrete examples in the literature. Kenney-Lazar argues with respect to land specifically that 'land types can be enclosed that are not easily categorized as communal or private, such as land belonging to the state that is legally tenured by individual households'.[113] Feldman and Geisler discuss 'the appropriation of government properties and embankments (dikes and levies)' and of canals; Wagle *et al* highlight the grabbing of water from the reservoirs of public dams; and Torres calls attention to the privatisation of dams and other water infrastructure as part of 'the latest phase of accumulation by dispossession'.[114] Whether these public assets—some of which were constructed in support of previous projects of capital accumulation—are best thought of as having been 'inside' or 'outside' capitalism before their seizure or privatisation depends very much on one's conception of capitalism. However, this is not (to my knowledge) an issue that the land grab literature has pursued.

Conclusions

The land grab literature has used primitive accumulation and accumulation by dispossession to analyse three main (and often overlapping) processes: dispossessory responses to capitalist crises, the use of extra-economic means of capital accumulation, and the creation, expansion and reproduction of capitalist social relations. Each of these processes is indeed central to the phenomena usually referred to as the 'global land grab', and land grab research contains highly productive analyses of each of them. The literature has made a substantial empirical contribution to debates over primitive accumulation and ABD in the context of rapid contemporary transformations in the global political economy. It has also pushed those debates ahead theoretically, especially through the work of Levien, Kelly and Adnan and the analysis of the relationship of enclosure and dispossession with 'control grabbing' and 'virtual grabs'. Key features of work on primitive accumulation and ABD during the first decade of the 2000s were that it shifted attention to 'ongoing' processes in the North and expanded the range of processes under consideration. The land grab literature has retained and built on these innovations while also firmly returning the debate to its traditional home in agrarian political economy.

I have tried in this paper both to highlight the contributions of primitive accumulation and ABD frameworks and to emphasise the challenges involved in using them. Prominent among the latter are assumptions that can skew empirical analysis of contemporary land acquisitions. Rather than running through these again, I emphasise a more basic point here. If primitive accumulation and/or ABD are to be understood in any of the three senses covered here, then those terms cannot be used as general characterisations of what the scholarly definitions I have surveyed call 'land grabbing' or 'the land grab'. The simplest reason for this is that the definitions all include capitalist-to-capitalist land purchases and leases, deals which do not involve extra-economic means of accumulation, do not bring anything 'into' capitalism, and which, while they may be responses to crisis, are not dispossessory ones.

One way for analyses of the land grab to deal with this issue would be to choose as the departure point of analysis *either* a definition of 'land grabbing' *or* an inquiry into contemporary primitive accumulation and ABD as they involve land. The scholarly definitions, which (with some variations) focus on large-scale contemporary land acquisitions for the purposes of crop production and natural resource use, all delimit significant and reasonably coherent objects of analysis. Similarly, the processes highlighted by the three core primitive accumulation and ABD frameworks are—notwithstanding the sometimes problematic assumptions that can be embedded within them—of the first order of importance in the analysis of contemporary capitalism. However, approaches that begin with the definitions should not assume that everything that falls under them is an instance of primitive accumulation and/or ABD, while those that begin with the application of the latter terms to contemporary land relations will need to study a broader range of phenomena than is captured by the main definitions of the 'global land grab' (including a much greater focus on acquisitions for urban development and industry). The tensions between the two starting points are revealed, it seems to me, by the diversity of empirical material covered in the land grab special issues. The literature (very productively) overflows the key definitions by taking up 'grabs' that are too small, from the wrong period, for the wrong purposes, carried out by the wrong actors, or only tenuously connected to 'multiple crises'.

This last observation suggests a return to the contested term 'land grab' itself. From one point of view research on land grabbing has exploded onto the academic scene. From a standing start in 2009, scholars had by mid-2013 written hundreds of papers on the topic. From another point of view, however, 'land grab' has taken its place in a list of other terms—including primitive accumulation and ABD themselves, but also enclosure, commodification, the double movement, displacement, and so on—that have been crucial to the past two decades of critical analysis of capitalism. The 'literature rush'[115] on land grabbing would hardly have been possible if there had not already been so many researchers doing theoretical and empirical work on land and dispossession before 2009. Like the other terms just mentioned, 'land grab' has been used in a variety of overlapping and often underspecified ways. The very power of the common-sense understanding of 'land grab' discussed in this paper may, indeed, make the term particularly tricky. While the choice to use 'land grab' over other terms like 'land acquisition' and 'land deal' is often explained in terms of preferences for a more politically charged term over a more neutral one,[116] the natural assumption that 'grabbing' involves force may lead to confusion when it is defined in a way that includes non-forceful acquisitions. Maintaining the political power of 'land grabbing' while avoiding these analytical problems is an ongoing challenge for the literature.

Notes

I received very helpful comments on earlier versions of this paper from Mez Baker, Hekia Bodwitch, Jennie Durant, Mike Dwyer, Marc Edelman, Elizabeth Havice, Alice Kelly, Lisa Kelley, Sarah Milne, Jason Morris-Jung, Carlos Oya, Nancy Peluso and two anonymous reviewers for TWQ. Any errors are my own.

1 K Marx, *Capital*, Vol 1, London: Penguin, 1976; and D Harvey, *The New Imperialism*, Oxford: Oxford University Press, 2003.

2 S Moyo, P Yeros & P Jha, 'Imperialism and primitive accumulation: notes on the new scramble for Africa', *Agrarian South: Journal of Political Economy*, 1(2), 2012, p 182. See also U Patnaik, 'The agrarian question in the neoliberal era', in U Patnaik & S Moyo (eds), *The Agrarian Question in the Neoliberal Era: Primitive Accumulation and the Peasantry*, Oxford: Pambazuka Press, 2011, p 11.

3 W Wolford, SM Borras Jr, R Hall, I Scoones & B White, 'Governing global land deals: the role of the state in the rush for land', *Development and Change*, 44(2), 2013, p 197; and SM Borras Jr & J Franco, 'Global land grabbing and trajectories of agrarian change: a preliminary analysis', *Journal of Agrarian Change*, 12(1), 2012, p 49.

4 L Mehta, GJ Veldwisch & J Franco, 'Water grabbing? Focus on the (re)appropriation of finite water resources', *Water Alternatives*, 5(2), 2012, p 195. See also Borras & Franco, 'Global land grabbing and trajectories of agrarian change', pp 35–36. It should be noted that some land grab research does not use a critical political economy framework.

5 B White, SM Borras Jr, R Hall, I Scoones & W Wolford, 'The new enclosures: critical perspectives on corporate land deals', *Journal of Peasant Studies*, 39(3–4), 2012, pp 621, 623.

6 *Ibid*; and L Alden Wily, 'Looking back to see forward: the legal niceties of land theft in land rushes', *Journal of Peasant Studies*, 39(3–4), 2012, pp 751–775.

7 Mehta *et al*, 'Water grabbing?'; and J Fairhead, M Leach & I Scoones, 'Green grabbing: a new appropriation of nature', *Journal of Peasant Studies*, 39(2), 2012, pp 237–261.

8 M Levien, 'The land question: special economic zones and the political economy of dispossession in India', *Journal of Peasant Studies*, 39(3–4), 2012, pp 937–940.

9 Borras & Franco, 'Global land grabbing and trajectories of agrarian change', p 38.

10 For key references, see D Hall, 'Rethinking primitive accumulation: theoretical tensions and rural Southeast Asian complexities', *Antipode*, 44(4), 2012, p 1190.

11 F Araghi, 'Accumulation by displacement: global enclosures, food crisis, and the ecological contradictions of capitalism', *Review: A Journal of the Fernand Braudel Center*, XXXII(1), 2009, pp 113–146.

12 P Patnaik, 'The accumulation process in the period of globalisation', *Economic and Political Weekly*, 43 (26–27), 2008, pp 108–113.

13 S Adnan, 'Land grabs and primitive accumulation in deltaic Bangladesh: interactions between neoliberal globalization, state interventions, power relations and peasant resistance', *Journal of Peasant Studies*, 40 (1), 2013, pp 87–128.

14 S Moyo, 'Primitive accumulation and the destruction of African peasantries', in Patnaik & Moyo, *The Agrarian Question in the Neoliberal Era*, p 64.

15 H Akram-Lodhi, 'Contextualising land grabbing: contemporary land deals, the global subsistence crisis and the world food system', *Canadian Journal of Development Studies*, 33(2), 2012, p 126; and T Perrault, 'Dispossession by accumulation? Mining, water and the nature of enclosure on the Bolivian Altiplano', *Antipode*, forthcoming.

16 Key examples are P McMichael, 'The land grab and corporate food regime restructuring', *Journal of Peasant Studies*, 39(3–4), 2012, pp 681–701; SM Borras Jr, C Kay, S Gómez & J Wilkinson, 'Land grabbing and capitalist accumulation: key features in Latin America', *Canadian Journal of Development Studies*, 33(4), 2012, pp 402–416; and Alden Wily, 'Looking back to see forward'.

17 For reviews, see J Glassman, 'Primitive accumulation, accumulation by dispossession, accumulation by "extra-economic" means', *Progress in Human Geography*, 30(5), 2006, pp 608–625; Hall, 'Rethinking primitive accumulation'; and Levien, 'The land question'.

18 The definitions (of 'land grabbing' or 'land grabs') can be found at Akram-Lodhi, 'Contextualising land grabbing', p 125; S Arduino, G Colombo, OM Ocampo & L Panzeri, 'Contamination of community potable water from land grabbing: a case study from rural Tanzania', *Water Alternatives*, 5(2), 2012, p 345; SM Borras Jr, JC Franco, S Gómez, C Kay & Max Spoor, 'Land grabbing in Latin America and the Caribbean', *Journal of Peasant Studies* 39(3–4), 2012, p 851; M Margulis, N McKeon & SM Borras Jr, 'Land grabbing and global governance: critical perspectives', *Globalizations*, 10(1), 2013, p 2; and White *et al*, 'The new enclosures', p 619. I take up Levien's use of 'land grab' below.

19 See A Zoomers, 'Globalisation and the foreignisation of space: seven processes driving the current global land grab', *Journal of Peasant Studies*, 37(2), 2010, pp 429–447.

20 Borras *et al*, 'Land grabbing and capitalist accumulation', p 404.

21 See Akram-Lodhi, 'Contextualising land grabbing', p 126; and Margulis *et al*, 'Land grabbing and global governance', p 2.

22 M Islar, 'Privatised hydropower development in Turkey: a case of water grabbing?', *Water Alternatives*, 5(2), 2012, p 386; Bakker cited in Fairhead *et al*, 'Green grabbing', p 243; and Akram-Lodhi, 'Contextualising land grabbing', pp 130–131.

23 For the former approach, see Adnan, 'Land grabs and primitive accumulation in deltaic Bangladesh', pp 95, 123; C Corson & KI MacDonald, 'Enclosing the global commons: the Convention on Biological Diversity and green grabbing', *Journal of Peasant Studies*, 39(2), 2012, pp 268–283; and TA Benjaminsen & I Bryceson, 'Conservation, green/blue grabbing and accumulation by dispossession in Tanzania', *Journal of Peasant Studies*, 39(2), 2012, p 336. For the latter, see Levien, 'The land question'; and Akram-Lodhi, 'Contextualising land grabbing', pp 130–131.

24 My analysis here is informed by M Levien, 'Special economic zones and accumulation by dispossession in India', *Journal of Agrarian Change*, 11(4), 2011, pp 454–483; and Levien, 'The land question'.

25 Levien, 'The land question', p 938.

26 Hall, 'Rethinking primitive accumulation', pp 1191–1196.

27 Harvey, *The New Imperialism*, pp 144, 149.

28 *Ibid*, p 151.

29 Some understandings are broader. See Glassman, 'Primitive accumulation, accumulation by dispossession, accumulation by "extra-economic" means', p 617.

30 Levien, 'The land question', p 940. See also S Sassen, 'A savage sorting of winners and losers: contemporary versions of primitive accumulation', *Globalizations*, 7(1–2), 2010, p 23.

31 Hall, 'Rethinking primitive accumulation', pp 1198–1199; Levien, 'The land question', pp 937–938; and Adnan, 'Land grabs and primitive accumulation in deltaic Bangladesh', pp 92–94.

32 M Kenney-Lazar, 'Plantation rubber, land grabbing and social-property transformation in southern Laos', *Journal of Peasant Studies*, 39(3–4), 2012, p 1021. See also EM Wood, 'Logics of power: a conversation with David Harvey', *Historical Materialism*, 14(4), 2006, p 23.

33 See M Sosa & M Zwarteveen, 'Exploring the politics of water grabbing: the case of large mining operations in the Peruvian Andes', *Water Alternatives*, 5(2), 2012, p 372; and M Keulertz, 'Land and water grabs and the green economy', in T Allan, M Keulertz, S Sojamo & J Warner (eds), *Handbook of Land and Water Grabs in Africa: Foreign Direct Investment and Food and Water Security*, London: Routledge, 2013, p 249.

34 McMichael, 'The land grab and corporate food regime restructuring', p 681.

35 Borras *et al*, 'Land grabbing in Latin America and the Caribbean', p 851, emphasis in the original.

36 *Ibid*, p 846. For another argument about crisis, see Akram-Lodhi, 'Contextualising land grabbing', p 135.

37 Fairhead *et al*, 'Green grabbing', p 243; and White *et al*, 'The new enclosures', p 627.

38 Corson & MacDonald, 'Enclosing the global commons', p 268.

39 Borras *et al*, 'Land grabbing and capitalist accumulation', pp 405–407; and Borras *et al*, 'Land grabbing in Latin America and the Caribbean', pp 859, 863.

40 M Edelman, 'Messy hectares: questions about the epistemology of land grabbing data', *Journal of Peasant Studies*, 40(3), 2013, p 488.

41 Borras & Franco, 'Global land grabbing and trajectories of agriaran change', pp 47, 49–50.

42 Indian figure cited in M Levien, 'Regimes of dispossession: from steel towns to special economic zones', *Development and Change*, 44(2), 2013, p 403. Chinese figure in YT Hsing, *The Great Urban Transformation: Politics of Land and Property in China*, Oxford: Oxford University Press, 2010, p 17.

43 M Fairbairn, 'Indirect dispossession: domestic power imbalances and foreign access to land in Mozambique', *Development and Change*, 44(3), 2013, p 335.

44 Akram-Lodhi, 'Contextualising land grabbing', p 135. On intentional analyses of primitive accumulation, see Hall, 'Rethinking primitive accumulation', p 1195; and Adnan, 'Land grabs and primitive accumulation in deltaic Bangladesh', pp 88, 93.

45 Patnaik, 'The agrarian question in the neoliberal era', p 11; and Corson & MacDonald, 'Enclosing the global commons', p 268.

46 P Woodhouse, 'New investment, old challenges: land deals and the water constraint in African agriculture', *Journal of Peasant Studies*, 39(3–4), 2012, p 779; R Smalley & E Corbera, 'Large-scale land deals from the inside out: findings from Kenya's Tana Delta', *Journal of Peasant Studies*, 39(3–4), 2012, pp 1041-2; and T Sikor, 'Tree plantations, politics of possession and the absence of land grabs in Vietnam', *Journal of Peasant Studies*, 39(4), 2012, p 1099.

47 NL Peluso & C Lund, 'New frontiers of land control: introduction', *Journal of Peasant Studies*, 38(4), 2011, p 669. See, similarly, JF McCarthy, JAC Vel & S Afiff, 'Trajectories of land acquisition and enclosure: development schemes, virtual land grabs, and green acquisitions in Indonesia's outer islands', *Journal of Peasant Studies*, 39(2), 2012, p 522.

48 T Lavers, 'Patterns of agrarian transformation in Ethiopia: state-mediated commercialisation and the "land grab"', *Journal of Peasant Studies*, 39(3–4), 2012, pp 795–822. For 'modify' and 'mediate', see Fairbairn, 'Indirect dispossession', pp 335–336.

49 Fairbairn, 'Indirect dispossession', p 351.

50 Borras *et al*, 'Land grabbing in Latin America and the Caribbean', p 847.

51 Levien, 'The land question', p 936; and Levien, 'Regimes of dispossession'.

52 S Feldman & C Geisler, 'Land expropriation and displacement in Bangladesh', *Journal of Peasant Studies*, 39(3–4), 2012, p 971.

53 D Hall, *Land*, Cambridge: Polity, 2013, pp 52–59.

54 Fairbairn, 'Indirect dispossession', p 342; and Akram-Lodhi, 'Contextualising land grabbing', p 127.

55 See, for instance, Lavers, 'Patterns of agrarian transformation in Ethiopia', pp 800–803.

56 McCarthy *et al*, 'Trajectories of land acquisition and enclosure'.

57 K Woods, 'Ceasefire capitalism: military–private partnerships, resource concessions and military-state building in the Burma–China borderlands', *Journal of Peasant Studies*, 38(4), 2011, pp 749, 752. See also MB Dwyer, 'Building the politics machine: tools for "resolving" the global land grab', *Development and Change*, 44(2), 2013, p 313; and G de LT Oliveira, 'Land regularization in Brazil and the global land grab', *Development and Change*, 44(2), 2013, pp 261–283.

58 O Visser, N Mamonova & M Spoor, 'Oligarchs, megafarms and land reserves: understanding land grabbing in Russia', *Journal of Peasant Studies*, 39(3–4), 2012, pp 911–912.

59 See Wasana La-orngplew, 'Living under the rubber boom: market integration and agrarian transformations in the Lao uplands', PhD dissertation, Department of Geography, Durham University, 2012; RA Cramb & PS Sujang, 'The mouse deer and the crocodile: oil palm smallholders and livelihood strategies in Sarawak, Malaysia', *Journal of Peasant Studies*, 40(1), 2013, pp 129–154; and McCarthy *et al*, 'Trajectories of land acquisition and enclosure'.

60 Borras & Franco, 'Global land grabbing and trajectories of agrarian change', pp 38–49.

61 McMichael, 'The land grab and corporate food regime restructuring', p 682; and KS Amanor, 'Global resource grabs, agribusiness concentration and the smallholder: two West African case studies', *Journal of Peasant Studies*, 39(3–4), 2012, pp 731–749.

62 D Hall, 'Where the streets are paved with prawns: crop booms and migration in Southeast Asia', *Critical Asian Studies*, 43(4), 2011, pp 507–530.

63 On smallholder oil palm, see Cramb & Sujang, 'The mouse deer and the crocodile'. On fast-growing trees, see Sikor, 'Tree plantations, politics of possession and the absence of land grabs in Vietnam'.

64 D Hall, 'Land grabs, land control, and Southeast Asian crop booms', *Journal of Peasant Studies*, 38(4), 2011, pp 811–831.

65 LC Becker, 'Land sales and the transformation of social relations and landscape in peri-urban Mali', *Geoforum*, 46, 2013, p 113.

66 On 'crop booms' see Hall, 'Land grabs, land control and Southeast Asian crop booms'. On frontiers, see Hall, *Land*, ch 3, and the references at pp 176–178.

67 Akram-Lodhi, 'Contextualising land grabbing', pp 130–131. See, relatedly, Borras & Franco, 'Global land grabbing and trajectories of agrarian change', p 46; and Fairhead *et al*, 'Green grabbing', p 238.

68 P Heather, *Empires and Barbarians: The Fall of Rome and the Birth of Europe*, Oxford: Oxford University Press, 2009.

69 Adnan, 'Land grabs and primitive accumulation in deltaic Bangladesh', p 94.

70 Levien, 'The land question', pp 941, 936.

71 See, in general, L Cotula, 'The international political economy of the global land rush: a critical appraisal of trends, scale, geography and drivers', *Journal of Peasant Studies*, 39(3–4), 2012, pp 654–655; and, for an example, LA Galeano, 'Paraguay and the expansion of Brazilian and Argentinian agribusiness frontiers', *Canadian Journal of Development Studies*, 33(4), 2012, p 465.

72 K Geary, *'Our Land, our Lives!' Time Out on the Global Land Grab*, Oxfam International, October 2012, at http://www.oxfam.org/en/grow/policy/'our-land-our-lives', p 5. For a partial exception, see Borras *et al*, 'Land grabbing and capitalist accumulation', p 406.

73 Borras *et al*, 'Land grabbing in Latin America and the Caribbean', p 850. See also Benjaminsen & Bryceson, 'Conservation, green/blue grabbing and accumulation by dispossession in Tanzania'; Fairhead *et al*, 'Green grabbing', p 239; and Wolford *et al*, 'Governing global land deals', p 195. On land control more broadly, see Peluso & Lund, 'New frontiers of land control'.

74 Levien, 'Special economic zones and accumulation by dispossession in India'; Levien, 'The land question'; and Levien 'Regimes of dispossession'.

75 Levien, 'The land question', p 940.

76 On such difficulties, see also Borras & Franco, 'Global land grabbing and trajectories of agrarian change', p 46.

77 D Hall, P Hirsch & TM Li, *Powers of Exclusion: Land Dilemmas in Southeast Asia*, Singapore/Honolulu: NUS Press/University of Hawai'i Press, 2011, pp 120–131. On similar dynamics in Bangladesh, see Adnan, 'Land grabs and primitive accumulation in deltaic Bangladesh', p 116; and Feldman & Geisler, 'Land expropriation and displacement in Bangladesh', p 986.

78 TM Li, 'To make live or let die? Rural dispossession and the protection of surplus populations', *Antipode*, 41(S1), 2009, pp 74–75. See also Akram-Lodhi, 'Contextualising land grabbing', pp 130–131.

79 Hall, 'Land grabs, land control, and Southeast Asian crop booms', p 845.

80 On the complex interplay between opportunity and coercion in such situations, see La-orngplew, 'Living under the rubber boom', pp 164–168.

81 See, for example, McCarthy *et al*, 'Trajectories of land acquisition and enclosure', p 533; and Smalley & Corbera, 'Large-scale land deals from the inside out', p 1053.

82 Harvey, *The New Imperialism*, pp 144, 147.

83 See Julia & B White, 'Gendered experiences of dispossession: oil palm expansion in a Dayak Hibun community in West Kalimantan', *Journal of Peasant Studies*, 39(3–4), 2012, pp 1004, 1010–1011; and McCarthy *et al*, 'Trajectories of land acquisition', pp 533–534.

84 Smalley & Corbera, 'Large-scale land deals from the inside out', pp 1056, 1058, 1066.

85 Wolford *et al*, 'Governing global land deals', p 197.

86 Mehta *et al*, 'Water grabbing?', p 198. Water grabbing is compared to other instances of primitive accumulation in Sosa & Zwarteveen, 'Exploring the politics of water grabbing', p 372. On water and primitive accumulation, see also Perrault, 'Dispossession by accumulation?'.

87 S Sassen, 'Land grabs today: feeding the disassembling of national territory', *Globalizations*, 10(1), 2013, p 27.

88 Borras & Franco, 'Global land grabbing and trajectories of agrarian change', p 39; and Akram-Lodhi, 'Contextualising land grabbing', p 134.

89 AB Kelly, 'Conservation practice as primitive accumulation', *Journal of Peasant Studies*, 38(4), 2011, p 688.

90 See, for instance, M de Angelis, 'Separating the doing and the deed: capital and the continuous character of enclosures', *Historical Materialism*, 12(2), 2004, p 57.

91 Alden Wily, 'Looking back to see forward', p 752; and Amanor, 'Global resource grabs, agribusiness concentration and the smallholder', p 732. See also Akram-Lodhi, 'Contextualising land grabbing', pp 126, 130.

92 See Alden Wily, 'Looking back to see forward', p 752; Cotula, 'The international political economy of the global land rush', pp 670–671; and Smalley & Corbera, 'Large-scale land deals from the inside out', p 1067.

93 Kelly, 'Conservation practice as primitive accumulation'. See also Benjaminsen & Bryceson, 'Conservation, green/blue grabbing and accumulation by dispossession in Tanzania', p 336; Corson & MacDonald, 'Enclosing the global commons'; and Fairhead *et al*, 'Green grabbing', p 238.

94 M Fairbairn, '"Like gold with yield": evolving intersections between farmland and finance,' paper prepared for the conference 'Food Sovereignty: A Critical Dialogue', Program in Agrarian Studies, Yale University, September 2013. See also S Daniel, 'Situating private equity capital in the land grab debate', *Journal of Peasant Studies*, 39(3–4), 2012, pp 703–729; McMichael, 'The land grab and corporate food regime restructuring', pp 688–691; and F Pearce, *The Land Grabbers: The New Fight over Who Owns the Earth*, Boston, MA: Beacon Press, 2012.

95 Corson & MacDonald, 'Enclosing the global commons', pp 268, 273; and M Leach, J Fairhead & J Fraser, 'Green grabs and biochar: revaluing African soils and farming in the new carbon economy', *Journal of Peasant Studies*, 39(2), 2012, pp 287–288, 295.

96 McCarthy *et al*, 'Trajectories of land acquisition', pp 521–524, 531–532.

97 Levien, 'Special economic zones and accumulation by dispossession in India'; and Levien, 'The land question'.

98 I Baird, 'Turning land into capital, turning people into labour: primitive accumulation and the arrival of large-scale economic land concessions in the Lao People's Democratic Republic', *New Proposals: Journal of Marxism and Interdisciplinary Inquiry*, 5(1), 2011, pp 10–26; and Kenney-Lazar, 'Plantation rubber, land grabbing and social-property transformation in southern Laos'.

99 TM Li, 'Centering labor in the land grab debate', *Journal of Peasant Studies*, 38(2), 2011, pp 281–298.
100 Araghi, 'Accumulation by displacement', pp 124, 127. See also Akram-Lodhi, 'Contextualising land grabbing', p 131.
101 Li, 'Centering labor in the land grab debate', p 286; and Kenney-Lazar, 'Plantation rubber, land grabbing and social-property transformation in southern Laos', p 1033. See also Benjaminsen & Bryceson, 'Conservation, blue/green grabbing and accumulation by dispossession in Tanzania', p 351; Li, 'To make live or let die?'; and White *et al*, 'The new enclosures', pp 624–625.
102 Baird, 'Turning land into capital', pp 19–20.
103 C Sneddon, 'Nature's materiality and the circuitous paths of accumulation: dispossession of freshwater fisheries in Cambodia', *Antipode*, 39(1), 2007, p 172.
104 Islar, 'Privatised hydropower development in Turkey', p 386.
105 Sosa & Zwarteveen, 'Exploring the politics of water grabbing', p 362.
106 Araghi, 'Accumulation by displacement', p 127.
107 Woodhouse, 'New investment', pp 785, 781–782. See also Fairbairn, 'Indirect dispossession', p 338.
108 Adnan, 'Land grabs and primitive accumulation in deltaic Bangladesh'.
109 Borras & Franco, 'Global land grabbing and trajectories of agrarian change'.
110 See Adnan, 'Land grabs and primitive accumulation in deltaic Bangladesh'; Amanor, 'Global resource grabs, agribusiness concentration and the smallholder', pp 739–742; Baird, 'Turning land into capital, turning people into labour', p 18; Galeano, 'Paraguay and the expansion of Brazilian and Argentinian agribusiness frontiers', pp 458, 463; Julia & White, 'Gendered experiences of dispossession', pp 998, 1004; and Smalley & Corbera, 'Large-scale land deals from the inside out', p 1052.
111 Baird, 'Turning land into capital, turning people into labour', p 11. See also Adnan, 'Land grabs and primitive accumulation in deltaic Bangladesh'.
112 White *et al*, 'The new enclosures', p 627.
113 Kenney-Lazar, 'Plantation rubber, land grabbing and social-property transformation in southern Laos'.
114 Feldman & Geisler, 'Land expropriation and displacement in Bangladesh', p 982; S Wagle, S Warghade & M Sathe, 'Exploiting policy obscurity for legalising water grabbing in the era of economic reform: the case of Maharashtra', *Water Alternatives*, 5(2), 2012; and IV Torres, 'Water grabbing in the Cauca Basin: the capitalist exploitation of water and dispossession of Afro-descendant communities', *Water Alternatives*, 5 (2), 2012, p 434.
115 C Oya, 'Methodological reflections on "land grab" databases and the "land grab" literature "rush"', *Journal of Peasant Studies*, 40(3), 2012, pp 503–520.
116 *Ibid*, p 504; and Smalley & Corbera, 'Large-scale land deals from the inside out', p 1040. Smalley and Corbera also point out that the term 'large-scale land acquisition', unlike 'land grabbing', 'allows for the possibility of a just transfer of land'.

Notes on Contributor

Derek Hall is an Associate Professor in the Department of Political Science and the Balsillie School of International Affairs, Wilfrid Laurier University. He researches the political economy of food, land, agriculture and the environment, with a focus on Japan and Southeast Asia. He is the author of *Land* (2013) and, with Philip Hirsch and Tania Murray Li, of *Powers of Exclusion: Land Dilemmas in Southeast Asia* (2011).

The New Enclosures? Polanyi, international investment law and the global land rush

LORENZO COTULA

Principal Researcher in Law and Sustainable Development, International Institute for Environment and Development, London, UK

ABSTRACT *Seven decades after its first publication, Karl Polanyi's* The Great Transformation *remains one of the most insightful readings about the socioeconomic changes associated with the Industrial Revolution, and the ways in which law facilitated, or countered, moves towards the commodification of land at that time. As today's global land rush brings competing land claims into contest, new transitions are occurring between more commodified and more 'socially embedded' conceptualisations of land. Using Polanyi's framework, this article analyses the role of international law in these processes. International investment law construes land as a commercial asset, can facilitate access to land for foreign investors and imposes discipline on the exercise of regulatory powers in land matters. But shifts in the political economy that underpins international investment law and growing recourse to international human rights law are creating new opportunities for reflecting the non-commercial (cultural, social, political) relations within which land rights remain embedded in many societies. When contrasting conceptualisations of land collide, the relative strength of legal rights and enforcement mechanisms become particularly important. Ultimately, the legitimacy of international law to mediate between competing land claims will depend on the extent to which it can recognise the multiple values that society attaches to land.*

Framing the issue

The period starting from the mid-2000s has seen a surge in the acquisition of long-term rights to land for plantation agriculture in Africa, Asia and Latin America. Agribusiness, financiers and foreign governments have been at the public forefront of transnational land deals, attracting sustained media attention. A changed global economic outlook has made farming a more attractive business proposition and land a precious asset that is widely expected to increase in value.

As the media spotlight on 'land grabbing' wanes, more in-depth analyses have emerged that emphasise the historical roots of this global land rush,[1] and the parallels and even continuities between today's deals and the enclosures of the commons that preceded the industrial transformation in 18th century England.[2] Within wider debates about the relationship between statehood and resource access,[3] and about the global governance of transnational deals,[4] the role played by the law in the global land rush has also received growing attention—both as an 'enabler' of the deals,[5] and as a source of opportunities, albeit limited and fragile, for citizens' pursuit of accountability and justice.[6]

These historical and legal perspectives on the global land rush intersect. Throughout history the law has enabled the more powerful to acquire common lands, or legalise illegal land grabs, in contexts as diverse as pre-industrial Scotland or colonial Africa.[7] In his classic *The Great Transformation*, Karl Polanyi discussed how legal processes facilitated the artificial reconfiguration of land and labour as tradable commodities before and during the Industrial Revolution, resulting in the private appropriation by elites of land previously held in common ('enclosures'), and in the creation of capitalistic labour markets.[8]

But history also provides numerous examples where the law has been used to resist and challenge adversity, or to protect societal interests. Polanyi's account of the Industrial Revolution in *The Great Transformation* is also the story of the emergence of social legislation—setting basic labour standards, for example—adopted to tame unregulated markets that were causing social dislocation as industrialisation deepened and extended its reach. This 'double movement' between facilitating 'commodification' (the reconfiguration of land and labour as commodities that could be bought and sold on the market), on the one hand, and restoring 'social embeddedness' (the subordination of market exchange to non-market modes of social integration, which have prevailed throughout human history[9]), on the other, is at the heart of Polanyi's account of the social transformation linked to the development of capitalism, and of his (largely implicit) thinking about the role of law in social change.

As today's global land rush unfolds, the law provides multiple arenas for negotiation and contestation between competing actors and authorities. These legal arenas are framed by local ('customary' but continuously evolving) land tenure systems, national legislation, international law and transnational legal processes. Actors and authorities rely on different norms to back their claims to land. Governments mobilise their formal ownership of land under national law to harness legitimacy and coercion for transnational land deals that promote 'agricultural modernisation', and that consolidate government control over marginal areas.[10] Companies leverage opportunities under national law to acquire long-term use rights over land; complex transnational corporate structures to minimise tax liabilities; and the legal protection provided by international investment law to shelter their assets and expectations from adverse public action.[11] Villagers and local-to-global alliances supporting them have resorted to national courts and international human rights bodies to halt, suspend or renegotiate the deals.[12]

Much public debate on the governance of transnational land deals has focused on national law, and on international guidelines and principles. But historical evolutions and current tensions within international law mark significant shifts in the way land is conceptualised. Under international investment law land is construed as a commercial asset valued in monetary terms, legal instruments facilitate access to land for foreign investors and stringent standards protecting the land rights acquired by those investors impose discipline on the exercise of regulatory powers. However, recent developments in international investment law and creative tensions with human rights law are establishing new spaces for government regulation, and new, if still embryonic, opportunities to reflect the non-commercial (cultural, social, political) relations within which land rights remain embedded in many agrarian societies.

Using Polanyi's framework, this article analyses the role of international investment law in transitions between more commodified and more socially embedded conceptualisations of land. The article first discusses the role of law in *The Great Transformation* and explores ruptures and continuities between today's global land rush and the longer-term process of land commodification described by Polanyi. It then examines historical shifts and current tensions within international investment law. The findings highlight the role of international investment law as an enabler of land commodification and a protector of accrued transitions towards commodification; but they also highlight evolutions—within investment law and in its interface with human rights law—that hold promise for reflecting the continued social embeddedness of land.

Law in *The Great Transformation*: a lawyer's reading of Polanyi's thesis

Seven decades after its first publication, *The Great Transformation* remains one of the most insightful readings about the socioeconomic changes associated with the Industrial Revolution. The book has also proved influential. Anthropologists and economic sociologists have particularly valued Polanyi's emphasis on the social and cultural context within which economic relations are embedded. But mainstream economists have largely ignored his work, and most lawyers and legal historians have probably never heard of Polanyi.[13] In recent years the enduring relevance of Polanyi's work has led to a renewed interest in *The Great Transformation*, including a new edition of the book with a foreword by well known economist Joseph Stiglitz, and several academic publications.[14]

Drawing on a vast body of anthropological and historical evidence, *The Great Transformation* argues that the Industrial Revolution that started in England in the 18th and 19th centuries represented a major rupture in the history of humanity—not only because technological progress triggered 'an almost miraculous improvement in the tools of production' (p 35), but also because the Industrial Revolution was associated with profound changes in the way human societies are organised. In England the enclosure of common lands in the centuries that had preceded the Industrial Revolution, coupled with far-reaching government intervention in labour relations, transformed societies traditionally characterised by a close connection between people and land into societies where land ownership was concentrated in fewer hands, and people 'released' from the countryside provided labour to the nascent industries.

In this process market exchange penetrated relations that had until then involved major social and political dimensions. For most of human history, Polanyi argued, the economy was 'embedded' within society. That is, economic relations were not primarily driven by individual maximisation of utility or profit, nor were they primarily coordinated by free markets and market prices. Rather, they were subordinated to non-market modes of social integration. A large share of consumption was based on subsistence production. People have traded since time immemorial, but much trading was part of wider socio-political relations between groups. Market exchange always existed. Its importance in economic organisation varied over time and space. But for most of human history, Polanyi argued, spot transactions based on purely economic considerations only played a subordinate role.

For Polanyi the Industrial Revolution and the development of a capitalist economy, coupled with the emergence of a political project that placed markets centre stage in human society, represented a radical departure from this historical trajectory. The market became the main mechanism for sourcing goods and services; economic calculus divorced from moral foundations came to be seen as the main driver of human relations; the self-regulating market gained preeminence as the model for organising economic relations. New pressures were unleashed for human activity (labour) and nature (land) themselves to be treated as commodities that could be freely bought and sold on the market. This process of commodification had far-reaching repercussions for societies. In Polanyi's words, 'instead of economy being embedded in social relations, social relations [became] embedded in the economic system' (p 60). While the Industrial Revolution expanded the frontier of material wealth, it also caused extensive social dislocation.

According to Polanyi, this historical expansion of market exchange did not happen spontaneously. Rather, it was the product of extensive state intervention, including through law making. In Polanyi's words, 'the road to the free market was opened and kept open by an enormous increase in continuous, centrally organized and controlled interventionism' (p 146). Polanyi argued that, in 19th century England, the Prescriptions Act, the Inheritance Act, the Real Property Act, the numerous Enclosures Acts and legal reforms that extended freedom of contract to land all contributed to the commodification of land. In addition, legal processes were part and parcel of the enclosures of the commons in the centuries before the Industrial Revolution, as elites manoeuvred the law to legitimise their appropriations.

But it is labour that provided the focus for much of Polanyi's discussion about the role of law in accelerating, or slowing, the artificial creation of new commodities. Polanyi examined in detail the Poor Law, a body of legislation that had regulated welfare provision since Tudor and Elizabethan England. In 1834 the Poor Law Amendment Act reformed the provision of welfare relief in ways that restricted access to support for the poor. In Polanyi's analysis this was the beginning of a capitalist system proper, because it forced the poor to sell their labour in order to make a living. The reform was the result of important changes in the prevailing political settlement: the Parliamentary Reform Act of 1832 had given greater electoral power to the rising bourgeoisie, which stood to gain from the unfolding capitalist system.

Yet the comprehensive commodification project reflected in these legal reforms, Polanyi argued, did not, and could not, fully succeed—at least in the most extreme form advanced by those who believed in a purely self-regulating market. For Polanyi certain goods like land and labour cannot be treated purely as commodities without causing widespread social dislocation. Letting labour relations be solely governed by unregulated markets, for example, would have devastating implications for human beings. Polanyi argued that the history of the emergence of capitalism has been accompanied by diverse forms of resistance to the changes brought by the spread of market mechanisms.

Already in the centuries that preceded England's Industrial Revolution, the Tudor monarchs were passing statutes to stop the enclosure of common lands. Politically this aimed to contain the power of an increasingly vocal aristocracy, and to appease grassroots resistance. These measures did not succeed, not least because it proved 'impossible to collect evidence against the enclosers, who often had their servants sworn upon the juries' (p 38). But this 'counter-movement' legislation was not completely ineffective, as it may have slowed down the pace of the enclosures. As Polanyi noted, 'the rate of change is often of no less importance that the direction of the change itself' (p 39), because time allows society to adjust to changing circumstances.

The deepening of the Industrial Revolution resulted in an array of social legislation that qualified the unrestrained operation of labour markets. For example, new mining legislation made it a criminal offence to employ children under 12 and not attending school, and to operate coal mines with a single shaft, while other laws required that workers be insured against damage suffered in the course of employment. Increased unionisation created new pressures for legal change, and social legislation was introduced in all leading European economies.

To sum up, in Polanyi's analysis law making emerges as a particular form of intervention by public authorities in economic relations: first to facilitate the creation of new commodities, then to rein in market forces. It is this 'double movement' between commodification and embeddedness that frames the relationship between law and social change in Polanyi's work. Law can both facilitate and restrain commodification. While legislative efforts to stem the tide of enclosures could only slow the unfolding of social processes driven by powerful vested interests, law making backed by strong political forces pushing toward commodification or embeddedness (the rising bourgeoisie and the emerging trade unions, respectively) proved more effective.

Polanyi's analysis has formed the object of critique over the years. Having been written at a difficult time in European history and Polanyi's life, *The Great Transformation* contains internal contradictions, and leaves important aspects unclear or underdeveloped.[15] Some scholars have contested parts of Polanyi's historical account, arguing, for example, that Polanyi's reading of world history is too Euro-centric;[16] that he downplayed the importance of market relations in pre-industrial societies;[17] and that much non-market organisation over history could be explained in terms of transaction costs and rational economic calculus.[18] It has been noted that markets are rarely devoid of social relations, and that culture and politics are important components of market processes.[19] Throughout history the organisation of economies has experienced multiple shifts in the combination of market and non-market mechanisms, resulting in periods of withdrawal as well as advancement of markets. Different patterns of both embeddedness and commodification may coexist in any given economy and tensions along the spectrum between embeddedness and commodification are usually a matter of degree more than of dichotomies.

The global land rush: a new frontier of commodification?

As a new phase of economic globalisation has extended the reach of international capital and markets to agrarian societies in the global South, 'great transformations' are sweeping across the developing world too—transformations that, on the surface at least, present parallels with the historical processes discussed by Polanyi. Debates about 'land grabbing' are a case in point. Proponents and detractors alike share a recognition that large-scale land deals, if sustained over time, can bring profound change to rural societies in recipient countries. Many commentators have seen in today's land deals a new phase of the same historical process of commodification that Polanyi described in relation to the Industrial Revolution in Europe.

It is not difficult to see why. Large land deals involve the economic transacting of land, which leads to the fencing off of areas that had previously been used as common property resources and according to non-commercial criteria.[20] When a company acquires land, land use tends to shift from multiple, overlapping local uses—farming, herding, foraging—to monoculture. At scale the deals accelerate a reconfiguration of relations between land, capital and labour, with small-scale farming giving ground to large plantations premised on the separation and commodification of the means of production (land, labour and capital).

This reconfiguration of land is particularly evident in the discourse developed in international investor circles. In order to make land an investible asset, the investment brokers who advertise land investments 'render [land] abstract, show its extent, indicate its value, and allow different physical, economic and social characteristics to be visualized together for the purpose of comparison'.[21] The social and political embeddedness that characterises land relations in the real world of local contexts, and the role of land as a basis of social identity and spiritual value that remains central in many agrarian societies, are absent in these narratives—land is just an 'asset class' to be invested in, alongside other commodities.

Governments too have done much to treat land as a commodity. Some have adopted development strategies that explicitly aim to 'turn land into capital'—in Laos, for example.[22] More generally the contracts that make land available to investors involve exchanges between land, on the one hand, and varying combinations of cash payments and in-kind commitments, on the other. These contracts effectively put a price tag on the land, which prospective investors can compare across countries. The commodification of land goes hand in hand with the monetisation of wider social relations: to make a living, farmers who lose land must now trade their labour for cash with landholding companies.

But while it is widely accepted that relations concerning more valuable lands are becoming increasingly commodified in many agrarian societies, caution is needed in identifying the transnational land deals with Polanyian processes of land commodification. Evidence suggests that public perceptions are likely to have overestimated the scale of recent transnational land deals, and that many of the deals signed have not been widely implemented.[23] Longer-term processes of agricultural commercialisation and land concentration in the hands of local and national elites are likely to have substantially greater impacts on the commodification of land than the much-debated transnational deals. More fundamentally simplistic views of the global land rush as a manifestation of the advancement of markets into agrarian societies are mistaken.

On the one hand, markets have been an important force in land relations for a long time, well before global debates about 'land grabbing'. In Africa, for example, land markets have existed since pre-colonial times, and local land relations are increasingly commercialised in many parts of the continent.[24] Similarly the link between people and land has been eroded for a long time. Perceptions of egalitarian land distributions under Africa's customary systems belie growing social differentiation both in rural areas and in national societies.[25] Where land is becoming scarcer, there are already growing numbers of landless people, especially among the youth. In these contexts the unfolding global land rush merely accelerates a pre-existing process of commodification and social differentiation.

On the other hand, today's transnational land deals are far from market transactions. It is true that the land rush is to a large extent the story of a restructuring of global agriculture in ways that favour large- over small-scale farming.[26] But public policies in both home and host states are also major drivers of the deals. Importantly companies mainly acquire land not on the open market, but through long-term leases with government or customary authorities. Land prices are often undervalued as a result of government policies to attract investment in pursuit of economic development, or of underdeveloped land markets. Some contracts for land deals include explicit commitments by the host government to negotiate protectionist exemptions from regional free-trade regimes—hardly the hallmark of the advance of markets.[27]

Further, 'anti-market' strategies that involve seizing large areas of land to blunt or neutralise competition are an important driver of land acquisition,[28] and many transnational land deals signal a transition from the sourcing of commodities from international markets to vertical integration strategies that involve intra-firm control over value chains. Where the deals involve the compulsory taking of land that has already formed the object of transactions on informal local markets, the global land rush entails the wiping out of local markets by transnational deals that are primarily framed as acts of public authority.

The shift in public discourses from the highly optimistic announcements of transnational land deals, which governments and companies made in the early phases of the global land rush, to today's widespread recognition that some form of regulation is necessary to ensure that the deals do not cause widespread dispossession, is another Polanyian dimension of the land rush. Early international regulatory efforts have centred on the Voluntary Guidelines on the Responsible Governance of Tenure of Land, Fisheries and Forests in the Context of National Food Security, which were endorsed by the UN Committee on World Food Security in May 2012; and on Principles on Responsible

Agricultural Investment, currently being discussed in the same Committee. Some countries have also taken measures under national law, for instance suspending land deals or tightening up rules and sanctions. This shift has been promoted by the mobilisation of peasant movements, non-governmental organisations, diaspora associations, opposition politicians, activist researchers and journalists. Positions still diverge widely between 'regulating to facilitate land deals', 'regulating to mitigate negative impacts and maximize opportunities' and 'regulating to stop and rollback'.[29] But there are signs that a Polanyian countermovement is underway.

International investment law and the commodification of land

Polanyi's historical account of the role of law in the reconfiguration of land focused on national legislation. Today's transnational land deals, and the commodification processes they represent, take place in a globalised world. By regulating land ownership and markets, national land law plays a critical role in mediating transitions between social embeddedness and commodification. But international law provides important arenas for advancing more commodified, or more socially embedded, conceptualisations of land, which have received little attention in scholarly writing. The role played by international investment law is a case in point.

Broadly speaking, international investment law protects foreign investment from adverse host-state interference, with the aim of promoting investment flows between states. It is based on customary international law and on international treaties. Customary law is created through state practice accompanied by *opinio juris*—that is, the belief of states that their practice reflects an international legal obligation. But it is international treaties that account for the bulk of the norms of investment law. Investment treaties have mainly been concluded between two states, but increasingly involve regional trade agreements that contain an investment chapter. The content of investment treaties varies, but mostly involves state commitments to treat foreign investment according to specified legal standards, and provisions allowing investors to seek compensation for alleged violations through investor-state arbitration—that is, dispute settlement by an international arbitral tribunal, leading to a binding and enforceable arbitral award. Shifts in international investment law, and tensions with other branches of international law, have a direct bearing on transitions between embeddedness and commodification.

The shifting political economy of international investment law

The historical development of international investment law reflects Polanyian shifts in politics and ideology.[30] For decades the standards of treatment to which foreign investment was entitled under customary international law formed the object of much disagreement between capital-exporting and -importing countries. In the 19th century investment disputes were a serious political matter, with capital-exporting states projecting military power to protect the interests of their nationals overseas. Many states came to see the creation of an international system based on the rule of law as a way to depoliticise disputes—and thus as a desirable shift away from 'gunboat diplomacy'. From the start this 'juridification' process was an attempt to dis-embed investment disputes from the politics of confrontation between sovereign states.[31] But there was no consensus on the content of applicable rules.

Capital-exporting countries from Europe and North America held that customary international law entitled foreign investors to an international minimum standard of treatment, irrespective of the protection available to nationals under domestic law. Capital-importing countries in Latin America resisted these demands, arguing that foreign investors should be entitled to no more than the legal protection available to nationals. Land struggles played an important part in bringing these two competing approaches into direct contest when some Latin American countries implemented agrarian reforms that expropriated and redistributed land owned by foreign nationals.

In Mexico Article 27 of the revolutionary Constitution of 1917, as originally formulated, prohibited foreign land ownership and triggered redistributive agrarian reform in favour of communities (*ejidos* and *comunidades*). When land expropriations affected US interests, disagreement over applicable standards of treatment (national treatment versus international minimum standard of treatment) emerged in correspondence between the Mexican and US authorities. In that correspondence US Secretary of State Cordell Hull held that customary international law required states to pay 'prompt, adequate and effective compensation' where foreign investment was expropriated, regardless of compensation standards applicable to local nationals (a standard that came to be known as the 'Hull formula').[32]

Meanwhile much of Africa and parts of Asia were ruled by European colonial powers and colonial law regulated investments in the colonies. After decolonisation capital-exporting countries became concerned with establishing international rules to protect the assets of their nationals now operating in independent countries. But a coalition of Latin American countries and of newly independent states in Africa and Asia began to emerge at the UN. This diverse grouping of states rejected the claims made by capital-exporting countries, demanded a New International Economic Order, and pushed landmark UN Resolutions that affirmed the sovereignty of states over their natural resources, and their right to regulate foreign investment.[33] While a multilateral regime has regulated international trade since the end of World War II, important aspects of international investment law formed the object of much contestation.

To overcome this impasse, capital-exporting countries started negotiating bilateral investment treaties (BITS) with individual capital-importing countries. While capital-importing countries as a group were challenging richer countries' demands for minimum standards of treatment, individually they were prepared to sign up to treaties that mainly reflected the demands of capital exporters. Some scholars have explained this apparent paradox as a collective action problem—with countries willing to make a principled stand collectively but happy to accept bilateral treaties that could improve their competitiveness in attracting investment.[34] In addition, diversity of interests and the debt crisis eroded the collective negotiating power of developing countries.

These processes led to the establishment of a vast network of investment treaties. It was in the 1990s, however, that the number of investment treaties boomed. Some 385 treaties were concluded worldwide up to 1989; by 2002 the figure had reached 2181 and, by the end of 2011, over 3000 investment treaties were in force globally, including a growing number of regional preferential trade agreements covering investment issues.[35] Several factors fostered this boom in treaty making. The fall of the Berlin Wall and the prevalence of neoliberal thinking led to a major shift in the roles of state, private sector and citizens in many low- and middle-income countries. Many governments came to see private capital as indispensable to promote economic development, and international investment law as a tool to attract foreign capital. In addition, over time divisions between capital-exporting and -importing countries became less clear-cut, and many investment treaties have been signed between developing countries themselves. The period starting in the 1990s has also witnessed a boom in the number of investor–state arbitrations. By the time the surge in transnational land deals took off, a sophisticated system of international investment law, coupled with functioning dispute settlement processes, had been established.

Recent years have witnessed shifts that bear the hallmarks of a Polanyian backlash against the rapid development of international investment law. The global context of investment treaty making has changed significantly compared with that of just 10 years ago. The economic crisis in the West has triggered a new phase of government intervention in the economy, challenging the belief that markets would do best and creating ripple effects in international investment law.[36] The shifting balance of global economic power (West to East and North to South) is altering the political economy of investment treaty making.[37]

Countries that have traditionally approached investment treaties as capital exporters now have to consider the implications of those treaties as capital importers too. High-income countries including the USA and Canada have seen their own public action challenged by foreign investors relying on international investment law. While in the past these countries promoted robust standards of investment protection, they have now developed model investment treaties that seek to balance investment protection with a concern for maintaining regulatory space.

Conversely some low and middle-income countries are becoming more assertive in investment treaty making. Bolivia, Ecuador and Venezuela have terminated BITs or withdrawn from the International Centre for the Settlement of Investment Disputes (ICSID), an important arbitration system. Fast-growing economies in Asia, particularly China and India, play an increasingly active role in investment treaty making, and are likely to change significantly the landscape of international investment law.

International investment law has also become increasingly contested in public discourses. In the late 1990s civil society mobilisation against the proposed Multilateral Agreement on Investment was one of the reasons for the failure of that project. In subsequent years campaigning groups largely focused efforts on trade negotiations at the World Trade Organization, paying scant attention to the continued proliferation of bilateral and regional investment treaties. More recently, however, growing scrutiny by non-governmental organisations (NGOS) has increased pressure on governments to take fuller account of non-commercial considerations in investment treaty making. NGO action has targeted international processes, challenging fundamental aspects of investment treaty making or dispute settlement,[38] but also national decision making on individual negotiations. In Thailand a coalition of NGOS leveraged a constitutional provision requiring disclosure of information and a public hearing for the negotiation of major economic treaties in order to call for open debate and public scrutiny on the negotiation of a preferential trade agreement with the European Union.[39]

As a result of these trends, international investment law is becoming more diverse and polycentric, and increasingly reflects a wider set of considerations beyond the early exclusive emphasis on investment protection.[40] The next two sections explore the implications of these evolutions in relation to two themes directly related to land commodification: the conceptualisation of land in investment treaties and arbitrations; and the channels through which international investment law can facilitate access to land for foreign investors and affects space for government regulation in land matters.

Land as a commercial asset

Investment treaties tend to define protected investment in very broad terms. A common approach is for treaties to combine a broad formula (eg 'every kind of asset') with an illustrative list of asset types (eg moveable and immoveable property, natural resource concessions, company shares). It is safe to say that the acquisition of rights over land for plantation agriculture—the essence of today's transnational land deals—would qualify as a protected investment under virtually all investment treaties, and also under customary international law. In fact, rights over land have formed the object of investment disputes since the early days of international dispute settlement.

The controversy arising from the Mexican agrarian reform has already been mentioned. An early arbitral proceeding between the USA and Panama, dating back to the 1930s, involved a legal challenge to the partial expropriation of a 3180-hectare farm in Panama.[41] The US government acted on behalf of a US national, who owned the expropriated farm. This land owner claimed compensation for the issuance, by the government of Panama, of land titles and temporary licences to third parties on part of the land. Nowadays investment arbitrations are initiated by investors directly, often based on arbitration clauses contained in investment treaties. While many investment disputes affecting low- and middle-income countries relate to extractive or service industries, agricultural investments continue to be a source of investment disputes, including investments focused on agro-processing and trading,[42] and on agricultural production.[43]

In disputes involving land rights acquired by investors, international investment law tends to emphasise the characteristics of land as a tradable, productive asset the value of which is conceptualised in monetary terms. This approach is a direct corollary of the wider concept of property rights followed under international investment law. Arbitral tribunals have held that international investment law protects 'all interests and rights which...may be evaluated in financial and economic terms'.[44] The arbitral tribunal in *Amoco International Finance Corp v Iran* was even more explicit: 'Expropriation...may extend to any right which can be the object of a commercial transaction, ie freely sold and bought, and thus has a monetary value'.[45] These awards concerned the expropriation of oil projects. But they illustrate how the defining feature of property rights protected under investment law is the possibility for the rights to be transacted and thus to be valued in monetary terms.

The conceptualisation of land as a commercial asset also emerges from an analysis of the arbitral jurisprudence concerning the standards of compensation applicable in case of expropriation or damage to property. Under international law, states have the sovereign right to expropriate assets within their jurisdiction. However, international law sets conditions with which expropriations of foreign investments must comply. Under customary international law and virtually all investment treaties, payment of compensation is one critical condition.[46] The standard of compensation remains a much-debated issue. But while different standards have emerged in international treaties and arbitral awards, international law tends to emphasise the market value of the assets taken, through formulae such as 'full equivalent of the property taken',[47] and 'prompt', 'adequate' and 'effective' compensation, taken to mean 'full compensation for the fair market value of the Property'.[48] The latter compensation standard reflects the 'Hull formula' (see above), which is now used in a large number of investment treaties.[49]

In addition to the standard of compensation, a key issue relates to valuation methods. Broadly speaking valuation methods guide the determination of the value of an asset, while compensation standards guide the determination of the portion of that value that must be compensated. Where expropriations have concerned income-generating assets, many arbitral tribunals have relied on future-oriented valuation methods (eg 'discounted cash flow') that are based on the ability of a company, as a unified whole, to earn revenues through use of its multiple assets and capabilities, including land. However, arbitral tribunals have not been consistent on the choice and application of valuation methods, and much depends on whether the venture has a sufficient history of positive results to justify the profit projections.[50]

A few examples of discussions about compensation and valuation in cases concerning agricultural ventures illustrate how, in investment arbitration, the arguments of the parties and the reasoning of arbitral tribunals reflect a commodified concept of land. In *Asian Agricultural Products Ltd v Democratic Socialist Republic of Sri Lanka*, an arbitration concerning the physical destruction of a shrimp farm within an armed conflict situation, the arbitral tribunal held that compensation must cover the 'full value' of the investment, and that this value must be based on the 'reasonable price' that a willing buyer would be prepared to pay for the investment in question; however, the tribunal did not specify the valuation methods it used to calculate the 'full value' of the investment (paras 88 and 97).

In *Tradex Hellas SA v Albania* the investor alleged that its stake in an agricultural joint venture had been expropriated through government measures and farm occupations, and sought compensation based on the 'net fair market value' of its share of the venture. However, the arbitral tribunal found that no expropriation had taken place, so the calculation of compensation became irrelevant. In *Ruby Roz Agricol LLP v The Republic of Kazakhstan*, the investor alleged expropriation of a poultry farm operation and claimed compensation based on 'discounted cash flow'. But the tribunal declined jurisdiction and made no finding on expropriation.

In *Bernardus Henricus Funnekotter and Others v Republic of Zimbabwe*, a case involving a legal challenge to the uncompensated expropriation of commercial farms as part of Zimbabwe's controversial fast-track land redistribution programme, the arbitral tribunal found that an uncompensated expropriation had occurred; that this violated the investment treaty concluded between The Netherlands (the investor's home country) and Zimbabwe; and that Zimbabwe must compensate the investors for losses suffered. Competing valuation methods were among the issues at stake: the claimants wanted the farms to be valued as going concerns, while the government of Zimbabwe calculated compensation as the sum of the value of land and the value of improvements. The arbitral tribunal observed that 'the genuine value of the properties does not correspond to the value of the arable land plus the estimated value of the various buildings and equipments which are necessary for the operation of the farms. Genuine value must be determined on the basis of the market value of the whole farm at the time of expropriation' (para 130).

The jurisprudence of arbitral tribunals suggests that, under international investment law, land—alone or as part of a wider 'going concern'—is conceptualised as a commercial asset valued in monetary terms. The possibility of generating income from a contested piece of land is centre stage in investment dispute settlement. This circumstance should not surprise. It reflects the fact that, because of the very nature of investment arbitrations, the land at stake in investment disputes is typically associated with commercial ventures. The legal relationship between investor and land allocator, which underlies the arbitration, was already premised on land being treated as a commodity. But even in the context of an established commercial venture, the land is not necessarily viewed as a commodity by all parties concerned. In allocating land to commercial investors, governments may dispossess local groups who claim customary rights to the same land. For these groups, the land may not just be a basis for economic activities, but also a source of social identity and cultural value; and landholding may be embedded in complex social, political and cultural relations.

Other bodies of international law, particularly human rights law, recognise these important non-commercial dimensions of land. To be sure, companies and individuals have relied on international human rights law to claim monetary compensation for infringements of property rights pertaining to commercial ventures, particularly under the European Convention on Human Rights and its First Protocol.[51] But from a human rights perspective access to land is closely linked to the protection of indigenous cultures and ways of life, and of fundamental human rights including the right to food, the right to property and the rights of minorities.[52]

Groups acting in Polanyian counter-movement mode have been harnessing international human rights law to advance a socially embedded notion of land. In 2009 transnational peasant movement La Via Campesina adopted a 'Declaration of Rights of Peasants—Women and Men', Article IV of which affirms the 'right to land and territory', triggering discussions at the UN Human Rights Council on a draft UN Declaration on the Rights of Peasants and Other People Working in Rural Areas.[53] Some NGOs have also advocated the development of a more explicit 'human right to land', conceptualised as the right to access land for food security, housing and cultural value.[54] In addition, indigenous peoples and local communities defending or reclaiming their land have initiated international human rights litigation to challenge government land allocations in favour of commercial investors. These suits, and the rulings that followed, have brought out the non-commercial connotations of land very strongly.[55]

These different legal constructions of land (as a basis for the realisation of human rights, on the one hand, and as a commercial asset protected under investment law, on the other) can come directly into contest. In the human rights law case *Sawhoyamaxa v Paraguay*, for example, an indigenous community claimed the restitution of their ancestral lands. The government of Paraguay resisted this claim, partly because the land belonged to a German investor protected under a BIT between Paraguay and Germany. According to the government of Paraguay, returning the land to the Sawhoyamaxa community would have required infringing upon the investor's property rights and violating the BIT (para 115(b) of the judgment). The Inter-American Court of Human Rights noted that, while the investment treaty contained a provision on expropriation, it did not prohibit expropriation altogether—it merely subjected its legality to certain conditions, including public purpose. The Court held that the public purpose requirement would be met where interfering with the investor's property rights is necessary to realise the human rights of third parties, including through land restitution programmes aimed at realising the human right to property of indigenous peoples (para 140).

Evolutions in international investment law, fuelled by the shifting political economy discussed in the previous section, have also created new spaces for raising the social embeddedness of land within investment arbitration itself. Responding to growing public demands for greater openness in investment arbitration, some states have taken steps to increase transparency and opportunities for public participation in arbitral proceedings. Following legal developments under the North American Free Trade Agreement (NAFTA), a new generation of investment treaties negotiated by the USA and by Canada with countries outside North America includes provisions that allow third parties to make submissions to arbitral tribunals where specified criteria are met, and to define specific procedures for those submissions.[56] Openings for greater public participation in arbitral proceedings have allowed third parties to bring their concerns and aspirations to arbitral tribunals, including by emphasising the spiritual or cultural value of contested land.

The NAFTA arbitration *Glamis Gold Ltd v United States of America* illustrates this trend. It concerned the alleged expropriation and unfair treatment of a mining project in the USA. The mining project was going to affect a sacred trail to which an Indian nation, the Quechan, felt a close spiritual connection. The focus of the tribunal's analysis was on whether measures taken by US government authorities, including those to protect that sacred trail, amounted to breaches of the applicable investment protection regime. But the Quechan filed a non-party submission with the tribunal to emphasise the spiritual value of the trail and the rights of indigenous peoples under international law.[57]

The *Glamis* award refers extensively to the spiritual value of the trail to local communities, though primarily in the presentation of the facts of the case.[58] And in a seemingly unprecedented move within investment arbitration, the tribunal referred to international instruments protecting cultural sites, including the 1972 World Heritage Convention, although this had no direct bearing on the outcome of the case.[59] The tribunal found that the economic impact of the US measures was not substantial enough for an expropriation to have occurred. It also dismissed the investor's claim that the challenged measures breached fair and equitable treatment.

Grand River Enterprises Six Nations, another NAFTA case brought against the USA, has also introduced new flavours into investor–state arbitration. The dispute did not raise any land issues, but the identity of the claimants had important implications. The case was filed by members of the Haudenosaunee, the Iroquois Confederation, who ran a business exporting tobacco products from Canada to the USA. The business was allegedly adversely affected by a settlement agreement between the US government and major tobacco companies, whereby the latter agreed to contribute to a fund for tobacco-related diseases in exchange for the former dropping all health-related lawsuits against the tobacco industry.[60] The claimants appointed Professor James Anaya, a specialist in indigenous peoples' rights and UN Special Rapporteur on the Rights of Indigenous Peoples, as one of the three arbitrators. It is very unusual for arbitral tribunals to have expertise in indigenous peoples' rights.

The claimants also relied on some unorthodox legal arguments within an investment arbitration context. They argued that, in interpreting the provisions of NAFTA, the tribunal had to take account of the 'customary law rules affecting indigenous peoples', and of the 18th century Jay Treaty, which gave natives a right of free passage across the Canada–US border. The claimants argued that their tobacco business was part of their traditional way of life, protected under international law; that the Jay Treaty created a 'reasonable expectation' that the claimants would be able to continue running their tobacco business without restrictions; and that the US measures breached fair and equitable treatment and amounted to expropriation. The tribunal dismissed these claims, and also found that taking account of other legal instruments cannot amount to 'import[ing] into NAFTA elements from other treaties', as the tribunal's jurisdiction was limited to claims arising from NAFTA. While the case was ultimately unsuccessful, it illustrates how arguments about indigenous peoples' traditional ways of life have started to penetrate investment arbitration.[61]

To sum up, international investment law embodies a conceptualisation of land as a commercial asset valued in monetary terms. Recent years have witnessed some attempts to reflect the social embeddedness of land within investor–state arbitration and—even more so—through recourse to international human rights law, paving the way for potential collisions between the fundamental values underpinning different branches of international law.

Investment protection and facilitation, and the global restructuring of land relations

In addition to the way in which land is conceptualised, two other aspects of international investment law are relevant to a discussion about shifts between embeddedness and commodification in land relations. The first relates to the extent to which investment law facilitates the acquisition of land rights by foreign investors. Under customary international law states have the sovereign right to regulate the admission of foreign investment within their territory. Investment treaties mainly concern the treatment of foreign investment *after* its entry into the territory of the host state. Most treaties do not establish an obligation on the host state to admit foreign investment into its territory. The regulation of land relations remains a prerogative linked to state sovereignty, and governments retain extensive latitude in restricting the right of foreigners to acquire land.

However, some investment treaties create enforceable obligations regarding the entry of foreign investment. In these 'pre-establishment' models the investment treaty requires governments not to discriminate against investors from the other state party in relation to admission. Specifically the treaty usually provides that the host state must apply to foreign investors a treatment no less favourable than that applied to its own nationals ('national treatment') and/or to nationals of other states ('most-favoured-nation treatment') in relation to the establishment, acquisition or expansion of an investment, with exceptions applying to specific sectors or measures. This pre-establishment approach is particularly common in the treaties concluded by the USA, Canada and Japan, while European investment treaties tend not to feature pre-establishment provisions.[62] The approach is also common in treaties that protect investment as part of wider preferential trade agreements.

The obligation not to discriminate against foreign investors does not constitute, in itself, full liberalisation of investment flows. Restrictions may still be imposed if they are applied in a non-discriminatory way. But the requirement not to discriminate between nationals and non-nationals means that foreign investors are, in principle, entitled to the same treatment provided to nationals. Unless exceptions apply, this means that foreign investors cannot be discriminated against in accessing land. However, non-discrimination requirements commonly apply only to future measures, so that existing regulations can remain in place; and treaties often exclude land tenure from the application of pre-establishment obligations.[63]

The signing of investment treaties with pre-establishment provisions can trigger, or accompany, national law reforms that reconfigure land relations in ways that facilitate land access for foreign investors. The profound revision of Mexico's agrarian legislation in the early 1990s, carried out in conjunction with the negotiation of NAFTA, is a case in point. As discussed above, for much of the 20th century land ownership in Mexico was characterised by a longstanding agrarian reform and by the spread of collective landholdings (namely, by *ejidos* and *comunidades*). In the early 1990s an amendment to Article 27 of the 1917 Constitution and a new Agrarian Law introduced privatisation and liberalisation measures that allowed *ejido* land sales, rentals and mortgages, and full land ownership by foreign corporations. These reforms have triggered transformations in landholding patterns, promoting greater land tenure individualisation within *ejido* lands and facilitating penetration by commercial operators.[64]

The second aspect of international investment law worth exploring in the discussion of land commodification concerns the much-debated tension between investment protection and regulatory powers. Investment law shelters foreign investment against the effects of host state measures that can adversely affect protected investments: should a government take action in violation of its legal obligations, it would have to compensate investors for losses suffered. Where public finances are under strain, the obligation to compensate investors could discourage states from taking action. This issue is not limited to low-income countries. The government of New Zealand recently announced that it would wait to see the outcome of an investment arbitration opposing a tobacco company and the government of Australia over cigarette marketing legislation adopted in Australia, before introducing similar legislation in New Zealand.[65]

The standard of 'fair and equitable treatment' illustrates the tensions that may arise between investment protection and public regulation. Fair and equitable treatment is required by many investment treaties and has been relied on in 'almost all claims brought to date by investors against States'.[66] It mandates the host state to treat foreign investment according to a minimum international standard of fairness, irrespective of the standards that the host state applies to domestic investment under its national law. In practice, assessing what is 'fair' and 'equitable' is not always straightforward. Some arbitral tribunals have interpreted this standard expansively, and have ordered governments to compensate investors whose business prospects have been adversely affected by public action. Respect for the legitimate expectations that the investor had when it made the investment is considered a central requirement of the fair and equitable treatment standard.[67] This requirement has been held to include, for example, consistency and transparency of government conduct,[68] and stability and predictability of the regulatory framework.[69]

Many government measures found in violation of fair and equitable treatment involve arbitrary and opportunistic conduct by government officials. But some commentators have raised concerns that broad interpretations of fair and equitable treatment may significantly constrain the exercise of sovereign powers in the host country. Regulatory measures that pursue legitimate public interests but adversely affect ongoing investments could be deemed to constitute inconsistency in government action, or to undermine the investor's expectations. In this sense international investment law could affect the ability of governments to regulate in Polanyian counter-movement mode—or else it could be invoked by governments to justify inaction, masking their limited political will or even vested interests in status quo. Reference to an investment treaty protecting the land reclaimed by an indigenous people, wielded by the government of Paraguay in the *Sawhoyamaxa* case to justify its inaction, is a case in point.

The legal protection of foreign investment would be relevant where regulatory measures affect the terms of an investor's land access. But it is even more dramatically relevant where land held by foreign investors is expropriated altogether. Besides providing insights on the way land is conceptualised, some of the arbitrations discussed above exemplify how international legal protection can be mobilised to challenge the legality of land redistribution measures (eg *de Sabla v Panama*; *Tradex Hellas v Albania*; *Funnekotter v Zimbabwe*).

Legal action before national courts may pursue similar ends. In the Namibian case *Günter Kessl, Heimaterde CC and Martin Joseph Riedmaier v Ministry of Lands and Resettlement and Others*, the applicants challenged the legality of farm expropriations as part of a land redistribution programme.[70] Much of the legal argumentation—in the judgment and throughout the case—concerned alleged violations of human rights recognised by the Constitution, and of procedural safeguards established by national land law. But the applicants, all German nationals, also argued that by targeting foreign nationals the expropriation violated the non-discrimination requirements of the Germany–Namibia BIT 1997. The court established that applicable rules had indeed been violated, set aside the relevant expropriation orders and provided guidance to the government on ways to implement expropriation-based land redistribution consistently with national and international law.

The contribution of international investment law in ensuring that land reforms comply with the rule of law is a welcome development. But questions have been raised where protection under investment law effectively crystallises historical injustices, or where land claims competing with those of foreign investors are not backed up by similarly effective international legal redress.[71]

Shifts in the political economy of international investment law have started altering the balance between investment protection and public regulation. For example, the new model investment treaties developed by Canada and the USA clarify that fair and equitable treatment is restricted to the international minimum standard of treatment required under customary international law. The customary law standard of treatment is typically interpreted relatively narrowly, as referring to conduct that is 'arbitrary, grossly unfair, unjust or idiosyncratic, is discriminatory...or involves a lack of due process'.[72] So equating fair and equitable treatment to the customary standard would restrict the scope of investment protection, and preserve greater space for government regulation. But some recent awards have emphasised that the customary standard is itself evolving, and have adopted broader interpretations of that standard.[73] So the extent to which these treaty formulations may make a difference remains to be seen. Also, many countries, for example in Europe, have continued to sign investment treaties that feature unqualified investment protection standards, including in relation to fair and equitable treatment.[74]

In addition to shifts in treaty making, there are signs that international arbitrators are displaying greater sensitivity to government concerns about regulatory space. For example, some arbitral tribunals have interpreted fair and equitable treatment in ways that place greater emphasis on the right of governments to regulate. To mention one case, the tribunal in *Saluka Investments BV v Czech Republic* stated that 'no investor may reasonably expect that the circumstances prevailing at the time the investment is made remain totally unchanged', and that 'the host State's legitimate right…to regulate domestic matters in the public interest must be taken into consideration'.[75] But arbitral practice is diverse, and recent awards feature examples of both restrictive and expansive approaches to interpreting 'fair and equitable treatment'.[76]

To sum up, the provisions of international investment law can facilitate the acquisition of land rights by foreign investors for the purposes of commercial operations. And by protecting foreign investment against state interference, investment law can restrict the scope or modes for 'counter-movement' public action. Recent evolutions in international investment law are altering the balance between investment protection and regulatory space, but the contours of this realignment remain uncertain.

Discussion

The global land rush constitutes a new frontier in historical shifts between social embeddedness and commodification in land relations. Important aspects of the deals being done—from the narratives deployed by governments and investors, through to key contractual terms—reflect and reinforce a process of commodification of land in low and middle-income countries. But the land rush cannot be reduced to a linear process of market expansion. The deals are importantly shaped by non-market forces, and reflect the continued operation of those forces in local-to-global land arenas. In fact, aspects of the land rush represent a withdrawal of market forces—as the sourcing of commodities from international markets gives way to vertical integration strategies, and as government land allocations swipe away local land markets. Concerns that large land deals will dispossess the rural poor have triggered a backlash against the deals. The outcomes of this counter-movement will depend on struggles that are still underway.

As in the processes described by Polanyi in *The Great Transformation*, extensive law making both facilitates the commodification of land and reflects early steps towards re-embedding those relations. Differently from Polanyi's account of the enclosures that preceded the Industrial Revolution, which focused on national law, in today's global land rush international law provides important arenas for negotiation and confrontation. Shifts within investment law, and in its interface with human rights law, illustrate transitions between social embeddedness and commodification—not just as a dichotomy between states of either embeddedness or commodification and a linear sequence along a trajectory involving change from embeddedness to commodification, and then again towards embeddedness, as suggested by Polanyi, but, rather, as a set of transitions along a spectrum between two ideological and regulatory poles. At any one point in time, competing normative references can be mobilised in different and even opposing directions—for example, conceptualising land as a commercial asset primarily valued in monetary terms, on the one hand, and as a basis for the realisation of fundamental human rights, on the other.

Investment law reflects a legal construction of land that is eminently commodified; can facilitate access to land for foreign investors; and protects the land rights acquired by those investors. To be clear, the argument developed here is not that there is cause and effect between international investment law and transnational land deals. Nor does the article argue that countries that have concluded more investment treaties necessarily also sign more land deals. But investment law effectively acts as an enabler of commodification, and as a protector of accrued transitions towards commodification.

Recent years have witnessed shifts in the political economy of international investment law that are redrawing the boundaries between investment promotion and regulatory space. The emerging narrower construction of some important investment protection standards illustrates this trend. And the *Glamis* and *Grand River* cases show that investment arbitration is not insulated from legal arguments reflecting social embeddedness, even though this development has to date delivered limited concrete results. The constellation of actors behind these shifts only partly overlaps with those involved in the counter-movement against transnational land deals, particularly given the important role of the state in promoting recent transitions within international investment law.

But insofar as land relations are concerned, shifts within international investment law have to date fallen short of a genuine Polanyian pushback. They have not fundamentally challenged the way in which investment law conceptualises land as a commercial asset, or the mechanisms through which it facilitates access to land for investors and protects the land rights they have acquired. More promising in counter-movement terms is the growing recourse to international human rights law to challenge commodification and reassert social embeddedness.

Where action under human rights law challenges foreign investment projects, the contrasting conceptualisations of land under investment and human rights law enter into direct collision. The relative strength of substantive protection and effectiveness of legal remedies will influence the ways in which law will mediate these tensions. Time will tell whether the mobilisation of human rights instruments can stem the tide, or only slow it—much like the Tudor anti-enclosure laws in the run-up to the Industrial Revolution. Imbalances in the strength of legal protection and enforcement mechanisms provided by international human rights and investment law, discussed at length elsewhere,[77] suggest that, short of effective political action to give real leverage to legal rights, the odds are not looking good. Also, the discipline that international investment law imposes on the exercise of state sovereignty could restrict scope for measures that, in Polanyian counter-movement mode, aim to reverse moves towards land commodification.

Another important dimension of (dis-)embeddedness concerns the relationship between law and politics. Historically international investment law has emerged through a process of 'de-politicisation' and 'juridification' of investment disputes. The exercise of traditionally important sovereign powers has become subordinated to an international rule of law that, while framed in legalistic terms, ultimately reflects political choices on the relationship between state and markets. Yet the importance of politics (the politics of international relations between sovereign states, and the politics of accountability through social mobilisation) returns to the fore in the all key turning points of the history of international investment law, including recent shifts that are reconfiguring the balance between investment protection and regulatory space.

Politically, Polanyi was a socialist. He saw self-regulating markets as utopian, and thought that reformist agendas could not work. Most commentators agree that Polanyi identified the solution in the de-commodification of land and labour through collective ownership of the means of production. But history has not evolved in the direction anticipated and desired by Polanyi. Actually existing socialisms have treated land and labour as commodities to be harnessed for state-led growth, and thus 'replaced one process of disembedding with another that, in some respects, was just as devastating as the original version'.[78] On the other hand, market economies have proved far more capable of adaptation than Polanyi had predicted, through extensive legislative and administrative interventions to correct the operation of market forces.[79] And in many parts of the developing world local organisations have indicated pathways for community-based development, and displayed effectiveness in their custodianship of the social embeddedness of land, although, as discussed, the terms of that embeddedness are evolving with socioeconomic change.

In relation to the global land rush, this discussion raises fundamental issues about development pathways that go well beyond legal aspects and international law. But as transnational land deals create encounters between competing land claims, and even between competing ways of conceptualising land, land disputes in a globalised world will see more engagement with international law, not less. Ultimately the perceived legitimacy of international law to mediate between competing land claims will depend on the extent to which it can reflect the multiple values that society attaches to land.

Notes

1 L Alden Wily, 'Looking back to see forward: the legal niceties of land theft in land rushes', *Journal of Peasant Studies*, 39(2), 2012, pp 751–776; and KS Amanor, *Land Governance in Africa: How Historical Context Has Shaped Key Contemporary Issues Relating to Policy on Land*, Rome: International Land Coalition, 2012.

2 B White, SM Borras Jr, R Hall, I Scoones & W Wolford, 'The new enclosures: critical perspectives on corporate land deals', *Journal of Peasant Studies*, 39(3–4), 2012, pp 619–647; and B Okot, 'Uganda: breaking the links between the land and the people', blog, 11 March 2013, at http://www.iied.org/uganda-breaking-links-between-land-people.

3 T Sikor & C Lund, 'Access and property: a question of power and authority', *Development and Change*, 40(1), 2009, pp 1–22; and 'Governing Global Land Deals: The Role of the State in the Rush for Land', special issue of *Development and Change*, 44(2), 2013, particularly the introductory essay with the same title by W Wolford, SM Borras Jr, R Hall, I Scoones & B White, pp 189–210.

4 'Land Grabbing and Global Governance', *Globalizations* (special issue), 10(1), 2013, esp ME Margulis, N McKeon & SM Borras Jr, 'Land grabbing and global governance: critical perspectives', pp 1–23 and SM Borras Jr, JC Franco & C Wang, 'The challenge of global governance of land grabbing: changing international agricultural context and competing views and strategies', pp 161–179.

5 W Anseeuw, L Alden Wily, L Cotula & M Taylor, *Land Rights and the Rush for Land: Findings of the Global Commercial Pressures on Land Research Project*, Rome: International Land Coalition, 2012, at http://www.landcoalition.org/cpl/CPL-synthesis-report; L Alden Wily, *The Tragedy of Public Lands: The Fate of the Commons under Global Commercial Pressure*, Rome: International Land Coalition, 2011, at http://www.landcoalition.org/publications/accelerate-legal-recognition-commons-group-owned-private-property-limit-involuntary-lan; and L Cotula, '"Land grabbing" in the shadow of the law: legal frameworks regulating the global land rush',

in R Rayfuse & N Weisfelt (eds), *The Challenge of Food Security: International Policy and Regulatory Frameworks*, Cheltenham: Edward Elgar, 2012, pp 206–228.

6 L Cotula, *Legal Empowerment for Local Resource Control: Securing Local Resource Rights within Foreign Investment Projects in Africa*, London: International Institute for Environment and Development (IIED), 2007; E Polack, L Cotula & M Côte, *Pathways to Accountability in Africa's Land Rush: What Role for Legal Empowerment?* London: IIED, 2013; and J Grajales, 'Speaking Law to Land Grabbing': Land Contention and Legal Repertoire in Colombia, LDPI Working Paper No 17, 2013, at http://www.iss.nl/file-admin/ASSETS/iss/Research_and_projects/Research_networks/LDPI/LDPI_WP_17.pdf.

7 See, respectively, A Wightman, *The Poor Had No Lawyers: Who Owns Scotland (And How They Got It)*, Edinburgh: Birlinn, 2011; and Alden Wily, 'Looking back to see forward'.

8 K Polanyi, *The Great Transformation: The Political and Economic Origins of Our Time*, Boston, MA: Beacon Press, 2001[1944]. All citations of Polanyi are from this second edition of the book.

9 A Ebner, 'Transnational markets and the Polanyi problem', in C Joerges & J Falke (eds), *Karl Polanyi, Globalisation and the Potential of Law in Transnational Markets*, Oxford/Portland: Hart Publishing, 2011, pp 19–40, p 33.

10 On the link between managing land access and establishing effective state control, see C Lund, 'Fragmented sovereignty: land reform and dispossession in Laos', *Journal of Peasant Studies*, 38(4), 2011, pp 885–905.

11 T Ferrando, 'Legitimizing accumulation by dispossession: the state/capital nexus in land-related investment agreements', 4 July 2013, at http://ssrn.com/abstract=2290022.

12 Polack *et al*, *Pathways to Accountability in Africa's Land Rush*; and Grajales, 'Speaking Law to Land Grabbing'.

13 Exceptions include A Perry-Kessaris, 'Reading the story of law and embeddedness through a community lens: a Polanyi-meets-Cotterell economic sociology of law?' *Northern Ireland Legal Quarterly*, 62(3) 2011, pp 401–13; and Joerges & Falke, *Karl Polanyi, Globalisation and the Potential of Law in Transnational Markets*.

14 J Stiglitz, 'Foreword', in Polanyi, *The Great Transformation*; F Block, 'Karl Polanyi and the writing of "The Great Transformation"', *Theory and Society*, 32(3), 2003, pp 275–306; K Polanyi-Levitt & K McRobbie (eds), *Karl Polanyi in Vienna: The Contemporary Significance of The Great Transformation*, Montreal: Black Rose Books, 2006; and R Sandbrook, 'Polanyi and post-neoliberalism in the global South: dilemmas of re-embedding the economy', *New Political Economy*, 16(4), 2011, pp 415–443.

15 Block, 'Karl Polanyi and the writing of "The Great Transformation"'.

16 K Hart, 'Karl Polanyi's legacy', *Development and Change*, 39(6), 2008, pp 1135–1143.

17 DN McCloskey, 'Polanyi was right, and wrong', *Eastern Economic Journal*, 23, 1997, pp 483–487.

18 DC North, 'Markets and other allocation systems in history: the challenge of Karl Polanyi', *Journal of European Economic History*, 6, 1977, pp 703–716.

19 Ebner, 'Transnational markets and the Polanyi problem'.

20 Alden Wily, *The Tragedy of Public Lands*.

21 T Li, 'What is land? An anthropological pespective on the global land rush', paper presented at the international conference on 'Global Land Grabbing II', Ithaca, NY, 17–19 October 2012, at http://www.cornell-landproject.org/papers/, p 12.

22 M Kenney-Lazar, 'Plantation rubber, land grabbing and social-property transformation in southern Laos', *Journal of Peasant Studies*, 39(3–4), 2012, pp 1017–1037.

23 See the evidence discussed in L Cotula, *The Great African Land Grab? Agricultural Investments and the Global Food System*, London: Zed Books, 2013; and L Cotula & C Oya, 'Ground-testing claims about land deals in Africa: summary findings from a multi-country study', *Journal of Development Studies*, forthcoming.

24 J-P Colin & P Woodhouse, 'Interpreting land markets in Africa', *Africa*, 80, 2010, pp 1–13.

25 PE Peters, 'Inequality and social conflict over land in Africa', *Journal of Agrarian Change*, 4(3), 2004, pp 269–314; and P Woodhouse, 'New investment, old challenges: land deals and the water constraint in African agriculture', *Journal of Peasant Studies*, 39(3–4), 2012, pp 777–794.

26 KS Amanor, 'Global resource grabs, agribusiness concentration and the smallholder: two West African case studies', *Journal of Peasant Studies*, 39(3–4), 2012, pp 731–749.

27 M Djiré with A Diawara & A Keita, *Agricultural Investment in Mali: Context, Trends and Case Studies*, London: IIED, 2012.

28 K Deininger & D Byerlee with J Lindsay, A Norton, H Selod & M Stickler, *Rising Global Interest in Farmland: Can it Yield Sustainable and Equitable Benefits?* Washington, DC: World Bank, 2011, at http://econ.worldbank.org/external/default/main?pagePK=64165259&theSitePK=469382&piPK=64165421&menuPK=64166322&entityID=000334955_20110208033706.

29 Borras *et al*, 'The challenge of global governance of land grabbing'.

30 The account of the early development of investment law draws on M Sornarajah, *The International Law on Foreign Investment*, Cambridge: Cambridge University Press, 2004; and A Newcombe & L Paradell,

Law and Practice of Investment Treaties: Standards of Treatment, Austin, TX: Kluwer Law International, 2009.

31 R Kreide, 'Re-embedding the market through law? The ambivalence of juridification in the international context', in Joerges & Falke, *Karl Polanyi, Globalisation and the Potential of Law in Transnational Markets*, pp 41–64.

32 A Reinisch, 'Legality of expropriations', in Reinisch (ed), *Standards of Investment Protection*, Oxford: Oxford University Press, 2008, p 196.

33 See particularly General Assembly Resolution 1803(XVII) of 14 December 1962 on Permanent Sovereignty of States over Natural Resources; and the Charter of Economic Rights and Duties of States, General Assembly Resolution 3281(XXIV) of 12 December 1974.

34 AT Guzman, 'Why LDCs sign treaties that hurt them: explaining the popularity of bilateral investment treaties', *Virginia Journal of International Law*, 38, 1996–97, pp 639–688.

35 Figures for 1989 and 2002 are from UNCTAD, *World Investment Report 2003—FDI Policies for Development: National and International Perspectives*, Geneva: United Nations Conference on Trade and Development, 2003. The figure for 2011 is from UNCTAD, *World Investment Report 2012: Towards a New Generation of Investment Policies*, Geneva: United Nations Conference on Trade and Development, 2012.

36 JE Alvarez, 'The return of the state', *Minnesota Journal of International Law*, 20(2), 2011, pp 223–264.

37 SW Schill & M Jacob, 'Trends in international investment agreements, 2010–2011: the increasing complexity of international investment law', in KP Sauvant (ed), *Yearbook on International Investment Law & Policy 2011–2012*, Oxford: Oxford University Press, 2013, pp 141–179.

38 See, for example, C Olivet & P Eberhardt, *Profiting from Injustice: How Law Firms, Arbitrators and Financiers are fuelling an Investment Arbitration Boom*, Amsterdam: Transnational Institute, 2012, at http://www.tni.org/briefing/profiting-injustice.

39 A Ashayagachat, 'Public hearing "required" before FTA talks', *Bangkok Post*, 8 August 2012, at http://www.bangkokpost.com/lite/topstories/306683/public-hearing-required-before-fta-talks.

40 Schill & Jacob, 'Trends in international investment agreements'.

41 *United States of America on Behalf of Marguerite de Joly de Sabla v The Republic of Panama*, US–Pan Arb Comm'n, 29 June 1933, reported in *American Journal of International Law*, 28, 1934, p 602.

42 See, for example, *Gustav F Hamester GmbH & Co KG v Republic of Ghana*, Award, 18 June 2010, ICSID Case No ARB/07/24, concerning a joint venture for the construction or upgrading of cocoa processing facilities in Ghana. See also the cases *Cargill Inc v United Mexican States*, Award, 18 September 2009, ICSID case No ARB(AF)/05/02; *Archer Daniels Midland Company and Tate & Lyle Ingredients Americas Inc v The United Mexican States*, Award, 21 November 2007, ICSID Case No ARB(AF)/04/05; and *Ruby Roz Agricol LLP v The Republic of Kazakhstan*, Award on Jurisdiction, 1 August 2013, Arbitration in accordance with the UNCITRAL Arbitration Rules.

43 See, for example, *Asian Agricultural Products Ltd v Democratic Socialist Republic of Sri Lanka*, Award, 27 June 1990, ICSID Case No ARB/87/3, (1991) 30 ILM 577; *Tradex Hellas SA v Albania*, Award, 29 April, 1999, ICSID Case No ARB/94/2; and *Bernardus Henricus Funnekotter and Others v Republic of Zimbabwe*, Award, 22 April 2009, ICSID Case No ARB/05/6.

44 *Libyan American Oil Company (Liamco) v The Government of the Libyan Arab Republic*, Award, 12 April 1977, 62 ILR 140, at 189.

45 *Amoco International Finance Corp v Islamic Republic of Iran and Others*, Partial Award, 14 July 1987, Iran–US Claims Tribunal, 15 Iran–US CTR 189, para 108.

46 Reinisch, 'Legality of expropriations'. See *German Interests in Polish Upper Silesia (Merits) (Germany v Poland)*, Judgment, 25 May 1926, (1926) PCIJ Ser A No 7, at 20–24; *Amoco International Finance Corp v Iran*, paras 113–117; and *Compañia del Desarrollo de Santa Elena SA v The Republic of Costa Rica*, Final Award, 17 February 2000, 39 ILM (2000) 1317, para 71.

47 *Phillips Petroleum Co v Islamic Republic of Iran*, Partial Award, Iran–US Claims Tribunal, 29 June 1989, 21 Iran–US CTR 79, paras 104–106.

48 *Compañia del Desarrollo de Santa Elena SA v Costa Rica*, paras 71–73.

49 For example, Cameroon–US BIT 1986, Article III; and Nigeria–South Korea BIT 1997, Article 5. On the emergence of the Hull formula as the increasingly dominant compensation standard under international law, see WM Reisman & RD Sloane, 'Indirect expropriation and its valuation in the BIT generation', *British Yearbook of International Law*, 74, 2003, pp 115–150.

50 TW Wälde & B Sabahi, 'Compensation, damages, and valuation', in P Muchlinski, R Ortino & C Schreuer (eds), *The Oxford Handbook of International Investment Law*, Oxford: Oxford University Press, 2008, pp 1049–1124.

51 For example, *Pine Valley Developments Ltd and Others v Ireland*, Judgment, 29 November 1991, European Court of Human Rights, 14 EHRR 319.

52 See *Large-Scale Land Acquisitions and Leases: A Set of Minimum Principles and Measures to Address the Human Rights Challenge*, Addendum to the Report of the Special Rapporteur on the Right to Food, Olivier De Schutter, 28 December 2009, UN Doc A/HRC//13/33/Add. See also *Chief Bernard Ominayak*

and the Lubicon Lake Band v Canada, UN Human Rights Committee, CCPR/C/38/D/167/1984, 26 March 1990, at http://www1.umn.edu/humanrts/undocs/session45/167-1984.htm.

53 http://viacampesina.net/downloads/PDF/EN-3.pdf and http://www.ohchr.org/EN/HRBodies/HRC/Rural Areas/Pages/WGRuralAreasIndex.aspx, respectively. See also M Edelman & J Carwill, 'Peasants' rights and the UN system: quixotic struggle? Or emancipatory idea whose time has come?' Journal of Peasant Studies, 38(1), 2011, pp 81–108.

54 R Künnemann & S Monsalve Suárez, 'International human rights and governing land grabbing: a view from global civil society', Globalizations, 10(1), 2013, pp 123–139.

55 For example, Mayagna (Sumo) Awas Tingni Community v Nicaragua, Judgement, 31 August 2001, Inter-American Court of Human Rights, at http://www1.umn.edu/humanrts/iachr/AwasTingnicase.html; Saramaka People v Suriname, Judgement, 28 November 2007, Inter-American Court on Human Rights, at http://www.corteidh.or.cr/docs/casos/articulos/seriec_172_ing.pdf; Sawhoyamaxa Indigenous Community v Paraguay, Judgement, 29 March 2006, Inter-American Court on Human Rights, at http://www1.umn.edu/humanrts/cases/12-03.html; and Yakye Axa Indigenous Community v Paraguay, Judgment, 17 June 2005, Inter-American Court on Human Rights, at www.corteidh.or.cr/docs/casos/articulos/seriec_125_ing.pdf.

56 For example, Canada–Tanzania BIT 2013 (not yet in force), Articles 30–31.

57 Glamis Gold Ltd v United States of America, Application for Leave to File a Non-Party Submission and Submission of the Quechan Indian Nation, 19 August 2005, at http://www.state.gov/documents/organization/52531.pdf.

58 Glamis Gold Ltd v United States of America, Award, 14 May 2009, at http://www.state.gov/documents/organization/125798.pdf.

59 Paras 83–84 of the award. On this point, see VS Vadi, 'When cultures collide: foreign direct investment, natural resources, and indigenous heritage in international investment law', Columbia Human Rights Law Review, 42, 2011, pp 797–889.

60 Vadi, 'When cultures collide', p 842.

61 Grand River Enterprises Six Nations, Ltd, et al, v United States of America, Award, 12 January 2011, at http://italaw.com/cases/documents/511, esp paras 66–71, 128–145. For a discussion of this case, see Vadi, 'When cultures collide'; and IA Laird, B Sabahi, FG Sourgens & NJ Birch, 'International investment law and arbitration: 2011 in review', in Sauvant (ed), Yearbook on International Investment Law & Policy, pp 41–140.

62 See, for example, Rwanda–US BIT 2008, Articles 3-4; Japan–Laos BIT 2008, Article 2; and Benin–Canada BIT 2013 (not yet in force), Articles 5–6.

63 For example Annex II of Benin–Canada BIT 2013; and Annex II(2) of Japan–Laos BIT 2008.

64 For a case study, see AL Luers, RL Naylor & PA Matson, 'A case study of land reform and coastal land transformation in southern Sonora, Mexico', Land Use Policy, 23, 2006, pp 436–447.

65 LE Peterson, 'First hearing in Philip Morris v Australia arbitration is pushed into 2014, as New Zealand reveals it is awaiting outcome of Australian cases', International Arbitration Reporter, 28 February 2013, at http://www.iareporter.com/articles/20130228_2.

66 UNCTAD, World Investment Report 2012, p 147.

67 Técnicas Medioambientales Tecmed, SA v United Mexican States, Award, 23 May 2003, ICSID Case No ARB(AF)/00/2, 43 ILM (2004) 133, para 154.

68 Ibid.

69 CMS Gas Transmission Company v The Argentine Republic, Award, ICSID Case No ARB/01/8, 12 May 2005, 44 ILM 1205, para 281; and LG&E Energy Corp, LG&E Capital Corp and LG&E International Inc v Argentine Republic, Decision on Liability, 3 October 2006, ICSID Case No ARB/02/1, 46 ILM 36 (2007), paras 132–139.

70 High Court, Judgment of 6 March 2008. Reproduced as annex in SL Harring & W Odendaal, Kessl: A New Jurisprudence for Land Reform in Namibia? Windhoek: Legal Assistance Centre and Namibian Economic Policy Research Unit, 2008, at http://www.lac.org.na/projects/lead/Pdf/kessl.pdf, which also provides a detailed commentary to the judgment.

71 LE Peterson & R Garland, Bilateral Investment Treaties and Land Reform in Southern Africa, Montreal: Rights & Democracy, 2010.

72 Waste Management, Inc (US) v United Mexican States, Award, 30 April 2004, ICSID Case No ARB(AF)/00/3, para 98.

73 Railroad Development Corporation (RDC) v Republic of Guatemala, Award, 29 June 2012, ICSID Case No ARB/07/23.

74 Schill & Jacob, 'Trends in international investment agreements'.

75 Partial Award, 17 March 2006, Permanent Court of Arbitration, at http://ita.law.uvic.ca/documents/SalukaPartialawardFinal.pdf, para 305.

76 El Paso Energy International Company v The Argentine Republic, Award, 31 October 2011, ICSID Case No ARB/03/15; and Merrill & Ring Forestry LP v The Government of Canada, Award, 31 March 2010, at http://italaw.com/cases/documents/1266. In this case, the tribunal defined fair and equitable treatment as

'protect[ing] against all such acts or behavior that might infringe a sense of fairness, equity and reasonableness' (para 210).

77 L Cotula, *Human Rights, Natural Resource and Investment Law in a Globalised World: Shades of Grey in the Shadow of the Law*, London: Routledge, 2012.
78 Sandbrook, 'Polanyi and post-neoliberalism in the global South', p 417.
79 JG Ruggie, 'International regimes, transactions, and change: embedded liberalism in the postwar economic order', *International Organization*, 36(2), 1982, pp 379–415; and Sandbrook, 'Polanyi and post-neoliberalism in the global South'.

Notes on Contributor

Lorenzo Cotula is Principal Researcher in Law and Sustainable Development, International Institute for Environment and Development, London. He has published extensively on natural resource investments and pressures on land in low and middle-income countries, and on the national, international and transnational legal frameworks that regulate these processes. Lorenzo also leads 'Legal Tools for Citizen Empowerment', an initiative to strengthen local rights and voices within natural resource investments. He holds a Law Degree from the University 'La Sapienza' of Rome, an MSc in Development Studies from the London School of Economics, a PhD in Law from the University of Edinburgh and a Postgraduate Certificate in Sustainable Business from the University of Cambridge.

Human Rights Responses to Land Grabbing: a right to food perspective

CHRISTOPHE GOLAY*a* & IRENE BIGLINO*a*

aGeneva Academy of International Humanitarian Law and Human Rights, Geneva, Switzerland

ABSTRACT   *This article approaches the debate on 'contemporary land grabbing' from a human rights perspective, focusing on one right that is particularly threatened: the right to food. It sketches an analytical framework grounded in international human rights law and the contribution such a framework can bring to the land-grabbing debate. Following a brief historical background on the right to food and its articulation in international human rights law, the paper expands on this by focusing on what can be called human rights responses to land grabbing from a right to food standpoint. The analysis considers the contributions of different actors in the human rights sphere and examines the role of the UN Committee on World Food Security and its recently adopted Voluntary Guidelines on the responsible governance of tenure of land, fisheries and forests. It also investigates how the phenomenon has been addressed by the UN human rights mechanisms, drawing on relevant practice of the UN treaty bodies and the Human Rights Council, with a focus on the Special Rapporteur on the right to food and the Special Rapporteur on the human rights situation in Cambodia. The engagement of regional human rights system with the issue of large-scale land transactions is also analysed.*

The overarching aim of this article is to approach the current debate on 'contemporary land grabbing' from a human rights perspective and, more specifically, to present an analysis of responses to land grabbing by different human rights actors. The discussion hinges on the recognition that land grabbing can be viewed as a human rights issue, and the chosen focus is on one right that is particularly threatened: the right to food.

The expressions 'land grab' or 'land grabbing' are used to describe the widespread, rapid increase of commercial land transactions that involve the acquisition or long-term lease of large areas of land by investors,[1] particularly when these are disproportionate to the average size of other land holdings in the area under scrutiny.[2] The transactions take a variety of forms, depending on the players involved, the drivers underlying the transactions, and the mechanisms through which these are carried out. As these different aspects are taken up in greater detail in other articles in this issue, it will suffice to acknowledge that the kinds of transactions which will inform the analysis range from acquisitions to leases, to land concessions and other contractual arrangements. For the purposes of this paper, therefore, a broad conception of the phenomenon is preferred and the term large-scale land transactions (LSLTs) will be used to describe it.

As scholars who have analysed the issue indicate, the use of a human rights lens to assess LSLTs rests on the premise that individuals and communities, as rights holders, are entitled to a set of rights and procedural safeguards that cannot be forfeited or 'traded away' in the context of such transactions.[3] In this regard a human rights-based approach is firmly anchored on the recognition that states have corresponding, binding obligations under international human rights law to respect, protect and fulfil human rights, and that LSLTs 'should under no circumstances be allowed to trump the human rights obligations of the states concerned'.[4] This is different from other approaches that promote voluntary commitments by states or business enterprises, such as corporate social responsibility.[5] As will be illustrated, and as S Narula also suggests, assessing the implications of LSLTs within a human rights framework also entails a distinct vision of land as a 'a productive, rights-fulfilling asset' which unlocks the realisation of many human rights, including the right to food.[6]

The first part of the article provides a brief historical background of the right to food and sets out its articulation in international human rights law. The second part focuses on human rights responses to LSLTs, specifically from a right to food standpoint. The key actors whose contribution is assessed are the UN Human Rights Council and its Special Rapporteurs, the UN treaty bodies, the UN Committee on World Food Security, and selected judicial and quasi-judicial human rights mechanisms at the regional level.[7]

The right to food

In order to provide a conceptual framework, this part of the article traces the legal and political recognition of the right to food at the international level.[8] The right's inclusion in regional human rights instruments and national constitutions is also touched upon.[9]

Legal and political recognition of the right to food

The right to food was first recognised as a human right in the Universal Declaration of Human Rights (UDHR) and the International Covenant on Economic, Social and Cultural Rights (ICESCR).[10] Article 25 of the UDHR provides that:

> Everyone has the right to a standard of living adequate for the health and well-being of himself and of his family, including food, clothing, housing and medical care and necessary social services, and the right to security in the event of unemployment, sickness, disability, widowhood, old age or other lack of livelihood in circumstances beyond his control.[11]

The ICESCR recognises 'the right of everyone to an adequate standard of living for himself and his family, including adequate food...and to the continuous improvement of living conditions' (Article 11, § 1) as well as 'the fundamental right of everyone to be free from hunger' (Article 11, § 2). At the international level the formal legal recognition of the right to food in the ICESCR—with its two main components being the right to adequate food and the fundamental right to be free from hunger—was not immediately followed by a strong commitment at the political level to ensure its full implementation. It was only in 1996, at the Food and Agriculture Organization (FAO) World Food Summit (WFS), that political leaders made a more solemn commitment towards the realisation of the right and requested the UN human rights system to better define it.[12] In response, the UN Committee on Economic, Social and Cultural Rights (CESCR) adopted its General Comment 12 in 1999,[13] in which it outlined the normative content of the right to food and states' corresponding obligations, while the UN Commission on Human Rights created the mandate of the first UN Special Rapporteur on the Right to Food in 2000.[14] At the second WFS, organised by FAO in 2002, states welcomed these developments and tasked an intergovernmental working group with the elaboration of Voluntary Guidelines to support the progressive realisation of the right to adequate food in the context of national food security (*Right to Food Guidelines*) in order to provide practical guidance for reducing hunger.[15] The *Right to Food Guidelines* are voluntary by nature but they represent an important political commitment to strengthen the implementation of the right to food. They were adopted unanimously by the FAO Council in November 2004 and, since then, have been used as practical tools by states that have chosen to address hunger through a rights-based approach.[16]

With the 2008 global food crisis, the UN Secretary General made a strong appeal to integrate the right to food more effectively in responses to food insecurity. At a high-level meeting on food security in 2009 the Secretary General stated:

> We must continue to meet urgent hunger and humanitarian needs by providing food and nutrition assistance and safety nets, while focusing on improving food production and smallholder agriculture. This is the twin-track approach...We should be ready to add a third track, the right to food, as a basis for analysis, action and accountability.[17]

The recognition of the right to food at the international level was not mirrored at the regional level, where the right appears explicitly in only one instrument, the Protocol of San Salvador completing the American Convention on Human Rights, which is characterised by weak enforcement mechanisms.[18] To fill this gap, other human rights, including the rights to life, health, environment, and property, have been used to protect the right to food indirectly in the African and Inter-American human rights systems.[19] At the national level the right to food has been incorporated in a growing number of constitutions in the past 20 years, most recently in Brazil, Bolivia, Ecuador and Kenya, and it is increasingly being adjudicated by courts.[20]

Definition of the right to food and states' corresponding obligations

In its General Comment 12, the CESCR provides the following definition of the right to food:

> The right to adequate food is realized when every man, woman and child, alone or in community with others, has physical and economic access at all times to adequate food or means for its procurement.[21]

According to this definition, all human beings have a right to food that is available in sufficient quantity, nutritionally and culturally adequate and physically and economically accessible.[22] Interpreting the right to food through the lens of human dignity, the UN Special Rapporteur on the Right to Food has underlined that it is the right of every human being to feed oneself and one's family with dignity.[23] As stated in the *Right to Food Guidelines*, this can be achieved by ensuring everyone's access to productive resources, in particular land, water and seeds, but also fisheries or forests, as well as access to labour or social assistance schemes.[24]

The corresponding obligations of states were first developed by human rights experts and subsequently defined by the CESCR, the UN Special Rapporteur on the Right to Food and by states through the adoption of the *Right to Food Guidelines*.[25] It is now generally accepted that state parties to the ICESCR have the obligation to respect, protect and fulfil the right to food, without any discrimination.[26] The obligation to *respect* is essentially an obligation to refrain from action that would interfere with the right to food. The obligation to *protect* requires states to ensure that enterprises and private individuals do not deprive individuals of their access to adequate food. The obligation to *fulfil* implies that states should, first of all, facilitate the realisation of the right to food by creating an environment that enables individuals and groups to feed themselves by their own means and, second, provide the right to food for those who are not capable of feeding themselves for reasons beyond their control.[27]

In respecting, protecting and fulfilling the right to food states must comply with human rights principles, in particular the principles of participation, accountability, non-discrimination, transparency, human dignity, empowerment and the rule of law.[28] When they develop and implement food security strategies, policies and programmes, states must therefore consult and inform all relevant actors, adopt and use budgets in a transparent manner, and take measures with the explicit aim of improving the realisation the right to food, especially with respect to vulnerable groups. States must also ensure that these steps empower rights holders to claim their rights and duty bearers to fulfil their obligations. Finally, under this framework access to justice must be available to victims of violations of the right to food.[29] In the context of LSLTs, the foregoing discussion entails that the conclusion and implementation of LSLTs should not lead to violations but, rather, to a better realisation of the right to food, and should be carried out in compliance with the foregoing human rights principles.[30]

Access to land and security of tenure as key components of the right to food

Access to land and security of tenure are guiding threads in the work of the CESCR,[31] and in the UN Special Rapporteur on the Right to Food, and clearly surface in the *Right to Food Guidelines*. The Special Rapporteur has stated, for example, that:

> The right to food requires that States refrain from taking measures that may deprive individuals of access to productive resources on which they depend when they produce food for themselves (the obligation to respect), that they protect such access from encroachment by other private parties (obligation to protect) and that they seek to strengthen people's access to and utilization of resources and means to ensure their livelihoods, including food security (the obligation to fulfil).

In two reports presented to the General Assembly in 2002 and 2010, the former and current Special Rapporteurs on the Right to Food emphasised the need to guarantee access to land and security of tenure, including through agrarian reform, to ensure the right to food of rural communities.[32] Both underlined the fact that access to land is essential for the majority of people suffering from hunger, who work as smallholder farmers or agricultural labourers because the land they have is not sufficient or otherwise inadequate.[33] Olivier De Schutter, in particular, has highlighted the special needs of indigenous peoples, smallholders, pastoralists and fisherfolk and concluded that, for many of them, private ownership of land and market-led land reforms are not the most suitable options. Instead, he recommended that states recognise the emergence of a human right to land and take measures to make it a reality through the recognition of different categories of land use, including communal property.[34]

The two Special Rapporteurs have also emphasised that women and indigenous people enjoy special protection in international law. Women's rights to land and property are recognised in the Convention on the Elimination of All Forms of Discrimination Against Women (CEDAW),[35] and the rights of indigenous peoples in the International Labour Organization (ILO) Convention No 169 concerning Indigenous and Tribal Peoples and the UN Declaration on the Rights of Indigenous Peoples.[36] Indigenous peoples' rights of ownership, possession and control of their land, territories and resources, and states' obligations to guarantee their effective protection, as well as the requirement of indigenous peoples' prior, free and informed consent, are particularly important in the context of LSLTS.[37] Finally, the need to protect access to land has also been a central element in the Special Rapporteur on the Right to Food's reports on his recent missions to China, Mexico, South Africa and Madagascar.[38]

Finally, when states adopted the *Right to Food Guidelines*, they recognised that the right to food protects the right of rural communities to access productive resources or the means of food production, including land.[39] The *Guidelines* provide that:

> States should pursue inclusive, non-discriminatory and sound economic, agriculture, fisheries, forestry, land use, and, as appropriate, land reform policies, all of which will permit farmers, fishers, foresters and other food producers, partic-

ularly women, to earn a fair return from their labour, capital and management, and encourage conservation and sustainable management of natural resources, including in marginal areas.[40]

The consensus of states with regard to their obligations to respect, protect and fulfil the right to food in the context of productive resources further emerges in the *Guidelines* as follows:

> States should respect and protect the rights of individuals with respect to resources such as land, water, forests, fisheries and livestock without any discrimination. Where necessary and appropriate, States should carry out land reforms and other policy reforms consistent with their human rights obligations and in accordance with the rule of law in order to secure efficient and equitable access to land and to strengthen pro-poor growth [...] States should also provide women with secure and equal access to, control over, and benefits from productive resources, including credit, land, water and appropriate technologies.[41]

Human rights responses to land grabbing

This section of the article considers the contributions of different actors operating within the UN human rights system with regard to LSLTs and what recommendations they have put forward in this remit. The role of selected regional mechanisms for human rights protection will also be outlined. It must be acknowledged that the majority of the actors examined were dealing with a variety of land-related issues from a human rights perspective even before the vocabulary of 'land grabbing' and its consolidation as a 'phenomenon' began to emerge against the backdrop of the 2008 global food crisis.[42] Access to land and natural resources, forced evictions, security of tenure, agrarian reform, free, prior informed consent and landlessness, among many other issues, have been scrutinised within the UN system and regional human rights systems. This means that a conceptual and analytical grounding for the application of a human rights-based approach to LSLTs already existed.

The United Nations human rights system

The first cluster of responses that will be examined originates from the UN system. The section will first focus on the UN human rights mechanisms by drawing on relevant examples from the work of the Human Rights Council and the UN treaty bodies. It will then proceed to assess the contribution of the FAO and the UN Committee on World Food Security.

The Human Rights Council and its mechanisms. The UN Special Procedures are a key mechanism established by the Human Rights Council for monitoring the promotion and protection of human rights. The Special Procedures mandate holders include special rapporteurs, independent experts and working groups. Their mandates can be thematic, for example on human rights defenders, or the right to food, or cover all human rights in a country.[43] In the following sections emphasis will be placed on how the human rights implications of LSLTS have been examined, in particular, by two special procedure mandate holders, the Special Rapporteur on the Right to Food and the Special Rapporteur on the Human Rights Situation in Cambodia. The work of the Advisory Committee of the Human Rights Council, which is the Council's 'think-tank', will also be presented.[44]

The first and current Special Rapporteurs on the Right to Food have strongly emphasised the need to protect access to natural resources, including land, to protect the right to food.[45] In March 2010, in response to the proliferation of LSLTS, Olivier De Schutter submitted a report to the Human Rights Council in which he described the phenomenon and its causes and presented a set of human rights principles applicable to large-scale land acquisitions and leases.[46] The report's objective was to delineate the 'minimum human rights obligations' that states, but also investors and financial institutions, must comply with when negotiating and concluding LSLTS. The Special Rapporteur emphasises that the principles 'are not optional; [but] follow from existing international human rights norms'.[47] In summary, these principles state that negotiations leading to LSLTS must comply with a number of procedural requirements, including the informed participation of local communities; that LSLTS must lead to adequate benefit sharing; and that under no circumstances should LSLTS be allowed to 'trump' the human rights obligations of states.[48] According to De Schutter,

> States would be acting in violation of the human right to food if, by leasing or selling land to investors (whether domestic or foreign), they were depriving the local population of access to productive resources indispensable to their livelihoods. They would also be violating the right to food if they negotiated such agreements without ensuring that this will not result in food insecurity, for instance because this would create a dependency on foreign aid or on increasingly volatile and unpredictable international markets (as large proportions of the food produced as a result of the foreign investment would be shipped to the country of origin of the investor or sold on the international markets), or because the revenues of the most marginal local farmers would decrease as a result of the competition consequent on the arrival of such investors.[49]

The 11 principles provide an excellent summary of the main elements of a human rights analysis of LSLTS. Part of the added value of the principles is that they extend available frameworks, such as the protection of indigenous peoples' right to land, or the requirement of free, prior and informed consent, to all potentially affected people, including smallholder farmers and rural labourers. Moreover, they cover a number of different situations and contexts in which LSLTS can take place.[50] The 11 principles include the obligation to conduct negotiations leading to LSLTS in a fully transparent manner and with the participation of local communities; the requirement of free, prior and informed consent of the local communities concerned; the general prohibition of forced evictions; the obligation to recognise and protect land tenure rights of local communities; the importance of sharing of revenues generated by LSLTS with the local population; the necessity of choosing labour-intensive farming systems in countries facing high levels of rural poverty and few employment opportunities in other sectors; the need to protect the environment; the necessity of including clear and detailed obligations for investors in the agreements, with sanctions for non-compliance; the need to include a clause providing that a certain minimum percentage of the crops produced will be sold in local markets in food-importing countries, to contribute to local food security; the necessity to undertake prior impact assessments, including on food security, environment and employment; the obligation to protect indigenous peoples' rights; and the obligation to respect the applicable ILO instruments.[51]

De Schutter's principles were not received unopposed and attracted some criticism from states and civil society organisations. In March 2010 member states of the Human Rights Council merely 'took note' of the principles 'with appreciation' but did not urge all actors to implement them.[52] As explained by Claeys and Vanloqueren, transnational agrarian movements and non-governmental organisations such as La Via Campesina, GRAIN, and FIAN, feared that the principles would 'legitimise' land grabbing, instead of contributing to halt the phenomenon.[53] In response, the Special Rapporteur insisted that these principles represented a minimum baseline aimed at making the right to food operational, and that LSLTS would not be justified simply because they complied with the principles. Moreover, the Special Rapporteur strongly advocated a paradigm shift towards investments in agriculture directed to smallholders rather than industrial agriculture for export.[54] De Schutter's principles have been used as a yardstick to assess the implications of LSLTS in practice. For example, in 2010 the Swiss government participated in a public symposium, alongside the Director of Addax Bioenergy, a Geneva-based company investing in Sierra Leone, and civil society organisations representing communities affected by LSLTS in Sierra Leone.[55] During the event the human rights impact of the proposed land transaction was discussed with reference to the Principles.

The engagement of the special procedures in the debate on human rights and LSLTS is not limited to the work of thematic mandate-holders, but is also detectable in the work of special rapporteurs entrusted with country mandates. While several earlier UN reports have examined problems generated by land concessions in Cambodia,[56] the 2012 report by the Special Rapporteur on the Human Rights Situation in Cambodia, Surya Subedi, provides the most detailed assessment to date.[57] The focus of the report is on one category of transactions, namely land concessions granted to private companies, both foreign and national, for large-scale agriculture, mining, infrastructure development, tourism and other purposes.[58] Although the report does not contain a separate heading specifically devoted to the right to food, this emerges as a recurring theme throughout, and a multitude of components of the right, first and foremost the impact such transactions have on livelihoods, surface with particular clarity.

For example, the Special Rapporteur explains how lack of access to natural resources has exposed communities to problems with food security, forcing many communities to leave their areas in search of work or food.[59] He further illustrates how concessions on indigenous peoples' land, in particular, impair their ability to gather food and forest products and to hunt and fish.[60] The report also examines how one consequence of LSLTS, the development of agro-industry, threatens the traditional agricultural systems of indigenous peoples, and therefore their food security.[61] Other highly relevant questions for the right to food and food security discussed by the Special Rapporteur include access to sufficient safe drinking water for personal and domestic uses, including food preparation.[62] The report also analyses the specific impact of LSLTS on women who, for cultural reasons, are often excluded even from those labour opportunities which arise in the context of agricultural land concessions. Moreover, in the case of urban land concessions resulting in eviction, women have lost jobs and sources of livelihood, in some cases more than men, especially when they are relocated far from city centres.[63] If such patterns persist, the Special Rapporteur warns that women will risk further marginalisation, impoverishment and undernourishment.

Among a large number of detailed recommendations, the Special Rapporteur calls on Cambodia to closely examine the impact of concessions on livelihood and income-generating opportunities of affected families through a set of concrete actions.[64] He further recommends that relevant government bodies and business enterprises comply with legal requirements for public consultations, and that standards of free, prior and informed consent be rigorously applied when consulting with all indigenous peoples.[65]

A further mechanism of the Human Rights Council we examine is its Advisory Committee. Building on the work of the Special Rapporteur on the Right to Food, the Human Rights Council took a number of initiatives in recent years that are relevant to the protection of the right to food in the context of LSLTS. In 2010 the Council, under considerable pressure from civil society actors, in particular La Via Campesina, mandated its Advisory Committee to produce a study on ways and means to further advance the rights of people working in rural areas.[66] In response to this request, the Advisory Committee presented its final study on the topic at the 19th session of the Human Rights Council in March 2012.[67] The study identified LSLTS as one of the most serious threats to the right to food and concluded that 'despite the existing human rights framework, peasants and other people working in rural areas are victims of multiple human rights violations that lead to their extreme vulnerability to hunger and poverty'.[68] In order to overcome this situation, the Advisory Committee recommended to the Human Rights Council 1) to better implement existing international norms; 2) to address the normative gaps under international human rights law, including by recognising the right to land; and 3) to elaborate a new legal instrument on the rights of people working in rural areas.[69] In the annex to its final study the Advisory Committee proposed a Declaration on the Rights of Peasants and Other People Working in Rural Areas, which recognises, inter alia, peasants' right to land and territory. The text of the Advisory Committee's Declaration is largely inspired by the Declaration on the Rights of Peasants —Women and Men adopted by La Via Campesina in 2008, which demonstrates the impact that social movements can have when they make use of a human rights framework.[70]

In September 2012 the Human Rights Council adopted a resolution on the promotion and protection of the human rights of peasants and other people working in rural areas. Through the Resolution the Council decided to create a Working Group to negotiate, finalise and present to the Human Rights Council a draft UN Declaration on the Rights of Peasants and Other People Working in Rural Areas, on the basis of the Declaration proposed by the Advisory Committee.[71] The first session of the Working Group took place in July 2013 and the elaboration of the UN Declaration is expected to take several years.[72]

The United Nations treaty bodies. The human rights treaty bodies are committees made up of independent experts, established under the international human rights treaties, which monitor the implementation of the treaties through the periodic review of reports submitted by state parties.[73] LSLTs have been scrutinised by different treaty bodies, including the CESCR, the Committee on the Elimination of Racial Discrimination (CERD), CEDAW and the Committee on the Rights of the Child (CRC). A number of closely interconnected, common threads run through their observations.

The first overarching concern relates to the actual or potential human rights implications of internal displacement and evictions caused by LSLTs, which often lead to drastic changes in livelihood opportunities. A connected concern is that in many cases the displaced groups are not resettled and compensated for their livelihood losses. Turning to concrete examples, in its review of Togo, CEDAW urged that country to ensure that 'land lease contracts with foreign companies do not result in forced eviction and internal displacement or the increased food insecurity and poverty of local populations, including women and girls, and that the company concerned and/or the State party provide the affected communities with adequate compensation and alternative land'.[74] An almost identical recommendation was issued in CEDAW's review of Ethiopia.[75] In its review of India the CESCR was similarly concerned about the effects of displacement and forced evictions occurring as a consequence of land acquisitions by private and state actors for the purposes of development projects, such as the construction of dams, as well as displacement following the designation of large areas of land as tax-free Special Economic Zones.[76]

In its evaluation of reports submitted with regard to Madagascar the CESCR noted with concern that legislation relating to investments allowing land acquisition by foreign investors, including for agricultural purposes, generated a number of adverse consequences regarding access of peasants and people living in rural areas to natural resources present on the land, with consequences for their ability to produce food.[77] The CESCR explicitly observed that the land acquisitions under scrutiny led to negative repercussions for the realisation of the right to food by the Malagasy population. It called on Madagascar to review the legislation in question in order to facilitate the acquisition of land by peasants and persons living in rural areas, as well as their access to natural resources.[78] It further recommended that the state party launch a national debate on investment in agriculture and seek, before any contracts with foreign companies, the free and informed consent of the persons concerned.[79] In its consideration of Cambodia, the CESCR examined issues relating to the human rights impact of LSLTs in quite some detail, explicitly reporting that 'authorities of the State party are *actively involved in land-grabbing*'.[80] The CESCR expressed grave concerns over the vast concessions granted to private companies and noted the increase in forced evictions and threats of eviction linked to such concessions,[81] expressing deep concern about the lack of effective consultation with persons affected by forced evictions. It called attention to the inadequate compensation or relocation provisions for families forcibly removed from their properties.[82]

The second common thread involves the impact of LSLTs on the livelihoods and right to food of indigenous peoples specifically. The latter has been central in the reviews of a large number of states, and has been tackled by virtually all treaty bodies. Emphasis is placed on the right to free, prior and informed consent of indigenous peoples to externally imposed policies and activities that directly affect their livelihoods. For example, as noted above, the CESCR examined the impact of land concessions on indigenous peoples during its assessments of Cambodia. In particular, the Committee highlighted in its recommendations the need to carry out environmental and social impact assessments and consultations with affected communities with regard to economic activities, including mining and oil explorations, 'with a view to ensuring that these activities do not deprive the indigenous peoples to the full enjoyment of their rights to their ancestral lands and natural resources'.[83] In further pointing out that legislation providing for the titling of indigenous communities' lands had not been implemented effectively, the CESCR urged Cambodia to provide for the implementation of the provisions without delay. Turning to other states, in a review of reports submitted by the Democratic Republic of Congo, the CESCR called for enforcement of an existing moratorium on mining concessions and urged the government to ensure that forest-related land concessions do not deprive indigenous peoples of the enjoyment of their lands and resources.[84] In the same vein the CESCR was concerned about the adverse effects of natural resource exploitation in indigenous territories in Chad and Mexico and made recommendations in this regard.[85]

The CERD has extensively examined the protection of livelihoods of indigenous populations. In 2007, for instance, it expressed concerns about 'the denial of indigenous peoples' rights' in Indonesia in connection with LSLTs for agro-industrial purposes, such as the expansion of oil palm plantations on indigenous territories.[86] The Committee called on Indonesia to secure indigenous peoples' ownership rights to their lands, territories and resources and to obtain their consent before further oil palm development.[87] The CERD voiced similar concerns the same year in its review of the Democratic Republic of Congo. The Committee considered that granting concessions for large-scale forestry projects constituted interference with the rights of indigenous communities, in particular those who depended on the forest for their livelihoods.[88] In its consideration of reports concerning the Lao People's Democratic Republic, the Committee reiterated the right of communities to free, prior and informed consent and called for the state to ensure that this is respected in the planning and implementation of large-scale projects affecting their lands and resources.[89] Express references were made to the importance of 'the cultural aspect of land, as an integral part of the identity of some ethnic groups'.[90] Similar considerations and recommendations were echoed in the reviews of Viet Nam, Suriname, Peru and Colombia.[91]

CERD also scrutinised the human rights impact of land concessions in Cambodia. The Committee noted that such transactions were in many cases being conducted 'to the detriment of particularly vulnerable communities such as indigenous peoples'.[92] Another concern related to reports that concessions affecting land traditionally occupied by indigenous peoples were being granted without full consideration, or exhaustion of procedures provided for by national legislation.[93] The Committee strongly encouraged the development of a series of protective measures, such as procedures to delay the issuing of concessions on indigenous lands and only pursuant to free, prior informed consent by the affected communities.[94] The reach of the Committee's recommendations extended even further, as it called on business entities negotiating concessions to take into consideration their corporate social responsibility as it relates to the rights and well-being of local populations.[95]

The foregoing discussion unearths another recurrent theme, namely the question of the disproportionately negative effect, in human rights terms, that LSLTS have on populations that are vulnerable to discrimination and face conditions of marginalisation or disadvantage. In addition to indigenous peoples, concerns have been raised about negative impacts on women, children, rural communities and small-scale farmers. CEDAW focused its attention on female heads of household in Cambodia who had lost their sources of livelihood because of the confiscation of land by private companies and were excluded from decision-making processes concerning land distribution.[96] Similarly, in its concluding observations on Cambodia in June 2011, the CRC expressed deep concern that thousands of children and families, especially the urban poor, small-scale farmers and indigenous communities, were continuing to be deprived of their land 'as a result of land grabbing and forced evictions carried out by people in positions of power'.[97] The Committee recommended the establishment of a 'national moratorium on evictions until the determination of the legality of land claims is made'.[98] Moreover, the CRC specifically called on Cambodia to fully implement the recommendations of the Special Rapporteur on the Situation of Human Rights in Cambodia regarding access to land and livelihood.[99] As an overarching recommendation in its assessment of Cambodia, CERD requested that a proper balance be struck between development objectives and the rights of citizens and that the former not be enacted 'at the expense of the rights of vulnerable persons and groups covered by the Convention [on the Elimination of All Forms of Racial Discrimination]'.[100] Following CEDAW's review of Laos, it was recommended that the state party ensure that development projects be implemented only after conducting gender impact assessments involving rural women.[101]

Finally, an issue that warrants a separate discussion relates to land policy reforms financed and promoted through development assistance, which in certain cases have been found to have negative impacts on the enjoyment of human rights, including the right to food.[102] A case that came to the CESCR's attention involves the German Agency for International Cooperation's financing of the land titling system in Cambodia. It has been suggested that the scheme contributed to weakening the tenure status of vulnerable and marginalised communities, exposing them to the risk of eviction as a result of LSLTS.[103] In tune with the foregoing considerations, in its review of Germany in 2011, the CESCR explicitly cited the land-titling scheme in Cambodia to illustrate the concern that 'the State party's development cooperation programme has supported projects that have reportedly resulted in the violation of economic, social and cultural rights.[104]

An overview of the treaty bodies' engagement must also briefly consider individual communications procedures. A number of treaties are supplemented by Optional Protocols allowing for the consideration of individual complaints, usually referred to as 'communications'.[105] Avenues that are potentially relevant for the right to food are those established by the Optional Protocol to the International Covenant on Civil and Political Rights, by Article 14 of the Convention on the Elimination of All Forms of Racial Discrimination, and the Optional Protocol CEDAW.[106] Turning to practical cases, there are some examples from the Human Rights Committee, the body entrusted with monitoring the International Covenant on Civil and Political Rights (ICCPR), in which indigenous communities have sought protection of their right to food through the protection of their way of life, their economic activities and their means of subsistence.[107] These cases, though not necessarily dealing with LSLTS as such, provide some useful lessons on how these mechanisms may be used in the future to challenge the actual or potential human rights ramifications of land grabbing.

A complaints procedure that has recently become available is the one established by the Optional Protocol to the International Covenant on Economic, Social and Cultural rights.[108] The Protocol, which entered into force on 5 May 2013, provides for the right of individuals and groups to submit complaints for violations of the rights contained in the Covenant. As seen in Part 2.1, the Covenant explicitly enshrines the right to food, making this complaint procedure ideally suited to submit right-to-food-based communications in connection with LSLTS in the future.

The UN Committee on World Food Security

The UN Committee on World Food Security was established in response to the 2008 food crisis, with the aim of becoming the principal international and intergovernmental platform on food security.[109] It is the result of a reform of the FAO Committee on World Food Security, which was created in 1974 and was composed of a selected number of states. The UN Committee on World Food Security comprises all states and allows for the participation of UN agencies, international and regional financial institutions, civil society organisations and international agricultural research institutions. It also includes a High Level Panel of Experts.

In May 2012, in response to the growing phenomenon of LSLTS and intense civil society pressure, the UN Committee on World Food Security adopted Voluntary Guidelines on the Responsible Governance of Tenure of Land, Fisheries and Forests in the Context of National Food Security (*Land Tenure Guidelines*).[110] The adoption of these Guidelines is the result of several years of negotiations among states, civil society organisations, peasant movements and the private sector, with the participation of the UN Special Rapporteur on the Right to Food.[111] The main objective of the *Land Tenure Guidelines* is to promote secure tenure rights and equitable access to land, fisheries and forests in order to reduce poverty and realise the right to food. Two central elements of the guidelines are the need to identify, record and respect legitimate tenure rights, whether formally recorded or not, and to protect tenure rights holders against forced evictions (guidelines 3.1.1 and 3.1.2). Special protection is to be accorded to smallholders and to indigenous peoples and other communities with customary tenure systems (guidelines 7.3).

The guidelines also recommend that states provide safeguards to protect legitimate tenure rights, human rights, livelihoods, food security and the environment from risks that could arise from LSLTS (guideline 12.6) and that responsible investments should do no harm, safeguard against dispossession of legitimate tenure right holders and environmental damage, and respect human rights (guideline 12.4). The guidelines further emphasise that redistributive reforms can facilitate broad and equitable access to land and inclusive rural development (guidelines 15.1). While it may be too soon to evaluate the impact of the *Land Tenure Guidelines*, it is clear that they offer a practical tool, of a voluntary nature but grounded in legally binding human rights obligations, to respond to LSLTS.

Regional human rights systems

At the regional level, human rights mechanisms in Africa and the Americas have displayed increasing activism in enforcing safeguards with respect to transactions or projects that affect indigenous peoples' and other communities' traditional lands and resources. In the cases cited below, the right to food has not been the direct subject of adjudication, but rather has been addressed within the context of other rights, such as the right to life, the right to an adequate standard of living, the right to personal integrity and the right to property. It must also be acknowledged that the vocabulary of 'land grabbing' does not surface as such in the judgments, and it is debatable whether or not some of the transactions may be considered 'large-scale'. However, the cases can yield valuable lessons and disclose possible entry points for litigation before the regional human rights mechanisms grounded on human rights violations in the context of LSLTS.

The Inter-American Court of Human Rights' case law reflects recognition of the special connection between indigenous peoples, land and subsistence activities. In a number of cases the Court interpreted the right to property of indigenous populations as including an implicit obligation on the part of the state to recognise and protect the right to collective ownership of land with a view to guaranteeing such communities' access to their means of subsistence. For example, in 2001 in *Mayagna (Sumo) Awas Tingni Community v Nicaragua*, for example, the Inter-American Court protected the access of over 100 families belonging to an indigenous community to their ancestral lands, which were threatened by a government concession to a Korean company.[112] The Court held that the state had violated its obligation to refrain from taking any action, whether direct or indirect, that could affect the lands on which members of the community lived and carried out their subsistence activities.[113]

In the 2007 case of *Saramaka v Suriname* the Saramaka community accused the state of violating the American Convention on Human Rights (the American Convention) because it failed to provide legal property title to its traditionally occupied lands.[114] It was argued that the state had granted logging and mining concessions on the land without consulting the community and without obtaining their free, prior informed consent. The applicants specifically contended that these activities placed 'a severe stress on the capacity of Saramaka lands and forests to meet basic subsistence needs'.[115] The Court drew on its previous case law and held that restrictions imposed on indigenous property give rise to violations of the American Convention when they entail 'a denial of the traditions and customs of the indigenous community in a manner that endangers the very survival of the group and its members'.[116] In the 2012 case of *Sarayaku v Ecuador*,[117] the Inter-American Court protected the rights of the Sarayaku indigenous community against a concession to an Argentinian oil corporation. The applicants contended that the forcible entry into their territory and the placement of explosives for the purposes of oil exploration in the forest where its members lived had serious repercussions for the community's right to food.[118] They further alleged that the oil extraction activities had the potential to severely affect the food security of the members of the community, as the activities were planned in areas they used for hunting, fishing and gathering.[119] Among other rights, the Court held that the right to life and the right to personal integrity had been violated.[120]

In the African system the African Commission on Human and Peoples' Rights has also addressed related issues. In *Centre for Minority Rights Development (Kenya) and Minority Rights Group International on behalf of Endorois Welfare Council v Kenya*, the applicants' claims challenged the establishment of a game reserve and a mining concession on traditional indigenous lands on human rights grounds. The African Commission found that Kenya had, among other rights, violated the Endorois' right to property, the right to development and the right of peoples to freely dispose of their wealth and natural resources.[121] The Commission acknowledged that, as a consequence of their dispossession, the community had been 'relegated to semi-arid land', which was unsuitable for pastoralism.[122] Grazing animals, a key means of subsistence, had been made *de facto* impossible and access to clean drinking water had also been seriously undermined as a result of loss of the land.[123]

Conclusions

As explained in the first part of this article, the right to food, as recognised in legally binding and soft law instruments, provides a solid basis for evaluating the impacts of LSLTS on the food security of affected communities from a human rights perspective. In particular, the *Right to Food Guidelines*, elaborated through a participatory process and accepted by all states, of a voluntary nature but grounded in legally binding human rights obligations, provide useful practical guidance on how to perform such an evaluation.

The second part of the article provided concrete evidence of a steadily increasing engagement with LSLTS by human rights actors and monitoring bodies. The adoption of the minimum human rights principles by the UN Special Rapporteur on the Right to Food and the Voluntary Guidelines on the Governance of Land Tenure by all states represents an effort of particular relevance. At present there is considerable potential to move further with the elaboration of a UN Declaration on the Rights of Peasants that would recognise a right to land for small-scale farmers and landless people.

The UN treaty bodies have also engaged with various aspects of LSLTS and issued recommendations to states. Several common threads can be extracted from the recommendations of the treaty bodies examined in the second part of the article. First, the actual or potential human rights implications of the internal displacement and evictions that occur as a consequence of LSLTS, which often threaten livelihood opportunities, have been repeatedly scrutinised. Second, the manner in which LSLTS may negatively influence the livelihoods of indigenous peoples and populations that are vulnerable to discrimination and face conditions of marginalisation or disadvantage have been identified by the treaty bodies as a key cause for concern. Finally, land policy reforms financed and promoted through development assistance have, in certain cases, been found by the treaty bodies to entail negative impacts on the enjoyment of human rights, including the right to food. As far as communications procedures under the treaty bodies are concerned, the recent entry into force of the Optional Protocol to the ICESCR paves the way for communications explicitly grounded on the right to food, even if at the moment this only concerns communities affected by LSLTS taking place in one of the 10 state parties to the Protocol.[124] At the regional level the Inter-American and African human rights mechanisms have also demonstrated a willingness to address human rights implications of LSLTS when such transactions affect indigenous peoples' and other communities' traditional lands, territories and resources connected to livelihood opportunities.

One issue that was not addressed in depth is the impact of these responses and the extent to which they have contributed to influencing state conduct and triggering change on the ground. Have the judgments of regional courts been enforced, have the Special Rapporteurs' and Treaty Bodies' recommendations been implemented? As this article was primarily concerned with outlining the responses and approaches adopted by the above actors, a thorough examination of their concrete impact exceeds its scope. However, tackling these questions remains of crucial importance in order to gauge the tangible contribution of a human rights-based approach in the LSLT arena. Beyond the human rights system another challenge remains to mainstream human rights in socioeconomic and food security analyses of LSLTS, so as to contribute to the acknowledgment of a compulsory—as opposed to optional or voluntary—legal reality for states and companies acquiring land and states agreeing to such transactions. In recent years few scholars have analysed LSLTS from a human rights or right to food perspective.[125] If not addressed systematically in future research efforts, potential avenues for preventing or remedying human rights violations may not receive the attention they warrant. Lack of emphasis on human rights approaches when addressing LSLTS may also obfuscate the reality that states have legal obligations under international human rights law and mistakenly relegate the responsibility of states and companies involved in land deals to the realm of voluntary commitments.

Notes

1 O De Schutter, 'How not to think of land-grabbing: three critiques of large-scale investments in farmland', *Journal of Peasant Studies*, 38(2), 2011, p 249.

2 FIAN International, *Land Grabbing in Kenya and Mozambique: A Report on Two Research Missions—and a Human Rights Analysis of Land Grabbing*, Heidelberg: FIAN International, 2010, p 7.
3 S Narula, 'The global land rush: markets, rights, and the politics of food', paper presented at the 'International Conference on Global Land Grabbing II', Cornell University, 17–19 October 2012, p 23.
4 Report of the Special Rapporteur on the right to food Mr Olivier De Schutter, UN Doc. A/HRC/13/33/Add.2, 28 December 2009, § 33.
5 See, for example, A Goetz, 'Private governance and land grabbing: the equator principles and the Roundtable on Sustainable Biofuels', *Globalizations*, 10(1), 2013, pp 199–204.
6 Narula, 'The global land rush', p 23.
7 Responses of civil society organisations to land grabbing are described in another article in this issue. See also R Künnemann & S Monsalve Suárez, 'International human rights and governing land grabbing: a view from global civil society', *Globalizations*, 10(1), 2013, pp 123–139; Brot für die Welt, ICCO & FIAN International, *Land Grabbing and Nutrition: A Challenge for Global Governance*, Right to Food and Nutrition Watch 2010, available at www.rtfn-watch.org.
8 See W Barth Eide & U Kracht (ed), *Food and Human Rights in Development: Legal and Institutional Dimensions and Selected Topics*, Antwerp: Intersentia, 2005; and J Ziegler, C Golay, C Mahon & S-A Way, *The Fight for the Right to Food: Lessons Learned*, London: Palgrave Macmillan, 2011.
9 C Golay, *The Right to Food and Access to Justice: Examples at the National, Regional and International Levels*, Rome: FAO, 2009.
10 These were adopted by the UN General Assembly on 10 December 1948, Resolution 217 A (III); and on 16 December 1966, Resolution 2200 A (XXI) (entering into force on 3 January 1976), respectively.
11 Emphasis added.
12 FAO, *Rome Declaration on World Food Security (13–17 November 1996)*, § 1; and *World Food Summit Plan of Action*, 1996, Goal 7.4, § 6.1.
13 CESCR, *General Comment 12: The Right to Adequate Food*, UN Doc. E/C.12/1999/5, 12 May 1999.
14 The mandate was created by resolution 2000/10 of the Commission on Human Rights. See websites of the mandate holders at www.righttofood.org and www.srfood.org.
15 FAO, *Declaration of the World Food Summit: Five Years Later*, Rome: FAO, § 10.
16 See FAO, *Right to Food: Making it Happen—Progress and Lessons Learned through Implementation*, Rome: FAO, 2011. See also www.fao.org/righttofood.
17 The speech is available at http://www.un.org/apps/news/infocus/sgspeeches/search_full.asp?statID=413.
18 The Protocol of San Salvador was adopted on 17 November 1988 by the General Assembly of the Organization of American States. See Articles 12, 15 and 17. Aside from the right to education and the right to organise and join unions, the rights recognised in the Protocol of San Salvador cannot be adjudicated before the Inter-American Commission or Court on Human Rights. See Article 19(6).
19 Golay, *The Right to Food and Access to Justice*, pp 37–46.
20 See L Knuth & M Vidar, *Constitutional and Legal Protection of the Right to Food around the World*, Rome: FAO, 2011; and Golay, *The Right to Food and Access to Justice*, pp 47–58.
21 CESCR, *General Comment 12*, § 6. This definition was clearly inspired by the definition of food security adopted by states in the 1996 WFS Plan of Action. FAO, *World Food Summit Plan of Action*, 1996, § 1.
22 CESCR, *General Comment 12*, §§ 6–8.
23 Report of the Special Rapporteur on the right to food Mr Jean Ziegler, UN Doc. A/HRC/7/5, 10 January 2008, § 18. *Right to Food Guidelines*, 1.1 provides that states should create the conditions 'in which individuals can feed themselves and their families in freedom and dignity'.
24 See *Right to Food Guidelines*, 8, 13, 14.
25 Commission on Human Rights, *The Right to Adequate Food and to be Free from Hunger: Updated Study on the Right to Food, Submitted by A Eide*, UN Doc. E/CN.4/Sub.2/1999/12, 28 June 1999.
26 See CESCR, *General Comment 12*, § 15; and Preface and Introduction to the *Right to Food Guidelines*, § 17.
27 Ziegler *et al*, *The Fight for the Right to Food*, pp 18–22.
28 O De Schutter, *Countries Tackling Hunger with a Right to Food Approach*, Briefing Note 1, Special Rapporteur on the right to food, 2010; and FAO, *Right to Food: Making it Happen—Progress and Lessons Learned through Implementation*, Rome: FAO, 2011, pp 6–7.
29 C Golay & M Büschi, *The Right to Food and Global Strategic Frameworks: The Global Strategic Framework for Food Security and Nutrition (GSF) and the UN Comprehensive Framework for Action (CFA)*, Rome: FAO, 2012, pp 13–17.
30 On the different roles played by states in dealing with LSLTS, see W Wolford, SM Borras Jr, R Hall, I Scoones & B White, 'Governing global land deals: the role of the state in the rush for land', *Development and Change*, 44(2), 2013, pp 189–210.
31 CESCR, *General Comment 12*, § 13.

32 Report of the Special Rapporteur on the right to food Mr Jean Ziegler, UN Doc. A/57/356, 27 August 2002, §§ 22–42; and Report of the Special Rapporteur on the right to food Mr Olivier De Schutter, UN Doc. A/65/281, 11 August 2011.

33 It is estimated that 50% of the world's hungry are smallholder farmers, 20% landless people and 10% herders, pastoralists or fisherfolk. UN Millenium Project, Task Force on Hunger, *Halving Hunger: It can be Done—Summary Version*, New York: UN Development Programme, 2005, pp 4–6.

34 Report of the Special Rapporteur on the right to food Mr Olivier De Schutter, UN Doc. A/65/281, 11 August 2011, §§ 39–43. See also O De Schutter, 'The emerging human right to land', *International Community Law Review*, 12, 2010, pp 303–334. This reference to the commons can be seen as part of a broader societal recognition of common property resources. See K Milun, *The Political Uncommons*, Farham: Ashgate, 2011.

35 See Articles 14(2) and 16 of CEDAW.

36 The Declaration on the Rights of Indigenous Peoples was adopted by the UN General Assembly on 13 September 2007, Resolution 61/295.

37 See, in particular, Articles 13–19 of the ILO Convention No 169 concerning Indigenous and Tribal Peoples; and Articles 8, 10 and 26 of the UN Declaration on the Rights of Indigenous Peoples.

38 Report of the Special Rapporteur on the right to food Mr Olivier De Schutter on his mission to China, UN Doc. A/HRC/19/59/Add.1, 20 January 2012; Report of the Special Rapporteur on the right to food Mr Olivier De Schutter on his mission to Mexico, UN Doc. A/HRC/19/59/Add.2, 17 January 2012; Report of the Special Rapporteur on the right to food Mr Olivier De Schutter on his mission to South Africa, UN Doc. A/HRC/19/59/Add.3, 13 January 2012; and Report of the Special Rapporteur on the right to food Mr Olivier De Schutter on his mission to Madagascar, UN Doc. A/HRC/19/59/Add.4, 26 December 2011.

39 *Right to Food Guidelines*, 8.

40 *Ibid*, 2.5.

41 *Ibid*, 8.1, 8.6.

42 P Clays & G Vanloqueren, 'The minimum human rights principles applicable to large-scale land acquisitions or leases', *Globalizations*, 10(1), 2013, p 193.

43 On the mandates and working methods of the special procedures, see C Golay, C Mahon & I Cismas, 'The impact of the UN special procedures on the development and implementation of economic, social and cultural rights', *International Journal of Human Rights*, 15(2), 2011, pp 299–318; S Subedi, S Wheatley, A Mukherjee & S Ngane, 'The role of the special rapporteurs of the United Nations Human Rights Council in the development and promotion of international human rights norms', *International Journal of Human Rights*, 15(2), 2011, pp 155–161; T Piccone, *Catalysts for Change: How the UN's Independent Experts Promote Human Rights*, Washington, DC: Brookings Institution Press, 2012; and I Nifosi, *The UN Special Procedures in the Field of Human Rights*, Antwerp: Intersentia, 2005.

44 The Advisory Committee of the Human Rights Council is composed of 18 independent human rights experts. It was created on the basis of UN General Assembly Resolution 60/251 creating the Human Rights Council, adopted on 15 March 2006.

45 See report of the Special Rapporteur on the right to food Mr Jean Ziegler, UN Doc. A/57/356, 27 August 2002, §§ 22-42; and the report of the Special Rapporteur on the right to food Mr Olivier De Schutter, UN Doc. A/65/281, 11 August 2011.

46 See annex to the report of the Special Rapporteur on the right to food Mr Olivier De Schutter on large-scale land acquisitions and leases: a set of minimum principles and measures to address the human rights challenge, UN Doc. A/HRC/13/33/Add.2, 28 December 2009.

47 Report of the Special Rapporteur on the right to food Mr Olivier De Schutter on large-scale land acquisitions and leases, § 5.

48 *Ibid*, Summary, p 1.

49 *Ibid*, § 15.

50 These include situations in which labour issues are central. See TM Li, 'Centering labor in the land grab debate', *Journal of Peasant Studies*, 32(8), 2011, pp 281–298.

51 Annex to the report of the Special Rapporteur on the right to food Mr Olivier De Schutter on large-scale land acquisitions and leases.

52 Resolution of the Human Rights Council on the right to food, UN Doc. A/HRC/RES/13/4, 24 March 2010, § 35.

53 Clays & Vanloqueren, 'The minimum human rights principles applicable to large-scale land acquisitions or leases', p 196.

54 *Ibid*, pp 196–197; O De Schutter, 'The green rush: the global race for farmland and the rights of land users', *Harvard International Law Journal*, 52(2), 2011, pp 504–559; and De Schutter, 'How not to think of land-grabbing'.

55 The symposium 'Business and Human Rights: Clearing the Path to Foster Corporate Accountability' took place on 18 October 2010 in Geneva. More information is available at http://www.reports-and-materials.org/Land-grabbing-symposium-Geneva-18-Oct-2010.pdf.

56 See http://cambodia.ohchr.org/EN/PagesFiles/Reports/SR-SRSG-Reports.htm.
57 Report of the Special Rapporteur on the human rights situation in Cambodia Surya Subedi, UN Doc. A/
    HRC/21/63/Add.1, 24 September 2012.
58 *Ibid*, § 11.
59 *Ibid*, §168.
60 *Ibid*, § 120.
61 *Ibid*, § 163.
62 *Ibid*, § 154.
63 *Ibid*, § 172.
64 *Ibid*, § 226.
65 *Ibid*, § 207.
66 Resolution of the Human Rights Council on the right to food, UN Doc. A/HRC/RES/13/4, 14 April 2010,
    § 44. See also M Edelman & C James, 'Peasants' rights and the UN system: quixotic struggle? Or
    emancipatory idea whose time has come?', *Journal of Peasant Studies*, 38(1), 2011, pp 81–108.
67 Final study of the Human Rights Council Advisory Committee on the advancement of the rights of
    peasants and other people working in rural areas, UN Doc. A/HRC/19/75, 24 February 2012.
68 *Ibid*, § 63.
69 *Ibid*, §§ 63, 74.
70 See S Monsalve Suarez, 'The human rights framework in contemporary agrarian struggles', *Journal of
    Peasant Studies*, 2012, pp 1–52; and E Holt Gimenez & A Shattuck, 'Food crises, food regimes and food
    movements: rumblings of reform or tides of transformation? ', *Journal of Peasant Studies*, 38(1), 2011,
    pp 109–144.
71 Resolution of the Human Rights Council on the promotion and protection of the human rights of peasants
    and other people working in rural areas, UN Doc. A/HRC/RES/21/19, 11 October 2012, § 1.
72 See http://www.ohchr.org/EN/HRBodies/HRC/RuralAreas/Pages/WGRuralAreasIndex.aspx.
73 H Keller & G Ulfstein (eds), *UN Human Rights Treaty Bodies: Law and Legitimacy*, Cambridge:
    Cambridge University Press, 2012; M Cherif Bassiouni & WA Schabas (eds), *New Challenges for the UN
    Human Rights Machinery: What Future for the UN Treaty Body System and the Human Rights Council
    Procedures?*, Cambridge: Intersentia, 2011, pp 137–148, 192–173; and W Vandehole, *The Procedures
    Before the UN Human Rights Bodies: Divergence or Convergence?*, Antwerp: Intersentia, 2004.
74 CEDAW, *Concluding Observations: Togo*, UN Doc. CEDAW/C/TGO/CO/6-7, 18 October 2012, § 37(e).
75 CEDAW, *Concluding Observations: Ethiopia*, UN Doc. CEDAW/C/ETH/CO/6-7, 27 July 2011, § 36.
76 CESCR, *Concluding Observations: India*, UN Doc. E/C.12/IND/CO/5, § 31.
77 CESCR, *Concluding Observations: Madagascar*, UN Doc. E/C.12/MDG/CO/2, 16 December 2009, §§ 12,
    33.
78 *Ibid*, § 12.
79 *Ibid*, § 12.
80 CESCR, *Concluding Observations: Cambodia*, UN Doc. E/C.12/KHM/CO/1, 12 June 2009, § 30, emphasis
    added.
81 *Ibid*.
82 *Ibid*.
83 *Ibid*, § 16.
84 CESCR, *Concluding Observations: Democratic Republic of Congo*, UN Doc. E/C.12/COD/CO/4, 20
    November 2009, § 14.
85 CESCR, *Concluding Observations: Chad*, UN Doc. E/C.12/TCD/CO/3, 16 December 2009 § 13; and CESCR,
    Concluding Observations: Mexico, UN Doc. E/C.12/MEX/CO/4, 9 June 2006, § 28.
86 Committee on the Elimination of Racial Discrimination (CERD), *Concluding Observations: Indonesia*, UN
    Doc. CERD/C/IDN/CO/3, 15 August 2007, §§ 17.
87 *Ibid*.
88 CERD, *Concluding Observations: Democratic Republic of Congo*, UN Doc. E/C.12/COD/CO/4, 20
    November 2009, § 14.
89 CERD, *Concluding Observations: Lao PDR*, UN Doc. CERD/C/LAO/CO/16-18, 9 March 2012, § 16–17.
90 *Ibid*, § 16.
91 CERD, *Concluding Observations: Viet Nam*, UN Doc. CERD/C/VNM/CO/10-14, 9 March 2012, § 15; CERD,
    Concluding Observations: Suriname, UN Doc. CERD /C /S U R /C O/12,3, 13 March 2009, §§ 12, 13,
    14; CERD, *Concluding Observations: Peru*, UN Doc. CERD/C/PER/CO/14-17, 3 September 2009, § 21, 13
    March 2010 ; and CERD, Concluding Observations: Colombia, UN Doc. CERD/C/COL/CO/14, 28
    August 2009, § 19.
92 CERD, *Concluding Observations: Cambodia*, UN Doc. CERD/C/KHM/CO/8-13, 1 April 2010, § 16.
93 *Ibid*.
94 *Ibid*.
95 *Ibid*.

96 CEDAW, *Concluding Observations: Cambodia*, UN Doc. CEDAW/C/KHM/CO/3, 25 January 2006, § 31.

97 Committee on the Rights of the Child (CRC), *Concluding Observations: Cambodia*, UN Doc. CRC/C/KHM/CO/2, 20 June 2011, §§ 61, 61.

98 *Ibid.*

99 *Ibid*, referring to reports A/HRC/4/36 and A/HRC/7/42, cited above.

100 CERD, *Concluding Observations: Cambodia*, UN Doc. CERD/C/KHM/CO/8-13, 1 April 2010, § 16.

101 CEDAW, *Concluding Observations: Lao People's Democratic Republic*, UN Doc. CEDAW/C/LAO/CO/7, 14 August 2009, § 44, 45.

102 Künnemann & Monsalve Suárez, 'International human rights and governing land grabbing', p 127.

103 *Ibid.*

104 CESCR, *Concluding Observations: Germany*, UN Doc. E/C.12/DEU/CO/5, 12 July 2011, § 11.

105 At the time of writing, six treaty monitoring bodies established within the UN human rights system can receive communications: CEDAW, CERD, CESCR, the Human Rights Committee, the Committee against Torture and the Committee on the Rights of Persons with Disabilities.

106 Golay, *The Right to Food and Access to Justice*, pp 32–33.

107 See, for example, Human Rights Committee, *Ángela Poma Poma v Peru*, Comm No 1457/2006, Views of 27 March 2009, UN Doc. CCPR/C/95/D/1457/2006; and *Apirana Mahuika et al v New Zealand*, Comm No 547/1993, Views of 27 October 2000, UN Doc. CCPR/C/70/D/541/1993. See also C Golay & M Ozden, *The Right of Peoples to Self-determination*, Geneva: CETIM, 2009, p 55.

108 See I Biglino & C Golay, *The Optional Protocol to the International Covenant on Economic, Social and Cultural Rights*, Geneva Academy In-Brief No 2, Geneva: Geneva Academy of International Humanitarian Law and Human Rights, 2013.

109 FAO, *Reform of the Committee on World Food Security*, Final version, Thirty-fifth Session of CFS, 14, 15 and 17 October 2009, FAO Doc. CFS:2009/2 Rev.2.

110 Voluntary Guidelines on the Responsible Governance of Tenure of Land, Fisheries and Forests in the Context of National Food Security, adopted by the FAO Committee on World Food Security on 11 May 2012.

111 See P Seufert, 'The FAO Voluntary Guidelines on the Responsible Governance of Tenure of Land, Fisheries and Forests', *Globalizations*, 10(1), pp 181–186; and S Monsalve Suarez, *Land: Not for Sale!*, Right to Food and Nutrition Watch, 2010, pp 33–37, available at www.rtfn-watch.org.

112 See Golay, *The Right to Food and Access to Justice*, pp 44–45.

113 Inter-American Court of Human Rights (IACHR), *Mayagna (Sumo) Awas Tingni Community v Nicaragua*, 31 August 2001, §§ 153, 164, 173.4.

114 IACHR, *Saramaka v Suriname*, 28 November 2007. The 'Saramaka people', are one of the six Maroon groups in Suriname whose ancestors were African slaves (§ 80). The Court reaffirmed that, similarly to indigenous communities, 'the members of the Saramaka people make up a tribal community whose social, cultural and economic characteristics are different from other sections of the national community, particularly because of their special relationship with their ancestral territories, and…their own norms, customs, and/or traditions' (§84).

115 *Ibid*, § 59.

116 *Ibid*, § 128

117 IACHR, *Kichwa Indigenous People of Sarayaku v Ecuador*, 27 June 2012.

118 *Ibid*, §§ 100, 134.

119 *Ibid*, § 174.

120 *Ibid*, § 341. The relevant rights are in Articles 4(1) and 5(1) of the American Convention on Human Rights.

121 Respectively, Articles 14, 22, and 21 of the African Charter on Human and Peoples' Rights.

122 African Commission on Human and Peoples' Rights, *Centre for Minority Rights Development (Kenya) and Minority Rights Group International on behalf of Endorois Welfare Council v Kenya*, 4 February 2010, §§ 286, 288.

123 *Ibid.*

124 The 10 countries that have ratified the Optional Protocol as of 1 August 2013 are Argentina, Bolivia, Bosnia and Herzegovina, Ecuador, El Salvador, Mongolia, Portugal, Slovakia, Spain and Uruguay. Thirty-two more countries have signed but not yet ratifiied the Optional Protocol. See Biglino & Golay, *The Optional Protocol*, 2013.

125 In addition to Olivier De Schutter's and Sofia Monsalve Suarez's publications cited above, see L Cotula, '"Land grabbing" in the shadow of the law: legal frameworks regulating the global land rush', in R Rayfuse & N Weisfelt (eds), *The Challenge of Food Security: International Policy and Regulatory Frameworks*, Cheltenham: Edward Elgar, 2012, pp 206–228; and Cotula (ed), *The Right to Food and Access to Natural Resources: Using Human Rights Arguments and Mechanisms to Improve Resource Access for the Rural Poor*, Rome: FAO, 2009.

Notes on Contributors

Christophe Golay is Research Fellow at the Geneva Academy of International Humanitarian Law and Human Rights and Lecturer at the Geneva Center for Education and Research in Humanitarian Action. He has published extensively on the right to food and is the author of *The Right to Food and Access to Justice: Examples at the National, Regional and International Levels* (2009) and co-author, with Jean Ziegler, Claire Mahon and Sally-Anne Way, of *The Fight for the Right to Food: Lessons Learned* (2011). He is also joint coordinator of the Swiss Network for International Studies-funded project 'Large-Scale Land Acquisitions in Southeast Asia: Rural Transformations between Global Agendas and Peoples' Right to Food'.

Irene Biglino is Research Fellow at the Geneva Academy of International Humanitarian Law and Human Rights. She is also a Legal Consultant with the International Development Law Organization, where she is conducting research on right to food litigation. She is currently working on the Swiss Network for International Studies-funded project 'Large-Scale Land Acquisitions in Southeast Asia: Rural Transformations between Global Agendas and Peoples' Right to Food'.

The Global Politics of Water Grabbing

JENNIFER FRANCO[a], LYLA MEHTA[b] & GERT JAN VELD WISCH[c]

[a]*Transnational Institute, Amsterdam and China Agricultural University, Beijing;* [b]*Institute of Development Studies, Brighton, UK and Noragric, Norway;* [c]*Water Resources Management Group, Wageningen University, The Netherlands*

ABSTRACT *The contestation and appropriation of water is not new, but it has been highlighted by recent global debates on land grabbing. Water grabbing takes place in a field that is locally and globally plural-legal. Formal law has been fostering both land and water grabs but formal water and land management have been separated from each other—an institutional void that makes encroachment even easier. Ambiguous processes of global water and land governance have increased local-level uncertainties and complexities that powerful players can navigate, making them into mechanisms of exclusion of poor and marginalised people. As in formal land management corporate influence has grown. For less powerful players resolving ambiguities in conflicting regulatory frameworks may require tipping the balance towards the most congenial. Yet, compared with land governance, global water governance is less contested from an equity and water justice perspective, even though land is fixed, while water is fluid and part of the hydrological cycle; therefore water grabbing potentially affects greater numbers of diverse water users. Water grabbing can be a powerful entry point for the contestation needed to build counterweights to the neoliberal, corporate business-led convergence in global resource governance discourses and processes. Elaborating a human right to water in response to water grabbing is urgently needed.*

The contestation and appropriation of water is not new, but in the contemporary context of a convergence of changing global dynamics around food, climate, energy and finance, and the resulting global debates on land grabbing, there is renewed interest in a water perspective on resources grabs.[1] Increasing attention to water has the potential to (re)invigorate inquiry and action along two lines simultaneously: 1) by casting new light on the global land grab phenomenon itself and related issues of land governance; and 2) by opening up new windows on old questions of political control, social justice and environmental sustainability in relation to the use and management of water. Since about 2010 evidence has been growing that the rush to control water resources is an important cause, as well as effect, of the phenomenon now commonly known as land grabbing. Specific attention to *water* grabbing has been prompted by the observation that while *land* grabbing has received a lot of attention, 'water as both a target and driver of this phenomenon has been largely ignored despite the interconnectedness of water and land'.[2]

In recent years various studies have put forward strong evidence for understanding land grabbing for agriculture (for food, feed, fuel and raw material for industrial use) as having important water dimensions. To illustrate, in many parts of sub-Saharan Africa rainfall is too erratic for high investment in agricultural production without securing access to reliable water. This is one of the reasons why land grabbing for agriculture almost by definition includes water grabbing, even when not explicitly specified in the land deals.[3] Globally most agricultural production is based purely on rainwater that has infiltrated the soil locally (so-called 'green water'), but diverted surface water and pumped-up groundwater (so-called 'blue water') are a far more reliable source for commercial agricultural production.[4] Hence the proliferation of political narratives on 'unexploited and underutilised' land and water resources, and how these 'need' new and large-scale investment to 'unlock' their potential and to awaken Africa's 'sleeping giant' and promote a blue revolution in Africa.[5] Even when investment plans do not specify a requirement for water beyond rain, experience shows that additional water will have to be mobilised for the crops to do well and this may typically be in the most water-scarce period and in competition with existing and/or potential future uses.[6]

Beyond agriculture, water grabbing extends into the water, energy, climate and mineral domains in ways that highlight the distinct material character of water. In short, water may be the context of a grab, it may be the object of a grab, or it may be both at the same time. To illustrate, in agriculture-driven grabs, water is a crucial context for land grabbing—determining for example 'which land located where' is desirable or most coveted by investors, usually having some irrigation potential. Water can also then become the object of what is primarily an agriculture-driven land grab.[7] In other cases water itself is the primary object of the grabbing, resulting in reallocations of formal and informal water rights and their benefits of use. For example, hydropower development in Turkey is made possible through neoliberal reforms that have transferred exclusive access rights to hundreds of rivers and streams to private companies for 49 years.[8] In Cajamarca, Peru, large-scale private mining operations are prompting big changes in how water rights are allocated, leading to detrimental changes in the amount and quality of water available to downstream users.[9]

As these diverse examples suggest, while land and water are interconnected, a focus on the grabbing of water resources helps to bring out an additional, distinct set of issues that are linked to the materiality of water. For instance, water availability fluctuates across time and space, flows within watershed boundaries and often has pronounced dislocated (downstream) effects, in terms of quantities and qualities. Moreover, a focus on the grabbing of this materially distinct and finite natural resource also uncovers additional analytical complexities that have major implications for both policy and political action. It is very difficult to pinpoint (the effects of) reallocations, among other reasons because of surface water–groundwater interactions and inter-annual variability, a fact which in some settings has important 'spillover' implications for policy and political action.[10] Meanwhile, in other settings, pointing out the *threat* of reallocation of a natural resource that is so crucial for human life may be enough to generate political resistance. The fluidity of water thus both complicates and potentially enriches the picture on land grabbing, both analytically and empirically—something which researchers looking at the contemporary global enclosures are just beginning to explore.

With these issues and the ongoing build-up of water-grabbing-focused case material in mind, we find this to be a good moment to take a more systematic look at land and water governance—especially at the global level—to see where we are in terms of generating knowledge and insights that have relevance for policy and political action. The global level of water related governance mechanisms is emphasised here as it has largely been absent from the discussions on the new global enclosures. The mechanism and processes through which water grabbing takes shape in practice, such as everyday politics and the role of water technologies, would also deserve further scrutiny and theorisation, but are outside the focus of this current article. Our analysis builds on discrete policy discussions over uneven access to and control of water that go back decades and are not necessarily linked to or coterminous with the agrarian question in which much land grabbing research is framed. Meanwhile, some of the more land-oriented global governance discussions, which likewise go back decades, are virtually silent on the question of water. Land and water are interconnected, but not the same, and their management and governance have often been constructed in isolation from one another historically. There are 'land experts/activists' and there are 'water experts/activists', but seldom do the two synergise in matters of governance. Bringing water issues to the fore in this context thus involves more than simply adding water to the land grab/land governance debate and stirring. It requires taking stock of ongoing debates around discrete questions of water rights, water management, the right to water and water governance, in both the land and water domains, and exploring how these potentially inform and eventually re-forge the current global debate on land grabbing into a broader and more integrated understanding of land and water issues and governance. Such an understanding is needed in order to build political contestation towards eventually tipping the balance of power in the direction of social and environmental justice. This article aims to contribute to a deeper understanding of these issues. We begin by defining how we understand water grabbing before exploring the tendency towards neoliberal processes in disparate global land and water governance mechanism that facilitate resource grabbing. We chart the specific neoliberal turn in water management, growing corporate influence in global policy making around water and how seemingly neutral processes such as Integrated Water Resources Management (IWRM) can serve powerful players' interests. We conclude with some thoughts on how social justice perspectives around land and water grabbing processes can be advanced.

Understanding water grabbing

Water grabbing is a process in which powerful actors are able to take control of, or reallocate to their own benefit, water resources used by local communities or which feed aquatic ecosystems on which their livelihoods are based.[11] It is one manifestation of a wider global trend involving large scale (re)allocations of natural resources more generally. Drawing insight from the discussion on land grabbing, we understand water grabbing as the capturing of control not just of the water itself, but also of the power to decide how this will be used—by whom, when, for how long and for what purposes—in order to control the benefits of use. The fast growing case material on land grabbing demonstrates a wider contemporary trend or cycle in the context of the intersection of global changes in the food–feed–fuel system, in climate, and in global finance and economy, which is driving the further expansion of large-scale capitalist control over natural resources for purposes of production, extraction and speculation. As many analysts and observers have noted, capture of land and water resources by powerful actors is nothing new, but has been happening for centuries. It is useful to situate and analyse different episodes of appropriation in their particular historical and institutional context. The current cycle is what we refer to as land and water grabbing.

A key feature of this phenomenon is that the underlying business deals are large scale, most visibly in terms of land area and the capital involved. There is a strong tendency in the literature on land grabbing to try to define it mainly in terms of the physical size of the land acquired.[12] By incorporating scale of capital into the analysis, land, water and other resources become visible as central in the operation of capital. A purely land-centred view overlooks the underlying logic and operation of capital accumulation.[13] For water grabbing, the fixation on size has a parallel in too narrow a focus on the volume of water involved, ignoring the fact that access to water concerns distribution in time and space.[14] In their study of water grabbing in the Office du Niger Hertzog et al demonstrate how important it is to thoroughly assess water requirements in space and time, rather than just looking at water volumes.[15] This also suggests a need to seriously take into account the notion of scale with regard to flows of water, in order to highlight and account more systematically for changes in water distribution and water quality.

We will return to this point later. For now it is useful to point out that our approach to water grabbing complements the work of Borras et al and is likewise grounded in a combined political economy, political ecology and political sociology approach.[16] As such, it seeks to move beyond narrow, proceduralist mainstream understandings of the 'grabbing' as illegal by definition, which have the disadvantage of emphasising the formal-legal quality of the transaction and from there limiting the lens on grabbing to those cases where state law is clearly contravened. Such an approach is problematic.

First, it tends to dismiss deeper interrogation of the actual nature and desirability of the outcomes of these 'transactions' in terms of the underlying development model that the new economic arrangements usher in, including, as pointed out by Borras and Franco, changes in land use and land property relations that often entail dispossession and ecological destruction.[17] How large-scale land and water grabs are prompting similar changes in and undermining existing use, management and social relations of water, has recently been explored by (among others) Williams et al in Ghana;[18] Bues and Theesfeld in

Ethiopia;[19] Houdret in Morocco;[20] Duvail *et al* in Kenya;[21] and Velez Torres in Colombia.[22]

Second, it tends to reduce the transaction itself essentially to a technical formal-legal procedure, at times even conflating financial accounting with political accountability, thereby underestimating (or ignoring) how the grabbing of natural resources is taking place in a historical–institutional field that is plural-legal, marked by power asymmetries and thus deeply political, as well as ignoring the fact that in many settings it is formal state law that has been fostering the grabs. Wily has shown how formal law that is supposed to protect vulnerable people can in practice 'oppress and dispossess' where land is concerned.[23] On the water front recent research shows how powerful actors use legal means as well as technical definitions to divert water and the benefits of its use away from local communities. In India sectoral reforms are used as a mechanism to legalise and legitimise water grabbing processes. The state also takes advantage of the opaqueness in the policy regime and when challenged on legal grounds, reform instruments are blatantly redefined.[24] In many cases state organisations bend or reinterpret existing rules and regulations that should actually prevent water grabbing, as in the case of Ethiopia, where the Water Resources Management Proclamation is supposed to protect local users.[25] In other cases and in various ways legally required Environmental Impact Assessments (EIAs) have served as mechanisms for 'window dressing' water grabbing activities.[26]

All these studies show that a litmus test of 'legality' ultimately offers little traction when trying to determine what counts as water (or land) grabbing. In fact, grabbers often make use of legally complex situations around water tenure. New commercial users usually coexist with complex non-registered users who are invisible. This legal pluralism can be both enabling and disabling, but it is often very difficult for local users to defend their claims. Companies often strengthen their informal social and political networks to influence governance processes. Hertzog *et al* refer to the latter as 'a fragmented negotiation process, whereby different investors have used different networks in the administrative and political apparatus in order to secure both suitable land and water arrangements'.[27] Meanwhile, formal water and land management are often separated from each other—an institutional void that also makes encroachment easier, while the separation of land and water rights can contribute to creating space for water grabbing to occur.[28]

Stepping back, one finds that water grabbing (like land grabbing) is diverse in its appearance. Water grabbing is 1) driven by varied forms of state–capital alliances; 2) not limited geographically; 3) happening in diverse agro-ecological contexts; 4) unfolding across various water–land property rights regimes; and 5) leading to diverse impacts. Each of these points is elaborated below using recent water grabbing-focused case study material.

First, the main actors behind diverse grabbing processes are varied forms of state–capital alliances, involving varied types of mechanisms and processes that are serving to make the grabs possible—among others state law and policy reforms;[29] state law and new policy interpretations;[30] violation of state law;[31] new public–private interest business coalitions;[32] exploiting legal complexity;[33] and bypassing democratic accountability processes.[34]

Second, water grabbing, like land grabbing, is happening across the globe. Many of the most prominent reports and studies, including those by Wood-house,[35] Woodhouse and Ganho,[36] and Skinner and Cotula,[37] tended to focus initially on water grabbing happening in Africa, perhaps reinforcing the impression (cultivated in the media) that it was mainly an African phenomenon. But empirical evidence shows it unfolding throughout Latin America;[38] across Asia,[39] in the Middle East and in Eurasia as well.[40]

Third, water grabbing is also happening across various agro-ecological contexts: river deltas and floodplains, inland rivers, freshwater lakes, wetlands, as well as semi-arid plains and savannah. Fourth, water grabbing, like land grabbing, is happening across diverse property rights regimes, including commons such as grazing corridors, as in the Tana Delta case;[41] communal/community tenure and resource management systems;[42] land- and waterscapes understood by local communities as territory;[43] and areas under individual private property rights regimes.[44]

Finally, the impacts of water grabbing are diverse. The impacts of land grabbing have been distinguished as two broad types: exclusion and adverse incorporation.[45] However, water grabbing and its impacts appear to be even more diverse and 'slippery' because of their dislocated, timing-relevant and quality-related effects.[46] Interventions in the water cycle can, for instance, 1) disturb the amount of groundwater and downstream water available for existing users (exclusion from the volume); 2) change the peak and base flows (exclusion in timing): 3) change the agro-ecological landscape (exclusion from ecosystem benefits that require, for example, occasional flooding); and 4) affect the quality of the water (exclusion from clean and safe water). In the latter case water grabbing does not necessarily involve diversion of water, but rather pollution of water resources by powerful upstream actors in a process marked by the externalisation of problems and costs (which are transferred from the causers to local communities downstream).[47] These 'watery' types of exclusion could also be understood in terms of adverse incorporation—ie the imposition of water use and management regimes that directly or indirectly 'incorporate' people into changed water regimes tied to the new economic arrangements.

Global land and water governance

Water grabbing takes place in a field that is plural-legal—ie characterised by the coexistence of varied and diverse regulatory frameworks and processes shaping who gets what kind of access to which water resources and for what purposes. As seen in the previous section, much of the empirical work of recent years emphasises this point from a local perspective.[48] But legal pluralism characterises the 'higher' levels of the political system too, including the global level where plural-legal resource 'governance-scapes' are becoming increasingly apparent. This is certainly the case in the land and water domains. As Mehta *et al* argue:

> the multiplication of institutional forms and sites of environmental governance and natural resource management itself generates greater uncertainty

as individuals, social groups, and organisations jostle for control over resources and their futures. The result is both that conventional theoretical divides between local and global, formal and informal have been made redundant, and that ambiguity, complexity and uncertainty increasingly characterise the conditions under which resources are governed and managed.[49]

Powerful players can navigate their way through such uncertainties, making them into mechanisms of exclusion for poor and marginalised people, and facilitate grabbing processes.

In this section we review the main global processes that govern and attempt to regulate water access, use and the distribution of benefits and burdens of these. We describe this scene in terms of an ongoing build-up of structures, institutions and discourses. This has been happening in a fragmented fashion historically, resulting in separate regulatory activities that are relatively unconnected. The discussion traces their disparate trajectories and tries to reveal what each may be contributing to the regulation of water grabbing. We argue that these global level ambiguities are reinforcing an overall regulatory setting which is highly permissive to water grabbing when political contestation from a social justice perspective is either weak or absent.

Globally numerous competing governance mechanisms have emerged around the issue of global capital engaging with local natural resources. High-profile governance initiatives addressing land use, management and access in relation to agriculture thus include the World Bank led 'Principles of Responsible Agricultural Investment' (PRAI); the Food and Agriculture Organization (FAO)-based 'Voluntary Guidelines on the Responsible Governance of Tenure of land, fisheries and forests in the context of national food security' (FAO-TG); the ongoing FAO- Responsible Agricultural Investment (FAO-RAI) process; and most recently the G8's 'Land Transparency Initiative' (G8LTI). None of these initiatives deals much with issues of water access, use or the distribution of benefits and burdens. Although 'land tenure security' is a major concern in all these initiatives, they do not necessarily refer to the same thing, while at the same time land remains the main focus of regulation. Despite the growing visibility of water grabbing, these agriculture-oriented governance initiatives have tended to neglect a wide and deep range of issues related to water.

The highly contentious political process that led to the recently adopted FAO-TGs warrants special attention, since it constitutes the most recent site of struggle in the 'proxy war' between competing views and interpretations of natural resources.[50] The FAO-TGs mark an important step forward in elaborating a human right to land, as they are 'the first international instrument which applies an ESC-Rights based approach to the governance of land'.[51] Although the understanding of land in these guidelines has its problems and contradictions, the situation is even worse with respect to water, since it was excluded from coverage.[52] During the final negotiations, the effort by civil society to get water into the guidelines ran up against opposition and resistance from other participants who denounced water and water governance as 'too complicated'.[53] For whatever the FAO-TGs are worth, this poses a major ambiguity since water is indeed deeply and inextricably interconnected with other natural resources.[54]

The FAO-TGS and other agriculture-oriented governance initiatives have emerged against the backdrop of competing (and still evolving) international regulatory frameworks. One of these is international human rights law, which served as a crucial source of inspiration, guidance and support for the civil society delegation throughout the FAO-TG formulation process, while seeming to provoke much discomfort and disdain from some government delegations. Although there is still a long way to go and progress has been uneven, international human rights law has been slowly moving towards authoritative establishment of land, water and associated resources such as fisheries and forests as matters of human rights. This has led to the inclusion of access to land as part of 'the right to feed oneself'.[55] Although there is as yet no distinct human right to land, the pressure to establish such a right remains.[56] There is a globally recognised right to water but it remains conceptually ambiguous and so far has had limited value as a countervailing force against grabbing processes.

The human right to water was the result of decades of intense global struggle and lobbying, as it was initially resisted by powerful players in the water domain and by countries such as Canada and the USA. It was not explicitly recognised in the 1948 Universal Declaration of Human Rights or in subsequent declarations. In July 2010 the UN General Assembly, and later in September 2010 the UN Human Rights Council, finally recognised access to clean water and sanitation as a human right. This official recognition was a great victory for the global water justice movement and has been used as a powerful mobilising tool for water struggles all around the world.

South Africa, Ecuador, Bolivia, Gambia, Tanzania, Uruguay and others have recognised the human right to water, thereby committing to respect, protect and fulfil the right of access to safe and affordable domestic water services. But all over the world there remains a considerable gap between human rights talk and human rights practice and governments are usually constrained in their financial commitments to achieving universal access to water and sanitation. There is often a clear tension between a government's commitment to rights and to market-based mechanisms, with the latter tending to prevail. Bolivia, for example, has been at the forefront of international campaigns to recognise the human right to water. Yet, domestically, the Morales government has been criticised for pursuing economic development policies based on industrialisation and extractive industry expansion that are elite-driven and often violate local people's human rights to water and water rights.[57] South Africa was the first country to provide constitutional recognition of the human right to water and in 2001 the Free Basic Water Policy was introduced, which aimed to provide a basic supply of water to all households free of charge. At the same time the South African water policies were also informed by market-driven approaches to water management, including an emphasis on cost recovery, user fees for water and controversial cut-offs which have violated poor people's basic rights to water.[58]

Human rights, like any rights, are open to interpretation, which makes ensuring a social justice interpretation a matter of political power and strategic political action. In the case of the human right to food, the office of the UN Special Rapporteur on the Right to Food has traditionally served as an important rallying point for civil society organisations and social movements seeking to realise a social justice interpretation. By contrast, the UN Special Rapporteur on the Right to Water has taken a quite different approach, issuing reports stating that 'the human rights framework does not express a preference over models of service provision' and that 'human rights are neutral as to economic models'.[59] Thus, it is not surprising that big global water corporations such as Suez have publicly declared that they 'strongly believe' in the right to water.[60] So far the human right to water has not been deployed to countervail water grabbing processes, partly because its scope is limited to domestic, rather than productive uses of water. Unlike the UN Special Rapporteur on the Right to Food, who has frequently commented on land grabs, the UN Special Rapporteur on the Right to Water has been reluctant to engage with water grabbing issues.

The other main competing international regulatory framework is being consolidated in an array of free trade agreements (FTAS) and bilateral trade agreements (BITS) building on legalist corporate business law discourses, principles, definitions and their underlying assumptions. Many social and environmental justice activists working on a wide range of concerns see these trade agreements as fundamentally at odds not only with human rights law, but also with democratic governance more broadly. They complicate national efforts to regulate environmental, labour, domestic content questions and treat national legislation on these matters as measures in restraint of trade, which are potentially actionable in the dispute resolution mechanisms of the FTAS or World Trade Organization (WTO).[61] The rise of a corporate-business law agenda in recent decades is the result of the project to institutionalise and consolidate neoliberalism internationally by strengthening markets while shrinking states,[62] and is expressed through law and policies on trade and investment, which 'play a crucial role in building the global supply chains that are part of the modern international economy'.[63] Narratives that justify land and water grabbing play an important role in facilitating these processes. In addition to the narrative of 'marginal' and 'idle' lands as 'underexploited resources', there is also the 'economic scarcity' narrative. Such narratives have been serving to justify the involvement of the private sector in irrigation on the twin argument that public funds are short while private funds are more efficient with regard to water use. Since the 1990s FTAS and BITS have been opening up new opportunities for foreign investors to bypass national laws and to question proposed government regulations before international tribunals if profits are threatened. National governments are known to refrain from (or resist) enacting human rights-based social and environmental regulation within their own borders. Linked to these developments are the reforms of the water and energy sectors promoted by multilateral and regional banks encouraging privatisation and deregulation, often in the name of efficiency.

If the most prominent contemporary global governance mechanisms shaping the land domain today offer little concrete guidance or practical insight on how to deal with land and water grabbing, neither do the main global governance mechanisms that exist more specifically for water. Contemporary water governance at the global level is an arena arguably characterised by a high degree of ambiguity, resulting from competing formal regulatory actors and official processes, with few agreed rules or procedures regarding decision making. Even the UN Watercourses Convention, the global water convention specifically related to the governance, use and management of watercourses, has not been ratified by sufficient countries to enter into force.[64] Because there are very few formal agreements, there is no single clear-cut global water regime with agreed-upon rules of the game providing normative prescriptions, clear expectations and institutionalised relationships.[65]

Partly this is because water is not really a global issue or a 'global public good'. Despite the existence of the global hydrological cycle, water remains highly localised or at best regional in scope. Water availability is variable across time and space and depends on factors such as climate, season and temperature, making it very difficult to provide blanket statements and solutions regarding the global state of water. Access to water between countries, within regions and countries, and between women and men is highly unequal and water shortages affect different social groups differently, while hitting the poorest hardest. Even though the 'global' nature of water is difficult to capture, and there is no single overall clear-cut global water regime, there is nonetheless an emerging global water regime.[66] This emerging water governance regime at the global level could best be described as plural-legal, encompassing several separate regulatory orders, each with its own field of action and institutional logic. Examples include the dams movement, convergences around the neo-liberalisation of water, international consensus around IWRM, and the water footprint discourse.

It is relevant to briefly look more closely here at the water footprint discourse. In assessing water grabbing 'water footprint accounting', which demonstrates flows of 'virtual water' as 'embedded' in products, has been suggested as a useful tool.[67] But water footprint tools have not taken account of the political nature of water distribution, especially at the local level.[68] For instance, water footprint accounting does show that, through the import of Peruvian asparagus, large amounts of virtual water are imported,[69] but it does not differentiate between an asparagus produced under industrial agriculture, with devastating effects on the local economy and depleting a non-renewable aquifer, on the one hand, and an asparagus produced under robust family farming with renewable (rain)water.[70] In that respect water footprint accounting has very limited value in the assessment of global water grabbing; in some cases it could even facilitate grabbing processes thanks to assumed 'higher water productivity'.

Zooming back out to look at the broader picture, each of the different global regulatory orders for water have their own networks of experts, including economists, engineers, policy professionals, consultants, and so on. Many supranational organisations, such as the World Commission on Dams, the World Water Council (WWC) and the Global Water Partnership (GWP) are currently addressing global problems and issues concerning water. Even though UN agencies have water programmes, there is no one major agency devoted to water and the one that does exist, UN Water, established in 2003 as a UN inter-agency coordination mechanism, remains a virtual institute with little influence. The GWP was founded in 1996 to champion the case of IWRM around the world. The World Water Council is a controversial elite international body based in Marseille, established by the World Bank, members of French water companies operating around the world and other water policy experts. Added to the mix is the current engagement of corporate players in water management, playing a key role in determining water security and insecurity. Even though these supranational organisations lack global legitimacy, they are powerful in shaping dominant debates and ongoing processes.

Amid increasing complexity and uncertainty, disparate global processes are interacting in a mutually reinforcing way to shape the way land and water are being allocated and reallocated. This is seen especially around processes of commodification and financialisation of natural resources, with land and water grabbing as both cause and effect.[71] This process has been termed liberal environmentalism or market environmentalism.[72] Land and water are increasingly taken strictly as an economic asset, either in productive, extractive or speculative directions. The convergence is therefore a reflection of the ideological ascendancy of neoliberal corporate power across domains. There is a danger that this leads to the establishment of an overarching global legal framework for natural resources that 'secures' rights to these from a corporate business and investor-protection perspective. Recent debates around the 'securitisation of the environment', accompanied by talk of future threats to human security and the 'food–energy–water nexus' driving new hydropower and energy developments and promoting the inclusion of new corporate players are all pointing in this direction.

Privatisation, commodification and water reforms

In this section we look more closely at the global processes that are interacting to shape the way water is allocated and reallocated and water grabbing is taking place. We do this by sketching the historical background of what marked the neoliberal turn in the water sector: the Dublin declaration and the subsequent processes of water privatisation, commodification and eventually also its financialisation (next subsection). The discourse of IWRM and its key principles have become highly influential all over the world. The ways in which IWRM policies and principles can form the playing field through which many of the water grabs take shape are elaborated in the following subsection before we conclude with a discussion on the growing influence of the corporate sector.

From Delhi to Dublin and the neoliberal turn in water

Water has been the focus of global collective action. Yet, despite repeated principles, declarations and meetings, nearly 800 million people lack access to safe water for drinking. The Mar del Plata Conference (1977) was the first—and still the only—global conference on water held under United Nations auspices. This led directly to the UN 'Water Decade' (1981–90), which aimed to achieve universal coverage for drinking water and sanitation by 1990. At the end of the decade the target remained distant. To assess what had happened and to look towards future pathways for collective action, in 1990 the UN held a global consultation in New Delhi hosted by the Indian government. Under the slogan, 'Some for all rather than all for some', the New Delhi Statement emphasised 1) protection of the environment and safeguarding of health through the integrated management of water resources and liquid and solid wastes; 2) institutional reforms promoting an integrated approach; 3) community management of services, backed by measures to strengthen local institutions; and 4) sound financial practices, achieved through better management of existing assets, and widespread use of appropriate technologies.[73]

The New Delhi Statement, with its focus on equity and universality, was rapidly overshadowed by the 'Dublin Statement' of 1992, an important turning point in the global discourse on water governance. This statement emerged from the International Conference on Water and the Environment (ICWE) held in Dublin in January 1992. It was organised by water experts and held under the auspices of the World Meteorological Organization. The conference culminated in the formulation of the Dublin principles which recognised the finite nature of water and its key role in sustaining life, development and the environment; the importance of participatory approaches in water development and management; the central role played by women in the provision, management and safeguarding of water; and the economic and competing values of water and the need to recognise it as an economic good. It is this final principle that has made Dublin a focus of policy differences and global fault lines ever since. Declaring water an 'economic good' in Dublin remains to this day deeply controversial. Many in the global water community still feel this not only legitimises the 'commodification' of a life-giving resource, but also continues to justify potential privatisation and resource capture (including water grabs). Strictly speaking, 'economic goods' are goods that are scarce and legitimise human action and market intervention.[74]

The controversial declaration of water as an economic good must be seen as a logical next step from the sustainability paradigm that had its roots in the late 1970s in combination with the neoliberal turn to economics more generally. The sustainability perspective raises the question of financial sustainability, ie the ability to generate finances to sustain and maintain a particular use. But there are some water needs and uses that lie outside the gamut of economic valuation. Through its focus on water as an economic good, Dublin provided a solid building block for a global discourse that evaluates water distribution in the first place on its economic value.

Corporate agriculture, mining, hydropower and other capital-intensive economic activities are often seen as more important contributors to economic growth than smallholder agriculture, community drinking water and traditional fisheries. The latter may have a place in national development policies, but usually are then framed within the realm of 'subsistence' rather than being seen as sectors that can provide a long-term sustainable contribution to a country's development. In other cases peasant agriculture and traditional fisheries are completely ignored and the areas in which these are important declared 'vacant', 'unused', 'empty' or at least 'underutilised'. For Mozambique Beekman and Veldwisch demonstrate how discourses and policies that favour foreign direct investment over investing in smallholder agriculture encourage local water grabbing processes.[75] There are many other cases in which these dichotomies between smallholders and commercial investments are clearly observable in national processes, policies and discourses.[76]

The shifts in paradigms around water provision and management as expressed in the Dublin statement must be viewed in conjunction with the rise of the neoliberal agenda of the early 1990s, which entailed a shift away from viewing governments as responsible for poor people's needs and problems. Instead, the state was required to play a facilitating and regulatory role without direct engagement. The Washington Consensus of the 1990s thus saw changes in how basic services such as water were governed, which included budget cutbacks, privatisation and deregulation, often legitimised through processes of economic liberalisation and structural adjustment. After Dublin the World Bank began to play a central role in water and sanitation and water has now moved from being viewed as a common good and a public service to a commodity being managed according to economic principles.[77] This has led to controversial water privatisations around the world, details of which cannot be discussed here.[78]

Twenty years on from the Dublin Conference, we are witnessing the privatisation not just of the service and infrastructure but of the resource itself. In recent years water has been transformed into a commodity tradable on large-scale global markets through water trading schemes, leading to the financialisation of water resources and the management of water in the hands of financial markets.[79] In Chile it has been possible to buy and sell different types of water rights since 1981 and the country's water market is considered an important policy model on which various other countries, such as Mexico, Argentina and Morocco, have based their policies.[80] In Uganda the controversial Bujagali dam, which is being resisted by local communities around the Nile, is being financed by the hedge fund Blackstone in partnership with the World Bank and the European Investment bank.[81] These and other examples highlighted in this section have demonstrated the diverse trajectories of neoliberalism that have led to the dominant discourse of water as an economic and tradable good whose market value supersedes its cultural and social values.

IWRM: fluidity of a concept

The concept of IWRM, as practised around the world for some two decades, emerged as an elaboration of the 1992 Dublin principles. The most frequently used definition of IWRM comes from the Global Water Partnership: 'a process which promotes the coordinated development and management of water, land and related resources, in order to maximise the resultant economic and social welfare in an equitable manner without compromising the sustainability of vital ecosystems'.[82] Despite these laudable aims, IWRM is a rather vague, diffuse and amorphous concept and it remains unclear what should be integrated and by whom.[83] However, it still remains a highly attractive concept precisely because of its capacious nature, which provides a lot of space for interpretation, and because of its ideal-typical nature of what good water management should look like.[84]

IWRM seeks to achieve a maximisation of economy, equity and ecosystems. However, it is rarely acknowledged that these goals are often 'antagonistic...that trade-offs are necessary and hard to achieve in such situations'.[85] IWRM thus 'obscure[s] the political nature of natural resources management; and [is] easily hijacked by groups seeking to legitimise their own agendas'.[86] All this can make IWRM an apolitical cloak for processes that are deeply transformative and involve the reallocation of limited water resources. In what follows we direct attention to two aspects of many IWRM-influenced water reforms that are important for water grabbing dynamics: first, decentralisation according to hydrographical boundaries and the involvement of water users water management and, second, the licensing of water abstraction. While these reforms may have contributed to democratising water management in some ways, our purpose here is to show how they can also unwittingly contribute to water grabbing.

Decentralisation of water management. In the water sector decentralisation in practice means the reorganisation of water governance from administrative units (eg districts) to units that coincide with hydrographical boundaries (eg basins). This provides an opportunity to deal with the dislocated effects of water use (eg pollution). Decentralisation policies and approaches often involve the setting up of Water Users Associations (WUAS) and/or River Basin Organisations (RBOS), which are now important exemplary 'models' in the water sector.

The WUA and RBO models include an emphasis on participation of water users in water management. A large body of literature highlights the mixed experiences with user involvement in water management at all levels of governance.[87] For example, the involvement of users in water management does not prevent strong actors from capturing unfair shares of water. Rather, user participation often becomes the forum through which the resource capture is taking shape, often facilitated by excluding the informal, legally unrecognised water users. Kemerink *et al* have analysed in detail for a case in South Africa where, despite the best of intentions, a policy of user participation in water management through the establishment of a WUA is used by the most powerful actors in the catchment to maintain the status quo of a highly unequal water distribution pattern established in the apartheid era.[88] Warner *et al* refer to various cases of participatory water management in which the process was used as a mechanism to delay decisions to the benefit of vested interests.[89]

More recently participatory processes have come to form the stage of appropriation processes and are used to legitimise water grabbing, though this does not mean that these processes cannot also be used to resist capture. In many countries licences for large-scale land and water investments are subject to an EIA that includes stakeholder consultations. When investors get a licence they may be expected to have passed through this stakeholder consultation process. However, such processes are often flawed and end up justifying the investment and silencing further resistance because of the completion of the stakeholder consultation exercises. Examples of such processes with regard to water grabbing have recently been documented in Ghana,[90] Mozambique,[91] and Kenya.[92]

Regulation and control through permit systems. Permit systems are an integral part of IWRM frameworks and have been drawn up in many countries. Van Koppen shows how formal administration-based water rights systems in sub-Saharan Africa have tended to dispossess the informal majority by design, as 'permit systems boil down to the formal dispossession of rural informal water users who manage their water under community-based arrangements'. Water rights that have historically been arranged locally are now declared subject to formalisation under national law. Existing rights are cancelled-out, with a promise to include them in the new law. In practice many of these rights are not (and often cannot) be included in the registration and licensing, leading to a weakening of the position of historical smallholder use. Complicated and expensive license application procedures ensure that water permits 'favour the administration-proficient'.[93] Dispossession through licensing is a prominent mechanism in the current era of global resource grabs.

Many of the colonial permit systems were designed to dispossess rural informal water users and van Koppen has argued that recently introduced or revised permit systems, based on such colonial logic, are *de facto* facilitating water grabs.[94] Small-scale water use, for drinking water and small productive use, is in many systems excluded from licensing, granting it a status of exemption, which according to Hodgson cannot be considered to be a right.[95] In practice this ignores pluralistic legal systems in which traditional legal systems govern the thousands of smallholders who are deemed uncontrollable under the registration system.[96] In South Africa general authorisations provide exemptions for larger volumes in designated areas.[97] In Mozambique these exempted uses are called *uso común*, or common use, and in Zimbabwe they are referred to as 'primary uses'.[98] In Islamic law rights to drinking water, formulated as 'rights to thirst' also have a priority.[99]

It is questionable whether these *de minimis* rights provide any security in practical terms, as this type of 'entitlement cannot lawfully prevent anyone else from also using the resource even if that use affects his own prior use/entitlement'.[100] Formal permits with state backing create first-class rights in comparison to any other right.[101] The exemption from a need for a permit keeps small-scale users from being registered as users, which makes it easier to overlook them in planning and allocation procedures, as for instance happened in a water grabbing case in Mozambique.[102] In Kenya nomadic livestock keepers and fisher folk without formal water licences were dispossessed of their traditional rights when large-scale investors started developing the Tana River Delta.[103] In many cases smallholders are even aware that their historic agricultural water rights are not recognised in national legal frameworks and that this has facilitated water grabbing. A formal right to abstraction of community drinking water does not guarantee that this cannot in practice be dispossessed through a land and water grab.[104] In Peru smallholder irrigators' formalised water right did not protect them against a water grab by a mining company.[105] In the context of limited registration of smallholder water use, poor hydrological knowledge and/or weak enforcement, permits provide an 'easy way in' for newcomers, while giving them the formal backing of the state.[106]

Growing corporate influence in water management

We now turn to the growing influence of corporate players in water resources management and water policy debates.[107] This is different from the privatisation of water supply services, which largely concerns urban water provision. Players include transnational corporations (TNCS), which use large volumes of water (to produce beverages, crops and services) and are engaging globally in debates about water management and protection of their access to supply in the face of growing shortages. The heads of 40 major TNCs recently issued a communiqué to heads of governments calling for decisive action to strengthen 'the enabling environment' for water resources management around the world.[108] Other groupings include the '2030 Water Resources Group', which is a platform of private sector companies, one international NGO (the World Wide Fund for Nature, WWF), some aid agencies and some national governments (eg those of China, India and Mexico). The 2030 Water Resources Group seeks to play a key role in water resources management at the basin scale, a function that is historically vested with the state. Instruments deployed include information sharing of data on water availability accrued through so-called 'water tool risks', a range of convening stakeholders, as well as engagement with communities.[109] However, business interests could triumph over altruistic ones. Water availability data can be framed to serve certain interests and stakeholder engagement may be merely symbolic. Finally, national governments may prioritise business interests and the scope of foreign revenue generation over local interests and questions of environmental integrity.

Companies are also spearheading innovation and action in water use in the beverages sector. One example is Coca-Cola, which operates in about 200 countries and has 300 bottling partners.[110] Coca-Cola set a target to improve water-use efficiency in its plants by 20% by 2012, against a 2004 baseline. The company claimed in 2010 that it had achieved six years of consecutive reduction along with a 16% reduction on the 2004 baseline.[111] But as Box 1 demonstrates, there are many contradictions in the way Coca-Cola actually operates in-country.

The activities of TNCs have largely been welcomed by dominant players in the water sector. In 2012 Pepsico and in 2011 Nestlé controversially won the Stockholm Industry Water Award for leadership, performance and efforts to improve water management in their supply chains and also for their work with local farmers at the World Water Week in Stockholm, the annual mecca of water experts worldwide.[112]

Nestlé is one of the world's largest corporations involved in food. Like Coca-Cola and Pepsico, it has massive structural and bargaining power over the world economy and trade policies, including virtual water flows embedded in trade.[113] Nestlé, like Coca-Cola, is playing a leading role in corporate water accountability, which includes paying attention to how farmers manage their water and active engagement in various corporate networks around water.[114] According to Genetic Resources Action International (GRAIN), companies such as Bunge (one of the world's largest agribusiness corporations) are also making direct investments in land as part of the global rush for land.[115] After winning an award at World Water Week in Stockholm in 2012 for water efficiency (20% per unit four years ahead of its 2012 goal), Pepsico announced the next day that it was seeking the right business model to significantly expand operations in Africa and 'thrive in this market of one billion people'.[116]

India

Across India, movements have emerged against Coca-Cola as a result of alleged water grabs and water contamination. According to local people, Coca-Cola was extracting 1.5 million litres of water per day in a plant located in Plachimada, resulting in a drop in the water table from 150 to 500 feet. Waste deposits from the plant also made the water in the surrounding wells, fields and canals unfit for drinking. The plant was closed on 17 February 2004. This movement triggered new demands against the 87 other Coca-Cola and Pepsi plants in India, where water had been depleted and polluted. Coca-Cola claims that these accusations are unjustified and points to an independent report undertaken by the Energy and Resources Institute, known as TERI, which assessed its practices in India. TERI found the plants to be complying with the government regulations. However, even this report states that Coca-Cola must take into account local community needs since in some plants excesses of bacteria and other pollutants were found.

Mexico

Mexico is currently the number one Coca-Cola consuming nation in the world. The beverage has attained religious significance in places like San Juan Chamula in the state of Chiapas, replacing traditional beverages used in religious ceremonies and as dowry payment for marriage (Rovira 2000). The company has strong political connections. Vicente Fox, México's former president was the President of the Coca-Cola Corporation of Mexico before coming to power and during his mandate Coca-Cola started to bottle water from water-rich Chiapas and the drink is often handed out for free during local elections by those in power.

However, the main reason for its immense consumption is the lack of potable water, making Mexico the second largest consumer of bottled water, most of which is largely owned by Coca-Cola. Since 2000 Coca-Cola has been allowed to extract water from 19 aquifers and 15 rivers and also has concessions to dump waste in public water. In 2003 the company paid $20,000 to compensate for over-extracting water while the profits of one bottling plant alone reached $40,000.

Box 1. Coca Cola in India and Mexico.
Sources: Shiva, V (2006) 'Resisting Water Privatisation, Building Water Democracy', a paper on the occasion of the World Water Forum in Mexico City March 2006.
Bokaie, J. (2007) 'Coke must prove it really cares', Marketing Jun 13: 19.
Bell, B. (2006) 'Cola Wars in Mexico', In these times http://inthesetimes.com/article/2840/ (accessed 1 May 2013).
Rovira, G. (2000) Women of Maize, Mexico: Editorial Era.
Wooters, M. (2008) 'Coca-Cola and Water Resources in Chiapas', Classic Newsletter 57, http://www.casacollective.org/story/newsletter/coca-cola-and-water-resources-chiapas (accessed 1 May 2013).

While some may argue that the growing corporate influence in water management does not yet have clear implications for water grabbing, these companies' emerging strategic influence on policy making does have risks and implications for current and future grabbing processes. These include the potential re-allocation of water to the 'highest economic value', with detrimental impacts on local lives, livelihoods and water and food security. Also there is a significant gap between the promotional instruments deployed by companies and what they are actually doing on the ground. The case of Coca-Cola illustrates these issues. Despite commitments to 'shared risks' and to sustainable water management, risks are often unequally shared and new water stresses may be created. Furthermore, companies are often more legally bound to be accountable to distant shareholders than to local stakeholders, who are often voiceless and powerless. Thanks to their structural bargaining power and influence over global and national policies and processes, they shape and frame powerful discourses, subjecting water governance institutions to processes of capture.[117]

Discussion and conclusions

The slippery nature of water grabbing means that it is difficult to pinpoint the effects of reallocations for reasons of surface water/groundwater interactions and inter-annual variability, among others. These characteristics of water have important implications for those interested in either regulating or contesting its management. This may partly explain why local communities have reacted in different ways to land and water grabbing. The fluidity of water (and dislocated effects of water grabbing) and the 'invisibility' of customary water rights systems can complicate the task of 'framing' water grabbing as really happening and as an injustice warranting a serious and systematic political response. Global governance mechanisms need to address these local complexities as well as two other challenges, namely the (in)visibility of customary access, use and management systems *vis-à-vis* formal state law, and the complexity of the regulatory field as both plural with overlapping regulatory orders and fragmented (separate state agencies for land vs water vs forests vs. fisheries).

As in the land sector, formalisation of rights in the water sector is increasingly seen as a universal solution; but the underlying issue is: formalising what? Rights that have historically been arranged locally are now declared subject to formalisation under national law, and in the context of limited registration of smallholder water use, poor hydrological knowledge and/or weak enforcement, permits provide an 'easy way in' for newcomers, while giving them the formal backing of the state.[118] Moreover, some of the security provided by customary arrangements to women and small-holders through informal and kinship arrangements are also being eroded, not to mention this being a highly bureaucratic process.

Even if formalisation could be a possible 'answer', it can truly only be an effective answer if what is being 'formalised' is water as a human right, *prioritising* the well-being and livelihoods of the poor, marginalised and vulnerable with regard to access, use and control. As has been noted, the human right to water was the result of decades of intense global struggle and lobbying, and this official recognition was a great victory for the global water justice movement. But so far debates around the right to water have had very limited effect on water resource management and have been very narrowly interpreted in the mainstream as the right to safe drinking water, neglecting the need for productive uses of water. The Special Rapporteur for the Right to Water and Sanitation also seems to be underserving the cause of human rights by claiming that rights are market-neutral and by remaining agnostic. Instead, human rights need to be actively used as a counterveiling force against commodification. Here we are calling for both a stronger social justice perspective to the right to water as well as a broader definition of the human right to water, encompassing both the domestic and the productive uses so integral for survival and well-being.

In this article we have explored the significance of global land and water governance initiatives for water grabbing at the national and local level. We demonstrated how disparate and seemingly isolated global processes have led to a domination of neoliberal discourses and trends. In the field of water management the Dublin conference provides the exemplar of a watershed moment and thus won out over earlier processes, such as Delhi, in which there was a stronger focus on equity and universality. The Dublin declaration and its popularity reflect the dominant Washington Consensus of the 1990s, which also influenced environmental governance. In water management this has led to clear neoliberal tendencies, elaborated alongside policies of integration, participation, water rights formalisation and basin management. After the privatisation of water services the privatisation and financialisation of the resource itself are now taking place. Similarly to IWRM policies, with their 20-year roots, new trends, such as drawing attention to the food–energy–water nexus, are reinforcing a call for integrated governance while at the same time legitimising increased corporate involvement. Fuzzy and ambiguous processes of global water and land governance are thus increasing local-level uncertainties and complexities. Usually powerful players can navigate their way through such uncertainties, making them into mechanisms of exclusion of poor and marginalised people.

For less powerful players resolving ambiguities in conflicting regulatory frameworks may require tipping the balance toward the most favourable. This may not be as impossible as it might seem. As Margulies *et al* point out, political-institutional uncertainties in global governance can also potentially become opportunities for previously excluded actors and ideas to be heard and make an impact, by creating unexpected 'opportunities for policy entrepreneurs and new ideas to enter global policy spaces that may set governance along new pathways'.[119]

How to convert this potential into actual gains from a social justice perspective is a major challenge. When understood as the capturing of control not just of the water itself, but also of the power to decide how this will be used and by whom, water grabbing is a potentially powerful entry point for increasing contestation and building resistance to the neoliberal, corporate business-led convergence in global resource governance discourses and processes. Control grabbing is perhaps best seen as a contingent process, marked by conflict, negotiation and friction, which can end up ratifying an existing balance of power. Although poor people often do lose out, under certain conditions their political action can make a positive difference. Yet, compared with land grabbing, water grabbing seems less contested from an equity and water justice perspective, much less an agrarian- and environmental justice perspective, even though the materiality of water means that water grabbing potentially affects greater numbers of diverse water users. If done systematically, applying a water lens to grabbing situations can help to open up vistas for possible political action that has the potential to challenge dominant governance processes:

- The far-reaching spillover effects of specifically water grabbing widen the space/time field of impacts and suggest the value of and need for more systematic horizontal and vertical alliance building among affected people. There is a need to go beyond the fixation with water volumes to focus on issues of access, quality, timing and control.
- Water has crucial importance for sustaining human life, which means that grabbing of land and water potentially affects all kinds of users directly in their sustenance of life. This reinforces the need to build alliances across land and water sectors.

It is unlikely that such a perspective will simply materialise on its own; social pressure and strategic political action are needed. The human right to food may also have potential as a basis for organising strategic political action and building cross-class and multi-sectoral alliances, similar to the way it has served as an important focal point for agrarian justice and land rights activism. For, whatever problems there are with the FAO-TGS, they can potentially still be used to pressure governments, since water is indeed deeply and inextricably interconnected with the other natural resources that are covered (land, fisheries and forests) and which are framed in the context of food security and the right to food.

Finally, our analysis points to a need for land and water rights advocates to begin more systematic engagements with each other around elaborating a human right to land and water that can off-set or build counterweights to the neoliberal corporate business-led convergence we are seeing in global resource governance discourses and processes, and which are imposing views of land and water as tradable economic assets. This would mean elaborating a human rights perspective to land and water that is both more interconnected, more social justice-oriented and which encompasses productive uses of water.

Notes

We are very grateful to Paola Velasco Herrejon and Beth Mudford for their fantastic help with research assistance and copyediting this paper. We thank the editors of this special issue, three anonymous reviewers and Rutgerd Boelens and Jeroen Vos for their useful comments. The usual disclaimers apply.

1 For an overview of discussions on this convergence of factors, see B White, SM Borras Jr, R Hall, I. Scoones & W Wolford, 'The new enclosures: critical perspectives on corporate land deals', *Journal of Peasant Studies*, 39(3–4), 2012, pp 619–647.
2 L Mehta, GJ Veldwisch & J Franco, 'Introduction to the Special Issue: water grabbing? Focus on the (re) appropriation of finite water resources', *Water Alternatives*, 5(2), 2012, pp 193–207.
3 P Woodhouse, 'New investment, old challenges: land deals and the water constraint in African agriculture', *Journal of Peasant Studies*, 39(3–4), 2012, pp 777–794; and J Skinner & L Cotula, *Are Land Deals Driving 'Water Grabs'? Briefing: The Global Land Rush*, London: International Institute for Environment and Development (IIED), 2011, at http://pubs.iied.org/17102IIED, accessed April 2012.
4 AY Hoekstra & MM Mekonnen, 'The water footprint of humanity', *Proceedings of the National Academy of Sciences*, 109(9), 2012, pp 3232–3237.

5 World Bank, *Rising Global Interest in Farmland: Can it Yield Sustainable and Equitable Results?*, Washington, DC: World Bank, 2010; and J Chu, 'A blue revolution for Africa? Large-scale irrigation projects and land and water "grabs"', in TA Allan, M Keulertz, S Sojamo, & J Warner (eds), *Handbook of Land and Water Grabs in Africa: Foreign Direct Investment and Food and Water Security*, London: Routledge, 2013, pp 207–220.

6 T Hertzog, A Adamczewski, F Molle, JC Poussin & JY Jamin, 'Ostrich-like strategies in sahelian sands? Land and water grabbing in the Office du Niger, Mali', *Water Alternatives*, 5(2), 2012, pp 304–321; Woodhouse, 'New investment, old challenges'; and S Duvail, C Médard, O Hamerlynck & DW Nyingi, 'Land and water grabbing in an East African coastal wetland: the case of the Tana Delta', *Water Alternatives*, 5(2), 2012, pp 322–343.

7 TO Williams, B Gyampoh, F Kizito & R Namara, 'Water implications of large-scale land acquisitions in Ghana', *Water Alternatives*, 5(2), 2012, pp 243–265.

8 M Islar, 'Privatised hydropower development in Turkey: a case of water grabbing?', *Water Alternatives*, 5 (2), 2012, pp 376–391.

9 M Sosa & M Zwarteveen, 'Exploring the politics of water grabbing: the case of large mining operations in the Peruvian Andes', *Water Alternatives*, 5(2), 2012, pp 360–375.

10 Mehta *et al*, 'Introduction to the Special Issue'.

11 *Ibid*.

12 World Bank, *Rising Global Interest in Farmland*; and Oxfam, *Land and Power: The Growing Scandal Surrounding the New Wave of Investments in Land*, Oxford: Oxfam-International, 2011.

13 S Borras Jr, J Franco, S Gomez, C Kay & M Spoor, 'Land grabbing in Latin America and the Caribbean', *Journal of Peasant Studies*, 39(3–4), 2012, pp 845–872.

14 MC Rulli, A Saviori & P D'Odorico, 'Global land and water grabbing', *Proceedings of the National Academy of Sciences*, 110(3), 2013, pp 892–897.

15 Hertzog *et al*, 'Ostrich-like strategies in sahelian sands?'.

16 SM Borras Jr, D Fig & SM Suárez, 'The politics of agrofuels and mega-land and water deals: insights from the ProCana case, Mozambique', *Review of African Political Economy*, 38(128), 2011, pp 215–234.

17 S Borras Jr & JC Franco, 'From threat to opportunity? Problems with the idea of a "Code of Conduct" for land-grabbing', *Yale Human Rights and Development Law Journal*, 13(2), 2010, pp 507–523.

18 Williams *et al*, 'Water implications of large-scale land acquisitions in Ghana'.

19 A Bues & I Theesfeld, 'Water grabbing and the role of power: shifting water governance in the light of agricultural foreign direct investment', *Water Alternatives*, 5(2), 2012, pp 266–283.

20 A Houdret, 'The water connection: irrigation, water grabbing and politics in southern Morocco', *Water Alternatives*, 5(2), 2012, pp 284–303.

21 Duvail *et al*, 'Land and water grabbing in an East African coastal wetland'.

22 I Velez Torres, 'Water grabbing in the Cauca basin: the capitalist exploitation of water and dispossession of afro-descendant communities', *Water Alternatives*, 5(2), 2012, pp 421–449.

23 LA Wily, 'Enclosure revisited: putting the global land rush in historical perspective', in Allan *et al*, *Handbook of Land and Water Grabs in Africa*, pp 11–24.

24 S Wagle, S Warghade & M Sathe, 'Exploiting policy obscurity for legalising water grabbing in the era of economic reform: the case of Maharashtra, India', *Water Alternatives*, 5(2), 2012, pp 412–430.

25 D Bossio, T Erkossa, Y Dile, M McCartney, F Killiches & H Hoff, 'Water implications of foreign direct investment in Ethiopia's agricultural sector', *Water Alternatives*, 5(2), 2012, pp 223–242.

26 N Matthews, 'Water grabbing in the Mekong Basin—an analysis of the winners and losers of Thailand's hydropower development in Lao PDR', *Water Alternatives*, 5(2), 2012, pp 392–411; and Duvail *et al*, 'Land and water grabbing in an East African coastal wetland'.

27 Hertzog *et al*, 'Ostrich-like strategies in sahelian sands?'.

28 Williams *et al*, 'Water implications of large-scale land acquisitions in Ghana'.

29 Islar, 'Privatised hydropower development in Turkey'; and Wagle *et al*, 'Exploiting policy obscurity for legalising water grabbing'.

30 Bues & Theesfeld, 'Water grabbing and the role of power'; and Bossio *et al*, 'Water implications of foreign direct investment'.

31 Duvail *et al*, 'Land and water grabbing in an East African coastal wetland'; and Matthews, 'Water grabbing in the Mekong Basin'.

32 Wagle *et al*, 'Exploiting policy obscurity for legalising water grabbing'; Velez Torres, 'Water grabbing in the Cauca basin'; and Sosa & Zwarteveen, 'Exploring the politics of water grabbing'.

33 Hertzog *et al*, 'Ostrich-like strategies in sahelian sands?'; and Williams *et al*, 'Water implications of large-scale land acquisitions in Ghana'.

34 Matthews, 'Water grabbing in the Mekong Basin'.

35 Woodhouse, 'New investment, old challenges'.

36 P Woodhouse & A-S Ganho, 'Is water the hidden agenda of agricultural land acquisition in sub-Saharan Africa?', paper presented at the 'International Conference on Global Land Grabbing', Institute of Development Studies and Future Agricultures Consortium, University of Sussex, 6–8 April 2011.

37 Skinner & Cotula, *Are Land Deals Driving 'Water grabs'?*.

38 Sosa & Zwarteveen, 'Exploring the politics of water grabbing'; and Velez Torres, 'Water grabbing in the Cauca basin'.

39 Matthews, 'Water grabbing in the Mekong Basin'; and Wagle *et al*, 'Exploiting policy obscurity for legalising water grabbing'.

40 S Gasteyer, J Isaac, J Hillal & S Walsh, 'Water grabbing in colonial perspective: land and water in Israel/Palestine', *Water Alternatives*, 5(2), 2012, pp 450–468; and Islar, 'Privatised hydropower development in Turkey'.

41 Duvail *et al*, 'Land and water grabbing in an East African coastal wetland'.

42 Matthews, 'Water grabbing in the Mekong Basin'; Williams *et al*, 'Water implications of large-scale land acquisitions in Ghana'; Duvail *et al*, 'Land and water grabbing in an East African coastal wetland'; and W Beekman & GJ Veldwisch, 'The evolution of the land struggle for smallholder irrigated rice production in Nante, Mozambique', *Physics and Chemistry of the Earth*, Parts A/B/C, Vol 50–52, pp 179–184, 2012.

43 Velez Torres, 'Water grabbing in the Cauca basin'; and Gasteyer *et al*, 'Water grabbing in colonial perspective'.

44 Houdret, 'The water connection'; and Sosa & Zwarteveen, 'Exploring the politics of water grabbing'.

45 SM Borras, JC Franco & C Wang, 'The challenge of global governance of land grabbing: changing international agricultural context and competing political views and strategies', *Globalizations*, 10(1), 2013, pp 161–179.

46 Mehta *et al*, 'Introduction to the Special Issue'.

47 S Arduino, G Colombo, OM Ocampo & L Panzeri, 'Contamination of community potable water from land grabbing: a case study from rural Tanzania', *Water Alternatives*, 5(2), 2012, pp 344–359; and Sosa & Zwarteveen, 'Exploring the politics of water grabbing'.

48 A legal pluralism lens helps to situate law as a complex and contested socio-political process that unfolds unevenly over time and space and generates variable and contingent results that are open to competing interpretations.

49 L Mehta et al *Exploring Understandings of Institutions and Uncertainty: New Directions in Natural Resources Management*, IDS Discussion Paper 372, Brighton: IDS, 1999, p 10.

50 SM Suárez, 'The human rights framework in contemporary agrarian struggles', *Journal of Peasant Studies*, 40(1), 2013, pp 239–290; and P Seufert, 'The FAO Voluntary Guidelines on the Responsible Governance of Tenure of Land, Fisheries and Forests', *Globalizations*, 10(1), 2013, pp 181–186.

51 SM Suarez, *The Recently Adopted Guidelines on the Responsible Governance of Tenure of Land, Fisheries and Forests: A Turning Point in the Governance of Natural Resources?*, Right to Food and Nutrition Watch 2012—Who Decides About Global Food and Nutrition?/Strategies to Regain Control/Bread for the World/FIAN International/Interchurch Organization for Development Cooperation (ICCO), Heidelberg, Germany: FIAN International, 2012, p 37.

52 No mention of water is made beyond a single reference to the governance of water and other 'associated natural resources', such as for instance fisheries, by national states on basis of their own 'different models and systems of governance'. Committee on World Food Security (CFS)-Food and Agriculture Organisation (FAO), 'Voluntary Guidelines on the Responsible Governance of Tenure of Land, Fisheries and Forests in the Context of National Food Security', Rome: FAO, 2012.

53 One of the authors was present when the proposal to include water was voted down by the governments as being 'too complicated'.

54 This leaves small-scale fishers vulnerable to other governance initiatives, which have the potential to facilitate 'ocean-grabbing'. See World Forum of Fisher Peoples & World Forum of Fish Harvesters and Fish Workers, 'Call for Governments to Stop Supporting the Global Partnership for Oceans (GPO) and Rights-based Fishing (RBF) Reforms', 2013, at http://masifundise.org.za/press-statement-by-the-world-forum-of-fisher-peoples-in-response-to-the-global-partnership-for-oceans/.

55 R Künnemann & SM Suárez, 'International human rights and governing land grabbing: a view from global civil society', *Globalizations*, 10(1), 2013, pp 123–139.

56 Borras Jr & Franco, 'From threat to opportunity?'.

57 R Bustamante, C Crespo & A Walnycki, 'Seeing through the concept of water as a human right in Bolivia', in F Sultana & A Loftus (eds), *The Right to Water: Politics, Governance and Social Struggles*, London: Earthscan, 2011, pp 223–240.

58 L Mehta, *Unpacking Rights and Wrongs: Do Human Rights make a Difference? The Case of Water Rights in India and South Africa*, IDS Working Paper 260, Brighton: IDS, 2005.

59 Office of the High Commissioner for Human Rights (OHCHR), *Report of the Independent Expert on the Issue of Human Rights Obligations related to Access to Safe Drinking Water and Sanitation*, A/HRC/15/31, Geneva: OHCHR, 2010.

60 http://www.suez-environnement.com/water/challenges/promoting-access-water-sanitation/, accessed 1 May 2013.

61 We thank an anonymous reviewer for pointing this out.

62 J Sumberg, J Thompson & P Woodhouse, 'Why agronomy in the developing world has become contentious', *Agriculture and Human Values*, 30(1), 2013, pp 71–83.

63 Seattle to Brussels Network, http://www.tni.org/briefing/beginners-guide-trade-0?context=70931, 2012, p 22.

64 www.gcint.org/what-we-do/water-peace/un-watercourses-convention , accessed 1 May 2013.

65 K Conca, *Governing Water: Contentious Transnational Politics and Global Institution Building*, Cambridge, MA: MIT Press, 2006.

66 *Ibid.*

67 Allan *et al*, *Handbook of Land and Water Grabs in Africa*.

68 AK Chapagain & D Tickner, 'Water footprint: help or hindrance?', *Water Alternatives*, 5(3), 2012, pp 563–581.

69 AY Hoekstra, *Water Footprint of Modern Consumer Society*, London: Taylor and Francis, 2013, p 288.

70 ND Hepworth, JC Postigo, B Güemes Delgado & P Kjell, *Drop by Drop: Understanding the Impacts of the UK's Water Footprint through a Case Study of Peruvian Asparagus*, London: Progressio/CEPES/Water Witness International, 2010.

71 D Harvey, *The New Imperialism*, Oxford: Oxford University Press, 2003; K Bakker, 'Neoliberalizing nature? Market environmentalism in water supply in England and Wales', *Annals of the Association of American Geographers*, 95(3), 2005, pp 542–565; and Borras *et al*, 'Land grabbing in Latin America'.

72 S Bernstein, *The Compromise of Liberal Environmentalism*, New York: Columbia University Press, 2001; and Bakker, 'Neoliberalizing nature?'.

73 A Nicol, L Mehta & J Allouche (eds), '"Some for all?" Politics and pathways in water and sanitation', IDS *Bulletin*, 43(2), 2012, pp 10–12.

74 L Mehta (ed), *The Limits to Scarcity*, London: Earthscan, 2010.

75 Beekman & Veldwisch, 'The evolution of the land struggle for smallholder irrigated rice production in Nante, Mozambique'.

76 Boelens & Vos, 'The danger of naturalizing water policy concepts: water productivity and efficiency discourses from field irrigation to virtual water trade', *Agricultural Water Management*, 108, 2012, pp 16–26; RM Friend, 'Fishing for influence: fisheries science and evidence in water resources development in the Mekong basin', *Water Alternatives*, 2(2), 2009, pp 167–182; and Duvail *et al*, 'Land and water grabbing in an East African coastal wetland'.

77 M Finger & J Allouche, *Water Privatisation: Transnational Corporations and the Re-regulation of the Global Water Industry*, London: Taylor and Francis, 2002.

78 *Ibid*; KJ Bakker, *Privatizing Water: Governance Failure and the World's Urban Water Crisis*, Ithaca, NY: Cornell University Press, 2010; and D Hall, E Lobina & R de la Motte, 'Public resistance to privatisation in water and energy', *Development in Practice*, 15(3–4), 2005, pp 286–301.

79 A Tricarico & C Amicucci, 'Background on financialisation of water', paper prepared by CRBM for the European meeting, 'For the Construction of the European Network for Public Water', Naples, 10–11 December 2012.

80 F Molle, 'Nirvana concepts, narratives and policy models: insights from the water sector', *Water Alternatives*, 1(1), 2008, pp 131–156.

81 *Ibid.*

82 Global Water Partnership, *Integrated Water Resources Management*, TAC Background Papers No 4, Stockholm: Global Water Partnership, 2000.

83 AK Biswas, 'Integrated water resources management: a reassessment', *Water International*, 29(2), 2004, pp 248–256.

84 Conca, *Governing Water*.

85 Molle, 'Nirvana concepts, narratives and policy models'.

86 *Ibid.*

87 F Cleaver, 'Paradoxes of participation: questioning participatory approaches to development', *Journal of International Development*, 11(4), 1999, pp 597–612; P Wester, DJ Merrey & M De Lange, 'Boundaries of consent: stakeholder representation in river basin management in Mexico and South Africa', *World Development*, 31(5), 2003, pp 797–812; R Boelens, *The Rules of the Game and the Game of the Rules: Normalization and Resistance in Andean Water Control*, Wageningen: Wageningen University, 2008; and J Warner, P Wester & A Bolding, 'Going with the flow: river basins as the natural units for water management', *Water Policy*, 10(S2), 2008, pp 121–138.

88 JS Kemerink, LE Méndez, R Ahlers, P Wester & P van der Zaag, 'The question of inclusion and representation in rural South Africa: challenging the concept of water user associations as a vehicle for transformation', *Water Policy*, 15(2), 2013, pp 243–257.

89 Warner *et al*, 'Going with the flow'.

90 Williams *et al*, 'Water implications of large-scale land acquisitions in Ghana'.

91 Borras *et al*, 'Land grabbing in Latin America'.

92 Duvail *et al*, 'Land and water grabbing in an East African coastal wetland'.

93 B van Koppen, *Dispossession at the Interface of Community-based Water Law and Permit Systems*, Community-based Water Law and Water Resource Management Reform in Developing Countries, http://ideas. repec.org/b/ags/iwmibo/138046.html, 2007, p 46.

94 *Ibid*, p 46

95 S Hodgson, *Land and Water: The Rights Interface*, Vol 84, Rome: FAO, 2004, p 92.

96 R Meinzen-Dick & L Nkonya, 'Understanding legal pluralism in water rights: lessons from Africa and Asia', paper prepared for the African Water Laws Workshop, 'Plural Legislative Frameworks for Rural Water Management in Africa', 2005.

97 B van Koppen, H Sally, M Aliber, B Cousins & B Tapela, *Water Resources Management, Rural Redress and Agrarian Reform*, Development Planning Division, Working Paper Series No 7, DBSA: Midrand. This paper is one of a set of papers on the theme of water security that the Development Planning Division of the DBSA commissioned in 2009. There is a list of these papers at the back of this document. Published by Development Planning Division Development Bank of Southern Africa, http://www.dbsa. org/Research/DPD%20Working%20papers%20documents/DPD%20No%207.pdf.

98 GJ Veldwisch, W Beekman & A Bolding, 'Smallholder irrigators, water rights and investments in agriculture: three cases from rural Mozambique', *Water Alternatives*, 6(1), 2013, pp 125–141.

99 Meinzen-Dick & Nkonya, 'Understanding legal pluralism in water rights'.

100 Hodgson, *Land and Water*.

101 van Koppen, *Dispossession at the Interface of Community-based Water Law and Permit Systems*, p 46.

102 P van der Zaag, D Juizo, A Vilanculos, A Bolding & NC Post Uiterweer, 'Does the Limpopo River Basin have sufficient water for massive irrigation development in the plains of Mozambique?', *Physics and Chemistry of the Earth*, Parts A/B/C, 35(13), 2010, pp 832–837; Borras *et al*, 'Land grabbing in Latin America'; and Veldwisch *et al*, 'Smallholder irrigators, water rights and investments in agriculture'.

103 Duvail *et al*, 'Land and water grabbing in an East African coastal wetland'.

104 Arduino *et al*, 'Contamination of community potable water'.

105 Sosa & Zwarteveen, 'Exploring the politics of water grabbing'.

106 Van Koppen, *Dispossession at the Interface of Community-based Water Law and Permit Systems*.

107 ND Hepworth, 'Open for business or opening Pandora's box? A constructive critique of corporate engagement in water policy—an introduction', *Water Alternatives*, 5(3), 2012, pp 543–562; P Newborne & N Mason, 'The private sector's contribution to water management: re-examining corporate purposes and company roles', *Water Alternatives*, 5(3), 2012, pp 603–618; and S Sojamo & EA Larson, 'Investigating food and agribusiness corporations as global water security, management and governance agents: the case of Nestlé, Bunge and Cargill', *Water Alternatives*, 5(3), 2012, pp 619–635.

108 Newborne & Mason, 'The private sector's contribution to water management'.

109 *Ibid*.

110 *Ibid*, p 610.

111 *Ibid*.

112 The Stockholm Industry Water Award recognises companies within the business sector that have demonstrated their commitment to advancing the world's water situation by achieving impressive performance in their water usage. See http://www.siwi.org/prizes/stockholm-industry-water-award.

113 Sojamo & Larson, 'Investigating food and agribusiness corporations'.

114 *Ibid*.

115 Genetic Resources Action International (GRAIN), *Land Grabs Data Set*, 2012, at http://www.grain.org/article/entries/4479-grain-releases-data-set-with-over-400-global-land-grabs, accessed 23 August 2013.

116 Newborne & Mason, 'The private sector's contribution to water management'.

117 Sojamo & Larson, 'Investigating food and agribusiness corporations'.

118 Van Koppen, *Dispossession at the Interface of Community-based Water Law and Permit Systems*.

119 ME Margulis & T Porter, 'Governing the global land grab: multipolarity, ideas, and complexity in transnational governance', *Globalizations*, 10(1), 2013, p 68.

Notes on Contributors

Jennifer Franco is coordinator of the Agrarian Justice program at the Transnational Institute, Netherlands, and an adjunct professor at the China Agricultural University in Beijing.

Lyla Mehta is a research fellow at the Institute of Development Studies at the University of Sussex, UK and a Visiting Professor at the Norwegian University of Life Sciences.

Gert Jan Veldwisch is assistant professor at the Water Resources Management Group of Wageningen University, The Netherlands.

Together they have edited a special issue of Water Alternatives on Water Grabbing.

Green Dreams: Myth and Reality in China's Agricultural Investment in Africa

DEBORAH BRÄUTIGAM[a] & HAISEN ZHANG[b]

[a]Department of Comparative Politics, University of Bergen, Norway and Johns Hopkins University's School of Advanced International Studies, Washington,DC, USA; [b]University of International Business and Economics, Beijing, China

ABSTRACT *What role does China play in the recent rush for land acquisition in Africa? Conventional wisdom suggests a large role for the Chinese government and its firms. Our research suggests the opposite. Land acquisitions by Chinese companies have so far been quite limited, and focused on production for African consumption. We trace the evolution of strategy and incentives for Chinese agricultural engagement in Africa, and examine more closely several of the more well known cases, sorting out the myths and the realities.*

In the first two decades of the 21st century Brazil, Russia, India and China (BRIC) emerged as highly visible traders and investors. This visibility was particularly noted in the rush of interest in agricultural investment following the global commodity price spike in 2008. A cycle emerged whereby news reports of foreign investor interest were collected in media-based databases, which became solidified in a conventional wisdom that the governments of certain countries—in particular, China and several Middle Eastern states—were attempting to secure large tracts of land in Africa to ensure their own food security.

This article analyses this cycle though a focus on China in Africa, where there is little direct evidence to support this conventional wisdom. It proceeds in several steps. First, we identify the initial, influential media reports of Chinese interest in African farmland. We then identify the ways in which these media reports were solidified in a conventional wisdom, and repeated uncritically by significant policy makers and respected scholars. Following this, we briefly outline the Chinese government's policies towards outward investment in agriculture, the history of agricultural engagement, and existing data on Chinese agricultural investment in Africa.[1] We follow this by several case studies in which we contrast the perception of large-scale land acquisition with the reality on the ground.

Our argument makes four key points. First, there is as of yet no evidence of a coordinated Chinese government effort to obtain land in Africa, for food security or for other agricultural investment. However, and second, a small number of Chinese agribusiness companies did pursue land acquisitions in Africa as part of China's general 'going global' surge of trade and outward foreign investment (these are the 'green dreams' of the title). In most cases the amounts of land at stake in these negotiations were far smaller than reported, and the projects themselves were either commercial, import-substitution production (mainly rice and sugar), or biofuels (oil palm, jatropha). Third, for a combination of political and economic reasons, this interest has not, so far, translated into significant land acquisitions in Africa. Finally, the key role of African agency—investors and governments—in this process has seldom been acknowledged. In the dominant narrative Africa and Africans appear primarily as passive bystanders, even victims, not active agents.

Sub-Saharan Africa contains multiple areas where large-scale agricultural investments could be risky for local people. Protection of poor people's property rights is inadequate in many countries, and women are especially at risk. These concerns have been behind the attention given to compiling lists of 'land grabbers' in Africa, lists that have (often erroneously) featured Chinese companies as large-scale, new investors. Our own research depends primarily on fieldwork conducted between 2007 and 2013 in China and a number of African countries, including the Democratic Republic of Congo (DRC), Ethiopia, Malawi, Mozambique, Republic of Congo, Sierra Leone, Sudan, Tanzania, Zambia and Zimbabwe. We supplement this fieldwork through interviews, secondary research by other scholars, and a careful review of information on the internet in Chinese, French, Portuguese and English. Our case studies join a new wave of scholarly literature that has criticised the methods employed by the media-based 'land grab' databases, the lack of attention to national investors, and the absence of agency on the part of host governments.[2]

How conventional wisdom was built

China's rise as a global investor country coincided with the global price increases of food, oil and many other commodities in 2007 and 2008. An intense media interest in China's role as an emerging investor, in the context of concern over global food security, led first to a spate of newspaper articles, blog postings and media reports. Many of these reports contained significant errors (discussed below) but were nonetheless circulated uncritically and became the foundation for databases and, later, scholarly analyses.

Media reports

One of the earliest reports appeared on the Swiss International Relations and Security Network website in August 2007.[3] The author, then a student in Singapore, claimed that 'Beijing and Maputo' had signed a Memorandum of Understanding (MOU) in 2006 to build 'a massive agricultural project in the Zambezi river valley' that would bring in 'as many as 20 000 Chinese settlers' to run farms 'to supply the ever more affluent Chinese market.[4] In April 2008 French television visited what they said was a 10 000 hectare (ha) Chinese farming project in Cameroon, claiming that the investors wanted to ship their rice production back to China.[5] The Associated Press published a story in May 2008 with the title: 'China farms the world to feed a ravenous economy'.[6] The article claimed: 'In the Democratic Republic of the Congo, a Chinese telecommunications giant, ZTE International, has bought more than 7 million acres of forest to plant oil palms. In Zimbabwe, state-owned China International Water and Electric Corp reportedly received rights from the government to farm 250 000 acres (101 174 ha) of corn in the south.'[7] The DRC story was repeated in an article on agricultural outsourcing in *The Economist* in July 2009, and this was cited by a number of researchers.[8] We discuss all these stories as case studies below.

It did not take long for the first collections and analyses of these media reports to appear, usually on websites hosted by think-tanks and NGOs. In October 2008 an NGO, GRAIN, published its first analysis of land-grabbing based on media reports.[9] The words 'China' or 'Chinese' were mentioned 47 times in the paper, mainly as one of a group of countries whose chief goal was to 'outsource their domestic food production by gaining control of farms in other countries'.[10] The analysis also claimed (erroneously) that the Chinese government had established a $5 billion fund to allow Chinese companies 'to invest in African agriculture'.[11]

By 2012 two major, international databases on 'land grabs' existed, along with two papers containing lists of Chinese 'land grabs' in Africa. GRAIN published its own collection in February 2012, assembling 400 alleged deals.[12] In GRAIN's database 15 African projects were reported to be Chinese, at various stages of commitment, involving 393 940 ha of land. A more ambitious effort was set up by a coalition of research institutions and NGOs that established the Land Matrix, a sophisticated online system to allow media reports of investor interest in land to be verified through 'crowd-sourcing'. The Beta version of the Land Matrix was started in 2009 and launched publicly at a major World Bank conference in 2012. It listed nine allegedly 'verified' Chinese 'deals' (including mining and other land-intensive investments) in Africa, covering a total of 3 131 491 ha.[13] In March 2012 the *Journal of Peasant Studies* published an article containing a different list of 'Chinese investments', including 55 African projects, many without an indication of size.[14] Finally, a paper published in 2012 by the Canadian International Institute for Sustainable Development (IISD) contained a list of Chinese overseas 'investments' in agriculture that counted 17 'confirmed' Chinese investments in Africa, totalling 463 000 ha.[15] Several bloggers immediately criticised the initial Land Matrix data as problematic, pointing to specific 'investments' that were included as originally described by media sources, even though they had later been thoroughly investigated and found to be significantly smaller, abandoned, never to have proceeded beyond an initial expression of interest or, sometimes, never to have existed at all.[16] Yet the (very) large discrepancy among these sources did not attract any attention from the media.

Therefore, by 2012, a misleading image of Chinese agricultural engagement in Africa appeared to have solidified in the public mind: the Chinese were very actively acquiring large amounts of farmland in Africa. The Chinese government was leading the effort, using its state owned enterprises (SOEs) and sovereign wealth funds. The purpose was to secure food for China's own food security. In August 2012 the chief economist of the African Development Bank posted a blog entry that reflected this belief. Referring to the April 2012 launch of the Land Matrix database, he commented: 'At a recent World Bank-organized conference, China was identified as the biggest land grabber in the world *and in Africa*'.[17] This conclusion was also echoed in a quasi-scientific article based on the Land Matrix 'data' and published by the prestigious US National Academy of Sciences.[18]

Fieldwork-based critiques of the 'Chinese land grab' discourse

Parallel to the efforts to compile lists of Chinese agricultural investments by the media, several researchers travelled to Africa to investigate these emerging reports in the field. In 2009 the Food and Agriculture Organization (FAO) sponsored a study on 'land grabs' by the London-based International Institute for Environment and Development (IIED), which drew on fieldwork in China, Ethiopia, Ghana, Madagascar, Mali, Mozambique, Tanzania and Zambia.[19] The IIED authors cautioned that, although there was clearly Chinese interest in agricultural investment, the conventional wisdom appeared to be incorrect: 'A common external perception is that China is supporting Chinese enterprises to acquire land abroad as part of a national food security strategy. Yet the evidence for this is highly questionable.'[20] The researchers also pointed out that 'as yet, there are no known examples of Chinese land acquisitions in Africa in excess of 50 000 hectares where deals have been concluded and projects implemented'.[21]

A book by one of the present authors, as well as a co-authored article published in *China Quarterly* in 2009, raised serious questions about some of the stories being accepted as conventional wisdom, including the idea that the Chinese had pledged to invest $800 million into rice in Mozambique and/or to bring in Chinese settlers, an alleged 101 174 ha Chinese maize farm in Zimbabwe, and the reported three million ha size of the DRC oil palm project.[22] Researchers at the Center for International Forestry Research (CIFOR) also conducted fieldwork in Africa to investigate large-scale farmland acquisition.[23] Their investigations, published in 2011, further confirmed that two of the most widely circulated stories (the 'Chinese' request for two million ha in Zambia, and the 2.8 million ha 'acquisition' in the DRC) were far smaller in reality than the media reports (see Table 1).[24] They concluded: 'China is not a dominant investor in plantation agriculture in Africa, in contrast to how it is often portrayed'.[25]

Much of this field research was available, on the internet, to organisations like GRAIN or the Land Matrix that were (justifiably) concerned with large-scale land acquisitions. Yet the almost exclusive focus on media reports and, in many cases, the mission of the organisation, meant that there was little investigation or follow-up on the initial 'land grab' reports before they were published,

TABLE 1. MOFCOM-approved Chinese farming investment proposals, Africa

Country	No of Chinese companies (total)	No of Chinese companies, farming sector	Grain crop (corn, rice, cassava, etc)	Cash crop (sisal, sugar, rubber, etc)	Livestock (chickens, eggs, etc)
Zambia	158	16	16	10	16
Zimbabwe	81	7	4	7	3
Nigeria	270	6	4	4	4
Sudan	83	6	4	6	2
Mozambique	58	6	3	4	1
Tanzania	112	5	1	5	1
South Africa	175	4	2	3	3
Mali	37	4	1	4	
Kenya	91	3	2	3	1
DR Congo	89	3	3	3	
Cameroon	36	3	2		3
Ethiopia	130	2	1	2	1
Ghana	115	2	1	2	
Angola	102	2	2	1	1
Rep of Congo	36	2	2	2	2
Gabon	26	2	2	2	2
Madagascar	26	2	1	1	
Liberia	24	2	2	2	2
Egypt	109	1			1
Uganda	57	1	1	1	1
Mauritius	45	1		1	
Togo	30	1		1	
Sierra Leone	29	1		1	
Benin	26	1		1	
Eq Guinea	20	1	1	1	
CAR	7	1	1	1	
Malawi	6	1		1	
Totals	2372	86	56	69	44

Note: The total number of Chinese companies includes those across all sectors, in all African countries. From these totals we identified the companies that are directly involved in grain or cash crop cultivation and animal husbandry and only include those countries. We do not include firms solely involved in agricultural trade, including those that do not have direct production, but provide credit to smallholders and purchase their crops. Some firms are simultaneously involved in two or three farming activities. *Source*: Ministry of Commerce (MOFCOM), People's Republic of China, Beijing, 2013.

becoming 'data' for others to analyse.[26] To be sure, these organisations had their own missions. In the case of GRAIN the organisation explained that it had specifically tried to attract attention to investor interest 'before the grabs happen', in the hope that activists could protest and derail the investment, and academics use the reports as a starting point for further investigation.[27] The Global Land Matrix desired to create a public tool, using community knowledge and crowdsourcing to raise awareness, while also verifying and amplifying reports.[28] The GRAIN database and the Global Land Matrix were also continually updated. Yet the nature of knowledge circulation is such that the first papers written on the initial analysis of (problematic) data often have much greater impact than papers written later, with revised and better data.[29] As one set of scholars has warned: 'the rapidity of easy access to "data" and the dangerous allure of Google have facilitated the recycling of facts long after their sell-by date'.[30] This is clearly the case with many of the 'facts' about Chinese engagement in agriculture in Africa.[31]

Chinese engagement in agriculture in Africa: an overview

China has been involved in agriculture in Africa since the 1960s. The Chinese government has featured agricultural technology transfer as a central component of its aid programme. As part of China's turn to the market in the 1980s, state-owned companies that had built state-owned farms and plantations for African governments often returned to manage them. In the 1990s these companies and others began to lease state-owned farms being privatised under structural adjustment programmes. By the new millennium the Chinese government had developed policy guidelines for outward investment in a number of sectors. Agricultural cooperation was one of the keystones of China's commitments under the Forum on China–Africa Cooperation and the January 2006 White Paper on China's Africa Policy. We elaborate on these below.

The origins of Chinese engagement in African agriculture: foreign aid

China's aid programme in Africa has always emphasised agriculture, a sector where Chinese expertise and African interest coincided.[32] The early years of the aid programme featured help for socialist governments in Africa to construct large, state-owned farms. In 1965, for example, Tanzania received Chinese help to build the Ruvu State Farm, 2834 ha of mixed farming, while Chinese technicians also built the Mahonda State Sugar Cane Farm on the island of Zanzibar, and the 5575 ha Mbarali Rice Farm Mbaye, which also featured poultry, dairy, hydropower and a rice mill.[33]

Large state farms became less frequent in the 1970s and 1980s, when Chinese teams began to take over agricultural projects abandoned by the Republic of China (Taiwan) when African countries switched diplomatic ties from Taipei to Beijing. By the end of 2009 Chinese teams had built at least 142 agricultural farms and demonstration centres for African governments, in 44 African countries, involving the development of a total of 61 500 ha.[34] Despite the political importance of agriculture, the Chinese found that it was hard to achieve sustainability for their rural projects. The World Bank, for example, reported a failure rate of 50% for its African rural development projects between 1965 and 1986.[35] The Chinese had similar difficulties.

During the 1990s the Chinese reformed their aid programme to enhance sustainability.[36] Turn-key projects with production potential could become joint ventures, rather than simply be given back to the host government, where they had generally failed to thrive.[37] In 2002 China's then vice minister in charge of foreign aid, Wei Jianguo, told a seminar encouraging Chinese agricultural investment in Africa that 'China–Africa agricultural co-operation in the new century *must be conducted by enterprises* and should be market-oriented'.[38] In agricultural aid the most visible sign of this new emphasis emerged in the launch of more than two dozen agro-technology demonstration centres across Africa. Chinese teams had built many agro-technology demonstration centres in past decades, only to watch them fail to be sustained. In 2006 they decided to experiment with a different model: getting Chinese companies and institutes, generally selected via a competitive tender system in China, to build and operate the centres for at least three years under a Chinese grant. During this time the companies were encouraged to seek out ways for the centres to earn income and become self-financing. They were also encouraged to investigate other business opportunities. Most centres were fairly small, less than 75 ha in size. In at least two cases, Cameroon and Mozambique, implementing companies have also made farming investments on their own.

Chinese investment in African agriculture: history and incentives

Chinese companies have been investing in agriculture in Africa since the mid-1980s. As China turned towards the market domestically, Chinese companies in Africa were encouraged to seek new sources of income. Most had arrived in Africa to carry out foreign aid projects, although some were sent by their parent companies to explore investment opportunities in agriculture, forestry and fisheries.[39] In the late 1980s and 1990s Chinese companies sought to lease several of the old Chinese aid projects that were being privatised under structural adjustment programmes: Segou sugar complex in Mali, Magbass sugar complex in Sierra Leone, Koba Farm in Guinea, Mpoli Farm in Mauritania, and so on. China State Farm Agribusiness Group (CSFAG) invested in two colonial-era sisal farms in Tanzania and began new agricultural investments in Zambia in 1989. By the new millennium CSFAG had seven agricultural investments in southeast Africa and West Africa, worth 290 million yuan (or roughly US$35 million).[40] These investments have continued in a pattern that has emphasised acquisitions of existing farms, as well as new, green-field investment. The largest Chinese agricultural acquisition in Africa occurred in 2008, when Chinese SOE Sinochem bought 51% of a Singapore rubber company, GMG Global. GMG Global had long term leases on rubber plantations in Cameroon and Côte d'Ivoire. Its largest concession comprised 41 000 ha in Cameroon (less than half under cultivation).[41]

The Chinese government has programmes to encourage agricultural investment overseas, although most of these are components of larger programmes promoting 'going global' across a number of sectors. Agriculture was included in the 'going global' programme as early as 2005, when the Ministry of Finance announced the establishment of special funds available to promote outbound foreign investment.[42] The Ministry of Agriculture and the China Development Bank signed an agreement in 2006 to work together in five areas, including development of projects using overseas land and water.[43] China Eximbank signed an agreement with the Ministry of Agriculture in 2008 to promote overseas investment in agriculture using export seller's credits and investment loans. In June 2010 China's top state-owned agribusiness group, China National Agricultural Development Corporation Group (CNADC) and the China–Africa Development Fund set up a joint venture, China–Africa Agriculture Investment

Co, Ltd (CAAIC). Funded at 1 billion yuan ($161 million), CAAIC was intended to be a platform to promote China's farming, fishing, animal husbandry, livestock, and agro-processing and marketing investments in Africa.[44] China's 12th five year plan (2011–15) encouraged Chinese firms to build productive capacity in developing countries with comparative advantage in agriculture, as part of the 'going global' strategy.[45] While most of these incentives were directed to state-owned firms, in 2010 the government announced that it would encourage private firms in the 'going global' effort.[46] Two years later China's State Council published notices outlining the new regulations for including private firms in the 'going global' framework.[47] Again, agriculture was included in the sectors eligible for special funds for foreign economic and technical cooperation.[48]

The focus of these incentives on Sino-African trade has yet to be felt. Chinese imports of African agricultural commodities are still relatively modest, and focused on agro-industrial imports: raw cotton (Burkina Faso), and tobacco (Zimbabwe). Indeed, some African countries import grain from China, including Eritrea, which is the second largest destination of Chinese maize exports. In 2011 African countries imported 101 968 metric tonnes (mt of cereals (wheat, rice, maize, etc) from China, while China imported less than one mt of cereals from Africa.[49] However, Chinese imports of oilseeds (mainly sesame seed from Ethiopia and groundnut from Senegal) are larger, with 366 954 mt imported into China from Africa in 2011, with a value of $489 million.[50]

According to China's State Council, as of the end of 2011, 2.5 per cent of the stock of China's foreign direct investment in Africa was in agriculture, which includes farming, forestry, animal husbandry, and fisheries, a total of $406 million.[51] For 2012, the annual figure was reported to be $82.47 million. However, we do not know the proportion of this that comes from farming alone. We include several estimates of the number of firms and the value of their investments, derived from surveys and from MOFCOM investment approval data. A survey done in 26 Chinese provinces and municipalities by the Foreign Economic Cooperation Centre of the Ministry of Agriculture estimated that, by the end of 2007, the average assets of medium-scale Chinese outward agricultural investments were about $2 million per company, with large-scale firms averaging about $10 million in assets per company.[52] We use this data to make estimates of the overall value of Chinese farming investments.

MOFCOM retains a database of approved Chinese overseas companies' investment proposals.[53] According to these data, there were 2372 African investments approved for medium and large-scale Chinese companies as of March 2013. Of these, 212 were somehow related to agriculture (grains, cash crops, animal husbandry, fisheries, forestry, agro-processing and commodity trade) in 37 African countries. Only 86 out of 2372 approved proposals were specifically related to farming (production of grains, cash crops or animal husbandry) in 27 African counties (see Table 1). The top four African countries for approved Chinese farming proposals—by number, not value—were Zambia (16), Zimbabwe (7), Mozambique (6), Nigeria (6) and Sudan (6). Not all of these approved proposals will be realised. Our fieldwork in Zambia and Zimbabwe showed that, as of June 2013, out of 16 farming investment proposals approved by MOFCOM for

Zambia, only eight were in operation, and some of these were very small. In Zimbabwe only two out of seven were actually producing, while other Chinese firms approved for farming were only operating as purchasers of cotton and tobacco. There are likely also to be some small investments under the minimum size for approval, and possibly other large acquisitions (such as Sinochem's GMG Global investment) that will not show up in the Africa data, as they were approved as investments in non-African countries, in this case Singapore.

Based on these numbers, we can say that the value of (approved) Chinese investment in farming in Africa is likely to be somewhere between $172 million (86 projects, at $2 million each) and $488.5 million ($406 million as of end-2011, plus the additional $82.5 million in 2012). The lower average may be the more realistic figure. Researcher James Keeley reported that in 2008, in one country, Zambia, a total of 23 Chinese farming investment proposals had been approved by the Zambian authorities, many from large state-owned enterprises. The total projected value was $10 million (or $435 000 per farm on average).[54]

This overview of Chinese data on Chinese companies and state incentives suggests several things. Chinese companies are interested in investing in farming in Africa. Yet the number of firms is small compared with companies in other sectors. Their investments are also still fairly small, with the exception of leasing existing plantations in places like Cameroon, Mali and Sierra Leone, and several newer farms in Zambia.[55] The new policies may foster additional interest by Chinese private firms in Africa investment. Yet risks remain high.

Case studies: investigating myth and reality in Chinese agricultural investments in Africa

In this section we review the evidence on several of the widely publicised cases that have featured on various 'land grab' lists. The case studies below illustrate the risks of agricultural investment, while also shedding light on several of the reasons why reality differs from the conventional wisdom.

Cameroon: Sino-Cam IKO

In the introduction we provided the case of the '10 000 ha Chinese rice investment' in Cameroon, visited by a French television crew who said that the Chinese were shipping the rice they produced back to China. Another French article, entitled 'Chinese raid on Cameroonian land,' predicted that the 'Chinese conquest of African farmland' would provide a solution for millions of Chinese peasants deprived of their land. 'In Cameroon', the article predicted, 'the Chinese could eventually control the chain of cereal production'.[56] These ominous statements need to be juxtaposed with a more complex reality.

What the television crew actually visited was a 120 ha rice demonstration centre near Nanga Eboko originally established as a foreign aid project by Taiwan in the 1960s, later abandoned, but brought back into production by a team of 10 agriculturalists from a state-owned company in Shaanxi Province.

Shaanxi Agriculture Group (SAG) arrived in 2005 at the invitation of the Minister of Agriculture of the Government of Cameroon, who had visited China.[57] SAG set up a subsidiary, Sino-Cam IKO (also known as China–Cameroon Yingkao Agriculture Development Co, Ltd), a subsidiary of Shaanxi Overseas Investment and Development Co, Ltd.

The Chinese firm (not the Chinese government) signed an MOU with the Cameroonian government. They obtained provisional agreement to acquire up to 10 000 hectares of land: 6000 hectares in Nanga Eboko and 4000 hectares in Santchou in the West Region, and they pledged to invest $60.5 million.[58] On the strength of this they set to work in 2006 testing rice and maize varieties at the old Taiwanese farm. In 2008 the company was selected to build one of the agro-technology training and demonstration stations pledged for Africa at the 2006 summit of the Forum on China–Africa Cooperation (FOCAC). With the agreement of the Cameroonians it built the station at Nanga Eboko. This reversed the original model, which was that the centre would serve as a springboard for further investment.

Another French team visited the station in 2010, writing an article with the title, 'When Cameroon feeds China'. This led with the sentence: 'The Cameroonian government has ceded land to an Asian enterprise that exploits local peasants to cultivate rice destined for China'.[59] The reporters interviewed the acting director of Sino-Cam IKO, who told them that 'the rice we produce is destined for consumption in Cameroon'. He said that the MOU the Chinese firm had signed in 2006 specified that all the rice would be milled and sold locally.[60]

The French reporters decided to believe local activists who showed them bags of rice for sale in the market of Nanga Eboko covered with Chinese characters. This, the activists argued, was proof that the rice was meant for the Chinese market, not Cameroon. At present, they said, volumes were too low for export: 'When they can fill a boat, the rice will leave for China'. Rice, they predicted, will 'follow the trail of bananas and cotton'. Yet this left unanswered a fundamental question: why would businessmen decide to come to Cameroon to produce rice and ship it to China, where rice prices are controlled by the government, and rice sells for about 44 US cents per kilo, when Cameroon was importing 500 000 metric tons of rice a year from Asia at a market price of 79 cents a kilo?[61]

Several field investigations during 2010 noted that the company still had not been able to obtain final authorisation for any additional land beyond the old Taiwanese-aided farm.[62] The farm manager complained to a journalist that it had implemented its side of the MOU, but that the Cameroonian government was waiting an inordinate amount of time to approve the transfer of land for large-scale rice production. After working for four years at the Taiwanese farm and building a training centre that could serve 300 agriculture students, 'we only have 100 hectares. We have also been exploited.'[63] In 2011 Cameroon's imports of rice rose by over 35% yet, as one study pointed out, '90% of land suitable for rice-farming remains unutilized'.[64]

Democratic Republic of the Congo: ZTE *and oil palm*

One single project accounts for most of the hectarage on lists of Chinese 'land investments' in Africa: the ZTE (Zhongxing Telecommunications, one of China's premier telecoms companies) alleged purchase of as much as three million ha in the DRC.[65] The size of the alleged transaction towers over that from any other company. As in the Cameroon case, there is a substantial core of reality to this story—yet far less than suggested by the headlines.

ZTE had been active in the DRC as a telecoms firm since 2000. Rumours about its interest in oil palm investment arose in May 2007 in local Congolese papers. One reported that ZTE desired to invest 'one billion dollars' in an oil palm biofuels venture estimated to cover '3 million hectares'.[66] Several months later, the project was approved by the DRC Council of Ministers, but only for 100 000 ha—a very large concession, but less than 4% of the figure discussed in the media.[67] Furthermore, no land was ever actually allocated for this project. Yet in 2008 a figure of '7 million acres' (about 2.8 million ha) was circulated in an Associated Press report on Chinese land investments globally (the reporters did not appear to have visited the DRC).[68] This story, published in the *International Herald Tribune* and other major papers, is the one usually cited as a source for this project.

How much land did ZTE *want* to acquire? ZTE officials made several confusing statements about their intentions, at least as reported in English translations. In 2009 an official from ZTE Agribusiness spoke of the company's plans to acquire a total of one million hectares of agricultural land overseas within 10 years, with a focus on Indonesia and Malaysia.[69] The same year, in a July 2009 interview with China's news agency Xinhua, ZTE's Africa regional manager, Zhang Peng, claimed that its planned project in the DRC alone would be 'one million ha'.[70] The Chinese ambassador said that the project would be 300 000 ha.[71] The convention signed in November 2007 specified 'at least' 100 000 ha.[72]

ZTE was clearly interested in investing, sending at least two separate delegations to discuss the project with the DRC's Ministry of Agriculture.[73] However, as of May 2013, the ZTE oil palm project remained moribund and there was no longer a mention of it on the website of ZTE Agribusiness. The company had invested in oil palm in Indonesia and Malaysia and, as of 2010, was reporting that it was exploring opportunities in West Africa. In Beijing Chinese officials commented privately to the authors that ZTE believed the transport costs would be too high in the DRC to make the project profitable.[74] Instead of 100 000 ha of oil palm, ZTE had established a much smaller area of 256 ha producing maize, soy, meat, chicken and eggs.[75]

Mozambique: 'China's rice bowl'?

At nearly the same time as the DRC story of ZTE Agribusiness began to circulate, another tale arose with a focus on land grabbing, Chinese settlers and huge investments in Mozambique. Like the story of China acquiring 3 million ha in the Congo, the widely circulated Mozambique tale would later be revealed to be largely a myth. Yet it was enormously influential, appearing in most of the 'land grab' databases in 2009, and referenced uncritically by a number of other overviews.

In Mozambique the storyline alleged that China was 'aggressively' seeking 'large land leases' in the Zambezi river valley, and that the Chinese and Mozambican governments had signed an agreement for Beijing to grow rice on a very large scale in Mozambique to ship back to China (since Mozambicans allegedly ate little rice).[76] Beijing would bring in tens of thousands of Chinese farmers. According to this story, 'local outrage' allegedly scuttled those plans, but the Chinese government nevertheless intended to move forward with an $800 million investment to modernise the rice sector in Mozambique. The story was summarised in 2008, in a report by GRAIN:

> According to a study by Loro Horta, the son of Timor L'Este's President Ramos Horta, the Chinese government has been investing in infrastructure development, policy reform, research, extension and training to develop rice production in Mozambique for export to China since 2006. Eximbank has already provided a loan of US$2bn and pledged an additional US$800m for these works, though more is expected. Some 10 000 Chinese settlers will be involved.[77]

Rather than a well researched study, the source of this story was a brief report that had appeared in different form—without any fact checking—on two think-tank internet websites. The author, a student who had lived in Mozambique as a child, apparently did not visit Mozambique for this research. Researchers who did visit Mozambique to investigate the story further in 2009 and 2010 were unable, over a collective period of months, to find anyone who had even heard of its central claims: the pledge of $800 million, an agreement between Beijing and Maputo to bring in Chinese settlers, or public outrage or opposition to such a reported plan.[78] (The alleged loan of US$2 billion was not about rice, but part of an early negotiation for a Chinese bank to finance, and a Chinese firm to build, a large dam and hydropower project desired by the Mozambicans. This did not materialise.)

As noted above, the IIED study sponsored in 2009 by the FAO raised questions about the Mozambique story—that China was negotiating for land as part of a food security strategy—saying: 'the accuracy of these reports is hard to verify'.[79] A scholarly article published in 2013 dismissed the story: 'Contrary to hyperbolic claims in the international media (Horta, 2008...) China's role in the Mozambican land grab is so far primarily indirect, operating via its demand for raw materials...Secondly, the production of staple grain crops to ensure home country food security is not a major driver of Mozambican land deals.'[80]

In fact, as one researcher noted, rather than China 'aggressively' seeking large land leases, 'the now abolished Zambeze valley office (Gabinete de Promoção do Vale de Zambêze, or GPZ) tried hard to get Chinese investment and failed'.[81] Indeed, the Mozambican government was eager to grant concessions to investors, as a 2012 Oakland Institute study showed. Between 2004 and 2009 over 2.5 million ha were granted to foreign investors, mainly from Europe and South Africa; Chinese investors were conspicuous only by their absence.[82]

On the other hand, as in the Cameroon example above, it is clear that increasing the production of rice was of interest to Mozambique. The original story made an important, but erroneous, assumption, arguing that 'Mozambique's increased rice production is clearly destined for export to the Chinese market, since the staple accounts for just a tiny fraction of the Mozambican diet.'[83] Annual rice consumption in Mozambique was in fact over 500 000 mt and in 2006 the country imported 382 300 mt of milled rice.[84] 'Rice', noted the International Rice Research Institute, 'is considered a strategic crop in Mozambique where it is expected to contribute to ensuring food security in the country'.[85]

The question of agency arises particularly strongly here. The conventional wisdom presented Mozambique as a passive recipient of Chinese demand for land. In actuality Mozambican policy makers had a goal to revive the country's historic experience of irrigated rice production under the Portuguese, becoming self-sufficient and moving into rice exports. Mozambique identified four rice production clusters (Xai-Xai, Beira, Quelimane and Nampula), in which private investment, improved seeds, and research and extension would be the pillars of the strategy. A number of foreign partners agreed to assist with this goal, including the Bill and Melinda Gates Foundation, the International Rice Research Institute and bilateral donors, including the Chinese.[86]

China's Hubei Province Farming Bureau sent a delegation to Mozambique in 2005. Directed by the Mozambican government, they visited several spots, including the 12 000 ha Xai-Xai production cluster in Gaza Province, far from the Zambezi River. Gaza Province arranged to set up a joint venture with Hubei Province, offering 1000 ha of disused, colonial-era, irrigated rice fields for Hubei to set up a demonstration farm.[87] The first stage of the Hubei–Gaza Friendship Farm was approved in 2007, with an estimated cost of $1.2 million.[88] In October that year Hubei Province Farming Bureau also won a tender held in Beijing to build one of the agro-technology demonstration centres pledged through the 2006 FOCAC.[89]

The demonstration centre, near the capital, Maputo, was completed in 2011, the same year that the Hubei–Gaza Friendship Farm completed the rehabilitation of 100 ha of irrigated rice. Yet the Hubei company found it difficult to carry out its agreed cooperation tasks.[90] Hubei was joined by a private Chinese grain processing and marketing company, Xiangyang Wanbao Grain and Oil Investment Group, which agreed to invest RMB10 million ($ 1.6 million) to develop another 333 ha of rice, and to test soybeans, vegetables and other cash crops. If all went well, it hoped to be able to expand to 100 000 mu (6667 hectares), while offering (paid) technical assistance to local farmers to develop 20 000 ha of irrigated rice.[91]

In 2012 researchers visiting the farm reported that Wanbao was now in charge of the project, and that local people had raised concerns about displacement, resettlement and competition for water use if the expansion occurred.[92] Despite discouraging results from the earlier phase, Wanbao and Gaza province officials remained optimistic that the company would be able to produce rice profitably. In 2013 the company announced a five-year plan to expand to 8000 ha of rice and an additional 2000 ha of sugarcane, while also setting up an agro-processing cluster.[93] Meanwhile, the establishment of a Brazilian–Japanese–Mozambican plan, ProSavana, to create a multi-use plan for 14 million hectares of land in Mozambique's Nacala corridor, shifted attention toward a different set of external actors with apparently far larger ambitions.[94]

Zimbabwe: CIWEC's ill-fated contract

In May 2013 the 'revised' Land Matrix database contained an entry for an alleged 'Chinese' land investment of 101 171 ha in Zimbabwe.[95] In various forms over the years this figure has appeared in a number of reports.[96] For example, a story on the Voice of America quoted a think-tank expert who said: 'There are a lot of Chinese farmers there now tilling Zimbabwean soil growing crops that are sent back to China while the people of Zimbabwe starve'.[97] The article described the project as 'a quarter of a million acres' leased by China 'for the growing of maize, which it exports back to China'. However, the reality of this story turned out to be quite different from the initial reports. This story shows how a small amount of digging can reveal the reality of a situation.

Maize output dropped substantially after the Mugabe government implemented its violent 'fast track' land reform early in the new millennium. Casting about for ways to increase output of this important staple crop, the government of Zimbabwe decided to develop part of the 300 000 ha Nuanetsi Ranch for flood-irrigation of maize and sorghum. The tender to clear and develop 250 000 acres (about 101 000 ha) of the ranch was won by China International Water and Electrical Corporation (CIWEC).[98] Although the contract was widely reported as a Chinese 'investment', the *Guardian* reporter who broke the story outside Africa made it clear that it was a contract: 'Harare has not revealed how much it will pay China for the development of the huge agricultural scheme'.[99] Local news media reported that the land was being cleared by the Chinese firm and that it would be allocated to local farmers.[100] In 2005 it became clear that the project was in trouble. CIWEC halted work on the project when it failed to receive its scheduled payments.[101] A senior government official from Zimbabwe commented: 'it now appears our government negotiated in bad faith'.[102]

Given Zimbabwe's dismal economic conditions, it is not surprising that there was little investment in agriculture from China, aside from several firms operating out-grower schemes with local tobacco and cotton farmers. However, as the economy began to improve with the introduction of the dollar and the formation of a government of national unity in 2008, Chinese interest picked up. The Anhui provincial branch of China State Farm Agribusiness Corporation (SFAC) in Zimbabwe arrived for a round of visits. A year later it returned to establish a joint farming venture on a farm belonging to Zimbabwe's Chinhoyi University of Technology. It sowed 750 ha of wheat in 2011 and announced grand plans to develop 50 000 ha between 2013 and 2015, starting with a pilot phase of 1800 ha.[103] A Chinese researcher who visited the project in early 2013 reported that the company was finding it difficult to find any additional land to lease.[104] Discussions with Anhui SFAC in June 2013 suggested that it was still optimistic, and had found strong interest from Zimbabwean government entities, including the Ministry of Defence, which had been allocated farms in the land reform but were unable to put them to good use.[105]

Conclusion

The continent of Africa has been a food deficit region for decades. For example, in 2009 countries in Africa imported 10 million tons of milled rice, costing at least $5 billion.[106] The goal of increasing production in Africa is not controversial, but the means certainly are. Irrigation and high-yielding varieties are looked at as solutions by some, and as problems by others. Commercial production, foreign investment, fertiliser, hybrid seeds and mechanisation all present risks as well as potential rewards.

The Chinese have a strategy to foster overseas investment, including in agriculture. Chinese food consumption will increasingly require imports, particularly as scarce land is lost to development, and as more Chinese move into the middle class, consuming more meat. These realities underpin the readiness with which NGOs and others believed the 'hyperbolic' media stories on Chinese 'land grabbing' in Africa, and filled their databases with cases that were often more chimera than real. Yet the details of these stories suggest that the way they have been interpreted needs to be revised. In particular, these investments do not appear to be part of a coordinated Chinese strategy to secure land in Africa to grow food for China. Rather, they reflect the uncoordinated strategies of a number of different firms to explore commercial investment opportunities across multiple sectors.

As noted in the introduction, we have made four key points in this article. First, we see a small but growing role for the Chinese government and its companies, whether state-owned or private, in promoting agricultural investment in Africa as part of a general effort to increase outbound investment. Second, farming investments—including contract farming—by Chinese companies have been occurring for several decades, but have grown more rapidly in recent years. In almost all cases the crops of interest are either for commercial import-substitution (rice, wheat, maize, vegetables) or industrial inputs and biofuel exports (sisal, sugar, oil palm). The evidence suggests that Chinese agricultural investment in Africa will increase, but that African land is unlikely to become the offshore guarantee for China's food security.

Third, China's existing farming investments have grown slowly in Africa. We know of only one case in which Chinese investors have been granted— and proceeded to develop—a new area of over 10 000 ha of land: N-Sukala, the extension of the Sukala sugar complex in Mali, founded as a Chinese aid project in 1965. Even this was not simply 'Chinese' but a joint venture between the government of Mali (40%) and a Chinese company (60%), which took over Sukala when it was privatised in 1996.[107] There are two central reasons why the very real Chinese interest has not led to substantial investment. Chinese firms believe that the business environment—including poor infrastructure and government inefficiency—in most land-rich African countries is substantially worse than in Southeast Asia, the traditional target for Chinese agricultural investments. Furthermore, according to the Ministry of Commerce, 58% of Chinese investors in Africa are small and medium-sized private firms from China's land-scarce coastal provinces.[108] In Zhejiang, according to the 2008 survey by the Foreign Economic Cooperation Centre of the Ministry of Agriculture, private firms accounted for 81.9% of outbound agricultural investment. Two-thirds of these firms complained that they were unable to get loans from China's policy banks, either because they lacked collateral, or because their investment was below the minimum size for the policy banks.[109]

Finally, African governments and citizens, are playing a far more active role in all of this than is often acknowledged. They are investing as joint venture partners with Chinese firms, travelling to China to solicit technology and investment and, in some cases, reacting with great caution, and going slowly in actually allocating land. In the real story, as opposed to the myths, they are active agents.

Notes

Deborah Bräutigam thanks Johns Hopkins University, American University, the Bill and Melinda Gates Foundation and the Smith Richardson Foundation, while Haisen Zhang thanks the NSFC–CGIAR International Cooperation Project 'Comparative Research on China–Africa Agricultural Public Investment and Rural Poverty' (2013–17, Grant Item Number: 71261140371) for financial support of this research. We also thank Tang Xiaoyang and Yuan Li for research assistance.

1 Throughout this paper we focus on farming investment and, where possible, do not include fisheries and forestry investment, conventionally included in Chinese agricultural investment statistics.

2 For examples, see M Edelman, 'Messy hectares: questions about the epistemology of land grabbing data', *Journal of Peasant Studies*, 40(3), 2012, pp 485–501; C Oya, 'Methodological reflections on "land grab" databases and the "land grab" literature "rush"', *Journal of Peasant Studies*, 40(3), 2013, pp 503–520; and I Scoones, R Hall, SM Borras Jr, B White & W Wolford, 'The politics of evidence: methodologies for understanding the global land rush', *Journal of Peasant Studies*, 40(3), 2013, pp 469–483. An article by L Cotula also addressed some of the problems with the database approach and the lack of attention to local agency. See Cotula, 'The international political economy of the global land rush: a critical appraisal of trends, scale, geography and drivers', *Journal of Peasant Studies*, 39(3–4), 2012, pp 649–680. Other recent studies that emphasis agency include a special issue on 'The Role of the State in Land Grabbing', *Development and Change*, March 2013; and T Lavers, '"Land grab" as development strategy? The political economy of agricultural investment in Ethiopia', *Journal of Peasant Studies*, 39(1), 2012, pp 105–132; and DA Alemu & I Scoones, 'Negotiating new relationships: how the Ethiopian state is involving China and Brazil in agriculture and rural development', *IDS Bulletin*, 44(4), 2013, pp 91–100.

3 L Horta, 'China–Mozambique: old friends, new business', at http://www.isn.ethz.ch/isn/Digital-Library/Articles/Detail/?id=53470&lng=en, accessed 10 May 2013. As of 2009 this story continued to be repeated by the writer. 'China and Mozambique invest in the Zambezi Valley to make Chinese "grain store"', says researcher', *Macau Hub*, 21 July 2009.

4 *Ibid*.

5 French TFI News, 'La Chine exploite le riz', at http://tinyurl.com/6ful9s, accessed 10 May 2013.

6 D Gray, 'China farms the world to feed a ravenous economy', Associated Press, 4 May 2008.

7 *Ibid*.

8 'Buying farmland abroad: outsourcing's third wave', *The Economist*, May 2009, at http://www.economist.com/node/13692889, accessed 10 May 2009. 'China secured the right to grow palm oil for biofuel on 2.8m hectares of Congo, which would be the world's largest palm-oil plantation.' The ZTE story was repeated almost verbatim by environmentalist Lester Brown, who wrote that China 'has secured rights to 2.8 million hectares in the Democratic Republic of the Congo'. L Brown, *Plan B 4.0: Mobilizing to Save Civilization*, New York: WW Norton, 2009, p 9. Columbia University Professor Saskia Sassen wrote that 'China secured the right to grow palm oil for biofuels on 2.8 million hectares of Congo, which would be the world's largest palm oil plantation'. S Sassen, 'Land grabs today: feeding the disassembling of national territory', *Globalizations*, 10(1), 2013, pp 25–46.

9 GRAIN, 'Seized: the 2008 landgrab for food and financial security', 24 October 2008, at http://www.grain.org/article/entries/93-seized-the-2008-landgrab-for-food-and-financial-security, accessed 10 May 2013.

10 *Ibid*, p 2. For comparison, there were no mentions of 'United States' or 'American', and only one mention of a British company.

11 *Ibid*, p 3. The Chinese government pledged to establish the China–Africa Development Fund, which at maturity will be a $5 billion equity fund. The fund will support Chinese investments and joint ventures in any economic sector, not simply agriculture.

12 GRAIN, 'GRAIN releases data set with over 400 global land grabs', 23 February 2012, at http://www.grain.org/fr/article/entries/4479-grain-releases-data-set-with-over-400-global-land-grabs.

13 As the original Land Matrix database has changed since its launch in 2012, these figures were obtained from the *Guardian* newspaper's website, which downloaded the original database. 'International land deals: who is investing and where—get the data', *Guardian*, at http://www.guardian.co.uk/global-development/datablog/2012/apr/27/international-land-deals-who-investing-what, accessed 10 May 2013.

14 I Hofman & P Ho, 'China's "developmental outsourcing": a critical examination of Chinese global "land grabs" discourse', *Journal of Peasant Studies*, 39(1), 2012, pp 1–48. Although this article was critical of the existing data, the annex it included, with the title 'Chinese investments', was a largely uncritical compilation of all Chinese agricultural activities (including small agricultural aid projects) that had been mentioned in the media, by NGOs, or in academic sources.

15 C Smaller, W Qiu & Y Liu, 'Farmland and water: China invests abroad', International Institute for Sustainable Development, Manitoba, August 2012, p 8.

16 For examples of blogs critical of these studies, see 'land grab' postings at 'China in Africa: The Real Story', and 'Rural Modernity'.

17 M Ncube, 'The expansion of Chinese influence in Africa—opportunities and risks', 14 August 2012, at http://www.afdb.org/en/blogs/afdb-championing-inclusive-growth-across-africa/post/the-expansion-of-chinese-influence-in-africa-opportunities-and-risks-9612/, accessed 10 May 2013. Authors' emphasis.

18 MC Rulli, A Saviori & P D'Odorico, 'Global land and water grabbing', *Proceedings of the National Academy of Sciences*, 110(3), 2013, pp 892–897.

19 L Cotula, S Vermeulen, R Leonard & J Keeley, *Land Grab or Development Opportunity? Agricultural Investment and International Land Deals in Africa*, London/Rome: IIED/FAO/IFAD, 2009, p 55.

20 *Ibid*, p 55.

21 *Ibid*, p 37.

22 D Brautigam, *The Dragon's Gift: The Real Story of China in Africa*, Oxford: Oxford University Press, 2009; D Bräutigam & X Tang, 'China's engagement in African agriculture: "down to the countryside"', *China Quarterly*, 199, 2009, pp 686–706.

23 L German, G Schoneveld & E Mwangi, *Contemporary Processes of Large-scale Land Acquisition by Investors: Case Studies from Sub-Saharan Africa*, Occasional Paper 68, Bogor, Indonesia: CIFOR, 2011. This paper also makes the case for African agency.

24 G Schoeneveld, *The Anatomy of Large-scale Farmland Acquisitions in Sub-Saharan Africa*, Working Paper 85, Bogor: CIFOR, 2011, p 2.

25 *Ibid*, p 7.

26 See, for example, a World Bank paper that was based on the media reports collected by GRAIN. K Deininger & D Byerlee, *Rising Global Interest in Farmland*, Washington, DC: World Bank, 2011.

27 GRAIN, 'Collating and dispersing: GRAIN's strategies and methods', *Journal of Peasant Studies*, 40(3), 2013, p 533.

28 W Anseeuw, J Lay, P Messerli, M Giger & M Taylor, 'Creating a public tool to assess and promote transparency in global land deals: the experience of the Land Matrix', *Journal of Peasant Studies*, 40(3), 2013, pp 521–530.

29 For example, the Beta version of the Land Matrix database underpinned the analytical paper written by some of the coalition members. W Anseeuw, M Boche, T Breu, M Giger, J Lay, P Messerli & K Nolte, *Transnational Land Deals for Agriculture in the Global South: Analytical Report based on the Land Matrix Database*, Bern/Montpellier/Hamburg: International Land Coalition (ILC)/Centre de Coopération Internationale en Recherche Agronomique pour le Développement (CIRAD)/Centre for Development and Environment (CDE)/German Institute for Global and Area Studies (GIGA)/Deutsche Gesellschaft für Internationale Zusammenarbeit (GIZ), 2012.

30 Scoones *et al*, 'The politics of evidence', p 473.

31 Although most of the recent literature on 'land grabs', including a special issue of *Globalizations* (March 2013) have touched on the many problematic assumptions about Chinese agricultural investments in Africa, few studies go into any details on China. Exceptions are: T Allan, M Keulertz, S Sojamo & J Warner, *Handbook of Land and Water Grabs in Africa*, London: Routledge, 2013, which contains a chapter by one of the authors of this article, D Bräutigam, 'Chinese engagement in African agriculture: fiction and fact', pp 91–113; and a collection of papers on China and Brazil in Africa in a special issue of the *IDS Bulletin*, 44(4), 2013.

32 D Bräutigam, *Chinese Aid and African Development: Exporting Green Revolution*, New York: St Martin's Press, 1998.

33 P Ai, 'From proletarian internationalism to mutual development: China's cooperation with Tanzania, 1965–95', in G Hyden & R Mukandala (eds), *Agencies in Foreign Aid: Comparing China, Sweden and the United States in Tanzania*, London: Macmillan Press, 1999, pp 156–201; and D Bräutigam & X Tang, *An Overview of Chinese Agricultural and Rural Engagement in Tanzania*, Discussion Paper 01214, Washington DC: Development Strategy and Governance Division, IFPRI, October 2012.

34 State Council of the People's Republic of China, 'China's Foreign Aid', Beijing, April 2011.

35 World Bank, cited in C Eicher, 'Flashback: 50 years of donor aid to African agriculture', paper presented at the InWEnt, IFPRI, NEPAD, CTA conference, 'Successes in African agriculture', Pretoria, 1–3 December 2003.

36 For a discussion of these changes, see Bräutigam, *The Dragon's Gift*, pp 232–272.

37 Bräutigam, *Chinese Aid and African Development*.

38 'Africa: top option for China's agricultural investment', Xinhua, 28 September 2002, emphasis added.

39 D Bräutigam, 'Doing well by doing good', *The China Business Review*, September–October 1983, pp 57–58; and Bräutigam, *Chinese Aid and African Development*.

40 C Wei, 'Zhongguo Nongye "Zou Chu Qu" De Xianzhuang, Wenti Ji Dui Ce' (Chinese agriculture "going global": situation, problems and countermeasures), *Guoji Jingji Hezuo* (International Economic Cooperation), 1, 2012, p 32.

41 GMG Global, 'Corporate profile', *GMG Global Annual Report 2011*. In October 2010 GMG Global established a second company in Cameroon to develop a 45 000 ha concession for rubber, but according to the GMG website, this concession is not yet in operation. GMG Global, 'Our business', at http://www.gmg.sg/business_divisions.html, accessed 11 May 2013. The *Annual Report 2012* listed a figure of 20 763 ha under cultivation in both Côte d'Ivoire and Cameroon (p 92).

42 Ministry of Finance, 'Duiwai Jingji Jishu Hezuo Zhuanxiang Zijin Guanli Banfa' (Regulations for management of the special fund for foreign economic and technical cooperation), Beijing, 9 December 2005, at http://qys.mof.gov.cn/czzxzyzf/201112/t20111206_613354.html, accessed 14 August 2013.

43 'China agri ministry, Development Bank support agri projects', *SinoCastChina Business Daily News*, 22 November 2006.

44 China–Africa Agriculture Investment Company, 'Guanyu women' (About us), at http://www.caaic.com.cn/Article_List.aspx?columnID=1, accessed 16 August 2013.

45 'China's twelfth Five Year Plan' (English Translation), at http://www.britishchamber.cn/content/chinas-twelfth-five-year-plan-2011-2015-full-english-version, accessed 25 May 2013; and National Development and Reform Commission, 'Shi Er Wuliong Waizi He Jingwai Touzi Guihua' (12th Five Year Plan of foreign capital utilization and overseas investment (2011–2015)), July 2012, at http://www.sdpc.gov.cn/gzdt/W020120724346802518900.pdf, accessed 12 August 2013.

46 State Council, 'Guanyu guli he yindao minying qiye jiji kaizhan jingwai touzi de shishi yijian' (Opinion on encouraging and guiding the implementation of the overseas investment of private enterprises), Beijing, 29 June 2012, at http://www.sdpc.gov.cn/zcfb/zcfbtz/2012tz/t20120703_489354.htm, accessed 16 August 2013.

47 State Council, 'Guanyu yinfa guli he yindao minying qiye jiji kaizhan jingwai touzi de shishi yijian' (Opinion on encouraging and guiding the implementation of the overseas investment of private enterprises), Beijing, 19 June 2012, at http://www.sdpc.gov.cn/zcfb/zcfbtz/2012tz/t20120703_489354.htm, accessed 14 August 2013.

48 Ministry of Commerce, Department of Outward Investment and Economic Cooperation, 'Guanyu zuo hao 2012 nian duiwai jingji jishu hezuo zhuanxiang zijin shenbao gongzuo de tongzhi' (Strengthening economic and technical cooperation in 2012: notice on special funds requirements), Beijing, 12 July 2012, *Cai Qi*, 141, 2012, accessed 13 August 2013. The programme on special funds for economic and technical cooperation allowed firms to apply for subsidies for fees, life and accident insurance. Several provincial governments, for example Anhui Province, also provided special funds for outward investment, including in agriculture.

49 People's Republic of China, Customs Statistics, 2013. Chinese exports of cereals to Africa include food aid. Additional details on China's food aid are available at World Food Program, International Food Aid Information System, at http://www.wfp.org/fais/reports/irma-by-recipient.

50 Customs Statistics.

51 Information Office of the State Council, 'China-Africa Economic and Trade Cooperation (2013), People's Republic of China, August, 2013.

52 Foreign Economic Cooperation Centre, 'Jingwai Nongye Ziyuan Kaifa Diaoyan Baogao' (Investigation report on Chinese overseas investment in agriculture resources), unpublished document, Ministry of Agriculture, People's Republic of China, Beijing, 2008. The survey covered investment in crops, animal husbandry and fisheries, but not forestry. All the companies were provincial and local state-owned companies; no central state-owned companies or private companies were included.

53 Ministry of Commerce, 'List of foreign-invested enterprises (institutions)', personal communication, May 2013.

54 S Marks, cited in B Sautman & H Yan, 'Chinese farms in Zambia: from socialist to "agro-imperialist" engagement?', *African and Asian Studies*, 9, 2010, p 314. Marks was reporting on a presentation by J Keeley (confirmed by personal email communication from Keeley, 7 June 2013).

55 B Sautman & H Yan 'Chinese farms in Zambia', pp 307–333.

56 P Fandio, 'Razzia chinoise sur terres camerounaises', *Arte*, 12 September 2009, at http://www.arte.tv/fr/razzia-chinoise-sur-terres-camerounaises/2837674,CmC=2837676.html, accessed 23 May 2013.

57 X Ren, 'Gengyun zai kamailong tudi shang—shanxi nongken shishi 'zouchu qu' zhanlue jishi' (Plough the land in Cameroon—Shaanxi Nongken's 'going out' strategy), 24 January 2007, at http://www.chinavalue.net/General/Blog/2007-1-24/4044.aspx, accessed 10 May 2013.

58 'China–Cameroon cooperation posts steady growth', Xinhua, 20 January 2007.

59 J-B Tagne & S Gouin, 'Quand le Cameroun nourrit la Chine', October 2010, at http//www.Politis.fr 21, accessed 22 May 2013. Unless otherwise indicated, all quotes in this paragraph are from this source.

60 C Ngorgang, 'Chinese in Cameroon: an agricultural misunderstanding', *Vita Magazine*, 30 December 2009.

61 Cameroon rice prices from 2008, at http://www.irinnews.org/Report/77971/CAMEROON-Lifting-of-import-taxes-fails-to-reduce-food-prices. Chinese rice prices from 2010.

62 GRAIN, 'Unpacking a Chinese company's land grab in Cameroon', October 2010, at http://farmlandgrab.org/16485 22 October 2010, accessed 10 May 2013.

63 J-B Tagne, 'Enquête sur la riziculture chinoise à Nanga-Eboko', *Le Jour* (Cameroon), 13 August 2010.

64 Economist Intelligence Unit (EIU), *Cameroon: Country Report*, London: EIU, March 2012, p 13.

65 Large Chinese firms not uncommonly diversify into what appear to be unrelated sectors. ZTE had established a subsidiary, ZTE Energy, which in turn set up a company, ZTE Agribusiness Corporation, to invest in biofuels.

66 F Kilubi, 'Un milliard Usd de Pékin pour des palmeraies à huile en République démocratique du Congo', *Le Phare*, 30 May 2007, at http://www.digitalcongo.net/article/44029, accessed 15 March 2010.

67 'Le Ministère de l'Agriculture et la Coopération [sic] ZTE ont signé une convention de partenariat', *Documentation et Information pour l'Afrique*, 2 November 2007.

68 Gray, 'China farms the world to feed a ravenous economy'.

69 'TEDA and ZTE Agribusiness Company Ltd sign an investment framework agreement', *Invest TEDA Newsletter*, 11 July 2009, at http://www.allroadsleadtochina.com/2009/07/11/invest-teda-newsletter/, accessed 15 March 2010.

70 B Tai, 'Chinese agribusiness company in DR Congo to offer thousands of jobs for locals', Xinhua, 10 July 2009, at http://news.xinhuanet.com/english/2009-07/10/content_11686244.htm, accessed 15 March 2010.

71 'L'ambassadeur Wu Zexian: la Chine n'a pas de vises impérialistes', interview in *Le Potential*, 14 January 2008, posted on the website of the Chinese embassy in the DRC, at http://cd.china-embassy.org/fra/xw/t399806.htm, accessed 8 December 2008.

72 L Putzel et al, *Chinese Trade and Investment and the Forests of the Congo Basin*, Working Paper 67, Bogor: CIFOR, 2011, p 33. See also 'Convention de Partenariat entre la RD Congo et la ZTE International Investment Co Ltd en vue de l'Implantation et de l'Exploitation d'une Palmaraie Industrielle', Ministry of Agriculture, DRC, 1 November 2007, p 2.

73 'Kinshasha's missing millions', *Africa-Asia Confidential*, 3(4), 2010.

74 Interview, Chinese official, Ministry of Agriculture, Beijing, 2011.

75 Putzel et al, *Chinese Trade and Investment and the Forests of the Congo Basin*, p 33.

76 Horta, 'China, Mozambique'; and Horta. 'The Zambezi Valley: China's first agricultural colony?', Center for Strategic and International Studies (CSIS), Africa Policy Forum Blog, 20 May 2008, at http://csis.org/publication/zambezi-valley-chinas-first-agricultural-colony, accessed 10 January 2012. All quotations are from these two sources.

77 GRAIN, 'Seized'.

78 S-MS Ekman, 'Leasing land overseas: a viable strategy for Chinese food security?', unpublished master's thesis, Department of Economics, Fudan University, Shanghai, 2010; and D Bräutigam & S-M Ekman, 'Rumours and realities of Chinese agricultural engagement in Mozambique', *African Affairs*, 111(444), 2012, pp 483–492.

79 L Cotula et al, *Land Grab or Development Opportunity?*, p 55.

80 M Fairbairn, 'Indirect dispossession: domestic power imbalances and foreign access to land in Mozambique', *Development and Change*, 2013, 44, pp 335–356.

81 Ekman cited in J Hanlon, 'Land moves up the political agenda', *Mozambique Political Process Bulletin*, 22 February 2011.

82 J Hanlon, *Understanding Land Investment Deals in Africa: Country Report Mozambique*, Oakland Institute, 2011, at http://www.oaklandinstitute.org/sites/oaklandinstitute.org/files/OI_country_report_mozambique_0.pdf, accessed 9 March 2012.

83 Horta, 'The Zambezi Valley'.

84 Coalition for African Rice Development (CARD), 'Mozambique's rice statistics', at http://www.riceforafrica.org/card-countries/g1/mozambique/353-mozambiques-rice-statistics, accessed 10 January 2012.

85 International Rice Research Institute (IRRI), 'Rice in Mozambique', at http://irri.org/partnerships/country-profiles/africa/mozambique/rice-in-mozambique, accessed 9 March 2012.

86 CARD, 'Mozambique's rice statistics'; IRRI, 'Rice in Mozambique'; and 'China to help Mozambique increase its rice production', *Macao Hub*, 31 March 2006.

87 X Teng, 'Policy proposals to buy and rent land overseas to grow grain submitted to the State Council,' *21st Century Business Herald*, 8 May 2008, at http://www.21cbh.com/, accessed 21 May 2008; and Y Zhang, 'Zhongguo Nongken Haiwai Tuohuang' (China State Farm Agribusiness Corporation farming overseas), *Oriental Outlook*, 12 June 2008. Unless otherwise noted, all information in this paragraph comes from these two sources.

88 S Chichava, *China in Mozambique's Agriculture Sector: Implications and Challenges*, Maputo: Institute of Social and Economic Studies (IESE), 2010, at http://www.iese.ac.mz/lib/noticias/2010/China%20in%20Mozambique_09.2010_SC.pdf, accessed 10 January 2012.

89 Centre for Chinese Studies, 'Evaluating China's FOCAC commitments to Africa and mapping the way ahead', University of Stellenbosch, January 2010, p 73.

90 S Chichava, J Duran, L Cabral, A Shankland, L Buckley, L Tang & Y Zhang, 'Brazil and China in Mozambican agriculture: emerging insights from the field', *IDS Bulletin*, 44(4), 2013, p 107.

91 Hubei Farm, 'Hubei–Gaza Friendship Farm agricultural development enters the phase of large-scale marketing operation', 29 July 2011.

92 S Chichava, J Duran, L Cabral, A Shankland, L Buckley, L Tang & Y Zhang, *Chinese and Brazilian Cooperation with African Agriculture: The Case of Mozambique*, Working Paper 49, London, Future Agricultures, March 2013.

93 'Zhuhu Feizhou Haiwai Nongchang Jianshi Tisu Zhuhu' (Africa overseas farms expand rapidly), 16 April 2013, at http://hubeifarm.com/news_show.asp?Class_Fid=140&Class_ID=6&ID=328, accessed 24 May 2013.

94 Chichava *et al*, *Chinese and Brazilian Cooperation with African Agriculture*.

95 http://landportal.info/landmatrix/get-the-detail/by-target-country/zimbabwe?investment_natures=A, accessed 24 May 2013.

96 For a sample, see C Friss & A Reenberg, 'Land grab in Africa: emerging land system drivers in a teleconnected world', Global Land Project, 2010, p 34, at http://www.globallandproject.org/arquivos/GLP_report_01.pdf; B Hurst, 'The twenty-first century land rush', American Enterprise Institute, 22 September 2010, at http://www.american.com/archive/2010/september/the-21st-century-land-rush, accessed 24 May 2013; Mo Ibrahim Foundation, *African Agriculture: From Meeting Needs to Creating Wealth*, November 2011, at http://www.moibrahimfoundation.org/en/media/get/20111113_Facts-and-Figures.pdf, p 19; and Smaller *et al*, 'Farmland and water', p 18.

97 P Pham, cited in W Ide, 'China supports global pariahs, gets resources and criticism in return', Voice of America News, 27 June, 2011, at http://www.voanews.com/content/china-supports-global-pariahs-gets-resources-and-criticism-in-return-124648814/141455.html, accessed 24 May 2013.

98 'Zhong shuidian gongsi zhongbiao jinba buwei zui da nongye kaifa xiangmu' (China International Water and Electricity Company wins largest agricultural development project in Zimbabwe), Ministry of Commerce, People's Republic of China, 23 February 2003, at http://www.mofcom.gov.cn/article/i/jyjl/k/200302/20030200070817.shtml, accessed 24 May 2013; and 'Zimbabwe: Minister Moyo denies Chinese group contracted to farm Nuanetsi Ranch', *The Herald* (Zimbabwe), 14 February 2003.

99 A Meldrum, 'Mugabe hires China to farm seized land', *Guardian*, 13 February 2003.

100 'Zimbabwe: Minister Moyo denies Chinese contracted to farm Nuanetsi Ranch'.

101 A Mukaro, 'Chinese firm abandons Nuanetsi project', *Zimbabwe Independent*, 8 April 2005, at http://www.theindependent.co.zw/local/12261.html, accessed 14 August 2008; and S Moyo, 'Land concentration and accumulation after redistributive reform in post-settler Zimbabwe', *Review of African Political Economy*, 38(128), 2009, p 269.

102 G du Venage, 'Harare's ties with Beijing begin to falter; China unhappy as unpaid bills mount up for aircraft, engineering work and construction projects across Zimbabwe', *South China Morning Post*, 19 May 2006.

103 G Bao , 'Anhui Nongken: "Zouchuqu" kaipi xintian di' (Anhui agribusiness: 'going out' to break new ground), *Zhongguo Nongchang* (China State Farms), 16 March 2012, at http://www.ahnk.com.cn/display.asp?id=6818, accessed 24 May 2013.

104 Interview, Chinese researcher, Beijing, 12 April 2013.

105 Interview, Anhui State Farm Agribusiness Corporation, Chinhoyi, Zimbabwe, June 2013.

106 Africa Rice, at http://www.africarice.org/arc2013/rationale.asp, accessed 25 May 2013.
107 At least 13 000 ha of land was allocated for this project. The factory was completed at the end of 2012, but the land development had not been completed as of this writing. F Maïga, 'Sucrerie: N-Sukala ouvre ses portes', *L'Essor*, 12 November 2012, at http://www.essor.ml/newspaper/sucrerie-n-sukala-ouvre-ses-portes.html; and interview, Chinese researcher, Beijing, 12 April 2013.
108 Data from MOFCOM, Beijing, April 2013.
109 Foreign Economic Cooperation Centre, 'Investigation report on Chinese overseas investment in agriculture resources'.

Notes on Contributors

Deborah Bräutigam is Professor II, Department of Comparative Politics, University of Bergen, Professor, School of Advanced International Studies, Johns Hopkins University, Washington, DC and Senior Research Fellow, International Food Policy Research Institute (IFPRI), Washington, DC. A specialist in the study of foreign aid, governance, state-building, and China's African engagement, her Ph.D. is from the Fletcher School of Law and Diplomacy, Tufts University. Her first book on China and Africa was Chinese Aid and African Development: Exporting Green Revolution (St. Martin's Press, 1998), and her most recent book is *The Dragon's Gift: The Real Story of China in Africa* (Oxford University Press, 2010). She thanks Johns Hopkins University, American University, the Bill and Melinda Gates Foundation, the Smith Richardson Foundation, and IFPRI for financial support of this research.

Haisen Zhang is Director of the Center for International Agricultural Cooperation and Development (CIACD) and an associate professor at the University of International Business and Economics (UIBE). The fields of his research include development aid, China-Africa food security, and international trade of agriculture. He received his PhD from China Agricultural University in 2005. Professor Zhang is a senior consultant of the International Agricultural Cooperation Committee of Ministry of Agriculture of China, and China Development Bank. He is an executive member of the Council of Chinese Foreign Agricultural Economic Research, and a senior expert of China Africa Research Institute. Professor Zhang was a visiting professor, School of International Service, American University (AU) and a visiting research fellow, International Food Policy Research Institute (IFPRI) in Washington D.C., U.S. from 2010 to 2011. In 2010, he was a senior international consultant for Africa-British-China trilateral cooperation employed by Department for International Development (DFID) of the United Kingdom. He thanks the NSFC-CGIAR International Cooperation Project 'Comparative Research on China-Africa Agricultural Public Investment and Rural Poverty' (2013-2017, Grant Item Number: 71261140371) for financial support of this research.

Cycles of Land Grabbing in Central America: an argument for history and a case study in the Bajo Aguán, Honduras

MARC EDELMAN[a] & ANDRÉS LEÓN[b]

[a]Department of Anthropology, Hunter College, City University of New York, New York, USA; [b]City University of New York, USA

ABSTRACT *The lack of historical perspective in many studies of land grabbing leads researchers to ignore or underestimate the extent to which pre-existing social relations shape rural spaces in which contemporary land deals occur. Bringing history back in to land grabbing research is essential for understanding antecedents, establishing baselines to measure impacts and restoring the agency of contending agrarian social classes. In Central America each of several cycles of land grabbing—liberal reforms, banana concessions and agrarian counter-reform—has profoundly shaped the period that succeeded it. In the Bajo Aguán region of Honduras—a centre of agrarian reform and then counter-reform—violent conflicts over land have been materially shaped by both peasant, landowner and state repertoires of contention and repression, as well as by peasants' memories of dispossession.*

Studies of the recent wave of land deals sometimes lack historical perspective. The most common approach to remedying this deficiency is to point to earlier processes of land concentration as a corrective to historically myopic claims about the 'newness' of today's land grabbing.[1] While the introduction of a longer temporal perspective and past cases is certainly welcome, this paper—which of necessity is highly synthetic—argues that there are at least three other, analytically more significant reasons for examining historical antecedents.

First, land grabbing tends to occur in cycles, or waves, depending on historically specific regional and global dynamics of capital accumulation. Each new cycle has had to take into account and is profoundly shaped by pre-existing social formations and local and regional particularities. These include formal and customary land tenure, historical configurations of class relations, family networks, gender and settlement patterns, environmental features, actual or potential infrastructure, state policies, international treaties and agreements, as well as forms of insertion in markets, among many other elements. The land deal literature, in other words, sometimes tends to 'forget' the historical social relations that produced the rural spaces in which 'new' grabs are occurring. Land grabbers—'foreign' or 'domestic', past and present—almost always have to operate within a context shaped by local practices, identities and meanings.[2]

While governments, corporations and multilateral institutions often justify contemporary land deals with assertions about the availability of *terra nullius* and the desirability of closing 'yield gaps' and developing 'empty lands', few if any such lands really exist anywhere in the world.[3] Indeed, so-called empty lands are typically 'produced'—geographically and discursively—through earlier processes of conflict or resistance which have displaced or excluded specific groups. Claims today about lands that belong to no one, or that are 'unproductive', hark back to previous waves of land grabbing and are suggestive of the continuities that link earlier processes to more recent ones.[4]

A second reason for historicising analyses of contemporary land deals relates to the need for baseline evidence to evaluate impacts. Recent studies of land grabbing have persuasively documented the deleterious consequences of particular deals (and conjectured about potential consequences), but there is also a tendency in the literature to reason from anecdotal evidence, to generalise on the basis of one or a few cases and to blame land grabbing for negative effects, such as proletarianisation or loss of water rights, which might plausibly have predated today's land deals, might have other causes or might have happened anyway. Information on land uses and livelihoods that existed before the implementation of a land deal is essential for assessing any transaction's short- or medium-term impact.[5]

The third reason for analysing land grabbing historically has less to do with introducing a deeper temporal frame than with viewing contemporary processes as the history—conceptually and methodologically speaking—of the present. This means viewing the present moment as an epiphenomenal result of earlier social and material processes and restoring the agency of contending social classes, rather than understanding their actions as entirely over-determined by the various *dei ex machina*—commodity booms or multilateral lending, for example—that figure so prominently in the land grabbing literature. It also means recognising that particular contexts are characterised by deeply ingrained, historical repertoires of class and gender contention and state repression that shape land conflicts and facilitate or impede large-scale deals. These elements in turn suggest that historical contingencies or choices made during 'critical junctures' of diverse kinds may play a role in agrarian outcomes and political outcomes more broadly.[6] This is as true of earlier processes of land concentration as it is of present-day land grabbing, whether in Central America or elsewhere.

Why Central America?

In addition to these reasons for historicising the land grabbing discussion, we argue that there are several reasons for focusing specifically on Central America, a region with a long history of agrarian conflicts to which today's land deal scholars have devoted relatively little attention.[7] First, the Central American countries share a broadly similar insertion in the global economy over the past two centuries yet are characterised by markedly contrasting political and agrarian outcomes.[8] The region—and most probably other regions as well—thus requires historically grounded analysis, as opposed to the deployment of monolithic assumptions about causality that characterised dependency and world-system paradigms in the 1960s and 1970s and that now undergird much of the recent literature on 'drivers' of land grabbing.[9]

Second, the Central American region is small; its five countries total 419 000 km^2, which is smaller than Spain, less than half of Venezuela and only 60% of Texas. While this diminutive extension could be seen as an indication of the region's irrelevance for understanding trends in global land grabbing, we argue instead that it actually contributes significantly to the discussion by facilitating a rethinking of issues of scale. The literature on recent large-scale land acquisitions—both scholarly and activist—has placed so much emphasis on the numbers of hectares 'grabbed' that it frequently loses sight of other key aspects of scale, notably the capital applied in any particular deal, the appropriation of other resources, such as water, and the actual or likely impacts on rural populations.[10] In particular, the geographic scale of a given land grab says little or nothing about the ways in which rural people will be excluded, incorporated or subsumed through other mechanisms to new forms of capital.[11] Central America has seen historical grabs of truly massive scale, and also in the recent period—and more importantly for our purposes—grabs that are of modest size by global standards but that have nonetheless generated major agrarian struggles. Indeed, outside of war-torn Colombia, the most acute agrarian conflicts in Latin America today are in the Central American region. We might ask why, if these confrontations result from small and medium-size grabs, the much larger grabs that have occurred in some South American countries have not produced similarly acute conflicts.

It is not just that antecedents and a more historical approach are important, but also that a geographically wider view of the sites of contemporary land grabbing may provide insights into broader tendencies and methodological problems. Much attention in the land grabbing literature has centred on sub-Saharan Africa, a phenomenon that doubtless reflects some combination (and probably an unknowable one) of genuine trends, on the one hand, and reporting or other biases in the main land deal databases, on the other. A focus on Central America points to a similar problem, albeit one 'writ small'.

Recently the United Nations Food and Agriculture Organization (FAO) carried out studies of land grabbing in 17 Latin American countries.[12] The FAO included three Central American countries—Costa Rica, Guatemala and Nicaragua—but, perhaps unintentionally, excluded Honduras—with Guatemala arguably the sites of the most acute agrarian conflicts in Latin America (outside of Colombia) in the past 15 years (about which more below).[13] Such choices in the construction of the 'sampling frame'—here as elsewhere—generate unacknowledged biases that in and of themselves produce a very particular reading of history. Along with an overly narrow definition of 'grabbing', which emphasised the role of foreign governments and investors and land appropriation for food production, this probably made it easier to arrive at the rather surprising conclusion that in Latin America 'the phenomenon of land grabbing is in an early stage and is restricted to two large countries: Argentina and Brazil'.[14]

The notion that the problem in the Americas is limited to Argentina and Brazil derives from the overly restrictive definition of land grabbing that other scholars have effectively critiqued.[15] The FAO's Central American studies point to large flows of regional (ie Central American) and Mexican capital into the sugar and oil palm sectors and smaller flows of extra-regional investment into these same sectors, as well as into cattle and forestry. They also make clear that small countries can be significant players in international markets and particularly profitable places in which to invest. 'Beginning in 2000', for example, 'Costa Rica, Honduras and Guatemala were among the 20 principal African palm oil exporters in the world and among the five largest in Latin America.'[16] In terms of yields Guatemalan plantations averaged five metric tons of fruit per hectare against a world average of 3.2 metric tons.[17] But because the FAO studies largely eschew on-the-ground investigations, focus almost exclusively on formal institutional changes and sometimes accord undue emphasis to the 'perceptions' of key 'actors', they tend to render invisible the frictions that the land concentration–dispossession dynamic produces, as well as the peasant resistance that this sometimes generates.[18]

This paper has two main sections. In the first, we explore three of the main cycles of land dispossession and grabbing in Central America in the postcolonial period: liberalism, the banana enclaves and the counter-reforms that followed agrarian reforms. We show how each of these cycles must be understood in the intersection between global forces placing the region in particular roles and local dynamics of dispossession and resistance. We also claim that, to understand each of these cycles, it is necessary to understand how the region and particular actors in each country emerged from the previous cycle. In the second part of the paper we examine the ongoing agrarian conflict that has convulsed the Bajo Aguán region in Honduras. This case raises significant questions about some widespread assumptions in the land grab literature, especially because it looks like a land grab without usually being identified as one. The Aguán case suggests, first, that to understand current agrarian conflicts, it is necessary to grasp the historical dynamics that created the conditions of possibility for current forms of both dispossession and resistance. Second, unlike the dominant emphasis in the land grab literature on 'foreign' capital, in the Aguán most of the grabs are by 'domestic' investors, albeit with support from institutions such as the International Financial Corporation (IFC).[19] Moreover, peasant organisations are also expanding the area in which African palm is grown, a crop commonly demonised in the literature and juxtaposed to basic food crops, which it is said to replace. To complicate the conventional land grab literature further, it is apparent—so far at least—that the expansion of palm is not attributable to the biofuel boom, as most of the production goes either towards the domestic market or to Mexico for the cosmetics industry.[20]

Liberalism and the first cycle

The first cycle of land grabbing in independent Central America occurred under Liberal Party regimes in the late 19th century. Analysing this process requires a brief outline of the situation in each country, but it also, more importantly, entails a consideration of the divergences between Liberal doctrine and practice, and between conventional interpretations of liberalism and evidence unearthed by more recent historical research. In the area of land policy two main phenomena are relevant to understanding this cycle of land grabbing: first, the privatisation—mostly for coffee production—of non-private property in the hands of small producers (*ejidos* or community lands, particularly in indigenous regions, and *cofradía* or religious sodality holdings, as well as other ecclesiastical lands);[21] and, in the second cycle, the granting of massive concessions, primarily to foreign banana and railway companies, but also to entrepreneurs in other sectors (eg rubber, mining, forestry, cattle).[22] These first and second cycles parallel what is known in food regime theory as the British-led 'first food regime' (circa 1870–1914). In the Central American region articulation with this first food regime was through the creation of a set of export-oriented 'dessert economies' (sugar, coffee and bananas) that brought cheap calories and stimulants to metropolitan working classes, a topic usually neglected in the food regimes literature, though amply covered in commodity-specific studies.[23]

While Central America experienced some processes of economic liberalisation as far back as the mid-18th century colonial Bourbon reforms, which continued under the Conservative and short-lived Liberal regimes of the early independence era, the period of concerted Liberal 'reform' commenced in the 1870s in Guatemala.[24] The Guatemalan 'reform' involved a three-stage process that included the seizure and privatisation of Church lands; the abolition of long-term leaseholds (*censo enfitéutico*), most of which were conceded by rural communities to outsiders; and the auctioning off of 'idle' state lands (*tierras baldías*), many of which were traditionally used by indigenous and ladino (ie non-Indian) peasants. In the 1880s a similar—albeit much more radical—process of land privatisation began in El Salvador, a country that had less ecclesiastical land and where—unlike in Guatemala (apart from Alta Verapaz Department)—the potential coffee zones were densely populated. Liberal regimes also came to power in Honduras (in the 1870s) and in Nicaragua (in the 1890s), but these reform processes were 'aborted', 'frustrated' and incomplete, in large part because of foreign intervention and geographical obstacles that limited access to potential coffee zones.[25] In Costa Rica, the region's first coffee-exporting country, the privatisation of Church and community properties began shortly before independence and proceeded gradually in a context of a small population and relatively abundant available land.[26]

The late 19th century apogee of Central American liberalism coincided with the emergence of strong states (and strong executive branches in particular) and heightened efforts to 'build nations'. Constructing states out of colonial provinces involved the creation of nominally constitutional regimes, the secularisation of society, and the administration, disciplining and political socialisation of the popular classes. Late 19th century Liberals considered thorough economic reform important, but not necessarily uppermost on the agenda. The 'dogmatic free trade liberalism' referred to in some accounts was dogmatic certainly, but most of the Liberals' zeal concerned issues other than trade. [27]

Nineteenth century Liberals sought to overcome the economically stifling legacy of a colonial regime which, among other things, had limited their societies' choice of trading partners, instituted commercial and financial monopolies, restricted the commodification of land and labour, and established onerous tax burdens, including large assessments for the Church (even though some of these restrictions diminished in the last century or so of Spanish rule). To 19th century Liberals 'free trade' meant overcoming limitations on elite economic activity left over from the colonial era. It did not necessarily signify 'getting the prices right' or 'opening up' economies by devaluing currencies, lowering or eliminating tariffs, or reducing government spending, as it does now (or as it may have then in Great Britain and elsewhere).[28] Free trade ideology under late 19th and early 20th century liberal regimes did not preclude distinctly non-liberal trade practices. Customs duties were one of these governments' main sources—if not *the* main source—of revenue.[29] Moreover, the main purpose of customs duties was to collect revenue (especially to pay debts to foreign—mainly British—banks) rather than to protect domestic manufactures, as was the case somewhat later in the larger Latin American countries.[30] The fragile fiscal foundation of the liberal state, along with liberal doctrine, was an impetus for land privatisation and concessions, both of which represented potentially lucrative flows of revenue to government coffers.

Given the draconian picture of the liberal reforms in influential accounts from the 1970s, as well as the arrogant names given to key laws—El Salvador's 1881 'Law of extinction of indigenous communities' (*Ley de extinción de comunidades indígenas*), for example—it may raise hackles to suggest that processes of commodification of land under 19th century liberalism were modest by today's standards.[31] Certainly they were not modest for those living in the zones most affected, especially in El Salvador, where they can reasonably be seen as proximate causes of later peasant unrest and rebellions, although under the strongest, most oppressive Liberal regimes, as in Guatemala, resistance was primarily of less dramatic, 'everyday' varieties.[32] Liberal reforms in late 19th century Guatemala—after El Salvador rightly regarded as the most extreme case—privatised various kinds of *ejido* and *cofradía* lands in what became the key piedmont coffee zones. But they also permitted the titling of hundreds of thousands of hectares of community lands where non-capitalist property and petty commodity forms of production persisted, albeit under intense pressure.[33] Between the Liberal 'revolution' of 1871 and 1883 close to 400 000 hectares of public lands in Guatemala were sold and another 74 250 hectares entered the market with the abolition of the *censo enfitéutico*, a type of 99-year lease that granted access to *ejido* lands in return for an annual rent of 2% or 3% of their value.[34] This is a lot of land (4742.5 km^2), and it clearly ended up in the hands of a small number of owners.[35] But the main importance of Liberal land privatisation may, as some recent analyses argue, lie less in its territorial extent than in the social relations that it destroyed and created and in the multiple ways it exposed subaltern groups to the discipline of the state, elites and the market.[36] In concrete terms liberal 'reform' in Guatemala and El Salvador (and to a lesser extent elsewhere) dispossessed indigenous populations, created a huge pool of landless 'free' workers, and solidified central states that deployed formidable apparatuses of labour control and repression. All this is crucial for understanding the second cycle of dispossession in the region.

The second cycle: bananas in the late 19th and early 20th centuries

The second major land grabbing cycle in Central America followed quickly on the heels of the liberal reforms. If the main motivation for these was to 'free' land and labour for coffee production, the impetus for the second wave, which involved US banana companies, was to modernise infrastructure (especially railways, ports, roads and electrical generation), to develop 'empty' lands, and to generate new sources of revenue from export taxes and concessions. Bananas thrived in the humid, fertile Atlantic lowlands—particularly in Costa Rica, Honduras and Guatemala—where malaria and yellow fever were endemic and human populations sparse (only in the 1930s did plantations appear on the Pacific littoral). These spaces—inhabited in most cases by scattered indigenous and Garifuna groups and mestizo peasants—were not strictly speaking *terra nullius*, but they did constitute a space, relatively 'empty' in development terms, for the creation of enclave economies. It is beyond the scope of this paper to analyse the often sordid history of US banana companies in Central America, about which a substantial literature exists. The important points, for our purposes, are 1) that the companies' activities in the late 19th and early 20th centuries frequently included major land acquisitions and that these—together with control over transport, finance, ports, electricity and shipping lines—gave them outsized influence over politics and a capacity to dominate both their labour force and small producers, in addition to creating new kinds of rural spaces and social groups that in turn shaped subsequent agrarian relations; and 2) that this labour force consisted significantly of fully or partially proletarianised workers dispossessed in the previous, liberal cycle of land grabbing.[37]

A key obstacle facing liberal elites was how to transport their coffee from the mountainous zones where it was produced to the coasts, whence it could be exported to Europe and North America. Not surprisingly, given this imperative, the first large banana plantations arose as corollaries of rail projects. In Costa Rica in 1871 US entrepreneurs Henry Meiggs and Minor Keith contracted to build a railway from the Atlantic coast to the capital San José. Thwarted by impenetrable tropical forests and recurring labour problems, the project proved more protracted and costly than anticipated and Keith—who assumed sole control after Meiggs' death in 1877—began to plant bananas along the railway sidings and to export them from Puerto Limón. In 1884, six years before the line was finally completed at a cost of nearly 5000 workers' lives, the Costa Rican government granted Keith a 99-year lease of the railway and 800 000 acres (323 887 hectares) of land in return for paying off the country's foreign debt.[38] Even though much of this land was eventually sold or returned to the government, the part that remained under Keith's control became the core of the Costa Rican operations of what was soon to become the United Fruit Company.

In succeeding years numerous contracts for building branch lines in the Atlantic lowlands—with Keith and others—resulted in additional land giveaways, including one that conceded 500 hectares for each kilometre of track constructed.[39]

In Guatemala, similarly, United Fruit's origins are inextricably linked to the International Railways of Central America, which later became its subsidiary, and to other rail projects. The early history of the country's railway to the Atlantic coast involved numerous contracts with diverse entrepreneurs, including lieutenants of Keith and eventually Keith himself. As in Costa Rica the government frequently granted lands as partial payment, albeit on a more modest scale ranging from 57 000 to 168 000 acres (23 077 to 68 016 hectares).[40] The largest concession, to Keith, in the lush Motagua Valley, became the centrepiece of United's empire in Guatemala.[41] By the mid-20th century United alone owned well over 200 000 hectares, making it by far the largest landowner in Guatemala.[42]

In the late 19th century Honduras had a flourishing smallholding banana sector, first in the Bay Islands and later along the North Coast. This drew the attention of the first foreign banana entrepreneurs, who were initially more involved in exporting fruit than in producing it. In contrast to Costa Rica and Guatemala, Honduras never succeeded in building a railway linking its capital to the coasts. A few short lines were built on the North Coast, but most of the monies borrowed for rail construction went on commissions and interest, leaving the country with a tremendous and rapidly growing debt. In 1888 one observer commented that at 'prevailing land values, Honduras could not repay such a debt by selling its entire national territory'.[43] Between 1900 and 1930, 57 concessions were granted to the major banana companies (or their predecessors), typically including lands and diverse kinds of tax exemptions.[44] This saddled the state with an ongoing fiscal crisis and made it notoriously vulnerable to powerful foreign influences. The Tela Railroad Company—a United Fruit subsidiary—came to control 194 992 hectares, much of it via a concession that gave it 500 hectares for every kilometre of track completed.[45] Standard Fruit received additional concessions, so that by the early 20th century just two companies controlled the production, transportation and export of bananas in Honduras, which emerged as the leading Central American exporter.[46]

By 1930 United Fruit alone owned over 1.1 million hectares of land in Central America, although only about 56 000 hectares were planted with bananas. Most of the rest was ostensibly held in reserve for future expansion, when soils or diseases required abandoning older plantations.[47] After World War II, however, the company began to divest itself of its landholdings, a process which accelerated in succeeding decades and which increasingly devolved risk onto smaller producers, who continued to sell it fruit for export.[48] Its 'idle' lands and its imperious treatment of its workers became increasingly charged issues throughout the isthmus.

Apart from noting the banana companies' land grabbing as an important antecedent, the significance of the enclaves for our argument is that they fomented powerful nationalist discourses which generated diverse kinds of resistance, most notably massive strikes (in Costa Rica in 1934 and Honduras in 1954) and widespread squatting. The companies' lands became scenarios for later conflicts and reforms, and their labour force—imbued with a heightened political consciousness from plantation struggles—became a new actor in struggles for land.

Twentieth-century agrarian reforms and counter-reforms

This section provides an overview and periodisation of agrarian reform and counter-reform in Central America, topics that are subjects of sizable literatures and cannot be covered thoroughly here. The contexts and motives for reforms in the different countries were diverse, as were the scope and impacts. The abortive reforms of Guatemala's 'democratic spring' (1945–54) first distributed lands expropriated from German nationals during World War II and then, in 1952, targeted idle lands in large properties.[49] The measure specified that expropriations would have to be completed in six weeks, a remarkably radical provision, although they continued for 18 months, until the CIA-directed invasion that deposed President Jacobo Arbenz. Estimates differ on the amount of land distributed, but it was probably around 884 000 hectares, of which 604 000 were from expropriations (16% of the country's idle land available for cultivation).[50] Of United Fruit's 222 580 hectares, the reform expropriated 146 000, a step that triggered the ire of the US government and became a major factor in precipitating the 1954 coup. An about-face came rapidly after the overthrow of Arbenz, with 99% of the agrarian reform land immediately returned to its previous owners.[51] The violence and repression that accompanied this reversal permanently scarred Guatemalan society and also have echoes in the counter-reforms of the 1990s in the rest of the isthmus (see below).

The 1961 Punta del Este conference that launched the Alliance for Progress was the next major turning point for agrarian reform in the Americas. The backdrop for the meeting was the radicalisation of the Cuban Revolution, which US policy makers feared could spread elsewhere in the hemisphere and which they hoped to head off with land reforms that would mollify a potentially rebellious peasantry. Within a few years virtually every Latin American government founded an agrarian reform agency and initiated land distribution. In Central America even the repressive regimes in Guatemala, El Salvador and Nicaragua carried out small colonisation programmes, settling landless peasants on public lands in remote zones (and at times displacing indigenous and other groups already there).[52] In Costa Rica the government initiated a modest agrarian reform (which continued into the mid-1980s, reaching a total of 226 558 hectares), which combined resolution of existing land occupations, land expropriation and distribution, and colonisation of remote zones.[53] In Honduras, as we discuss in more detail below, a tepid reform in the 1960s accelerated in the mid-1970s under a populist military regime and growing pressure from a highly organised peasantry. In Nicaragua, shortly after the Sandinistas toppled the Somoza dictatorship in 1979, the government seized 781 324 hectares of properties that had belonged to the ruling family and its close allies, creating a vast sector of state farms and cooperatives. In the 1980s a new agrarian reform law led to further expropriations of large, underutilised properties, although by 1989 the Sandinista authorities halted the programme in an effort to reduce social polarisation and end the civil war.[54] In El Salvador the USA, fearing contagion from Nicaragua, encouraged a radical albeit counterinsurgency-oriented reform in the 1980s, which established a constitutional 245-hectare ceiling on landholdings. By the late 1980s peasant cooperatives held 207 868 hectares and individual reform beneficiaries had received an additional 69 231 hectares.[55] Further land distributions to ex-combatants occurred as part of the settlement of the civil war in 1992, but by then the formerly agrarian elite had largely shifted out of agriculture and into industry and finance.[56]

The agrarian reforms of the 1960s–80s had several effects relevant to our analysis. First, they created a large and at times dynamic sector of producers ensconced in spaces that sometimes included the best agricultural lands. Second, they cemented a social contract between beneficiaries and the state that generated rising expectations and new conceptions of rights. Third, they encouraged 'flex' crops and the know-how needed to cultivate them, particularly African palm (also sugarcane), which in the 1990s became major drivers of private-sector land grabbing.[57] And fourth, in all cases the reforms were undermined by the beneficiaries' obligation to pay for the land they received, by the globalisation of agricultural markets and by states' failure to facilitate sufficient complementary resources for them to succeed: technical assistance, administrative training, irrigation, insurance, credit, post-harvest storage and processing, and marketing. By the early 1990s the growing globalisation of agricultural trade, the implementation of neoliberal reforms across the entire region and increased incentives for non-traditional agricultural exports set the stage for a profound reconfiguration of what had been agrarian reform space.

The demise of the Central American agrarian reforms opened the way and created an institutional framework for a massive privatisation of peasant enterprises' and individual beneficiaries' holdings—in effect a 'land grab before land grabbing'. Some informal privatisation of the reform sector was already evident in Costa Rica in the early 1980s.[58] In Nicaragua, shortly before the Sandinista Front left power in 1990, privatisation began on a huge scale, first as a result of the Sandinistas' Law 88, which permitted the sale of agrarian reform lands, then from the '*piñata*' or seizing of public-sector resources by departing Sandinista leaders, and then—most significantly—from a reinvigorated land market that saw Nicaraguan and foreign investors gobbling up holdings of indebted *campesinos* at risible prices.[59] One 1995 estimate suggested that Nicaraguan and foreign landowners had wrested effective control of some 350 000 hectares of land from the peasants and ex-combatants to whom it was originally distributed.[60] The mechanisms of this appropriation relied less on full titling of reform lands than on various kinds of flexible contracting and renting arrangements, some of dubious legal status.

In Honduras the counter-reform occurred with similar rapidity and thoroughness. Between 1962 and 1990, as we detail below, the Honduran state distributed over 376 000 hectares of land to some 66 000 rural families.[61] In 1990 the government announced plans for a structural adjustment programme. Two years later the 'Agricultural Modernisation Law' took effect, permitting private titling and sales of agrarian reform lands.[62] In 1992 alone, the law's first year, official data show that some 17% of reform beneficiaries had abandoned and/or sold their land.[63] As the counter-reform accelerated, the extent of the dispossession and the associated violence mounted. Nowhere was this more apparent than in the Bajo Aguán.

Agrarian conflict in the Bajo Aguán

During the 1960s and 1970s the Bajo Aguán region was the centrepiece of the Honduran agrarian reform and the nucleus of the strongest peasant movement in Central America.[64] In the 1990s it became the country's 'capital of agrarian counter-reform'.[65] Since the 2009 coup that toppled the elected government of José Manuel ('Mel') Zelaya, the Bajo Aguán has seen a dramatic escalation of agrarian conflict and violence against peasant communities. At least 50 assassinations have occurred as a result of the conflict in the region. The victims have been largely peasant activists, but the toll also includes a journalist, a human rights lawyer, and lawyers and guards working for the large landowners.[66] The struggle pits a set of peasant organisations and communities, heirs to the powerful peasant movements of the 1960s and 1970s, against a small group of large landowners, who enriched themselves as industrialists in the 1970s and 1980s.[67]

At first glance the conflict seems to be a clash between subsistence-oriented peasants and transnationally oriented landowners interested in expanding the production of African palm, one of the quintessential 'flex crops', with end uses that include edible oil, biofuel and cosmetic production, as well as additional benefits, in some cases, in the form of tradable carbon emission reduction credits under the Kyoto Protocol's Clean Development Mechanism.[68] This framing of the ongoing conflict in the Aguán Valley has every appearance of a land grab. However, because of the relatively small size of the land 'grabbed' at the beginning of the 1990s—some 21 000 hectares—and the fact that it predates the 2008 spike in land grabbing, most recent literature on land deals ignores the conflict in the Aguán Valley.[69] Also, since most of the investment in land in the region is 'domestic', it falls outside the FAO's definition of 'land grab', which might be one reason why Honduras was left outside of the FAO's 17-country study of Latin America.

For the historical roots of the current conflict in the Aguán we must look back at the first half of the previous century. The Truxillo Railroad Company—one of United Fruit's two Honduran subsidiaries—began to move into the region in the early 1920s, felling vast quantities of valuable hardwoods and planting thousands of hectares of bananas. In its early years in the Aguán the Company purchased most of the bananas it exported from small producers. But by the early 1940s the spread of Panama disease (a plant fungus) was leading to the abandonment of dozens of farms.[70] By the end of World Word II the companies had all but abandoned these lands and ex-banana and railway workers, Garifuna communities, and landless Salvadoran migrants began to settle them, remaining largely beyond the influence of the state.[71] After 1945 Standard Fruit acquired large properties in the region, but had only limited success in bringing the Panama-disease-infested soils back into cultivation.[72]

In May 1954 a general strike broke out involving 35 000 workers in the nearby North Coast banana plantations.[73] In August and September strong rains and flooding destroyed many of the banana farms there and the companies again abandoned large amounts of land and introduced technological changes that led to the dismissal of around 13 000 workers (almost half the total workforce). This combination of idle land and massive landlessness fuelled the growth of combative peasant movements that not only sought access to land, but also protection for their tenure against landowners' attempts to evict them. From this moment on, the North Coast, where most of the banana plantations were based, became the centre of the national peasant movement and land invasions became the main way of obtaining land and improving peasants' living conditions.[74]

In 1962, following the US-sponsored Punta del Este meeting that established the Alliance for Progress, Honduras passed its first modern agrarian reform law, based primarily on the distribution of state and *ejidal* or municipal lands, including those that had been illegally occupied by large or small producers.[75] Even though the measure guaranteed private property and did not set a ceiling on land ownership, it generated intense opposition from landowning groups and from the United Fruit Company, which succeeded in pressuring President Ramón Villeda Morales to amend the law so that private property could not be expropriated.[76] For over a decade the law's results were meagre, with only 35 961 hectares distributed to 6271 peasant families in the entire country.[77]

In 1972 a 'progressive' military regime (influenced by similar regimes in Peru, Panama and elsewhere) took control of Honduras and in 1974–75—faced with ever increasing pressure from landless peasants, tenant farmers and former banana workers—it decreed a sweeping agrarian reform. The new law created and strengthened both state agencies and the framework for creating peasant enterprises. It established a ceiling on the size of land holdings and provisions for expropriating 'idle' or underutilised private and 'national' lands for resettling the landless peasantry. The pace of land distribution accelerated in the 1970s. By 1980, 8% of the total farmland—some 207 433 hectares—had been distributed to 46 890 rural families or 12% of the total; 22% of the country's landless people had become beneficiaries, making the Honduran reform the most radical in Central America up to that time.[78] Nonetheless, only 3.8% of the beneficiaries were women, one of the lowest levels of any Latin American agrarian reform.[79]

Like most agrarian reforms in Latin America in this period the Honduran reform affected few large landowners and focused instead on colonisation programmes on state lands in 'empty areas', even though many were hardly empty and at times entire communities were evicted to open space for peasant enterprises. The Aguán Valley became the centrepiece of the colonisation programme; indeed, 31% of the total land distributed was in the Bajo Aguán alone.[80] The state offered land expropriated from local inhabitants or from the banana companies to thousands of landless and land-poor families from all over the country for planned and supported colonisation on the plains, the most fertile lands, and spontaneous settlement on the hills, which even then were quite vulnerable to environmental hazards.[81]

The government's National Agrarian Institute (Instituto Nacional Agraria, INA) created a large number of 'peasant enterprises' (*empresas asociativas campesinas*) and cooperatives. With a US$200 million loan from the Inter-American Development Bank (IADB) it then implemented a massive export-oriented development project, which ended up turning most of the cooperative members mainly into producers of African palm and secondarily of citrus fruits and bananas.[82] The project was fundamental in creating conditions for the expansion of African palm cultivation over the next four decades. This impressive transformation of the Valley's landscape, however, the result of inflows of both capital and labour, rarely translated into significant improvements in the peasants' lives, either in the plains or the hills. Owners in name only and in debt for the land they had received, the peasants saw most palm oil profits drained from the peasant enterprises and used to pay debts or simply lost in labyrinthine webs of embezzlement and fraudulent accounting that proved lucrative for a few corrupt male 'leaders'.

The relationship between the peasant sector and the state was never simple. By the late 1970s, as revolution convulsed Nicaragua and violence and repression escalated in El Salvador and Guatemala, the Honduran government increasingly subscribed to the logic of Washington's 'National Security Doctrine', which held that the West was locked in an inexorable struggle with domestic and international 'subversion' and that left-wing movements had to be controlled through surveillance and 'low-intensity conflict'.[83] In the Aguán the government kept a close eye on the peasant enterprises, repressing anything that smacked of the 'red threat' and severely curtailing the cooperatives' autonomy. In 1977, for example, the military occupied the Isletas Peasant Enterprise (Empresa Asociativa Campesina Isletas, EACI), a major banana producer, and incarcerated some of its leaders after a group of associates began to promote cultivation of staple food crops and animal husbandry (maize, rice and pig production) as ways of gaining some economic autonomy in their relation with the Standard Fruit Company.[84]

Following a regional trend by the 1980s the agrarian reform sector was stagnating, mainly as a result of corruption and inadequate government support. By the early 1990s the dominant government discourse was that the agrarian reform had failed and that the market ought to take over.[85] President Rafael Leonardo Callejas (1990–94), referring to agrarian reform beneficiaries, asked:

> Why are they not going to sell if it has been their lifetime work and effort? …I do not agree with those who believe that it is a step back for the Agrarian Reform. On the contrary, it is the culmination of a process. Now, a peasant can receive 500 000 Lempiras for his hard work.[86]

In this context, two important laws were passed. First, in 1983 a massive land titling programme, bankrolled by the US Agency for International Development (USAID), was put in place as a precondition for a competitive land market. Second, in 1992 the Congress passed the Law for the Development and Modernisation of the Agricultural Sector (Ley para la Modernización y Desarrollo del Sector Agrícola, LMDSA). Popularly known as the 'Ley Norton' after US economist Roger Norton, who helped write the law, the LMDSA must be understood within the larger context of neoliberal structural adjustment in Central America. Neoliberals argued that the state should roll back its support of the 'inefficient' peasant sector and promote the region's 'competitive advantages', particularly cheap labour and natural resources, including land. In terms of agrarian structure, this meant emphasising exports over production for the domestic market, devaluing national currencies to make exports more competitive and lifting agricultural tariffs. These policies glutted local markets with artificially cheap subsidised staples, such as rice and maize, from the USA.[87] At the same time the liberalisation of agricultural trade within Central America hit Honduran basic grains producers harder than those in any other country.[88]

The LMDSA reversed the 1974 agrarian reform law, removing the ceiling on large properties and making it possible for agrarian reform land to be put on the market, thus opening the floodgates for a massive process of agrarian counter-reform. Between 1990 and 1994 more than half of the land distributed during the agrarian reform was sold. This number rises to over 70% in the Aguán, where over 20 930 of the 28 365 hectares initially distributed—ie 73.8%—were alienated in this same period.[89] The LMDSA allowed for joint husband-and-wife titles (and for couples in officially recognised consensual unions), but in practice this had little effect, since the state had largely ceased distributing land and instead concentrated on titling existing holdings.[90]

The process of agrarian counter-reform in the Aguán was sometimes voluntary, sometimes violent, as the already impoverished peasant enterprises, abandoned by the state, were 'invited' to sell their lands either by hook or by crook.[91] Most of this land came to be concentrated in the hands of a few wealthy landowners, of whom Miguel Facussé and his Dinant Corporation was the most notorious.[92] Taking advantage of public investments in infrastructure in the region built over the preceding two decades, as well as of the existence of a pool of cheap labour already experienced in palm production consisting of 'freed' cooperative members and impoverished landless and land-poor peasants from the nearby hills, Facussé expanded the area devoted to palm and invested in oil-processing factories (much as other landowners and the surviving cooperatives were also doing).

By the late 1990s the Aguán Valley landscape was a massive monoculture, with palm plantations stretching as far as the eye could see. It consisted of three main sectors: what was left of the agrarian reform enterprises—'those who did not sell'—dedicated mainly to the production of palm oil for the domestic market; the wealthy landowners and their corporations, producing palm oil for the domestic market and for export, mainly to Mexico; and a large landless peasantry, barely surviving as either wage labourers in the palm plantations or as tenants clinging to the hills of the Valley.

In October–November 1998 Hurricane Mitch slammed into Central America's Caribbean coast. In Honduras, already one of the poorest countries in the continent, Mitch caused enormous destruction and significant loss of life. This exacerbated the already harsh living conditions of the Honduran peasantry and particularly the landless. With little support from the state and corruption and embezzlement of aid funds by government officials, peasant communities had to turn to their own organisations for relief and solidarity.[93] In the Bajo Aguán, with support from the *Pastoral Social*, a Church agency, the communities organised into Local Emergency Committees as a way of channelling relief funds from organisations such as Catholic Relief Services. These forms of community organisation would become crucial in the aftermath of the hurricane, as they allowed peasants to come into contact with each other and gain organising and collective action experience. By then all the pieces seemed to be in place for a new cycle of resistance against elite land encroachment. The destruction from Mitch had three main effects. First, it eroded the social contract between peasants and the state, showing the former that for the situation to change they needed to go on the offensive. Second, then President Carlos Roberto Flores Facussé (nephew of landowner Miguel Facussé) claimed in a donors' conference in Stockholm that the government would relaunch the agrarian reform as a way of helping in the reconstruction of the country, thus opening space for sectors in INA and the Catholic Church to act in favour of the landless. Finally, bringing together this landless peasantry triggered memories of resistance, connecting new struggles with those of the great 1954 banana plantation strike and the 'golden age' of the peasant movement during the 1970s. The post-Mitch crisis also prompted 'memories of dispossession' in the form of narratives that challenged the legality of the early 1990s sales of agrarian reform lands and calls to revive the 1970s peasant movement 'spirit' and for the recovery of what was legally theirs.[94] Furthermore, as Jennifer Casolo shows, the idea that women would not have sold also resonated, reminding both women and men that female labour had also gone into the construction of the Aguán landscape, and that men had orchestrated many of the changes without women's consent.[95] The result was a massive wave of land recuperations that signalled the resurgence of the national peasant movement and the increasing prominence of women activists within it.[96]

One of the most significant of these land recuperations targeted the former Regional Center for Military Training (CREM), a US base created in 1983 to train Central American militaries and the Nicaraguan 'contras'.[97] In the 1990s, having served its purpose, the CREM's more than 5000 hectares were returned to the Honduran state for agrarian reform purposes. Before the land could be distributed, however, the municipality of Trujillo illegally sold it to local ranchers and politicians. In 1999, in the post-Mitch period, the *Pastoral Social* in the nearby city of Trujillo began organising the landless into peasant enterprises in different parts of the Valley and the surrounding hills. They were joined by the INA and the three largest national peasant federations (ANACH, CNTC and ACAN).[98] These in turn came together to form the Peasant Movement of the Aguán (Movimiento Campesino del Aguán, MCA). On 14 May 2000 some 700 families from the MCA entered and peacefully occupied the CREM, creating the community of Guadalupe Carney.[99] Memories of the last cycle of dispossession clearly informed the actions of the occupants, who required not only that those joining new peasant enterprises meet the agrarian law's criteria for reform beneficiaries, but also that they must not have sold their land during the counter-reform. These memories had an important gender dimension as six months after the occupation, Guadalupe Carney's leadership and representative assembly, at that time 95 per cent male, cast a historic vote. They approved land rights and assembly membership for single women heads of households, joint title and assembly membership for both adults in the case of couples, and political education and skill-training workshops for families.[100]

During this period other peasant groups also began to organise and staged peaceful occupations to pressure the government into negotiating with the large landowners and 'returning' erstwhile agrarian reform lands to organised landless peasants. This was far from a simple or bloodless process, but a gleam of light appeared in 2008, when the soon-to-be-deposed President 'Mel' Zelaya signed Decree Law 18-2008, which would have given the MCA, as well as other peasant organisations (eg the Peasant Movement of Rigores), legal title over lands they occupied. Further, just before Zelaya was ousted in the June 2009 coup, he reached an agreement with a new organisation, the Unified Peasant Movement of the Aguán (Movimiento Unificado Campesino del Aguán, MUCA), to buy back their land from Facussé.[101] This momentum for resolving the agrarian crisis collapsed, however, when the military kidnapped Zelaya and flew him to Costa Rica on 28 June 2009. As if to illustrate the deep connection between political power and agrarian structure in Central America, that same day the army surrounded the community of Guadalupe Carney to prevent any sort of uprising and to give a clear sign of what was to come.

Led initially by Roberto Micheletti and then by Porfirio Lobo, the post-coup regime's answer to agrarian conflict in the Aguán was to militarise the Valley and give a free hand to the landowners to protect their property however they saw fit. The result has been a rising body count, with dozens assassinated and peasant activists suffering most of the casualties.[102] The peasant organisations have faced a campaign of criminalisation. More than 200 activists face different types of criminal charges. However, the violence and repression unleashed by the coup, and enacted by the combined forces of the landowner's private security forces and the military and police, has also strengthened the resolve of the peasant organisations to right the wrongs of the past. Phrases such as 'the coup opened our eyes', 'thanks to the coup we peasants have lost our fear of the army', or 'how can we stop now when we have lost so many friends and partners' can often be heard when speaking to people of the communities. Further, although the bloody repression of the peasant movement has slowed the pace and extent of land 'recuperations', these have not stopped and movements such as MUCA have been supporting land occupations in places outside the Aguán.

Increasingly international human rights organisations have investigated and condemned the violence in the region.[103] This scrutiny has had internal effects, as local residents feel that levels of repression have diminished, particularly since the creation of the locally based and peasant-run Permanent Human Rights Observatory of the Aguán (Observatorio Permanente de Derechos Humanos del Aguán). Internationally, in 2011, human rights advocacy by organisations such as FIAN International and Salva la Selva led the German Development

Corporation (Deutsche Investitions und Entwicklungsgesellschaft, DEG, part of the KfW Bankengruppe) to cancel a \$20-million loan to Facussé's Dinant Corporation.[104]

African palm in the Bajo Aguán

With these historical elements in place we can turn our attention to the production of African palm in the region. Nationally, according to the National Federation of Palm Producers of Honduras (Federación Nacional de Productores de Palma Africana de Honduras), the area dedicated to this crop jumped from around 40 000 hectares in 1990 to almost 90 000 in 2006 and around 132 000 in 2011.[105] Palm oil is now the country's third most important export after coffee and bananas, generating \$300 million in 2013.[106] Producers aspire to make Honduras the most important producer in Latin America by increasing palm area to 650 000 hectares, which would surpass Colombia, now the largest producer.[107]

In the late 1920s Standard Fruit Company started experimental production of African palm in Honduras, but the crop only took off in the 1970s with investments by the state and IADB loans. In the 1990s, in the context of the agrarian counter-reform, production started to shift to private firms with significant backing from international financial institutions. For example, in 2009, around the time of the biofuel boom, IFC invested \$30 million in Dinant's oil palm enterprise, which also enjoyed support from the IADB, the World Bank and BCIE (although some of these credits were subsequently cancelled, as occurred with the DEG loan mentioned above). The corporation also received carbon credits under the Clean Development Mechanism of the Kyoto Protocol on global climate change.[108]

Importantly in the Aguán no simple differentiation can be made between foreign and domestic investment. African palm production largely predates the global boom. Also, most of the installations and investment were already in place from the colonisation and agrarian reform programmes of the 1970s. Apart from some biodiesel use by Dinant's transport fleet and a pilot programme with Tegucigalpa's urban bus system, there is not really a domestic biofuels market. Further, according to a Dinant spokesperson, there are no plans to shift output towards biofuels in the near future.[109]

Moreover, while most of the killings in the region appeared to be directly related to African palm cultivation, there is no opposition to the crop itself, but rather to who is producing it and how. Many peasant organisations in the region either grow or plan to grow African palm, to the detriment of staples such as rice or maize.[110] Further, since the first land recuperations in the late 1990s, the idea of promoting a co-investment model has gained traction. The idea is simple: peasant enterprises should focus solely on producing raw materials (African palm fruit), while the big private plants will process and market the palm oil. Both private producers, such as Facussé (2011), and the government (early 2000s) have promoted this model and sectors of the peasant movement are favourably disposed. Honduran activists, however, are critical, since this contract farming approach would reproduce the dependency of the Isletas enterprise in the 1970s and 1980s, which forced peasants to assume all production risks, while allowing private investors to accrue the value added in processing.[111] Further, as in other contexts, the monopsony power of processing plants allows them to set prices, permitting a small number of intermediaries and exporters to control the entire production chain.[112] In this way a 'control grab' has in effect occurred—ie the control of huge amounts of productive land for monoculture—but without actually buying or leasing the land.[113] This, again, points to blind spots in much of the land grab literature.

It needs to be emphasised, moreover, that peasants are producing and expanding the area in African palm for both cultural and economic reasons. Most peasant organisations are still paying for the land they occupy and African palm is one of the few viable cash crops in the region (in terms of market access, production knowledge, and financial and technical support). African palm production has become prestigious in the Aguán, evoking images of a better life related to effects of the land reform of the 1970s and 1980s, as well as to the image of success attached to those cooperatives (and the communities linked to them) that were not dismantled in the early 1990s, such as the Salama Cooperative. Signs of the cultural esteem and prestige accorded African palm can be seen all over the Valley. Tocoa, the principal city in the Valley, is traditionally called 'the city of palms'. Its soccer team's insignia has big palm trees in it and every year in July it hosts the 'National Palm Festival', where 'palm culture' is celebrated with a parade and floats. At a more profound level in this region the palm tree has become a sign of development, to the point where two or three of them can be found in the backyard of many homes. As Derek Hall, Philip Hirsch and Tania Li suggest for Southeast Asia, 'the legitimation supplied by visions of development, modernity, [and] civilization... has a pervasive effect on land use and exclusion'.[114]

Conversely, the lack of palm trees signals underdevelopment. When children in rural communities were asked about what their community had that no other one did, they responded negatively that they lacked electricity, running water and palm trees. When peasants farmers were queried as to why they prefer African palm to other crops such as plantains or rice, besides the most direct economically oriented responses ('because it has a better market price'), they pointed out that palm trees are a safer investment, since floods and strong winds could not topple them. The meaning and value of planting African palm thus transcends simple economic rationality and has to do also with local environmental understandings, which are shaped by memories of the devastation wrought by Hurricanes Katrina (2005), Mitch (1998) and Fifi (1974), as well as by fears—well-founded or not—about other hazards, particularly floods and droughts.

These considerations suggest that crops and land are never simply 'things', but are deeply embedded in and are manifestations of social relations of power historically instituted in particular social settings. Crops and agricultural technologies may also be symbols that speak to rural people of their history and aspirations and that promise delivery from poverty and domination, even at the cost of new dependencies.[115] Understanding and reconstructing these social relations is essential for grasping why particular crops expand or disappear, the range of productive forms that they entail, and the impacts they have on local populations.[116] Land deals *per se*, and certain types of crops, do not create totally new situations from scratch, with totally new forms of production and exploitation.

Conclusions

Land grabbing is a cyclical phenomenon and a product of global accumulation processes, of rising demand for particular commodities and of on-the-ground processes that create both space for capital and new social groups (eg entrepreneurial sectors, labourers, displaced people, contract farmers). When land grabs generate conflict, the outcomes depend importantly on historically specific repertoires of resistance and repression. These, in turn, shape possibilities for future land grabs. Claims about 'empty' or 'undeveloped' lands are usually discursive constructions which refer to spaces that capital has not yet been able or wanted to penetrate, not spaces devoid of people. A greater historicisation of the land grab discussion is necessary not just to acknowledge antecedents or to understand impacts, but also to conceive of the present as an outcome of past processes of contention.

Central America has experienced several cycles of land grabbing in the post-independence period. Late 19th century liberal regimes sought to overcome the economically stifling legacy of three centuries of Spanish rule; to modernise infrastructure and banking; and to turn what had been colonial provinces into consolidated nation-states. Rising international demand for coffee had a number of impacts. Governments sought to build railways from the interior to the coasts, to create markets in land and labour, and to discipline and subordinate the popular classes. The private appropriation of previously non-private land was a central piece of this political-economic project, although the 'frustrated' liberalism of Honduras left large swathes of municipal and state land intact. Liberalism called into being new social groups: coffee and merchant elites of domestic and foreign origin, proletarianised and semi-proletarianised rural workers, and 'comprador' groups that allied with foreign capital. The fragile fiscal foundation of the liberal states led them to view concessions to foreign investors as both an essential source of revenue and a quick route to modernisation. The first cycle of land grabbing—for coffee—was thus a precondition for the second, banana plantation, cycle. The transition from the first to the second cycles also involved a shift between foreign hegemons. While British banks were the primary source of loans for the liberal states' early railway and other modernisation projects, US financial capital became increasingly important as US-based banana giants gained a foothold in the region.

The second cycle of land grabbing by foreign banana companies (and associated railways) reconfigured rural spaces, gave rise to new social groups and ideologies and shifted the country's economic centre of gravity from the interior to the North Coast. Foreign enclaves fuelled nationalistic sensibilities that became a central ideological pillar of labour and agrarian movements, along with heightened class consciousness of both a working-class and peasant sort. In the Bajo Aguán, for example, peasants today continue to emphasise the 'foreignness' of Facussé and other large investors who usurped agrarian reform lands.

The continued existence of municipal and national lands even in the early 21st century—a product of Honduras's 'failed' 19th century liberalism and the combativeness and tenacity of the 20th century peasant movement—has had two effects that are important for our argument. First, Honduran peasants have a living memory of having had land, if not in the present generation then in the generation of their parents or grandparents. Second, in contrast to other Central American countries, in Honduras the peasant movements have always focused on the recuperation of erstwhile agrarian reform lands or national lands rather than on private property.

In the Aguán older people frequently recall how their situation was better in the 1980s, when they were still in the cooperatives. Young and old see the surviving cooperatives and the higher living standards of their associates as reminders of the world they lost and as an aspiration animating current struggles. Tales circulate in the communities about how the leaders of the old cooperatives were given the choice of selling or getting shot. In some of the organisations (eg the Movimiento Auténtico Reivindicador Campesino del Aguán) people insist that they never sold the land, which was illegally taken from them, and express pride in being the daughters and sons of members of the original cooperatives. These memories have found their way into the institutional organisation of the peasant enterprises, as one of the requirements for taking part in land recuperations was not having participated in the sales of the 1990s. Lived histories of dispossession and memories of land grabbing cycles have become a material force that affects contemporary agrarian outcomes and shapes the possibilities of future land grabs.

Notes

Research was supported by the US National Science Foundation (grant #1024017 to Edelman) and the Wenner-Gren Foundation for Anthropological Research (grant #8594 to León). The authors greatly appreciate receiving constructive criticisms on an earlier version from Saturnino Borras, Jr, Jefferson Boyer and Carlos Oya.

1 LA Wily, 'Enclosure revisited: putting the global land rush in historical perspective', in T Allan, M Keulertz, S Sojamo & J Warner, (eds), *Handbook of Land and Water Grabs in Africa: Foreign Direct Investment and Food and Water Security*, Abingdon: Routledge, 2012, pp 11–23; C Huggins, 'A historical perspective on the "global land rush"', International Land Coalition, 2011, at http://www.landcoalition. org/sites/default/files/publication/904/HUGGINS_History_web_11.03.11.pdf, accessed 14 March 2012; and PF Luna, 'Latifundia, haciendas et landgrabbing, en perspective historique', *Histoire(s) de l'Amérique latine*, 8, 2013, pp 1–8.

2 See, for example, CC LeGrand, 'Living in Macondo: economy and culture in a United Fruit Company banana enclave in Colombia', in GM Joseph, CC LeGrand & RD Salvatore (eds), *Close Encounters of Empire: Writing the Cultural History of US–Latin American Relations*, Durham, NC: Duke University Press, 1998, pp 336–337.

3 On assertions about 'yield gaps' and the 'availability' of uncultivated land, see KW Deininger & D Byerlee, *Rising Global Interest in Farmland: Can it Yield Sustainable and Equitable Benefits?*, Washington, DC: World Bank, 2011. On *terra nullius*, see K Milun, *The Political Uncommons: The Cross-cultural Logic of the Global Commons*, Farnham: Ashgate, 2011, pp 57–69.

4 In Argentina's 19th century genocidal 'wars of the desert', for example, '*desierto*' did not refer to arid lands (some were humid forests, called 'the green desert'), but rather to spaces that elites regarded as 'empty geographies with enormous yet dormant economic potential defined by their absence of civilization, market relations and state presence…[T]hese were 'deserts' inhabited by armed indigenous groups

that had yet to be defeated.' See G Gordillo, *Landscapes of Devils: Tensions of Place and Memory in the Argentinean Chaco*, Durham, NC: Duke University Press, 2004, pp 46–48.

5   C Oya, 'Methodological reflections on "land grab" databases and the "land grab" literature "rush"', *Journal of Peasant Studies*, 40(3), 2013, pp 503–520.

6   J Mahoney, *The Legacies of Liberalism: Path Dependence and Political Regimes in Central America*, Baltimore, MD: Johns Hopkins University Press, 2001.

7   H Pérez Brignoli, *Breve historia de Centroamérica*, Madrid: Alianza Editorial, 1985, pp 9–12, provides a useful outline of various approaches to defining 'Central America'. For the purposes of this analysis, we consider this region to include the five republics that emerged out of Spanish Central America: Guatemala, Honduras, El Salvador, Nicaragua and Costa Rica. Belize and Panama are geographically part of the region, but have very distinct histories as a former British colony and a province of Colombia, respectively. Recent analyses of land grabbing in Central America include A Alonso-Fradejas, 'Land control-grabbing in Guatemala: the political economy of contemporary agrarian change', *Canadian Journal of Development Studies*, 33(4), 2012, pp 509–528; L Grandia, 'Road mapping: megaprojects and land grabs in the northern Guatemalan lowlands', *Development and Change*, 44(2), 2013, pp 233–259; and, especially, L Grandia, *Enclosed: Conservation, Cattle, and Commerce Among the Q'eqchi' Maya Lowlanders*, Seattle, WA: University of Washington Press, 2012. The latter takes the type of long-term historical view for which this paper argues.

8   CFS Cardoso, 'Historia económica del café en Centroamérica (siglo XIX): estudio comparativo', *Estudios Sociales Centroamericanos*, 10, 1975, pp 9–55; L Gudmundson, 'Lord and peasant in the making of modern Central America', in E Huber & F Safford (eds), *Agrarian Structure and Political Power: Landlord and Peasant in the Making of Latin America*, Pittsburgh: University of Pittsburgh Press, 1995, pp 151–176; and S Martí i Puig, *Tiranías, rebeliones y democracia: itinerarios políticos comparados en Centroamérica*, Barcelona: Edicions Bellaterra, 2004.

9   See SJ Stern, 'The decentered center and the expansionist periphery: the paradoxes of foreign–local encounter', in Joseph *et al*, *Close Encounters of Empire*.

10 SM Borras, C Kay, S Gómez, & J Wilkinson 'Land grabbing and global capitalist accumulation: key features in Latin America', *Canadian Journal of Development Studies*, 33(4), 2012, pp 402–416; M Edelman, 'Messy hectares: questions about the epistemology of land grabbing data', *Journal of Peasant Studies*, 40(3), 2013, pp 485–501; and Oya, 'Methodological reflections on "land grab" databases and the "land grab" literature "rush"'.

11 TM Li, 'Centering labor in the land grab debate', *Journal of Peasant Studies*, 38(2), 2011, pp 281–298.

12 S Gómez, 'Acaparamiento de tierras: reflexiones sobre la dinámica reciente del mercado de la tierra en América Latina', FAO, 2011, at http://www.rlc.fao.org/fileadmin/content/events/semtierras/estudios/gomez.pdf, accessed 2 January 2013; and F Soto Baquero & S Gómez (eds), *Dinámicas del mercado de la tierra en América Latina y el Caribe: concentración y extranjerización*, Rome: FAO, 2012.

13 The FAO project also included a study of Panama, although the criteria for selecting cases are not specified.

14 Gómez, 'Acaparamiento de tierras', p 13.

15 SM Borras, JC Franco *et al* 'Land grabbing in Latin America and the Caribbean', *Journal of Peasant Studies*, 39(3–4), 2012, pp 845–872; and Borras *et al*, 'Land grabbing and global accumulation'.

16 JA Carrera C & JL Carrera Campos, 'El caso de Guatemala', in F Soto Baquero & S Gómez (eds), *Dinámicas del mercado de la tierra en América Latina y el Caribe: concentración y extranjerización*, Rome: FAO, 2012, p 269.

17 *Ibid*, p 272.

18 The methodologically impoverished tendency to accept uncritically the authority of state functionaries is exemplified in the Costa Rican case study, which notes approvingly that 'according to information from Agriculture Ministry functionaries, the phenomenon of land grabbing is not a reality that affects the productive process'. See ST Donoso, 'El caso de Costa Rica', in Soto Baquero & Gómez, *Dinámicas del mercado de la tierra en América Latina y el Caribe*, p 211.

19 A prevalent discourse in Honduras nonetheless represents these investors—in particular, Miguel Facussé, Reynaldo Canales and René Morales—as 'foreign'. In the case of Facussé, owner of Dinant Corporation and the main figure behind the 1990s agrarian counter-reform, these claims are based on his Palestinian ancestry, although the Facussé family has been in Honduras for over a century. See NL González, *Dollar, Dove, and Eagle: One Hundred Years of Palestinian Migration to Honduras*, Ann Arbor, MI: University of Michigan Press, 1993, p 191. Morales was born in Nicaragua but lived in Honduras after 1979. His brother, Jaime Morales Carazo, also lived in Honduras in 1979–96 and was Daniel Ortega's vice president from 2007 to 2012. Finally, Reynaldo Canales is often identified as of Salvadoran descent. Drawing distinctions between 'foreign' and 'domestic' actors is clearly fraught with ambiguities.

20 The largest landowners' processing plants are, however, capable of producing biodiesel. See TM Kerssen, *Grabbing Power: The New Struggles for Land, Food and Democracy in Northern Honduras*, Oakland, CA: Food First Books, 2013, p 66. The human rights literature also sometimes assumes that palm is

for biofuels. See D Frank, 'WikiLeaks Honduras: US linked to brutal businessman', *The Nation*, 21 October 2011, at http://www.thenation.com/article/164120/wikileaks-honduras-us-linked-brutal-businessman# axzz2YZGRvb3q, accessed 10 June 2013.

21 The variety of property forms are detailed in D McCreery, *Rural Guatemala, 1760–1940*, Stanford, CA: Stanford University Press, 1994, pp 49–84, 236–242.

22 As in more recent cycles of land grabbing elsewhere, some large concessions were never put into production. In 1882 a French concessionaire who held a contract to build a canal between Nicaragua's two large lakes claimed to have received a grant of 50 000 manzanas (34 500 hectares) for rubber production. A-P Blanchet, *Le caoutchouc: son emploi, sa production naturelle & sa plantation au Nicaragua—création d'une compagnie pour son exploitation*, Paris: Librairie Jules Lecuir, 1882, p 6.

23 On food regimes, see H Friedmann & P McMichael, 'Agriculture and the state system: the rise and decline of national agricultures, 1870 to the present', *Sociologia Ruralis*, 29(2), 1989, pp 93–117; P McMichael, 'The land grab and corporate food regime restructuring', *Journal of Peasant Studies*, 39 (3–4), 2012, pp 681–701; B Pritchard, 'The long hangover from the second food regime: a world-historical interpretation of the collapse of the WTO Doha Round', *Agriculture and Human Values*, 26(4), 2009, pp 297–307; and B Winders, 'The vanishing free market: the formation and spread of the British and US food regime', *Journal of Agrarian Change*, 9(3), 2009, pp 315–344. Key works on the 'dessert economies' include SW Mintz, *Sweetness and Power: The Place of Sugar in Modern History*, New York: Penguin Books, 1986; MJ Jiménez, '"From plantation to cup": coffee and capitalism in the United States, 1830–1939', in W Roseberry, L Gudmundson & M Samper Kutschbach (eds), *Coffee, Society, and Power in Latin America*, Baltimore, MD: Johns Hopkins University Press, 1995, pp 38–64; and J Soluri, *Banana Cultures: Agriculture, Consumption, and Environmental Change in Honduras and the United States*, Austin, TX: University of Texas Press, 2005. Stimulant consumption powered not just industrial working classes, but also imperial war machines. See M Haft & H Suarez, 'The marine's secret weapon: coffee', *New York Times*, 2013, at http://atwar.blogs.nytimes.com/2013/08/16/the-marines-secret-weapon-coffee/?_r=0, accessed 17 August 2013.

24 Key overviews include L Gudmundson & H Lindo-Fuentes, *Central America, 1821–1871: Liberalism before Liberal Reform*, Tuscaloosa, AL: University of Alabama Press, 1995; C Hall & H Pérez Brignoli, *Historical Atlas of Central America*, Norman, OK: University of Oklahoma Press, 2003; Mahoney, *The Legacies of Liberalism*; Pérez Brignoli, *Breve historia de Centroamérica*; and RG Williams, *States and Social Evolution: Coffee and the Rise of National Governments in Central America*, Chapel Hill, NC: University of North Carolina Press, 1994.

25 DA Euraque, *Reinterpreting the Banana Republic: Region and State in Honduras, 1870–1972*, Chapel Hill, NC: University of North Carolina Press, 1996; A Lanuza, JL Vázquez, A Barahona & A Chamorro *Economía y sociedad en la construcción del Estado en Nicaragua*, San José: Instituto Centroamericano de Administración Pública, 1983; and Mahoney, *The Legacies of Liberalism*.

26 L Gudmundson, 'The expropriation of pious and corporate properties in Costa Rica, 1805–1860: patterns in the consolidation of a national elite', *The Americas*, 39(3), 1983, pp 281–303.

27 F Mallon, 'Economic liberalism: where we are and where we need to go', in JL Love & N Jacobsen (eds), *Guiding the Invisible Hand: Economic Liberalism and the State in Latin American History*, New York: Praeger, 1988, p 180.

28 V Bulmer-Thomas, *The Economic History of Latin America Since Independence*, Cambridge: Cambridge University Press, 1994, p 140.

29 H Lindo-Fuentes, 'Consecuencias económicas de la independencia en Centroamérica', in L Prados de la Escosura & S Amaral (eds), *La Independencia americana: consecuencias económicas*, Madrid: Alianza Editorial, 1993, pp 54–79.

30 The exceptions to this generalisation reveal similar objectives at work. The Liberal regime of José Santos Zelaya, for example, protected the turn-of-the-century Nicaraguan sugar industry. This was, however, an attempt to favour political allies and generate revenue through the alcohol distilling monopoly. See JL Gould, *To Lead as Equals: Rural Protest and Political Consciousness in Chinandega, Nicaragua, 1912–1979*, Chapel Hill, NC: University of North Carolina Press, 1990, pp 23–24. The second largest source of government revenue in late 19th century Central America generally consisted of taxes on (or sales and franchise income from) *aguardiente* and other spirits. In some countries, such as Costa Rica, El Salvador and Honduras, the state maintained ownership of all alcohol production, a continuation of the colonial-era institution of *estancos* or monopolistic franchises.

31 Interpretations of liberalism as an extreme process of dispossession and primitive accumulation include R Menjívar, *Acumulación originaria y desarrollo del capitalismo en El Salvador*, San José: EDUCA, 1980; and E Torres-Rivas, *Interpretación del desarrollo social centroamericano*, San José: EDUCA, 1971. More recent historiography generally maintains, with greater attention to empirical evidence, that the pace of late 19th and early 20th century land expropriations was less abrupt and their territorial extent less drastic than previously believed. A Lauria-Santiago, *An Agrarian Republic: Commercial Agriculture and the Politics of Peasant Communities in El Salvador, 1823–1914*, Pittsburgh, PA: University of Pittsburgh

Press, 1999; and H Lindo-Fuentes, *Weak Foundations: The Economy of El Salvador in the Nineteenth Century*, Berkeley, CA: University of California Press, 1990.

32 JL Gould & A Lauria-Santiago, *To Rise in Darkness: Revolution, Repression, and Memory in El Salvador, 1920–1932*, Durham, NC: Duke University Press, 2008; J Handy, *Gift of the Devil: a History of Guatemala*, Boston, MA: South End Press, 1984; and McCreery, *Rural Guatemala*.

33 McCreery, *Rural Guatemala*, p 252.

34 Cardoso, 'Historia económica del café en Centroamérica', pp 21–22; Handy, *Gift of the Devil*, p 69; and R Wagner, *Historia del café de Guatemala*, Bogotá: Villegas Editores, 2001, p 93. Guatemalan Liberals sought to abolish a 99-year lease because they viewed it as a manifestation of economic stagnation, while contemporary land grabbers rejoice in much shorter leases in places such as Ethiopia, where all land formally belongs to the state. See T Lavers, '"Land grab" as development strategy? The political economy of agricultural investment in Ethiopia', *Journal of Peasant Studies*, 39(1), 2012, p 113. Obviously the key difference has to do with the velocity at which capital reproduces in each period. Today a much shorter lease is sufficient for recouping a major investment and generating a profit. In late 19th century Guatemala, on the other hand, leases in effect removed land from an emerging property market.

35 J Castellanos Cambranes, *Coffee and Peasants in Guatemala: The Origins of the Modern Plantation Economy in Guatemala, 1853–1897*, Stockholm: Institute of Latin American Studies, 1985, p 297.

36 E Dore, 'Property, households and public regulation of domestic life: Diriomo, Nicaragua 1840–1900', *Journal of Latin American Studies*, 29(3), 1997, pp 591–611; JL Gould, *To Die in This Way: Nicaraguan Indians and the Myth of Mestizaje, 1880–1965*, Durham, NC: Duke University Press, 1998; Lindo-Fuentes, *Weak Foundations*; and H Ronsbo, 'State formation and property: reflections on the political technologies of space in Central America', *Journal of Historical Sociology*, 10(1), 1997, pp 56–73.

37 In their early years the enclaves also employed large numbers of English-speaking Caribbean migrants. See PI Bourgois, *Ethnicity at Work: Divided Labor on a Central American Banana Plantation*, Baltimore, MD: Johns Hopkins University Press, 1989.

38 'Aprobación del Contrato Soto-Keith sobre deuda exterior y ferrocarril, 1884', in *Documentos fundamentales del siglo XIX*, Biblioteca Patria, San José: Editorial Costa Rica, 1978, XVI, pp 321–330; and W Stewart, *Keith and Costa Rica: The Biography of Minor Cooper Keith, American Entrepreneur*, Albuquerque, NM: University of New Mexico Press, 1964.

39 J Casey Gaspar, *Limón 1880–1940: un estudio de la industria bananera en Costa Rica*, San José: Editorial Costa Rica, 1979, pp 25–32.

40 PJ Dosal, *Doing Business with the Dictators: A Political History of United Fruit in Guatemala, 1899–1944*, Wilmington, NC: SR Books, 1993, pp 17–40.

41 *Ibid*, p 44.

42 RH Immerman, *The CIA in Guatemala: The Foreign Policy of Intervention*, Austin, TX: University of Texas Press, 1988, p 80.

43 Quoted in Euraque, *Reinterpreting the Banana Republic*, p 4.

44 *Ibid*, p 7.

45 E Flores Valeriano, *La explotación bananera en Honduras*, Tegucigalpa: Universidad Nacional Autónoma de Honduras, 1987, p 26.

46 Soluri, *Banana Cultures*, pp 8, 33.

47 M Moberg & S Striffler, 'Introduction', in S Striffler & M Moberg (eds), *Banana Wars: Power, Production, and History in the Americas*, Durham, NC: Duke University Press, 2003, p 12. The company also acquired large lowland haciendas to fatten cattle and breed mules for the plantations. See M Edelman, *The Logic of the Latifundio: The Large Estates of Northwestern Costa Rica Since the Late Nineteenth Century*, Stanford, CA: Stanford University Press, 1992, pp 395–396.

48 M Bucheli, 'United Fruit Company in Latin America', in Striffler & Moberg, *Banana Wars*, pp 82–85.

49 Some analysts assert that 'The [1952] law was more moderate in almost every respect than the Mexican agrarian reform bill that preceded it by over a decade, and in fact would have been acceptable under the American Alliance for Progress seven years later'. SC Schlesinger & S Kinzer, *Bitter Fruit: The Untold Story of the American Coup in Guatemala*, Garden City, NY: Anchor Books, 1983, p 55.

50 T Melville & M Melville, *Guatemala: The Politics of Land Ownership*, New York: Free Press, 1971, pp 54–57.

51 WC Thiesenhusen, *Broken Promises: Agrarian Reform and the Latin American Campesino*, Boulder, CO: Westview Press, 1995, pp 79–80.

52 *Ibid*, pp 132, 144; and L Grandia, 'Raw hides: hegemony and cattle in Guatemala's northern lowlands', *Geoforum*, 40(5), 2009, p 724.

53 I Román Vega & R Rivera Araya, *Tierra con fronteras (treinta años de política de distribución de tierras en Costa Rica)*, San José: CEPAS, 1990, p 15.

54 C Blokland, *Participación campesina en el desarrollo económico: la Unión Nacional de Agricultores y Ganaderos de Nicaragua durante la revolución sandinista*, Doetinchem: Paulo Freire Stichting, 1992, pp 88–90.

55 A Montoya, *El agro salvadoreño antes y después de la reforma agraria*, Cuadernos de Investigación 9, San Salvador: DIES-CENITEC, 1991, p 53.

56 A Segovia, 'Centroamérica después del café: el fin del modelo agroexportador tradicional y el surgimiento de un nuevo modelo', *Revista Centroamericana de Ciencias Sociales*, 1, 2004, pp 5–38; Segovia, 'Integración real y grupos centroamericanos de poder económico: implicaciones para la democracia y el desarrollo regional', *Estudios Centroamericanos*, 61, 2006, pp 517–582; and WI Robinson, *Transnational Conflicts: Central America, Social Change, and Globalization*, London: Verso, 2003, pp 93–94.

57 On 'flex' crops, which have multiple uses as food, feed, fuel and industrial inputs, see SM Borras, JC Franco & C Wang, 'The challenge of global governance of land grabbing: changing international agricultural context and competing political views and strategies', *Globalizations*, 10(1), 2013, pp 161–179.

58 M Edelman, 'Illegal renting of agrarian reform plots: a Costa Rican case study', *Human Organization*, 48 (2), 1989, pp 172–180.

59 F Amador & G Ribbink, 'El mercado de tierra en Nicaragua y el sector reformado', *Revista de Economía Agrícola*, 6, 1993, pp 3–15; J Jonakin, 'Agrarian policy', in TW Walker (ed), *Nicaragua without Illusions: Regime Transition and Structural Adjustment in the 1990s*, Wilmington, NC: SR Books, 1997, pp 100–102; and Robinson, *Transnational Conflicts*, pp 79–81.

60 O Núñez Soto, *La economía popular asociativa y autogestionaria*, Managua: CIPRES, 1995, p 41.

61 M Sierra Mejía & M Ramírez Mejía, 'El papel del estado en el desarrollo del sector rural de Honduras hacia el año 2000', in HN Pino, P Jiménez & A Thorpe (eds), *¿Estado o mercado? Perspectivas para el desarrollo agrícola centroamericano hacia el año 2000*, Tegucigalpa: POSCAE-UNAH, 1994, p 59.

62 Honduras Poder Legislativo, 'Decreto número 31-92, Ley para la modernización y el desarrollo del sector agrícola', 1992, at http://www.honduraslegal.com/legislacion/legi104.htm, accessed 25 March 2013.

63 A Thorpe *et al El impacto del ajuste en el agro hondureño*, Tegucigalpa: POSCAE-UNAH, 1995, p 113. Some estimates indicate that as early as 1985 'over one-fifth' of beneficiaries had abandoned the land. See P Dorner, *Latin American Land Reforms in Theory and Practice: A Retrospective Analysis*, Madison, WI: University of Wisconsin Press, 1992, p 43.

64 With a total extension of over 6000 km², the Valley takes its name from the Aguán River, 395 km long, and contains some of the most fertile lands in the country. It is typically divided into three sub-regions: the lower, mid and upper Aguán. In administrative terms the Aguán Valley extends through the Departments of Colón and Yoro.

65 M Macías, *La capital de la contrarreforma agraria: el Bajo-Aguán de Honduras*, Tegucigalpa: Editorial Guaymuras, 2001.

66 CONADEH, 'Informe anual 2011', Comisionado Nacional de los Derechos Humanos, 2012, at http://www.conadeh.hn/index.php/7-conadeh/31-informe-anual-2011, accessed 20 March 2012; and 'Asesinan a dos abogados en menos de cinco días en Colón', *Conexihon*, 2013, at http://conexihon.info/site/noticia/derechos-humanos/derechos-humanos-conflicto-agrario-y-minero/asesinan-dos-abogados-en-menos, accessed 17 July 2013.

67 M Posas, *El movimiento campesino hondureño: una perspectiva general*, Tegucigalpa: Editorial Guaymuras, 1981; JM Ruhl, 'Agrarian structure and political stability in Honduras', *Journal of Interamerican Studies and World Affairs*, 26(1), 1984, pp 33–68; and V Meza *et al, Honduras: poderes fácticos y sistema político*, Tegucigalpa: Centro de Documentación de Honduras, 2008.

68 Borras *et al*, 'Land grabbing in Latin America and the Caribbean'; Kerssen, *Grabbing Power*, pp 68–73; and R Wong, 'The oxygen trade: leaving Hondurans gasping for air', *Foreign Policy in Focus*, 2013, at http://www.fpif.org/articles/the_oxygen_trade_leaving_hondurans_gasping_for_air?utm_source=feedburner&utm_medium=feed&utm_campaign=Feed%3A+FPIF+%28Foreign+Policy+In+Focus+%28All+News%29%29%, accessed 19 June 2013.

69 But see Kerssen, *Grabbing Power*.

70 Soluri, *Banana Cultures*, pp 50, 77–80.

71 J Casolo, 'Gender levees: rethinking women's land rights in northeastern Honduras', *Journal of Agrarian Change*, 9(3), 2009, pp 392–420.

72 Soluri, *Banana Cultures*, pp 50, 77–80, 168–171.

73 M Argueta, *La gran huelga bananera: los 69 días que estremecieron a Honduras*, Tegucigalpa: Editorial Universitaria, 1995; R MacCameron, *Bananas, Labor, and Politics in Honduras: 1954–1963*, Syracuse, NY: Maxwell School, Syracuse University, 1983; M Posas, *Luchas del movimiento obrero hondureño*, San José: Editorial Universitaria Centroamericana, 1981; and A Robleda Castro, *40 años después: la verdad de la huelga de 1954 y de la formación del SITRATERCO*, Tegucigalpa: Ediciones del SEDAL, 1995.

74 Posas, *El movimiento campesino hondureño*; and Ruhl, 'Agrarian structure and political stability in Honduras', p 51.

75 Thiesenhusen, *Broken Promises*, p 87; and R Ruben & F Fúnez, *La compra-venta de tierras de la reforma agraria*, Tegucigalpa: Editorial Guaymuras, 1993, p 13.

76 DE Schulz & DS Schulz, *The United States, Honduras, and the Crisis in Central America*, Boulder, CO: Westview Press, 1994, pp 29–30.

77 Ruhl, 'Agrarian structure and political stability in Honduras', p 53.

78 *Ibid*, p 53.

79 CD Deere & M León, 'Revertir la reforma agraria con exclusión de género: lecciones a partir de América Latina', *El Otro Derecho*, 31–32, 2004, p 191.

80 Ruhl, 'Agrarian structure and political stability in Honduras', p 54; and Macías, *La capital de la contrarreforma agraria*.

81 Casolo, 'Gender levees'; and C Brockett, 'Public policy, peasants, and rural development in Honduras', *Journal of Latin American Studies*, 19(1), 1988, pp 69–86.

82 Ruben & Fúnez, *La compra-venta de tierras de la reforma agraria*; and AA Castro Rubio, *Un plan de desarrollo: el Bajo Aguán en Honduras*, Mexico, DF: Universidad Iberoamericana, 1994.

83 S Landau, *The Dangerous Doctrine: National Security and US Foreign Policy*, Boulder, CO: Westview Press, 1988, pp 145–146; and Schulz & Schulz, *The United States, Honduras, and the Crisis in Central America*, p 73.

84 Macías, *La capital de la contrarreforma agraria*, p 39. In 1974, after Hurricane Fifi crashed into the North Coast and destroyed the banana plantations, the INA and the Corporación Hondureña del Banano created the EACI on lands that had belonged to the Standard Fruit Company. See Flores Valeriano, *La explotación bananera en Honduras*, pp 83–84; M Posas, *Autogestión en el agro: el caso de la Empresa Asociativa Isletas*, Tegucigalpa: Editorial de la Universidad Nacional Autónoma de Honduras, 1992; and D Slutzky & E Alonso, *Empresas transnacionales y agricultura: el caso del enclave bananero en Honduras*, Tegucigalpa: Editorial Universitaria, 1982, pp 64–91. With little support from the state, the EACI rehabilitated the banana fields and signed contracts with Standard in which, in exchange for technical and financial support, it agreed to grow bananas and sell all of its production to the banana company.

85 J Suazo, *Honduras: ¿30 años de política agraria en democracia?*, Tegucigalpa: ASOHDEICO, 2012.

86 Quoted in *ibid*, p 73. In 1992 US$1.00 was worth 5.83 lempiras.

87 This was part of a broader shift towards a more flexible global 'food regime'. See Winders, 'The vanishing free market'.

88 F Rueda-Junquera, 'Regional integration and agricultural trade in Central America', *World Development*, 26(2), 1998, pp 345–362.

89 COCOCH, 'Reforma agraria, agricultura y medio rural en honduras: la agenda pendiente del sector campesino', Consejo Coordinador de Organizaciones Campesinas de Honduras, 2010, p 24, at http://www.landcoalition.org/pdf/08_COCOCH_Reforma_Agraria_en_Honduras.pdf.

90 CD Deere & M León, 'Gender, land, and water: from reform to counter-reform in Latin America', *Agriculture and Human Values*, 15(4), 1998, pp 379–380.

91 Ruben & Fúnez, *La compra-venta de tierras de la reforma agraria*; and Macías, *La capital de la contrarreforma agraria*.

92 T Wilkinson, 'In Honduras, a controversial tycoon responds to critics', *Los Angeles Times*, 21 December 2012, at http://articles.latimes.com/2012/dec/21/world/la-fg-honduras-facusse-20121221, accessed 23 December 2012. See also Frank, 'WikiLeaks Honduras'; and H Herrera, '¿Quién es Miguel Facussé?', *Socialismo o Barbarie Honduras*, 2011, at http://www.sobhonduras.org/index.php?option=com_content&view=article&id=176%3Aiquien-es-miguel-facusse&catid=63%3Aets-85&Itemid=66, accessed 30 January 2013.

93 See P Jeffrey, 'Una mirada introspectiva: la respuesta al huracán Mitch en el Valle del Bajo Aguán', in M Torres Calderón *et al* (eds), *Descifrando a Honduras: cuatro puntos de vista sobre la realidad política tras el huracán Mitch*, Cambridge, MA: Hemisphere Initiatives, 2002, pp 44–57.

94 G Hart, 'Denaturalizing dispossession: critical ethnography in the age of resurgent imperialism', *Antipode*, 38(5), 2006, pp 978–1004.

95 Casolo, 'Gender levees'.

96 Because liberal reform in Honduras was never as 'successful' as in El Salvador and Guatemala, large amounts of communal and public land survived until well into the 20th century; indeed, the Honduran state continued to create new *ejidos* in the late 19th and early 20th centuries even as El Salvador and Guatemala abolished them. See M Samper, 'Café, trabajo y sociedad en Centroamérica (1870–1930): una historia común y divergente', in VH Acuña Ortega (ed), *Historia general de Centroamérica*, Madrid: Sociedad Estatal Quinto Centenario & FLACSO, 1993, IV, p 22.

97 CEDOH, 'Instalado el CREM', *Boletín Informativo Centro de Documentación de Honduras*, June 1983, pp 1, 4–5; and Jeffrey, 'Una mirada introspectiva', p 56.

98 ACAN is the Asociación Campesina Nacional, ANACH is the Asociación Nacional de Campesinos Hondureños, and CNTC is the Central Nacional de Trabajadores del Campo.

99 Carney was a US-born Jesuit priest who spent two decades in Honduras ministering to the poor and organising cooperatives in the Aguán. He was expelled in 1979 and killed four years later when he joined an ill-fated guerrilla incursion in Olancho Department. See JG Carney, *To Be a Revolutionary: An Autobiography*, San Francisco: Harper & Row, 1985. For a vivid description of the occupation, see R Falla, 'Honduras: una toma de tierras abre puertas a la reforma agraria', *Envío*, September 2000, pp 1–3.

100 Casolo, 'Gender levees' p 408.

101 The conflict in the Aguán Valley involves more than 13 different peasant movements with quite different roots. For example, the MCA is the result of the struggle to recuperate the CREM lands and was originally made up mainly of peasants who did not have anything to do with the cooperatives of the 1970s and 1980s. MUCA, in contrast, originates in the early 2000s; its members identify themselves as the sons and daughters of those who sold and lost their lands during the 1990s. See MUCA, *Machete de esperanza*, Tocoa: Movimiento Unificado Campesino del Aguán, 2010.

102 It is hard to come up with an exact number of people murdered in relation to the agrarian conflict, as different estimates range from around 50 to more than 100.

103 A Bird, 'Human rights violations attributed to military forces in the Bajo Aguan Valley in Honduras', Rights Action, 2013, at http://rightsaction.org/sites/default/files/Rpt_130220_Aguan_Final.pdf, accessed 6 May 2013; Salva la Selva, 'Acción terminada—gobierno británico y ¿derechos humanos?: comercio de carbono ensangrentado en Honduras', Salva la Selva, 2011, at https://www.salvalaselva.org/mailalert/691/gobierno-britanico-y-derechos-humanos-comercio-de-carbono-ensangrentado-en-hondurasFirefoxHTML%5CShell%5COpen%5CCommand, accessed 11 July 2013.

104 Salva la Selva, 'Honduras: instituciones retiran apoyo financiero a la expansión sangrienta de la palma', Salva la Selva, 2011, at http://www.salvalaselva.org/exitos/3502/honduras-instituciones-retiran-apoyo-financiero-a-la-expansion-sangrienta-de-la-palma, accessed 17 June 2013.

105 'Productores de granos ahora cosecharán palma africana', *La Tribuna* (San Pedro Sula), 16 January 2013, at http://www.latribuna.hn/2013/01/16/productores-de-granos-ahora-cosecharan-palma-africana/, accessed 19 January 2013.

106 'Palma africana gana terreno en Honduras', *Central America Link*, 2013, at http://www.centralamerica-link.com/es/Noticias/Palma_africana_gana_terreno_en_Honduras/, accessed 30 January 2013.

107 'Honduras podría convertirse en principal productor de palma africana de América Latina', *Proceso Digital*, 2013, at http://www.proceso.hn/2012/01/21/Econom%C3%ADa/Honduras.podr.C/47405.html, accessed 30 January 2013.

108 Salva la Selva, 'Acción terminada'; Kerssen, *Grabbing Power*; and Wong, 'The oxygen trade'.

109 R Pineda, interview with one of the authors (A León), Tegucigalpa, 13 September 2012.

110 'Productores de granos ahora cosecharán palma africana'.

111 G Ríos, 'El caso MUCA, la reforma agraria y el neoliberalismo', *FIAN Honduras*, 2010, at http://www.fian.hn/v1/index.php?option=com_k2&view=item&id=26:el-conflicto-agrarioFirefoxHTML/Shell/Open/Command, accessed 11 June 2013; and Posas, *La autogestión en el agro*.

112 S Striffler, *In the Shadows of State and Capital: The United Fruit Company, Popular Struggle, and Agrarian Restructuring in Ecuador, 1900–1995*, Durham, NC: Duke University Press, 2002; and PD Little & Michael Watts (eds), *Living Under Contract: Contract Farming and Agrarian Transformation in Sub-Saharan Africa*, Madison, WI: University of Wisconsin Press, 1994.

113 See Borras *et al*, 'Land grabbing and global capitalist accumulation', p 404.

114 D Hall, P Hirsch & TM Li, *Powers of Exclusion: Land Dilemmas in Southeast Asia*, Honolulu, HI: University of Hawai'i Press, 2011, p 196.

115 A Bebbington, 'Movements, modernizations, and markets: indigenous organizations and agrarian strategies in Ecuador', in R Peet & Michael Watts (eds), *Liberation Ecologies: Environment, Development, Social Movements*, London: Routledge, 1996, pp 91–92.

116 TM Li, 'To make live or let die? Rural dispossession and the protection of surplus populations', *Antipode*, 41(s1), 2010, pp 66–93; and VK Gidwani, *Capital, Interrupted Agrarian Development and the Politics of Work in India*, Minneapolis, MN: University of Minnesota Press, 2008.

Notes on Contributors

Marc Edelman is professor of anthropology at Hunter College and the Graduate Center, City University of New York. His books include *The Logic of the Latifundio* (1992), *Peasants Against Globalization* (1999), *Social Democracy in the Global Periphery* (coauthored, 2007), and *Transnational Agrarian Movements Confronting Globalization* (coedited, 2008).

Andrés León is a doctoral candidate in anthropology at the City University of New York and a professor in the Political Science Department at the University of Costa Rica. He is the author of *Neoliberalismo y destrucción creativa en Costa Rica: el caso de la región Huetar Norte durante el período de ajuste estructural, 1985–2005* (forthcoming).

Global Land Grabbing and Political Reactions 'From Below'

SATURNINO M BORRAS JR[a]* & JENNIFER C FRANCO[b]

[a]International Institute of Social Studies (ISS), The Hague, The Netherlands; [b]Transnational Institute (TNI), Amsterdam, TheNetherlands

ABSTRACT *Contemporary large-scale land deals are widely understood as involving the expulsion of people who, in turn, struggle instinctively to resist dispossession This is certainly true in many instances. Yet this chain of events evidently does not always occur: large-scale land deals do not always result in people losing the land, and many of those who face expulsion do not necessarily respond with the kind of resistance often expected of them. Indeed, much evidence shows that the nature of and responses to big land deals can (and do) vary across and within 'local communities'. Taking off analytically from a relatively narrow selection of cases, the expulsion–resistance scenario is too often assumed rather than demonstrated, thereby leaving many inconvenient facts undetected and unexplained. This suggests a need to step back and problematise the variable and uneven responses 'from below' to land grabbing, both within and between communities. This paper offers an initial exploration into why poor people affected by contemporary land deals (re)act the way they do, noting how issues and processes unite and divide them. This helps explain variation in political trajectories in the context of land grabbing today.*

Across the globe today a major revaluation of land is underway, the result in part of a convergence of global dynamics (or 'crises') around food, energy/fuel, climate and finance,[1] and leading to a resurgence of what some observers refer to as 'land grabbing'. For others, certainly, 'land grabbing' is an unacceptable term for what they see as legitimate business transactions. For still others the large-scale (private) investment in rural spaces that these transactions might bring is needed, but at the same time can be risky, and so the term would apply only to those big land deals that fail to uphold criteria of 'responsible investment' and 'good governance'. For the latter, one underlying assumption is crucial: that the solution to today's multiple global crises lies in the putative discovery of vast quantities of previously overlooked, supposedly marginal, underutilised or empty land. The amount of such land is estimated to be a minimum of 445 million ha.[2] (Re)framed in these ways, land is now increasingly (and conveniently) presented as 'available' for transformation into new economic arrangements that, according to mainstream economic and political elites, are deemed necessary not just for 'development', but for the very survival of a growing human population. In this way, and against the back-drop of multiple global crises, land grabbing of various sorts is being actively reimagined in mainstream discourse as necessary and 'responsible investment'.

This attempt to make land grabbing seem acceptable has not gone uncontested, and many voices have been raising critical questions about both the phenomenon and the public relations makeover surrounding it. Initially behind, the academic community has started to catch up with the earlier efforts made by news media and NGOs seeking to raise public awareness and to engage in critical debate. Today there is a growing—but still limited—body of academic research that has contributed significantly to a better understanding of land grab-bing.[3] Complicated by its still-unfolding and fluid character, the study of land grabbing is further constrained by unresolved issues around how to define, and conduct research on, the phenomenon.[4]

One still underexplored dimension of contemporary land grabbing has to do with the political reactions 'from below'—eg among groups of poor, vulnerable and marginalised people and peoples who are affected by large-scale land deals. How do those most affected actually perceive and react to these large-scale land deals and why? On this issue public debate is quite polarised. Whether for or against, there is a strong tendency to assume *a priori*, rather than to demonstrate, what the reactions of affected groups of people are or would be. On the one hand, those in favour of large-scale land deals generally assume that poor people would naturally want the opportunities that such investments are purported to bring. On the other hand, those opposed to the deals generally assume that if only those same poor people knew what they were really getting into, they would reject the deals outright. The problem is that evidence can always be marshalled for both sides, so it would seem that, while neither side can be 'right', neither side can be 'wrong' either.

Stepping back from this political impasse, however, one can begin to see serious analytical shortcomings with both sides. Characterising both in our view is a shared, largely implicit assumption of the homogeneous nature of affected local communities: that the 'local communities' affected (or potentially affected) by these land deals exist in homogeneous spaces, and that at stake for the people who inhabit these spaces are very similar (if not identical) interests, identities and aspirations for the future.

If there is one thing that the spectre of land grabbing has shown, however, it is that local communities are socially differentiated and consequently the impact on and within communities will likewise be differentiated, leading in turn to an *array* of diverse responses. It is not just that different people will be affected differently. Rather, what adds further complexity to the whole thing is that different people will perceive and interpret the experience differently, based on a whole range of variable and relative economic, political, social and cultural factors, conditions and calculations that are often not well understood and in any case would require much deeper inquiry than is often given. In short, the individual and collective political reactions of people and peoples affected by land deals cannot be taken for granted.

Imagine two books of account, one listing all the reported land grabs and the other listing all the reported protests against land grabs. Comparing these two lists would probably reveal a curious thing: that they do not add up to the same total. This is obviously an imagined account, but there is evidently no automatic 1:1 ratio between land grabs and protest against them – otherwise we would have seen Cambodia or Ethiopia erupting in conflagrations of protest. It is clear that the reported protests against land deals are far fewer than the reported land grabs themselves. There may be a number of very interesting explanations for this discrepancy that warrant a closer look. First, some reported land deals ultimately do not (or will not) push through as initially planned or intended, but instead are redirected, abandoned mid-stream, cancelled, stalled or blocked, perhaps as a result of what Anna Tsing would call 'frictional encounters', or 'the awkward, unequal, unstable, and creative qualities of interconnection across difference'.[5] This is not so surprising in a politically charged context where what is often initially reported (or announced) in the media are the business agreements, rather than the actual transfers of control. Second, looking from another angle, it is likely that many protests go unseen, unrecognised and unreported. Maybe they are overlooked or dismissed as insignificant; or maybe they escape attention because of what James Scott calls the 'friction of terrain', or 'geographical resistance': often these places are not easy to reach or are completely out of range for those who want to report cases of resistance.[6] Third, some combination of both sorts of scenarios is also possible. But in any case what is suggested here is that there is still much left to be unpacked on this score, and thus more systematic empirical research is warranted.

This paper aims to contribute to this challenge by offering an initial discussion around a possible broad framework that can be useful in researching and understanding this topic more fully. While the 'collective action problem' in classical sociology tried to explain why it is that people mobilise to defend their interests,[7] this article poses the opposite question, ie why people fail or refuse to mobilise in the face of attacks on their livelihoods. It builds on earlier critiques, including those by Marc Edelman,[8] as well as on the rich scholarship on agrarian politics that has attempted to explain the trigger for peasant collective action.[9] Another important starting point for this purpose is a reiteration of what we mean by 'land grabbing': the capturing of control of relatively vast tracts of land and other natural resources through a variety of mechanisms and forms, carried out through extra-economic coercion that involves large-scale capital, which often shifts resource use orientation into extraction, whether for international or domestic purposes, as capital's response to the convergence of food, energy and financial crises, climate change mitigation imperatives, and demands for resources from newer hubs of global capital.[10] Even though the term 'land grabbing' carries a lot of baggage and remains problematic, in our view it still has the advantage of 1) focusing attention on the core issues of politics and power relations; and 2) underscoring the dimension of extra-economic coercion involved in land deals.[11]

The contextual and definitional discussion above helps situate our discussion on political reactions from below. Against this backdrop many questions arise: what is the particular range of political reactions from below to land grabbing in a given case? Why and how do various social groups react the way they do to particular types of land deals, and with what outcomes, in specific situations? What are the issues that unite and divide social groups? What are the political tensions and synergies within and between communities? How and to what extent are such political contestations (re)shaping the trajectory of global land deals? These are some of the questions that come to mind, and that have been left largely unanswered so far in the emerging body of literature on land grabbing.[12]

The remainder of this paper proceeds as follows: the next section explores the contested meaning of land and the role of the state. The following section discusses struggles against expulsion; the fourth section is on struggles for incorporation, the following one on struggles against land appropriation and concentration, and for redistribution and recognition; section six examines struggles across geographical and institutional spaces, before some concluding discussion is offered in the final section.

Contested meaning of land and role of the state

The contested meaning of land is a key starting point. On many occasions competing views about the meaning of land underpin land-based political contestations, but this is only implicitly suggested. Land has multiple meanings to different groups of people. For some, including the corporate world, it is a scarce factor of economic production valued in monetary terms, and measured partly in terms of yield. In this context it is a resource that is used to produce primary commodities such as food and timber for commercial purposes. For many agrarian communities, land is a resource base that guarantees subsistence, and provides a cushion from occasional external food price shocks by enabling them to produce some or all of the food they need for consumption. While land is indeed an important natural resource, it is a special one since it is also key to gaining *access to other* natural resources. One needs to control land in order to capture water, in order to extract subsoil resources, in order to calculate, capture and commoditise carbon, and so on. On some occasions, because land is not a movable investment asset, some form of land control is necessary in order to deny access to land to peasants so that they are forced to look for work—and/or to capture the cheap labour through a variety of plantation set-up and/or contract farming schemes. For others still, including indigenous communities, land is also a territory where their ancestors lived as a people, and where they continue to live and reproduce as a people, engaging with their immediate natural environment. Others may value land principally because of its being a habitat for other species, a necessary host for biodiversity, a landscape, for its aesthetic beauty.

To reduce the meaning and value of land to just one of these many functions oblivious of other overlapping meanings is absurd, and provokes or aggravates much of contemporary land-based political conflicts and contestations. Often heated debates and political conflicts appear unresolvable because the contesting parties are coming from different perspectives and talking about land from very different starting points.

At the local level different groups are related to land, but they are linked to land differently. Some groups belong to landed elites with or without private titles. They can be private landlords, warlords, or narco-syndicates using land to launder money, or elite clans or local chiefs in charge of local allocation of land.[13] Cashing in from land deals either by selling or renting out land can be, and in many places has become, a lucrative enterprise. Indeed there is a discernible pattern of an emerging class of what can be termed 'land grabbing entrepreneurs'—they are the land brokers, speculators and scammers who have taken advantage of pre-existing institutional arrangement of land control in order to cash in on the ongoing global land rush. There are also capitalist landowners who may want to further transform their land either by directly capitalising on the emerging market or by forging partnerships with foreign companies looking for local partners, partly because of laws prohibiting foreign companies from purchasing land or from full ownership of a company, as in the case of Argentina.[14] The latter is particular attractive to local partners who are 'land rich and cash poor' elites.[15] Others depend on land for their livelihoods but do not have (formal) ownership and/or control of the land they work: tenants, farmers on public lands, indigenous communities, pastoralists, forest dwellers, or forest non-timber product gatherers. In some cases these groups of people may or may not be present in official state censuses to begin with.

In many settings these relatively stable, broad patterns of social relationships to land are gender-based and ethnic-oriented. When land deals hit these communities, the impact is not uniform among these various groups. Some benefit, others do not; some are adversely affected, others are not. Concepts such as 'local community' and 'local people' are useful to our understanding of the phenomenon but only to a limited extent. These concepts conceal more than reveal the uneven and differentiated impacts of land deals on such communities and people. Conceptual lenses around class and other parallel and/or overlapping social divides are thus indispensable. The overlap and intersection between class and other identities are summarised and explained in Bernstein: 'class relations are universal but not exclusive "determination" of social practices in capitalism. They intersect and combine with other social differences and divisions, of which gender is the most widespread and which can also include oppressive and exclusionary relations of race and ethnicity, religion and caste'.[16] The cumulative impact of multiple forms of oppression over the course of a lifetime may have a lot to say about whether individuals or groups will mobilise around a particular issue.[17]

Other relevant dimensions are the geography, ecology and institutional character of land deals. Contemporary large-scale land deals privilege or target specific geographical locations: lands that are proximate to sources of water, existing roads and other transportation channels.[18] Some land deals, specifically those that are linked to green grabbing, such as Reducing Emissions from Deforestation and Forest Degradation (REDD+), specifically look for forested terrain.[19] Others are more interested in the subsoil resources, with little regard for the communities that may happen to be sitting on top of a coal field, for instance. Finally, land deals are often directed to specific lands through state-created institutional maps: carved out tracts of land specifically reserved for land deals such as the Economic Land Concessions (ELCs) in Cambodia, or the contemporary initiative in Gambella region in Ethiopia.[20]

Different state policies are implicated in land deals in different ways. What this implies is that traditional conceptual tools that are specific to particular geographic or institutional spaces may have only limited relevance in explaining political reactions from below. For example, a block of land may have been allocated for a land concession with a big agricultural company, at the same time that it has been identified as a mining site, at the same time that it has been declared as a REDD+ project site. These institutional overlaps, layerings and intersections partly shape the political calculations of affected social groups in deciding about their political actions: eg where and with which state agency to engage, which institutional space to bring their political struggle to, and which formal and informal institutional traditions and state policies to invoke to frame their demands as just, reasonable and/or legal.[21]

Amid such complexity it is rare to find local communities reacting and mobilising in relation to a land deal in a unified fashion. Some who have been expelled from their lands, or are being threatened with expulsion, resist land deals or mobilise to seek better compensation. At the same time there may be others who mobilise not to resist land deals—but to demand incorporation into the emerging enterprises either as workers or as contract farmers. Yet others may mobilise in order to demand improvements in the terms of their incorporation into these emerging investment enclaves (more working days, higher wages, better working conditions, fairer growership terms, and so on). Such differences can also create new or exacerbate existing political tensions between groups within and between communities.

Political mobilisations for or against land deals by affected social groups do not emerge automatically, despite the changing objective conditions, a topic that has been the subject of research in agrarian studies and social movement/collective action studies for quite some time now. Some individuals and groups are able to resist through covert actions, more fluid and pervasive at times. Some groups are able to resist and succeed. Some mobilisations are localised and isolated, while others are able to link up with national groups. Still others are able to forge links between local, national and international actors and mount globally coordinated campaigns, the outcomes of which maybe varied.[22] Ultimately groups that are able to galvanise broad unity within and between affected communities, able to recruit and mobilise influential allies from within their communities and beyond (including international actors), within and outside the state, and able to generate sympathetic media attention are likely to succeed, even if just partially, in their political struggles in the context either of struggle against expulsion or of adverse incorporation.

The role of the state

The history of the development of global capitalism is a history of varying combinations of state and capital alliances, where accumulation and dispossession have advanced and occurred hand in hand.[23] As in past cycles of enclosures the state has a central role in facilitating contemporary global land grabbing.[24] Therefore, it has to be a significant part of any analysis of the politics around land deals, even when it appears to be largely absent on the ground. In our examination of various cases of land grabbing, we observe that states engaged in systematic policy and administrative tasks aimed at capturing so-called 'marginal lands' and turning them into an investable commodity.[25] Each task is a step towards eventual full capture of land control. Each task is inherently political. These are the operational mechanisms towards land dispossession. The tasks of the state include a combination or all of the following: 1) invention or justification of the need for large-scale land investments; 2) definition, reclassification and quantification of what are 'marginal, under-utilized and empty' lands; 3) identification of these particular types of land; 4) assertion of the state's absolute authority over these lands; 5) acquisition or appropriation of these lands; and 6) re-allocation or disposition of these lands to investors.[26] In most settings only the state has the absolute authority and the capacity to carry out these key legal–administrative steps to facilitate land deals. These mechanisms of land dispossession separately and altogether constitute varying shades and degrees of extra-economic coercion by the state. Often stories of such dispossession are indeed, in Marx's words, written in 'blood and fire'.

More broadly there are three distinct but interlinked areas of state actions that are relevant in understanding contemporary land grabs: 1) a state simplification process; 2) the assertion of sovereignty and authority over territory; and 3) coercion through police and (para)military force to enforce compliance, extend territorialisation and broker private capital accumulation. First, in order to administer and govern, states engage in a simplification process to render complex social processes legible to the state. The creation of cadastres, land records and titles are attempts at simplifying land-based social relations that are otherwise too complex for state administration.[27] This in turn brings us back to the notion of 'available marginal, empty lands'. The trends in state discourse around land grabs seem to be: if the land is not formally titled or privatised, then it is state-owned; if the census does not show significant formal settlements, then these are empty lands or, if it does not show formal farm production activities, then these are unused lands. Second, beyond the economic benefits of land investment, land deals are also viewed as an essential component of state-building processes, where sovereignty and authority are extended to previously 'non-state spaces'.[28] Third, coercion and violence, usually with the use of police, (para)military and the courts to enforce compliance with state simplification projects and the broader state-building process, have accompanied land deals in various parts of the world.[29]

Based on the discussion above, Jonathan Fox's formulation of the two permanent contradictory tasks of the state, namely, to facilitate capital accumulation but at the same time to maintain a historically determined minimum level of political legitimacy, provides a useful perspective on why and how the state engages with large-scale land deals, and why and how it is both part of the problem of and the solution to land grabbing.[30] It will push and push hard for large-scale land deals and on most occasions is even the one directly engaged in the actual land grabbing—but occasional 'brakes' will be applied when the character and extent of accumulation and dispossession processes threaten the legitimacy of the state.[31] This explains the occasional moratorium on land deals and some forms of regulation, as in the cases of Cambodia and Ukraine (moratorium) and Tanzania (land deal-size ceiling) more recently, for example, with varying outcomes. It is in this broader and historical context that we should understand the political dynamics around the Food and Agriculture Organization (FAO) Tenure Guidelines.[32]

Broad types of political conflicts and terrain of contestations

Looking at the intersections of conflict and terrain of contestations will help us understand how poor people who engage in contentious politics understand their issue, identify their adversary, frame their demands, and choose the forms of their collective action. There are at least three intersections of political contestations within and between the state and social forces around current land grabbing that are relevant to our analysis, namely, poor people versus corporate actors, poor people versus the state, and poor people versus poor people.

Poor people versus corporate actors tends to be more common in cases where the issue is about incorporation into an enterprise, or is about improvement of the terms of poor people's inclusion ('struggles against exploitation'-type of contestations). Issues are usually framed within demands for companies to make good on promised jobs, uphold labour standards, or improve the terms of growership arrangements. Increasingly, we also see in this type of conflict the rise of environmental issues: poor people taking issue against companies on pollution or chemical contamination issues. Poor people-versus-the state is much more common in cases involving actual or potential expulsion of people from their land, or terms of relocation and resettlement arrangements. It brings us back to the centrality of the role of the state in land appropriation discussed above ('struggles against dispossession'-type of contestations). Poor people versus poor people—of inter- and intra-class types—are probably more common than the popular literature would acknowledge. This links back to the differentiated impacts of land deals on social groups within and between communities. In a community it is common to see mobilisations *against* a land deal parallel to counter-mobilisations *in favour* of the same deal.

On many occasions we see political contestations around a particular land deal where contentious politics have multiple intersections—all three types discussed above are simultaneously at work. The two main types of struggles by working classes—struggles against dispossession (largely of 'struggles against expulsion from the land'-type, as well as the broader, more encompassing type of 'struggles in defence of the commons') and struggles against exploitation (or 'struggles against adverse incorporation'[33])—are more usefully examined in a relational way, rather than in isolation from each other.

The key point is that it is not useful to casually claim that conflicts around current land deals are either just between 'local communities' and foreign companies, or between 'local communities' and the central government. The configuration of actors and the intersections, character and trajectory of political contestations are far more diverse and complex than casual claims in the current

TABLE 1. Overview of struggle fronts and political trajectories, in terms of frequency

Four broad arenas of struggle	Key struggle fronts	Campaign/advocacy/lobby principal target			
		National state	Foreign states	International financial and/ or development institutions	Corporations (foreign and/or domestic)
Struggle against expulsion	Agrarian justice, environmental justice, human rights, indigenous peoples' rights	High	Medium	Low	High
Struggles for, and within, incorporation	Labour justice, agrarian justice	High	Medium	Low	High
Struggle against land concentration and/or redistribution and/or recognition	Agrarian justice, environmental justice, human rights, indigenous peoples' rights	High	Low–medium	Medium	High
Struggles across interlinked geographic and institutional spaces	Agrarian justice, environmental justice, labour justice, indigenous peoples, human rights	High	Medium–high	Medium	High

media and popular literature on land deals would suggest. The discussion so far can be partly summarised in Table 1, which offers a broad typology of struggle fronts and political trajectories. The categories we entered (in terms of frequency) are indicative—meant to serve as signposts for more systematic research in the future, rather than a definitive assessment. This is elaborated in the succeeding sections.

Struggles against expulsion

When the land is needed, but the labour is not, the most likely outcome of a land deal is the expulsion of people from the land.[34] It is a double whammy if and when expelled people have no place to go and no possibility of jobs. Many of them end up in city slums. Many contemporary land deals have needed large tracts of land and are establishing monocrop large farms that are highly mechanised. These types of farms are inherently labour expelling or labour saving.

Throughout this section we are concerned about struggles against expulsion from the land—and not the more generic and broader formulation of struggles against dispossession (the latter can encompass a much broader meaning and not just dispossession of land property). Struggles against expulsion from the land have accompanied the histories of peoples worldwide, whether in the context of 'primitive accumulation' or 'accumulation by dispossession'.

There are different types and trajectories of expulsion of people from the land. The subsequent political reactions of affected social groups from below depend partly on the type of expulsion that occurs. There are at least three discernible broad types in the current context: 1) expelled people have nowhere to go and are not absorbed in any other productive sectors of the economy; 2) expelled people are absorbed in other productive sectors of the economy; and 3) expelled people are relocated somewhere to continue what they were previously doing. A single land deal can have more than one of these trajectories. In addition, people may be compensated for their expulsion or not. Having some kind of formal or community-recognised rights over the appropriated land may increase the possibility of expulsion-with-compensation, although not automatically. The gravest scenario is the first one, where people are expelled without (any significant) compensation, and have no place to go and no jobs to do. The other two types, especially when done with significant compensation, may not be as bad as the first type—at least as far as the affected social groups are concerned. The last type, expulsion-with-relocation, is more common in land-abundant countries, such as in many parts of Africa. It can be seen on a smaller scale, such as in the case of Procana sugarcane plantation in Mozambique during its original inception around 2008–10, or on a large-scale resettlement project in order to capture a vast tract of land for reallocation to corporate investors, as in the case of Gambella region in Ethiopia.[35]

There is no automatic relationship between each of the three types of expulsion (with or without compensation) and certain types of political reactions from affected social groups. The gravity of the situation, especially when it leads to, or threatens to lead to, subsistence crisis, partly determines the political reactions of people who have been evicted from their land. A useful conceptual reminder in this context is James Scott's framing: often it is not about how much was taken but how much was left that is crucial to providing a trigger to poor people's decision to engage in contentious politics.[36] Moreover, in some cases it is not only economic subsistence that provokes poor people to engage in contentious politics. At times when non-economic considerations, such as their identity, culture or tradition, are threatened or, indeed, if there is a perceived threat to what is considered 'public goods' (water source, landscape, community forest) poor people may also engage in political contention. Recent protests by Mapuche people and many other environmentalists against the 900 000 ha acquisition made by the United Colours of Benetton in Patagonia is an example.

But as the rich critical agrarian studies literature has shown, the objective existence of unjust treatment or exploitation of poor people does not automatically translate to affected social groups mobilising and engaging in contentious politics—otherwise we should have already seen a conflagration of uprisings against land grabbing worldwide. Changing political opportunity structure can partly influence poor people's decision to engage in overt political contention to struggle around their expulsion, either against their expulsion or to demand some kind of compensation or better terms of compensation. Tarrow identified four important political opportunities: access to power, shifting alignments, availability of influential elites, and cleavages within and among elites.[37] The availability of all or some of these opportunities can create possibilities that even weak and disorganised actors can take advantage of; conversely, the strong may also grow weak.[38] Key is poor people's ability to perceive and take advantage of the shifts in political opportunity structure, or to create changes in the opportunity structure if there are none. The emergence of collective perception about a possible threat to their community landscape or ecology can arguably be an important shift in the structure of political opportunity or threat that can bring different groups of people together to oppose a land deal. The contradictory role of the state—in maintaining political legitimacy while advancing capital accumulation[39]—often triggers shifts in the political opportunity structure, including divisions among the ranks of state officials. The emergence of elite allies within and outside the state is central to rural poor people's ability to engage in contentious politics. For example, the most popular tactic employed by Chinese local villagers protesting at contemporary land grabbing is to pry open the latent division between central and local state officials, accusing the latter of being corrupt while pleading for support from the former, who are represented as 'reform-oriented'. This can also be seen in the framing of rights by the same rural villagers protesting at land expropriation: they invoke the official promises of the state to demand disciplining of those who are disloyal to the official state narrative, and mobilise around this political master frame, in what O'Brien and Li call 'rightful resistance'.[40]

Let us examine more closely an illustrative case. In Kampong Speu, Cambodia, two concession contracts each with close to 10 000 ha were awarded to two companies owned by a politically powerful, well connected member of the Cambodian elite.[41] The 10 000 ha size of each concession is not an accident; it is obviously meant to circumvent a law that limits a concession to a maximum of

10 000 ha. The land was part of the tracts allocated to ELCs. These lands are assumed to fit the mainstream global narrative about marginal, empty, under- or unutilised—and available—lands. It turned out that, when the company moved in, the combined 20 000 ha of land were inhabited and worked by hundreds of people either living and/or farming within the allocated land. Many farms (some estimated to be up to 2000 ha in size) were highly productive, irrigated riceland that followed criss-crossing creeks. The 20 000 ha plot can be likened to a Swiss cheese—with so many holes (patches of irrigated ricelands) inside. There were also patches of community forest that were the source of non-timber products for the villagers. There were up to 1000 villagers affected by the land deal. Most of them had lived in this place for more than a generation. There is a handful of new arrivals, however, post-1994.

The company was to plant a single crop, sugarcane, in a large-scale, industrial, mechanised way. This involved a tie-up with a Thai corporation aimed at capitalising on the EU's 'Everything But Arms' (EBA) special tariff arrangement for goods exported to the EU. The company needed to flatten the moderately sloping terrain, close existing creeks, clear the secondary growth forest, and destroy all patches of irrigated rice lands inside the 20 000 ha plot. The first people to be evicted, their houses and garden plots destroyed, without much of a whimper, were the post-1994 settled households. They were dumped outside the edge of the newly drawn plantation boundary, at the foot of a hill without any infrastructure for a village settlement. They were given US$25 each as one-off compensation for their expulsion. The more difficult eviction was the one involving the farms of the original villagers whose residence is just outside the newly constructed plantation boundary. The company at first preserved the patches of farms but cut off completely any access routes to these farms, then eventually destroyed the farms. Everything was burned down and flattened. The company offered $100–$200 compensation per hectare, which the villagers rejected, arguing that they earned more from farming.

Villagers resisted. They started with combined covert and overt forms of resistance, including sabotage, arson, and stoning of bulldozers, but addressed their main demands to the Cambodian government. The case started to attract sympathisers from the capital and internationally: human rights, environmental and agrarian activists started to assist the villagers, which in turn emboldened them to escalate their resistance to more overt and defiant acts: trooping to police headquarters and court, highway blockades, and so on. Their leaders were thrown in jail a number of times and harassment escalated. The struggle has been going on since 2010 amid rapid development of the 20 000 ha plot into a modern, monocrop, large-scale industrial sugarcane plantation. This industrial character of the plantation required only a few labourers, many of whom are employed just for seasonal work. The company recruited a handful of local villagers, some of whom were previously affected by expulsion. But the bulk of the current workers are recruited from outside the ranks of the villagers previously affected by the land deal, and several mill workers are from Thailand.[42] The affected villagers and their allies have resorted to a campaign in the EU to stop providing special trade preference through EBA to what they call 'blood sugar', sugar produced from sites of land grabbing.[43]

Struggles for, and/or around the terms of, incorporation

There is an implicit tendency in the emerging literature on contemporary land grabbing towards viewing the issue of land deals via an 'exclusion versus inclusion' dichotomy. A land deal is a land grab when it excludes and expels people. It is assumed to be otherwise when people are included in some way in the farm enterprises that emerge. It is essentially a procedural definition of land grabbing. This is of course appropriate and important, but only partly. Our present discussion is informed by both a procedural and substantive definition of land grabbing, as explained at the beginning of this paper.

Resorting to large-scale monocrop plantations that are highly mechanised is one way to save on labour and labour management costs and is thus desirable to corporations. But there are just as many situations where capital has needed the land *and* cheap labour. Capture of cheap labour can be done in a variety of ways, including the incorporation of people as landless workers in the emerging enterprises, or as small-scale farmer-growers contracted to sell their produce to the company. When and where this happens, the character of political contestations gravitates around the issue of incorporation and the *terms* of such inclusion.

Poor people who struggle to become incorporated into the emerging enterprises, or are demanding improvements in the terms of their inclusion, can be those whose lands were acquired by companies by purchase or lease; often it is the latter—be it a lease arrangement between the corporation on the one hand, and the people or the state on the other. This is illustrated in the case of some 11 000 ha Ecofuel sugarcane ethanol investment in Isabela, Philippines, where several hundred beneficiaries of recent government land redistribution programmes (land reform, formalisation of land rights programme) were left without any follow-up support services to develop their lands. It is not surprising then that they were relatively eager to lease their lands to the company in exchange for regular income from land rent, or growership arrangements for some, and promised jobs for others.[44] This is despite well known forms of subsumption in which small owners of land do not lose their land but become completely dependent on the company for credit, technology, marketing, and even daily subsistence needs.

The people who engage in political struggles for incorporation may also be those who failed to demonstrate their formal rights over the acquired lands, and are therefore relatively more vulnerable than those who have formal claims to land; they may thus not always choose the path of struggle against expulsion. It is probably a matter of a 'second best option' for them. When the Philippine government allocated one million ha in 2008 to San Miguel Corporation in the Philippines, it was assumed that these lands were empty—at least that was what the official records in Manila would show. But many of these lands turned out to be inhabited and farmed by a variety of rural poor people, whose 'invisibility' in the official records allows them to work the land without giving any rent to anyone or tax to the government. When the deal with San Miguel got underway, their 'squatting' was put under a spotlight, their situation rendered politically vulnerable. The government and company instead offered some form of growership arrangement, and many of them agreed and in the process negotiated the terms of their incorporation.[45]

But the people who engage in political struggles can also be poor people who were not inserted in any pre-existing social relations of landed property, people who have no claim whatsoever over the land but are landless in and around the land deal site, or indeed, in some cases, from far away but who are being recruited as workers. The diverse provenance of this group of people shapes the multiple framings of their demand for inclusion, or for improvement in the terms of their incorporation. When the sugar company started to operate its plantation and mill in Kampong Speu, (see above), the workers who were recruited came from a variety of origins. The earlier struggle against expulsion seemed to make no significant connection with them.

There are at least two types of struggles around the issue of incorporation: agrarian and trade union. Agrarian struggles often have something to do with land-based social relations. These include those involving poor people who were expelled from their lands on a variety of (legal, institutional) bases and are demanding to be incorporated into the business enterprise as workers; and poor people who have leased their lands and are demanding improvements in the terms of the lease contract, often associated with arrangements over labour employment in the plantation. They also include poor people in and around the land deal site wanting to be incorporated through growership arrangements whereby they remain small-scale farmers selling their products to the company. Agrarian justice struggles for inclusion and/or against 'adverse incorporation' thus cut across land and labour issues, as demonstrated more commonly in the oil palm sector in Indonesia.[46] 'Propertied proletariats', in this context, have two fronts to anchor their struggles: their property (land) and their labour, often around issues of rent, wages or terms of exchange.

Labour justice struggles are distinct struggles, despite often being linked to land. Regardless of their provenance, workers raise labour issues: extent of employment generated by a land deal, wage issues and conditions at the work place. It is not uncommon to see the overlap between the two, as in the case of Isabela, Philippines (discussed above), where small-holders who leased their individual plots to the company were promised the opportunity to become some kind of regular (part-time) plantation or mill workers and/or contracted growers.[47] Hence, groups of people are simultaneously confronted by agrarian *and* labour justice issues, and framing political struggles in complex situations like this is not straightforward. Recent and still unfolding struggles among land reform beneficiaries in the plantation belt of the Southern Philippines (in Mindanao), especially in the banana sector, have shown similar complicated struggles around agrarian-labour and social justice.[48] There are also situations where we see parallel and, arguably, political and institutional intersecting processes between agrarian justice and labour justice issues—as in the case, more broadly, of the sugarcane sector in Brazil: workers' unions tend to emphasise demands for labour issues addressed to sugarcane plantation owners, while peasant movements like Via Campesina Brazil demand the redistribution of these plantations for conversion into small family farming plots. These two streams of poor people's campaigns do not always interact with each other.[49]

In short, agrarian and labour justice struggles are inherently marked by issues that unite and divide, by tension and synergy, within and between social groups in affected communities. The poor people versus poor people axis of political contestations is not uncommon in the agrarian-labour justice intersection. This is also where serious dilemmas are found, partly because of the 'multi-class' character of some rural poor involved in this situation: some are still part-time farmers who moonlight as seasonal plantation workers, and so on. Their class political standpoints cannot be reduced simplistically as either a peasant or a worker standpoint.

The struggle for incorporation or for the improvement of the terms of incorporation is diverse, and it is impossible for a single case, however iconic, to capture the diversity of issues. With this caveat in mind, let us examine more closely the case of Chikweti Forest in Niassa, Mozambique, a case that involves a consortium of investors, including a Swedish investment fund and a Dutch pension fund.[50] A few years ago the Mozambican government promised a company more than 100 000 ha of land to be developed into an industrial tree plantation, on lease agreement for 50 years, renewable for another 50 years. By 2013 51 000 ha of land have been taken by the company, and planted with eucalyptus intended for industrial commodities for domestic and regional trade, as well as for an anticipated REDD+ programme. This was billed as a 'win-win' investment where local villagers would find additional jobs to augment their largely subsistence-oriented farming livelihoods. A few years later, there has been a significant gap between what was promised and what was delivered. There are two principal issues for the villagers: undermining of their subsistence farms and questions of jobs that were promised. On the one hand, villagers accused the company of having encroached into their subsistence farms and sources of livelihoods in at least four ways: 1) directly taking over their plots; 2) taking over lands that they had purposely kept fallow based on their more mobile, rotating way of farming; 3) planting trees too close to the farms, which in turn block the sun; and 4) destroying the nearby forests and thus their sources of non-timber products.

One immediate effect of these encroachments is that peasants are forced to go much further from their homes to look for plots to farm. On the one hand, they felt cornered and their autonomy and capacity to construct subsistence livelihoods significantly undermined. In 2011 villagers chopped and burned up to 60 000 trees in protest. On the other hand, the villagers felt that the promised jobs were not fully delivered, and this condition can be seen in a number of ways, including fewer jobs than initially promised (around 1000 by late 2012), a decreasing trend following the initial surge of jobs thanks to clearing and planting work, which rapidly disappeared once this was done, and too few working days, too seasonal, and thus much less aggregate working days, as well as the fact that wages were quite low. Between these two clusters of agrarian and labour justice issues, villagers put forward a set of demands: respect their subsistence plots and sources of subsistence livelihoods and deliver the promised jobs at fairer wages and working conditions. To date, there has never been any significant, organised call by the villagers for the company to pull out of their land. Some global justice activist groups have been tempted to raise the call to demand investors to pull out from Niassa, in line with the call to stop land grabbing more generally. But they are cautious since this is clearly not what the affected local population wanted.

Struggles against land concentration, and for redistribution and recognition

The first two broad types of struggles discussed above are among the most commonly known struggles directly related to contemporary global land grabbing—a political process in which extra-economic coercion is an important component. But while land grabbing is a key land issue, it is not the only critical land issue in the world today. The generic issue of land concentration remains an urgent and important one for many—probably a majority of—poor people in the rural world today. The character, demands and trajectories of political struggles around this issue are, and will be, different from the land grabbing-related political struggles.

Pre-existing land monopolies and recent trends towards a greater degree of land concentration are caused, conditioned and perpetuated by pre-existing agrarian structures and institutions (see the related discussion in Edelman and Leon, this issue). The revaluation of land as a result of the recent convergence of multiple crises discussed at the beginning of this paper has, in many places in the world, driven the process towards an even greater concentration of land in the hands of the few landed and corporate elites. Dispossession by social differentiation is the common mechanism of this concentration.

It is also critical to emphasise the relevance of looking at land grabbing in the context of parallel and overlapping generic land concentration in a region, as underscored in the Edelman, Oya and Borras, introduction to this collection.[51] Land concentration is the main land issue in the global North, as in the case of Europe, alongside a creeping phenomenon of land grabbing starting in its Eastern front.[52]

Poor people's struggles against land concentration have taken on different characters, led to different framings of demands, and charted different political trajectories. Where land concentration is greatest, the demand for conventional redistributive land policies, eg land reform, restitution, leasehold and forest reallocation policies has occupied the centre-stage of political struggles. This is the case, for instance, in Brazil or in Indonesia, where radical rural social movements have taken the most prominent profiles in the struggles there.[53] In settings where calls for conventional land reform may not gain any immediate political or policy traction, these calls have been focused on the driver of land concentration. Such have been the land struggles in the EU, where the subsidy scheme in the EU's Common Agricultural Policy (CAP) is the principal target of rural social movement organisations. In societies where indigenous peoples live, the demand against creeping land appropriation or concentration usually takes the form of demanding *recognition* of claims over territory, and respect for and compliance with some relevant global governance principles such as free, prior, informed consent (FPIC) in the context of the UN Declaration on the Rights of Indigenous Peoples (UNDRIP), and the campaigns concerning the land rights of Afro-Colombians. Demands for redistribution and/or recognition in these political settings are just as profound as the demands to stop the expulsion of people from their lands as a result of contemporary corporate enclosures.[54]

Struggles across overlapping/intersecting geographical and institutional spaces

The convergence of multiple crises has brought together various sectors of the world's economy in a global land rush—with various corporate sectors rushing in to join the bandwagon: chemical, oil, biotechnology, automobile, biofuels, seed, pulp, banking and finance, among others. This also means overlaps and intersections between agrarian, labour and environmental issues in different settings, and thus of struggle fronts. What we see are different elite (state, corporate) actors coveting the same, or adjoining, plots of land/territory, and exploring and employing different institutional channels and instruments to get to their coveted object. Their race to the same or adjoining tracts of land results in increasing competition over this resource, and may create spillover effects to adjoining plots of land or territory. For example it has become more common to see a plot of land or adjoining plots allocated by different agencies of a national government to different entities for different purposes—economic land concession for agricultural production, mining, or conservation such as REDD+, invoking various national laws and policies—affecting a common set of people—ie various groups that have otherwise different socioeconomic interests but are unified by a common adverse impact of the land deals. Resolution of resource conflict in one plot and under one institutional umbrella has become increasingly difficult, if not impossible. These conflicts are usually associated with competing, overlapping or intersecting agrarian, labour and environmental justice issues.

The convergence of issues—eg expulsion of peasants from the land, labour issues in mining, or ecological issues in the land deal site—may be tackled by different groups of poor people, depending on their take on each of the issues, which in turn depends on which issue affects them most. Further, the decision on collective action targets and institutional frameworks for campaigns depends on the campaign master frame: struggle against expulsion (specifically, or the broader struggle against dispossession) or struggle against exploitation (broadly cast) or struggle against land concentration. Perhaps it will be the ministry of land and forestry if the case is against dispossession, the ministry of agriculture if framed on agricultural issues, probably the ministry of labour if framed about labour standards, or the ministry of mines and/or the environment if about extractive industry issues, maybe the water ministry if the issue is centrally about water, despite being apparently a land issue, and so on – or, indeed, it may be all of the above, simultaneously. Multi-layered, overlapping, competing and intersecting agencies, laws, policies—and sectoral traditions of campaign master frames and repertoire of collective actions—are likely to surface in these types of settings. They will expose both tensions and synergies within and between groups of affected people—and the targeted state agencies—and how they react politically to land deals. Hence, cross-sectoral, cross- or multi-class, cross-institutional and landscape-type of struggle fronts may become more common. If so, adjusting our analytical lenses to study the emerging politics around land deals becomes an even more urgent challenge. The complication explained here is captured partly in a case in Oddar Meanchey in Cambodia, one of the world's first REDD+ pilot areas, underscoring simultaneous political and institutional processes occurring in one landscape and affecting various groups of people therein, and its implications for poor people's political reactions 'from below':

> Recent ELCs seek long-term leases to convert forestland to plantation crops including sugarcane... In 2007, 44 000 hectares of forestland was granted to large concessionaires... ELC issuance frequently results in ... rapid and extensive deforestation of the concession area, while displacing forest-dependent populations that transfer pressures that degrade or deforest neighbouring areas. In the case of Oddar Meanchey, ELC applicants and cfmcs [Community Forest Management Committees] were in direct competition for the control of some of the proposed forest blocks in the REDD project area... Mitigating the impact of ELCs on deforestation is certainly beyond the capacity of communities and RE project design teams.[55]

In short, and essentially, we reiterate the relevance of the broader framing of struggles against dispossession ('dispossession' broadly defined, beyond land expulsion), also often phrased as contemporary struggles in defence of the commons ('commons' here broadly cast[56]). But, here again, we restate the importance of taking a closer look at the necessarily cross- or multi-class character of emerging struggle fronts, where various social groups and classes which have otherwise different (and even competing) socioeconomic interests might be affected similarly, negatively, by various land deals.

Concluding discussion

There are multiple implications that can be drawn from the initial discussion in this paper. We pick six points for further discussion that we think are critical to addressing the challenge of understanding the political reactions from below to global land rush.

Land property relations change and beyond

Changes in the social relations of landed property have been a central theme in the emerging global land rush literature. Who is getting dispossessed of their access to land and who gets to control these lands are two of the most critical questions in current land deal studies. The act of expelling people from the land is usually done by the state, deploying extra-economic coercive mechanisms. But, as discussed above, deploying concepts such as 'local community' or 'local people' and a priori assumptions their political reactions, ie either for or against land deals, are not helpful. More nuanced empirical research is required to advance our understanding of this matter. Conceptual lenses such as class, and conceptual frameworks such as struggles against dispossession in the broader context of the two broad types of struggles, with struggles against exploitation as the other type, are important analytical handles to deploy.[57] These will help us appreciate the broader meanings and implications of specific case studies.

However, there are situations where the state and corporations have needed the land and the cheap labour. On some occasions this is a better bargain for capital in dealing with the problem of the crisis of over-accumulation, to significantly bring down the cost of inputs,[58] and in this case of land and labour. In situations like this we are dealing with a very specific kind of dispossession—that which does not require expulsion of people from the land. This can happen in a variety of ways, including peasants still the nominal owners of their land but who have ceased to have any effective control over it after having been recruited to a growership arrangement. Hence, a 'landed property relations-centred' analysis risks overlooking the actually existing changing social relations dynamics because, while on paper peasants were not expelled from their lands, they may have been effectively dispossessed, subordinated to the emerging capitalist plantation enclave. In cases like this one may therefore not see any struggle against expulsion. What we may see are different forms of emerging political contention around struggles over the terms of incorporation. While this is likely to be 'adverse incorporation', there is a danger of this template being used in an either/or fashion, since we are actually referring to the terms of incorporation, which is better seen as a matter of degree, not a matter of either completely adverse nor completely non-adverse.

In sum, our point is that the unit of inquiry should be the *dynamics of change in social relations* as a result of large-scale land deals, regardless of what the official documents may tell us.[59] That should be the basic starting point towards a better understanding of why and how affected rural under-classes react the way they do to large-scale land deals in relation to questions of social relations of land property.

'Land grabbing' and beyond

'Land grabbing' has grabbed popular attention worldwide and, as Carlos Oya has explained, the global land rush has also ushered in a global 'land grab literature rush'.[60] This is important, in our view, especially in the context of 'engaged research'; research that aims to have societal relevance and impact, to help interpret—and change—existing situations. It is important therefore that the level of interest in land grabbing among media practitioners, policy makers, civil society organisations and academics remains high—pushing it further to understand better the varied political reactions among affected social groups.

But looking at land grabbing and the politics around it in isolation from other relevant land issues and political contestations will not only miss a significant portion of what transpires in the rural world, but may even lead to only partial understanding of the land grabbing phenomenon itself. As we mentioned earlier, land grabbing is an important and urgent issue, but it is not the only urgent land issue today. The generic land concentration through market mechanisms and without significant extra-economic coercion is just as profound and is probably even more widespread—with a similar impact on the lives and livelihoods of subordinated groups in the countryside. The political struggles around the generic land concentration issue are necessarily of a different character than those against expulsion from the land, the set of demands necessarily different. When is capital content with its accumulation processes through the 'normal' course of social differentiation via commoditisation, and when is it pushed to resort to extra-economic coercive measures, including forcibly and often violently expelling people from their lands? These are key contextual questions that help shed light on the questions that we are interested in: the political reactions by affected social groups to these different processes of dispossession. In more concrete terms, this will help us make sense of why, for example, within the international peasant and farmers' movement *La Via Campesina*, there tends to be different emphasis by various regional groups, with the African section more actively engaged in an explicitly anti-land grabbing framework, while the Latin American group as well as the North Atlantic groups seem to be more keen on framing their issues within the generic land concentration perspective. What are the political implications of these varying master frames in terms of capturing the diversity of political configuration around land deals in various regions? What are the sources and implications of tensions and synergies within and between agrarian movements? These are some of the empirical questions that need to be investigated further. And it is best done not by looking at land grabbing and land concentration as two separate and unrelated processes—but as likely to be organically linked.[61]

Corporate land grabbers and beyond

Despite the growing prominence of the state and its role in land grabbing in the emerging literature on the subject, the main attention remains on corporate, often foreign, grabbers. But as we have discussed above, the state plays a central, albeit contradictory, role in all crucial steps in securing land for corporate investors. This puts the state centre-stage in terms of the politics of land deals and as a principal target of the various social groups affected by land deals. Recent studies have contributed a lot to our better understanding of this matter. It might be useful if further empirical research and conceptualisation are done in terms of disaggregating the 'state-subordinated classes' political interactions around land deals based on the broad types of struggle: against dispossession/expulsion, against exploitation, and against land concentration and for redistribution and recognition, as discussed earlier in the paper.

'Local communities' and 'local people' and beyond: inter- and intra-class political dynamics

This is probably where empirical research remains faced with a daunting challenge. To date, there has been hardly any systematic research into the dynamics of inter- and intra-class tensions and synergies (the issues that unite and divide), nor any moving away from not-so-useful categories, such as 'local community' and 'local people', that conceal more than reveal actual dynamics of politics. The relatively easier area to study in the future is to see the emerging politics by clearly defined social groups and the variegated ways they are becoming inserted into plantation enclaves: eg peasants expelled from their lands, peasants who have leased their lands but have not secured wage-earning jobs elsewhere (dispossession without proletarianisation), peasants who leased their lands and secured wage-earning jobs, and migrant workers recruited to join the workforce of the newly established plantation. Latent and actual political divides are relatively easy to discern, and fronts of struggles not difficult to figure out. Nevertheless more systematic empirical research needs to be done within this framework.

But, as we also know, there are individuals who cannot be reduced simplistically to a single class—they are small-scale farmers, but they are also workers in a plantation, and so on—and there are situations that are more complex than others, such as the case of 'propertied proletarians'. Hence a simplistic view of a class political standpoint will run into some difficult cases like this. It is likely that there are more situations reflecting these complexities; these demand careful and rigorous conceptualisation and methodological approaches in studying (class) politics.

Local, case-oriented country studies and beyond

The Land Deal Politics Initiative (LDPI, see www.iss.nl/ldpi) International Conference on Global Land Grabbing II held in October 2012 at Cornell University was the first time that a critical mass of academic papers was made available that had something to do with political reactions among affected social groups towards land deals. Many of the papers were empirical, looking at specific country or land deal case studies. This is a critical piece of the puzzle. In our view it is important to accumulate a critical mass of good, solid empirical cases of political reactions to land deals. This remains a challenge, and so should remain a growth pole in the emerging academic literature on land grabbing. However, studies of local, case-oriented politics need to be accompanied by big picture studies of multi-scale politics around land grabs. Again, this will help us grapple with tensions and synergies, the issues that have united and divide social groups and movements, and which will be missed in our analysis if we limit ourselves to local and case-oriented analyses of politics. And it is a similar problem with the other side of the story: studies that look only into the dynamics of political contention at the (inter)national level, and which are not sufficiently grounded at the local, land-grab site level, will miss the empirical richness (ie contradictions) of land deal-related politics.

State and corporate self-regulation governance instruments and beyond

So much attention and momentum have focused recently around global governance instruments, specifically the Tenure Guidelines (TGs),[62] and related instruments like transparency instruments, all in response to the emerging political reactions of various affected social groups towards large-scale land deals. This is an all-important and welcome development, academically and politically. But studies of the politics of land deals should therefore accompany the process of policy debates around the TGs and related matters. The more effective way of doing this to avoid a depoliticised, administrative and technical take on matters that are essentially political is to embed one's research framework and methodology within the first five points we have raised above.[63]

Notes

We thank the anonymous reviewers for this journal for their tough but very constructive and helpful comments and suggestions. We also thank Marc Edelman, Carlos Oya, Dianne Rocheleau and Eric Gutierrez for their critical comments and suggestions.

1 P McMichael, 'The land grab and corporate food regime restructuring', *Journal of Peasant Studies*, 39(3–4), 2012, pp 681–701.

2 K Deininger, 'Challenges posed by the new wave of farmland investment', *Journal of Peasant Studies*, 38 (2), 2011, pp 217–247.

3 Important academic journal collections include the 'Forum on Global Land Grabbing: Part 1', *Journal of Peasant Studies* 38(2), 2011, which outlines key ideological and analytical strands and includes a contribution by O de Schutter, 'How not to think of land-grabbing: three critiques of large-scale investments in farmland', pp 249–279; J Fairhead, M Leach & I Scoones (eds), *Journal of Peasant Studies*, 39(2), 2012; B White et al (eds), 'The New Enclosures: Critical Perspectives on Corporate-driven Land Deals', *Journal of Peasant Studies*, 39(3–4), 2012; L Mehta et al (eds), 'Water Grabbing? Focus on the (Re)appropriation of Finite Water Resources', *Water Alternatives*, 5(2), 2012; W Wolford et al (eds), 'Governing Global Land Deals: The Role of the State in Rush for Land', *Development and Change*, 44(2), 20013; M Margulis, N McKeon & S M Borras Jr (eds), 'Land Grabbing and Global Governance', *Globalizations*, 10(1), 2013; and S M Borras Jr, C Kay & J Wilkinson (eds), 'Land Grabbing in Latin America', *Canadian Journal of Development Studies*, 33(4), 2012.

4 On the latter, the 'Forum on Global Land Grabbing: Part 2', *Journal of Peasant Studies*, 40(3), 2013 has been dedicated to jump-starting a more rigorous debate on this matter. See, specifically, I Scoones et al, 'The politics of evidence: methodologies for understanding the global land rush', *Journal of Peasant Studies*, 40(3), 2013 pp 469–483; M Edelman, 'Messy hectares: questions about the epistemology of land area and ownership', pp 485–501; and C Oya, 'Methodological reflections on land "grab" databases and the land "grab" literature "rush"', *Journal of Peasant Studies*, 40(3), 2013, pp 503–520.

5 A Tsing, *Friction*, Princeton, NJ: Princeton University Press, 2005, p xx.

6 J Scott, *The Art of Not Being Governed*, New Haven, CT: Yale University Press, 2009.

7 M Olsen, *The Logic of Collective Action: Public Goods and the Theory of Groups*, Cambridge, MA: Harvard University Press, 1965.

8 M Edelman, 'Social movements: changing paradigms and forms of politics', *Annual Review of Anthropology*, 30, 2001, pp 285–317. See also related discussions in A Walder, 'Political sociology and social movements', *Annual Review of Sociology*, 35, 2009, pp 393–412. We thank Marc Edelman for pointing this out to us.

9 See, for example, various works by J Scott (above and below); B Kerkvliet, 'Everyday politics in peasant societies (and ours)', *Journal of Peasant Studies*, 36(1), 2009, pp 227–243; and J Paige, *Agrarian Revolution*, New York: Free Press, 1975.

10 S Borras, J Franco, S Gómez, C Kay & M Spoor, 'Land grabbing in Latin America and the Caribbean', *Journal of Peasant Studies*, 39(3–4), 2012, pp 845–872.

11 We refer to some case studies to illustrate some of the analytical points we are trying to put forward. These case studies were generated through joint and individual field visits by the authors to several land grabbing sites in several countries (including the Philippines, Indonesia, Cambodia, China, Brazil, Mali and Mozambique), with each field visit lasting around two weeks. These are therefore not exhaustive case studies, but sufficient for our current purpose.

12 Among the few exceptions are S Adnan, 'Land grabs and primitive accumulation in deltaic Bangladesh: interactions between neoliberal globalization, state interventions, power relations and peasant resistance', *Journal of Peasant Studies*, 40(1), 2013, pp 87–128.

13 See, for example, K Woods, 'Ceasefire capitalism: military–private partnerships, resource concessions and military–state building in the Burma–China borderlands', *Journal of Peasant Studies*, 38(4), 2011, pp 747–770; J Grajales, 'The rifle and the title: paramilitary violence and land control in Colombia', *Journal of Peasant Studies*, 38(4), 2011, pp 771–792.

14 See M Murmis & M Murmis, 'Land concentration and foreign land ownership in Argentina in the context of global land grabbing', *Canadian Journal of Development Studies*, 33(4), 2012, pp 490–508.

15 We thank Marc Edelman for pointing this out to us.

16 H Bernstein, *Class Dynamics of Agrarian Change*, Halifax: Fernwood, 2010, p 115.

17 We thank Marc Edelman for pointing this out to us.
18 L Mehta, GJ Veldwisch & J Franco, 'Water grabbing: editorial introduction', *Water Alternatives*, 5(2), 2012, pp 193–207; J Franco, L Mehta & GJ Veldwisch, 'The global politics of water grabbing', this issue; and P Woodhouse, 'New investment, old challenges: land deals and the water constraint in African agriculture', *Journal of Peasant Studies*, 39(3–4), 2012, pp 777–794.
19 J Fairhead, M Leach & I Scoones, 'Green grabbing: a new appropriation of nature?', *Journal of Peasant Studies*, 39(2), 2012, pp 237–261.
20 T Lavers, '"Land grab" as development strategy? The political economy of agricultural investment in Ethiopia', *Journal of Peasant Studies*, 39(1), 2012, pp 105–132.
21 This can also be seen in the context of land reform implementation in the Philippines where more than 20 government agencies are directly involved, with very different histories of interaction with peasant mobilisations from below. This in turn influences the choices of institutional targets of peasant mobilisations for land. See J Franco, *Bound by Law*, Manila: Ateneo de Manila University Press, 2011.
22 S Borras, M Edelman & C Kay (eds), *Transnational Agrarian Movements Confronting Globalization*, Oxford: Wiley–Blackwell, 2008.
23 G Arrighi, *The Long Twentieth Century*, New York: Verso, 1994; K Marx, *Capital: I*, London: Penguin, 1976; and D Harvey, *The New Imperialism*, New York: Oxford University Press, 2003.
24 W Wolford et al, 'Land grabbing and global governance: introduction', *Development and Change*, 44(2), 2013, pp 189–210; and M Levien, 'Regimes of dispossession: from steel towns to Special Economic Zones', *Development and Change*, 44(2), 2013, pp 381–407.
25 It is relevant to note that lands that were once marginal may become less so with a different crop mix and new technologies. The marginal claims are sometimes connected to new cash crops that do well on poor soils, eg jatropha, or new kinds of millets in India or Africa. We thank Marc Edelman for pointing this out to us.
26 S Borras, J Franco & C Wang, 'The challenge of global governance of land grabbing: changing international agricultural context and competing political views and strategies', *Globalizations*, 10(1), 2013, pp 161–179.
27 J Scott, *Seeing Like a State*, New Haven, CT: Yale University Press, 1998.
28 *Ibid*.
29 Grajales, 'The rifle and the title'; Woods, 'Ceasefire capitalism'; N Peluso & C Lund (eds), 'New frontiers of land control', *Journal of Peasant Studies* (special issue), 38(4), 2011; and Scott, *Seeing Like a State*.
30 J Fox, *Food Politics*, Ithaca, NY: Cornell University Press, 1993, esp ch 2. For related discussion, see Harvey, *The New Imperialism*; and G Arrighi, *The Long Twentieth Century*, esp his concept of 'capitalists and territorialists'.
31 Balancing the issue of the 'legitimacy of the state' includes calculations of resistance from entrenched (local) elites. We thank Eric Gutierrez for pointing this out.
32 Borras *et al*, 'The challenge of global governance of land grabbing'.
33 A Du Toit, *Forgotten by the Highway: Globalisation, Adverse Incorporation and Chronic Poverty in a Commercial Farming District of South Africa*, Cape Town: PLAAS Chronic Poverty and Development Policy Series No 4.
34 T Li, 'Centering labour in the land grab debate', *Journal of Peasant Studies*, 38(2), 2011, pp 281–298.
35 S Borras, S Monsalve & D Fig, 'The politics of agrofuels and mega-land and water deals: insights from the ProCana case, Mozambique', *Review of African Political Economy*, 38(128), 2011, pp 215–234; and Lavers, '"Land grab" as development strategy'.
36 J Scott, *The Moral Economy of the Peasant*, New Haven, CT: Yale University Press, 1976.
37 S Tarrow, *Power in Movement*, Cambridge: Cambridge University Press, 1998.
38 We are aware of the debate in the social movements literature about the Political Opportunity Structure (POS) school of thought. In this paper we use this concept of POS in its generic sense, ie the relevance of changing structures of political opportunities and threats that are critical contexts for collective actions. It is thus relevant to any analytical tools, whether class-based, identity politics or political process/resource mobilisation perspectives. For an excellent analytical overview, see Edelman, 'Social movements'.
39 Fox, *Food Politics*, ch 2.
40 K O'Brien, & L Li, *Rightful Resistance*, Cambridge: Cambridge University Press, 2006.
41 The information for this short write-up of the case is based on Borras' field visit to the contested site in 2010, facilitated by Foodfirst Information and Action Network (FIAN) and the Cambodian human rights organization, LICADHO. Together with fian's Roman Herre, Borras interviewed key actors in the case, especially villagers in the contested site and various NGOS and donor agencies.
42 Information from fian's Roman Herre, with whom Borras went to the site in 2010 and who went back in late 2012 for another field visit.
43 D Pred, 'Is the European Commission sweet on land grabbing? Trade benefits, sugarcane concessions and dispossession in Cambodia', at http://terra0nullius.wordpress.com/2012/07/23/is-the-european-commission-

sweet-on-land-grabbing-how-trade-benefits-to-sugar-companies-displace-cambodian-farmers/, accessed 28 August 2013.

44 J Franco, D Carranza & J Fernandes, *New Bio-fuel Project in Isabela: Boon or Bane for Local People?*, Amsterdam: Transnational Institute, 2011; and L Alano, 'Opportunities and vulnerabilities amidst changing property and labor regimes', paper presented at the 'Land Deals and Rural Transformations Workshop', Bogor Agricultural University, 25 March 2013.

45 This is based on the field visits and interviews with key informants in Davao in 2011 done by Borras, together with Lisa Alano.

46 J McCarthy, 'Processes of inclusion and adverse incorporation: oil palm and agrarian change in Sumatra, Indonesia', *Journal of Peasant Studies*, 37(4), 2010, pp 821–850; and O Pye, 'The biofuel connection—transnational activism and the palm oil boom', *Journal of Peasant Studies*, 37(4), 2010, pp 851–874.

47 See also related discussion in M Edelman & A Leon, 'Cycles of land grabbing in Central America: an argument for history and a case study in the Bajo Aguán, Honduras', this collection.

48 Franco, *Bound by Law*.

49 This observation is largely based on Borras' field visit to Brazil in 2008, especially to the State of Sao Paulo, where discussions were held with several key social movements groups, both agrarian and trade union.

50 FIAN, *The Human Rights Impacts of Tree Plantations in Niassa Province, Mozambique: A Report*, Heidelberg: Foodfirst Information and Action Network, 2012.

51 See also S Borras, S Gomez, C Kay & J Wilkinson, 'Land grabbing and global capitalist accumulation: key features in Latin America', *Canadian Journal of Development Studies*, 33(4), 2012, pp 402–416; and Borras *et al*, 'Land grabbing in Latin America'.

52 J Franco & S Borras (eds), *Land Concentration, Land Grabbing and People's Struggles in Europe: A Report by the European Coordination Via Campesina (ECVC) and Hands-Off The Land (HOTL)*, Amsterdam: Transnational Institute (TNI), 2013.

53 S Borras & J Franco, 'Towards a land sovereignty alternative?', TNI discussion paper, Amsterdam, July 2012; and P Rosset (ed), 'Grassroots Voices: The Evolution of Social Movement Thinking on Agrarian Reform, Land and Territory', *Journal of Peasant Studies* 40(4), 2013, pp 721–775.

54 M Edelman & C James, 'Peasants' rights and the UN system: quixotic struggle? Or emancipatory idea whose time has come?', *Journal of Peasant Studies*, 39(1), 2011, pp 81–108; and Sofia Monsalve, guest editor, 'Grassroots voices: the human rights framework in contemporary agrarians struggles', *Journal of Peasant Studies*, 40(1), 2013, pp 239–290.

55 M Poffenberger, 'Cambodia's forests and climate change: mitigating drivers of deforestation', *Natural Resources Forum*, 33, 2009, pp 285–296.

56 See Harvey, *The New Imperialism*. For relevant discussions on the 'commons', see K Milun, *The Political Uncommons: The Cross-cultural Logic of the Global Commons*, Farnham, UK: Ashgate, 2011; P Barnes, *Capitalism 3.0: A Guide to Reclaiming the Commons*, San Francisco: Berrett-Koehler, 2006; and D Mosse, 'Collective action, common property, and social capital in South India: an anthropological commentary', *Economic Development and Cultural Change*, 54(3), 2006, pp 695–724

57 See Harvey, *The New Imperialism*; S Spronk & J Webber, 'Struggles against accumulation by dispossession in Bolivia: the political economy of natural resource contention', *Latin American Perspectives*, 34(2), 2007, pp 31–47; and B Kaup, 'In spaces of marginalization: dispossession, incorporation, and resistance in Bolivia', *Journal of World Systems Research*, XIX(1), 2013, pp 108–129.

58 Harvey, *The New Imperialism*.

59 H Bernstein, *Class Dynamics of Agrarian Change*; and S Borras & J Franco, 'Contemporary discourses and political contestations around pro-poor land policies and land governance', *Journal of Agrarian Change*, 10(1), 2010, pp 1–32.

60 Oya, 'Methodological reflections on land "grab" databases'.

61 Edelman & Leon, 'Cycles of land grabbing in Latin America'. This collection, is a good example of the way forward.

62 Philip Seufert, 'Voluntary guidelines on the responsible governance of tenure of land, fisheries and forests, *Globalizations*, 2013.

63 See Borras *et al*, 'The challenge of global governance of land grabbing'.

Notes on Contributors

Saturnino M Borras Jr is Associate Professor at the International Institute of Social Studies (ISS), The Hague, and Adjunct Professor at China Agricultural University, Beijing, Fellow at the Transnational Institute (TNI) in Amsterdam and Food First in California. He is co-editor *of Land Grabbing and Global*

Governance (Routledge, 2013, with M. Margulis and N. McKeon) and *Governing Global Land Deals: the Role of the State in the Rush for Land* (2013, Wiley-Blackwell, with W Wolford, R Hall, I Scoones, and B White), and co-coordinator of the Land Deal Politics Initiative (LDPI, www.iss.nl/ldpi).

Jennifer C Franco is at the Transnational Institute (TNI), Amsterdam and College of Humanities and Development Studies (COHD) at China Agricultural University, Beijing. Guest Editor (with L. Mehta and G J Veldwisch), 'Water grabbing? Focus on the (re)appropriation of finite water resources,' *Water Alternatives* journal special issue, 2012. Her latest book is *Bound by Law: Filipino Rural Poor and the Search for Justice in a Plural-legal Landscape* (2011, Manila: Ateneo de Manila University Press; Honolulu: University of Hawaii Press).

Index

For Product Safety Concerns and Information please contact our
EU representative GPSR@taylorandfrancis.com Taylor & Francis
Verlag GmbH, Kaufingerstraße 24, 80331 München, Germany